P9-DWJ-548

BREAKING
BREAD

Day said, "We know Christ in each other in the breaking of bread." St. Joseph's House of Hospitality, New York City. Photo by William Carter. Courtesy Marquette University Archives.

BREAKING BREAD

The Catholic Worker
and the Origin of
Catholic Radicalism in America

Mel Piehl

TEMPLE UNIVERSITY PRESS
PHILADELPHIA

Library of Congress Cataloging in Publication Data

Piehl, Mel.
  Breaking bread.

  Bibliography: p.
  Includes index.
  1. Catholic Worker Movement—History.   2. Catholic Church—United States—
History—20th century.   3. Radicalism—United States—History—20th century.
4. Day, Dorothy, 1897–   5. Maurin, Peter.   I. Title.
BX810.C393P53   1982   267'.182   82-10327
ISBN 0-87722-257-6

Temple University Press, Philadelphia 19122
© 1982 by Temple University. All rights reserved
Published 1982
Printed in the United States of America

To Eileen

Contents

Preface

In the 1960s Americans received a new image of Catholicism from the radical social activism of Daniel and Philip Berrigan and others in the Catholic Left. To most, the idea that Catholics could be radicals came as something of a surprise; yet Catholic radicalism has existed in the United States since 1933, when Dorothy Day and Peter Maurin founded a newspaper and a social movement both called the Catholic Worker.

This is a study of the Catholic Worker and the origin of Catholic radicalism in America. "Origin" means beginning, and it is also the root of "original," meaning fresh, independent, novel. The Catholic Worker movement marked the beginning of the American Catholic radicalism that burgeoned in the sixties, but it was also a true original. Rather than the simple germ of something larger, the Catholic Worker was a complex phenomenon, blending Catholicism and radicalism into an enduring composition of great subtlety and strength.

Unraveling the elements that make up the Catholic Worker and tracing the movement's development after 1933 are thus the first tasks for a historian of Catholic radicalism. The central problem in interpreting the Catholic Worker is the seeming paradox of its radical social outlook and its conservative Catholic religiosity. Determining whether that paradox was apparent or real means trying to uncover the nature of the connections between the Catholic Worker's religion and its social outlook as these existed in both theory and practice.

It also means coming to terms with Dorothy Day, the remarkable woman who guided the Catholic Worker throughout its history. When Miss Day ("Dorothy" to nearly everyone who knew her) died on November 29, 1980, she was widely hailed as a great pioneer of American social Catholicism. Her long life was certainly as varied and interesting as her character. Born into a newspaper family before the turn of the century, she became a youthful radical in pre–World War I Greenwich Village. In 1927 she converted to Catholicism, and six years later she founded the Catholic Worker with Peter Maurin, a French peasant. After 1933 she made her home in Catholic Worker Houses of Hospitality and farms. Besides her extensive writing for the *Catholic Worker*, she was the author of six books and over fifty articles.

The complex impulses at work in the Catholic Worker were crystallized in the person of Dorothy Day. She was at once thoroughly modern and deeply traditional, socially committed yet uninterested in power, devoted to ideas yet absorbed by elemental concerns, ambitious yet unassuming, completely American and Catholic to her fingertips. When some began calling her a modern saint, she scorned what she called "premature canonization" as a device to blunt her radical social criticism, adding that becoming a saint "costs too much." Almost everyone who met Dorothy Day has testified to her enormous personal magnetism; many were fascinated by her.

This book is not, however, a biography of Dorothy Day. My topic is the Catholic Worker and American Catholic radicalism; Day is considered only insofar as she contributed to these movements. But even by that criterion, her place in this study is necessarily large. The Catholic Worker—and therefore American Catholic radicalism—was Dorothy Day's invention, and she pervaded its history for so long that a social, religious, and intellectual history of American Catholic radicalism up to 1965 turns out to be, in significant measure, an interpretation of the social outlook, religion, and ideas of this one person. To use the comparison first made by Dwight Macdonald, writing a history of the Catholic Worker without giving a major share of attention to Dorothy Day would be like writing a history of the Federal Bureau of Investigation without giving close attention to J. Edgar Hoover.

The problem would be simplified if the Catholic Worker were an authoritarian institution or simply the person vehicle of its founder. Although some have regarded the Catholic Worker as virtually an extension of Dorothy Day, and have thus largely overlooked others in the movement, I have found this an inaccurate conception. The Catholic Worker was a decentralized anarchist movement, and Day's charismatic leadership functioned not to exclude others but rather to attract collaborators, like her co-founder, Peter Maurin, who complemented her own abilities. Although the movement has maintained its basic identity and ideological viewpoint with remarkable consistency through the years, there was also, as this study shows, considerable internal diversity and conflict. While this analysis focuses on Dorothy Day, it also emphasizes the contributions of other Catholic Workers, including those outside the main Worker headquarters in New York.

Because the Catholic Worker has been such a lively, complicated movement—and has produced so many colorful characters—it is tempting to write about it in isolation. But such a microscopic approach would create a distorted view of the Worker phenomenon. Although a small movement, the Catholic Worker has always been in touch with larger historical developments. While carrying out a specific mission to the poor, the Worker has operated within the environment of modern American Catholicism and has addressed major questions of religion, culture, and politics affecting American society at large.

The history of the Catholic Worker, therefore, must be set in a larger context. Since the Worker's religious orthodoxy is crucial to its identity and social outlook, the most pertinent context is that of American Catholicism. In 1933 American Catholicism was an ungainly youngster, still absorbed by the adolescent question of identity: How is it possible to be both American and Catholic? Catholic social thought at that time was also immature, but unconscious attitudes growing out of Catholics' American experience disposed them toward certain views of the social consequences of their faith. The Catholic Worker made its mark by extending and challenging those views, and by offering a radically alternative model of what it might mean to be both American and Catholic.

Two comparisons help illumine the problem of religion and social thought as it emerged in American Catholicism. First, the Protestant Social Gospel presented, early in this century, a significant instance of an attempted marriage of faith and social reform. The Protestant example is particularly helpful for an understanding of the Catholic Worker because it included a small radical element. Second, a look at European Catholicism also provides a basis for insight into the social thought of American Catholics. No extended comparison of American and European Catholicism is attempted here, but some attention to the European standard is vital because American Catholicism was still close to its European parent, and because Catholics everywhere were obligated to look to Rome for guidance on social questions.

In putting the Catholic Worker and Catholic radicalism into a larger context, the knottiest problem is striking a proper balance among social, religious, and intellectual factors. The ordinary difficulties of relating these elements are enhanced when considering a Catholic movement in a modern world that has tended to confine religion, and ideas generated from religion, to certain spheres of life. Not the least item of the Catholic Worker's radical dissent was its protest against this segregated ordering of human affairs. Present-day historians often deemphasize the importance of religion and ideas as autonomous forces in history, but the Catholic Worker seems a prime example of a religious impulse set against the dominant social ethos of a period. How it was possible for such a movement to remain relevant to modern American life is one of the important questions addressed here.

Two further questions run through these pages: What has been unique about the Catholic Worker, and what has been its influence on American Catholicism and American culture generally? The first question is answered partly through a dissection of the "Catholic Worker idea," and partly through an analytical narrative that shows what allegiance to that idea has amounted to in practice. Several themes emerge from this account, but the dominant one is probably the distinctiveness of the Catholic Worker's effort to join traditional contemplative Catholic spirituality and modern forms of social action.

The question of influence is more difficult. Because it has dealt primarily in religion and ideas rather than more tangible commodities, the impact of Day's movement is not easy to measure. Apart from those it sheltered and fed, the Worker's most direct effects were on the many individuals who passed through the movement and went on to other kinds of social activism, and on several closely related Catholic reform movements and journals. These are discussed in Chapters 5 and 6. The Catholic Worker was also the predecessor of the wider Catholic radicalism of the sixties. This study ends about 1965, when the new Catholic Left emerged amidst a general crisis in American Catholicism. It concludes with a question: What kind of larger influence can a committed religious minority like the Catholic Worker exert on a modern mass society like that of the United States?

When I first went to look for the *Catholic Worker* in the Stanford Library stacks some years ago, I could not find it. Only after some hunting around did I turn up unbound copies of the paper, buried under a bottom shelf in the basement. In some ways the Catholic Worker movement itself still seems to me as elusive as those old, yellowed papers. Not a thing to be neatly classified and stuck up on the shelf, the Worker stays partly hidden in the most dusty, out-of-the-way places. That may be where it belongs. But if this study is able to shed a little light on it there, and give others a better glimpse of an unusual phenomenon of our times, it will have served its purpose.

Acknowledgments

Before I attempted this work, I used to wonder how authors could really have received help from all the people they customarily thanked in their acknowledgments. Now I know. Without the ideas, practical assistance, and encouragement of many people a book like this simply does not get written. Besides those listed below who directly aided in the research, writing, and final preparation of the manuscript, there are many others not mentioned who provided help and friendly criticism somewhere along the way. To all of them I owe genuine thanks.

My teachers and advisers at Stanford University not only educated me in history, but exhibited the fine intellectual and personal qualities that inspired me and many others who have studied with them. As I now recognize even more clearly, their view of historical scholarship as a branch of humanistic learning that is best carried out in a humane atmosphere is by no means common. I feel fortunate indeed to have known them, and I hope this work reflects some of their tutelage. I am especially grateful to: Carl N. Degler, Don E. Fehrenbacher, Linda Kerber, George Knoles, the late David M. Potter, Barton J. Bernstein, and Robert McAfee Brown.

Two people were especially important while this study was in preparation as a dissertation at Stanford. Lorraine Sinclair was a true friend in need to me, as she has been to so many others. Her ability to assist with practical details while providing vital morale boosts was truly wonderful.

David M. Kennedy was more responsible than anyone else for the successful completion of this work. It was his unwavering support for this study and his untiring advice and encouragement that saw me through the difficult process of writing and revision. His determination to make me live up to his own high standards of excellence and his continuing emphasis on the larger significance of the subject made this a better work. Always a friend as well as an adviser, he combined the two roles with a deft hand. I cannot thank him enough.

Many people helped in my research on the Catholic Worker. The unusual character of the subject undoubtedly had something to do with the unusual generosity of those who went out of their way to help an outsider to the Catholic Worker and Catholicism. Among those who aided me were: Father Alex Avitabile, John C. Cort, Ed Marciniak, Anthony Novitsky, and Peter Steinfels.

My special thanks to the people at the Catholic Worker farm and House of Hospitality in New York who took time from more important work to help a visiting "scholar." No one who ever spent even a brief time with the late Stanley Vishnewski is likely to forget the encounter; he was a great embodiment of the Catholic Worker spirit. I am grateful to Peggy Scherer and Dan Mauk for helping me gain access to restricted materials at the Catholic Worker archives.

The Worker papers are in good hands at Marquette. The many people there who aided my work, and in some cases literally made me at home during research trips to Milwaukee, could not have been more kind: Paul Gratke, the late Father Raphael Hamilton, Chuck Elston, and Phillip Runkel. A special mention must be made of Professor William Miller. All those who study the Catholic Worker now and in the future are in debt to Dr. Miller for his pioneering scholarship and for assembling the rich historical materials now available on the Catholic Worker. Professor Miller's generosity to me during visits to Milwaukee went far beyond the bounds of ordinary academic courtesy. I deeply appreciate his help.

My knowledge of the burgeoning field of American Catholic history owes much to my participation, during much of the time I was writing, in various conferences and seminars generously sponsored by the Cushwa Center for the Study of American Catholicism at Notre Dame. Among those who through formal work and, equally important, informal conversation shared with me their vast understanding of American Catholicism are Jay Dolan, Philip Gleason, Patricia McNeal Dolan, Father Tom Blantz, and Jeff Burns. While neither they nor the Cushwa Center are responsible for any of the views or errors in this book, they were responsible for reading and commenting on some of my work, including an earlier version of Chapter 5 presented as a paper at the American Catholic Studies Seminar.

Several friends and colleagues read portions of this book at various stages and provided valuable comments and criticism: David Danbom, Anthony Novitsky, and R. Keith Schoppa. I have also benefited from exchanging views about many historical subjects with Charles K. Piehl; if friends may not always be honest critics, one can be sure that brothers are. Mark Schwehn has been not only a friendly critic of my work, but a critical friend over many years. His scintillating mind and wise counsel on many matters contributed to this work in ways not easily reckoned.

Librarians and archivists at Stanford, the University of Chicago, the University of Michigan, Notre Dame, and Valparaiso helped in my research. The Danforth Foundation provided financial assistance during the writing of the dissertation. Valparaiso University helped with funds for typing and preparation of the final manuscript. Deborah Lamb typed the final copy. Dr. Richard Baepler gave encouragement and support for this project over several years. Many of my other colleagues at Valparaiso University and Christ College contributed in direct or indirect ways to this work. I want to thank especially Professors Willis Boyd and Kenneth Klein, who first taught me the values of history and scholarship; Dean Arlin G. Meyer, who understood and helped balance the burdens of teaching and writing; and Warren G. Rubel, who listened to a writer's woes with unfailing sympathy and good cheer.

A special kind of thanks goes to Valerie Piehl and Stephanie Piehl. Although they sometimes questioned the seemingly endless hours spent on "Daddy's papers," they never stopped giving happily of their time and love to a slightly distracted father. Their contribution was very large, and I shall always be grateful to them.

Finally, this book is dedicated to Eileen. Her humor, wisdom, and love are remarkable. She has shared in the making of this book, as in everything else.

BREAKING BREAD

CHAPTER ONE

Dorothy Day

I

"This first number of the *Catholic Worker* was planned, written, and edited in the kitchen of a tenement on Fifteenth Street, on subway platforms, on the 'L', on the ferry," stated the little eight-page tabloid that appeared in New York's Union Square on May Day, 1933. "The money for the first issue was raised by begging small contributions from friends. . . . The rest of it the editors squeezed out of their own earnings." The crude typography and rough stock confirmed the claim of poverty and suggested that editorial concern about a possible "fly-by-night existence" might be justified. But the little paper related its own precarious condition to that of its intended audience, "those who are walking the streets in the all but futile search for work, those who think there is no hope for the future."[1]

In 1972 W. H. Auden began a review by saying that he would "assume that all readers of the *New York Review of Books* know something about the activities of the Catholic Worker movement."[2] After forty years the *Catholic Worker* could still proclaim its poverty, but ephemerality was no longer a threat. The *Catholic Worker* had long since become one of the fixtures of American journalism, while the Catholic Worker movement exerted a continuing influence that extended far beyond the paper's faithful readership.

In 1933 perhaps only a keen judge of character could have guessed at such a result. The author of that first editorial, Dorothy Day, was a thirty-five-year-old journalist and Catholic convert. Day was born in Brooklyn on November 8, 1897. Her father, John Day, was a sports writer for a number of newspapers in major cities around the turn of the century. In 1904 Day took his family to San Francisco, but when the earthquake of 1906 destroyed the plant of his paper, the *Morning Telegraph*, the family had to move again, this time to Chicago. Dorothy Day later linked the earthquake with some of her earliest religious feelings:

I began to be afraid of God, of death, of eternity. As soon as I closed my eyes at night the blackness of death surrounded me. What would it be like to sink into that immensity? If I fell asleep God became in my ears a great noise that became louder and louder, and approached nearer and nearer to me until I woke up sweating with fear and shrieking for my mother. I fell asleep with her hand in mine, her warm presence by my bed. . . . The very remembrance of the noise, which kept getting louder and louder, and the keen fear of death, makes me think now that it might have been due only to the earthquake.[3]

Whether or not such dreams were occasioned by the earthquake, the memory accurately recalled two elements of young Dorothy Day's personality—her sense of loneliness and her concern with things metaphysical.

In Chicago the Day family lived for a time in a drab six-room flat above a tavern on the South Side. Eventually, after John Day became established on the *Chicago Inter-Ocean*, they moved up to a comfortable home on the North Side. The frequent moves reinforced Dorothy's seriousness and sense of isolation. In a later novel she has her main character say: "And it made me mad that we were always moving around from one place to another so that we never had any friends."[4]

John Day's strict Victorian control of his daughters' lives further isolated Dorothy from the world. Attempts to shelter families from the rawer side of life were common in the Chicago middle class of that time, but the crusty, remote Day went to extremes, practically forbidding his children companions.[5] "He had the old-fashioned impulse to protect innocence," Dorothy later recalled, "and he believed that the place for women and children was in the home."[6] Although Dorothy eventually escaped these restrictions, there would always remain for her an "old-fashioned" longing for the security of a home and loving family, a tendency that seemed to contradict her equally strong inclinations to rebelliousness and defiance of social convention.

Day's secure but quite lonely childhood may also have contributed to other of her character traits—her intellectual bent, her interest in religion, and her thirst for "experience." Reading provided practically the only amusement for young Dorothy. Her father permitted no "trash" in the house, so the girl grew up on the volumes of Dickens, Poe, Hugo, Cooper, and Scott that lined the shelves in the home. By her early teens, Dorothy was an avid and precocious reader, particularly of fiction. She dipped into weighty nonfiction as well; Spencer, Kant, and Spinoza "baffled" her, but she "enjoyed" Darwin and Huxley. She was bored by historical tomes, but an enthusiastic high school classics teacher prompted her to explore Virgil and Cicero on her own.[7]

Most important was her discovery of religious classics; the sermons of Wesley and Edwards, the Anglican prayer book, and St. Augustine's *Confessions*. Familiarity with such works lent substance to young Dorothy's budding religiosity. Her parents, of Episcopalian and Presbyterian background, were indifferent to religion and puzzled by their daughter's intent fascination with whatever manifestations of piety she came across in playmates or neighbors. Not unnaturally, religion became an outlet for Dorothy, an expression of emotional independence in her undemonstrative home environment. In California she had attended a Methodist church for a time with a friend. Then at age twelve she went to an Episcopal church in Chicago and became familiar with the Bible, catechism, and liturgy. "I loved the Psalms and Collect prayers and learned many of them by heart," she wrote. "I had never heard anything so beautiful as the *Benedicite* and the *Te Deum*. . . . The Psalms were an outlet for the enthusiasm of joy or grief."[8]

As an adolescent, Dorothy Day had already become what she was to remain throughout life—a prodigious and retentive reader of fine literature. Despite her lack of advanced education, she developed a discriminating taste in fiction, drama, and religious writing that served her well as a writer, editor, and friend of intellectuals. She was always surrounded by books, and enjoyed nothing more than discussing her reading with anyone who happened to be around.

For Day, producing the written word went along with consuming it. "I have been a compulsive writer ever since I was eight years old," she reflected. Like religion, writing was an "outlet" for emotion and a way to overcome her isolation. "If you get to the point where you can write about suffering, analyzing and explaining it to others, it has already been alleviated. Putting it down on paper has externalized it somehow, put it away from one's self. It helps to write about it. Psychiatrists know that."[9] She began keeping a diary at an early age, and even though her brothers constantly stole it and "read aloud torrid passages, with religious ecstasies included," she kept it up because she "was lonesome and the little red book was her only comfort."[10] By age twelve the girl was turning out serials for a neighborhood newspaper, and in school she wrote numerous stories and poems, including "a tale of the martyrdom of Russian revolutionaries which must have surprised the staid little woman who taught us English."[11] When she graduated from high school at the age of sixteen, Day had already decided to become a writer; she lacked only the "experience" to fill her stories.

Until she could acquire experience, her subject had to be her own life. A letter to a girl friend written at age fifteen shows her adolescent self-absorption, but also her conscious effort to translate raw feelings into "literary" prose:

> We went to the park Friday and Della and I went on the merri-go-round and the lake boat. We each had fifty cents and it was with regret that I saw the money go. But then I realized there was more for God's children and it will come to them when they need it. "Be careful for nothing. . . ." "Take no thought for the morrow." So I just spent it with the others and enjoyed myself very much. . . .
>
> This afternoon it took us two hours to do the dishes and now that they are done, I suppose I'll have to take the baby out for a long walk. How I love the park in winter. So solitary and awful in the truest meaning of the word. God is there. Of course, He is everywhere, but under the trees and looking over the wide expanse of lake He communicates Himself to me and fills me with a deep quiet peace. I need those hours alone in the afternoon with the baby, and I feel as though the troubles of life are lifted until I return to the house and it all comes back to me.
>
> Maybe if I stayed away from books more this restlessness would pass. I am reading Dostoevski and last night I stayed up late. This morning I had to get up early and I feel that my soul is like lead. . . . I am sitting in my bedroom in my comfortable chair by the window. The wind is cold and seeps in around the glass so that I have to wrap my bathrobe around me as I write. I should be reading the Bible because it is Sunday afternoon. But I don't want to. I'd rather write.[12]

While self and religion were her first topics, Day's reading had already widened her horizons beyond the middle-class family parlor. She was coming of intellectual age in the Progressive Era, when much of American society talked of reform and the young intelligentsia was taking an active interest in social problems. Contemporary writers like Jack London, Upton Sinclair, Frank Harris, Peter Kropotkin, and Vera Figner awakened Day's social conscience and stimulated an interest in the poor. And, of course, poverty was not entirely foreign to her; she remembered how the Day family's tight financial condition had exposed the raw surfaces of existence. "My mother had to do all her own work, washing for six in a large common basement which stretched the length of the block and was like a series of caverns. Outside was a cement-paved yard with neither tree nor blade of grass. The household tasks were too much for my mother, who after her four children had a series of miscarriages."[13] By her teenage years Dorothy Day's family had become comfortable, but she now saw economic hardship through the eyes of the class-conscious writers of the day. The fact that Upton Sinclair and others wrote about her hometown sharpened her curiosity. She began diverting carriage strolls with her baby brother from the pleasant lakefront and parks to the immigrant slums of Chicago's West Side:

> We explored until we were footsore, going up and down interminable gray streets, fascinating in their dreary sameness, past tavern after tavern, where I envisaged such scenes as that of the Polish wedding party in Sinclair's story, past houses which were sunk down a whole story below street level for block after block.
>
> There were tiny flower gardens and vegetable patches in the yards. I collected odors in my memory, the one beauty in those drab streets. The odor of geranium leaves, tomato plants, marigolds; the smell of lumber, of tar, of roasting coffee; the smell of good bread and rolls and coffee cake coming from the small German bakers. Here was enough beauty to satisfy me.[14]

Her "experience" of the world was still indirect, but what she learned confirmed Day in her rejection of shibboleths about the poor and inspired her belief that things should be different. "I felt even at fifteen . . . that we did not need to have quite so much destitution and misery as I saw all around."[15] That was not an uncommon sentiment in the Progressive Era, but young Dorothy Day endorsed it with unusual intensity. In poverty she had found not only a doorway to the experience she craved, but a subject for her writing and an outlet for her moral idealism.

These emerging themes of Day's life—devotion to reading and writing, social concern, and the desire for wider experience—came into sharper focus during her two-year stay at the University of Illinois. She owed her chance at college to the Hearst paper in Chicago, which sponsored a scholarship competition that Dorothy won at age sixteen. Free at last of the severe paternal restraints, she was "happy as a lark" and "filled with a great sense of independence." As a scholarship student with a fine record she might have been studious and deferential, but except for one English class, she found the courses lifeless and inimical to what Henry Adams called "accidental education." "I felt so intensely alive that the importance of the here and now absorbed me. . . . It was experience in general that I wanted."[16] Wanting to read and write on her own schedule, she began cutting classes, keeping odd hours, and spending all her money on books. To earn money for more, she turned to arduous and poorly paid housekeeping and baby-sitting jobs, rejecting easier campus work because such jobs were controlled by the "bourgeois" YMCA. Increasingly divorced from normal student life, she took comfort only in the friendship of the few bright, avant-garde, frequently Jewish, literary types on campus, who admired the short stories she published in the student newspaper and invited her into their literary club, the Scribblers. As with a number of other young midwesterners of the period, the experience of friendship with Jews deepened Dorothy's awareness of anti-Semitism and further alienated her from conventional society.[17]

Day's growing disaffection with the world around her led to a rebellion that was typically youthful and American—highly personal and nonideological, yet morally passionate and dedicated to making over the world with new ideas and direct action. By taking up unconventional ideas, values, and associations she could express a hope for social change while satisfying her personal drive for self-assertion and experience. "I was tearing myself away from home, living my own life," she said.[18] Some of the values of "home" would eventually reassert themselves in Day's life, but now she enjoyed the delicious sensations of freedom.

Although she visited the placidly academic Socialist party in Urbana, it was her writing that best expressed Day's growing social awareness. Her articles in the local paper criticized the pay and working conditions of the poorer students, who were exploited as cheap labor by local businesses and even some faculty members. She supported her argument by describing in detail her own experience of going without food for three days when she was short of cash. The paper printed these critical articles but refused other pieces indicting "the whole social order." Thus, amidst the unlikely circumstances of a pleasant, midwestern college town, seventeen-year-old Dorothy Day began to display the essential ingredients of her subsequent career as a journalist: an obsession with the facts of poverty in affluent America, a personal willingness to share the circumstances of the deprived, and the need to communicate her findings and feelings to a wide public.

The missing piece in the pattern of Day's future career was religion. Although religion had strongly attracted Dorothy, and served her as a way to assert independence against her parents, she now turned against it, seeing it as part of the complacent and self-deluded world of the comfortable classes. Expelling piety and propriety proved a difficult personal challenge. "I started to swear, quite consciously began to take God's name in vain. . . . I shocked myself as I did it, but I felt that it was a strong gesture I was making to push religion from me." She now saw Christianity as a particularly seductive religion of weakness and social quietism; her own attraction to it became evidence of a dangerous sentimentality and shrinking from life. "Jesus said, 'Blessed are the meek,' but I could not be meek at the thought of injustice. For me Christ no longer walked the streets of this world. He was two thousand years dead and new prophets had risen up in his place."[19] For the romantic young rebel, social justice was a new faith requiring the passion, struggle, and heroic sacrifices of earlier religions. In turn-of-the century America it was not hard to find models of such heroism. They existed in the romantic tradition of the new industrial radicalism—in the Haymarket martyrs, in Eugene Debs, in the anonymous strikers in mills and mines who represented the stirring of "the masses." Contemporary Christianity had nothing to compare with this.

After her second year, Day left college and went to New York City. Like thousands of other discontented young people who flocked to the metropolis in the remarkable migration just before World War I, she was attracted to what historian Henry May has called "the great rebellion." The city fairly crackled with energy, as a generation of young American intellectuals proclaimed their exuberant experiment in radical politics, culture, and personal behavior. Centered in Greenwich Village, the prewar intellectual movement crystallized trends and ideals that had been gathering force within American culture for some time. Although it contained complex and often contradictory elements, two basic features defined the new radicalism: a rejection of everything "bourgeois," and an experimental approach to life and art that expressed what the radicals saw as the freedom and wholeness of human existence. Politically, this meant a commitment to social justice, an identification with the underdog working classes and non-Anglo-Saxon immigrants, and opposition to corporate capitalism. Culturally, it meant an assault on the reigning genteel tradition, with its didactic progressivism, polite conventions, and pious certainties about man and his place in the universe, using the weapons of irreverent humor and artistic modernism. And in lifestyles it meant a bohemian challenge to the supposedly hypocritical standards of official Victorian morality, especially as they concerned women and sexuality.

As an avant-garde cultural community, Greenwich Village represented something genuinely new in American life, and those who study such matters as literature, art, birth control, and feminism have rightfully discovered there "the first years of our own time." But the political trends with which these developments were closely linked were not so much innovations as twentieth century versions of traditional American moral and political idealism. Although some of its adherents flirted with Marxism, Fabianism, syndicalism, or even more exotic imported ideologies, the real force of the new radicalism's social propaganda lay in its thoroughly American appeal to extend, more rapidly and completely than others wanted, the widely shared democratic values of liberty, equality, and opportunity for all. Those who have looked closely at these young radicals have discovered, behind their mockery of the established bourgeois Protestant order, the kind of earnest moral idealism that American intellectuals seem to draw in with their mothers' milk. The young rebels' passion for social justice, their individualistic hatred of bureaucratic power in business and government, their quest for utopian community, and even their thirst for intense personal experience all reflected drives deeply rooted in their American and Protestant heritage. As historian John Diggins observes, ". . . if they rejected the capitalist ethos of striving to make good, many retained the religious ethic of striving to *be* good." Certainly such representative figures of the period as John Reed, Floyd Dell, and Max Eastman—the latter the son of two Congregationalist ministers—often approached politics, art, and sex with the fervor of religious commitment.[20]

Like most of the young participants in the radical movement, Dorothy Day had no sophisticated grasp of its full dimensions or significance. Yet she was already in tune with its major premises when she arrived in New York, and before long she took up most of its characteristic attitudes and activities. The city itself provided an education in current American social thought and action, for it was alive with immigrant clubs, progressive schools, birth control groups, settlement houses, and every kind of radical politics. When Day was taken on as a reporter for the *New York Call*, a Socialist daily, she found herself in a perfect vantage point to watch all the excitement. Like many of the bright, young newcomers, she was caught up in the general spirit of exuberant dissent, happily observing and sampling a wide variety of groups and movements without feeling called on to join any one of them.

As it happened, she owed her job on the *Call* to the same knack for participatory journalism she had shown in Urbana. Members of the police department were staging a highly publicized "Diet Squad" to show how cheaply one could live in New York. Day volunteered as a "diet squad of one" for the radical *Call* to satirize the police effort and meanwhile examine the real hardships faced by the poor in the city. She took a tiny tenement apartment on the Lower East Side and immediately began relating her experience. "Dull monotony and yet more monotony in the way of food," she recorded. "How can one afford anything but such monotony on five dollars a week?"[21] She later described her bleak slum surroundings, which harbored an appalling poverty amidst the variety of immigrant life. "Above all the smell from the tenements, coming up from basements and areaways, from dank halls, horrified me," she wrote.

"It is a smell like no other in the world. . . . One's very clothes smell of it. It is not the smell of life, but the smell of the grave."[22]

The debunking diet squad reports concluded that the police effort was fraudulent and that "a working girl cannot live in New York on the $1.82 a week that organized charity allows her." Day then turned to other assignments which became, for her, an education in contemporary American dissent. She covered major strikes, the peace movement, the Wobblies, the numerous anarchist groups. She analyzed city health department pamphlets urging the poor to save on fuel by eating raw rice and interviewed subjects from Leon Trotsky to Mrs. Vincent Astor's butler. Day quickly became skilled in the techniques of partisan journalism, excelling in emotional descriptions of the poverty she saw around her in the immigrant slum neighborhood. A typical description of a protest of East Side mothers:

> Some of the women talked quietly, others so energetically that strands of gray, drab hair tousled around their faces. Their whole bodies quivered and tears streamed down their cheeks. Then they would suddenly stop, realize that they had been saying the same old, hard facts—just what everybody else had said—that potatoes and onions and meat had gone up, that their children were starving. And a cold despair would take the place of the fire in their words and looks, and they would get down and let some other hungry soul take their place.[23]

This was the classic prose of American muckrakers: the pungent details, the barely suppressed anger, the invitation to identify with the poor and oppressed. Stylistically it is in the tradition of "romantic realism," in which "hard" facts and descriptions are used to evoke emotion, and the echoes of London and Sinclair, Dickens and Dostoevsky, are clear.

As these fictional models suggest, there was a thin line between committed journalism and deceptive propaganda. For the radical journalist it was easy to step over that line. In her columns on poverty, Day scored "sensational journals" that "exaggerate the problems of the working girl while ignoring her real difficulties."[24] But she later admitted that she had distorted a few facts herself in her reports on Mrs. Ethel Byrne, sister of birth control advocate Margaret Sanger, who went on a hunger strike to protest her treatment in prison. In Day's stories in the *Call*, Mrs. Byrne was described on her return as having "cheeks and features that were pinched and colorless. The whole appearance was that of a corpse." Actually, Day acknowledged, "she did not suffer from her hunger strike and was perfectly well and strong when released from jail;

but my job was to paint a picture of a woman at the point of death." Though she submitted to the apparent demands of propaganda, the young reporter grew more disturbed at such "committed morality." "It irked me that my job was always to picture the darker side of life, ignoring all the light touches, the gay and joyful sides of the stories as I came across them." She left the *Call* in April 1917 to go to work for the Anti-Conscription League, but she found a similar difficulty there and quit when the group "over-reached themselves in providing sensational stories for the press."[25] Day's lessons in the moral failings of even righteous causes contributed to her development as an ethical rather than a political radical, one who would not look for complete virtue in any class, cause, or institution, no matter how appealing.

Through her work on the *Call* Day had come to know several young literary and political radicals. In May 1917, the prominent Greenwich Village writer Floyd Dell offered her a position as assistant editor of his magazine, *The Masses*. Dell was very taken with Day; in his autobiography he called her "an awkward and charming young enthusiast, with beautiful slanting eyes."[26] Dell taught Day the technical side of editing and made her responsible for selecting poetry and fiction for the journal. When Dell went off on vacation a few months later and the other editor, Max Eastman, left on a speaking trip, twenty-year-old Dorothy Day found herself unexpectedly in charge of one of the most daring, sophisticated, and influential little magazines in the United States. Although this heady experience lasted only three months, it brought her into contact with such well-known radicals as John Reed, Maurice Becker, Charles Wood, and Art Young, and it gave her valuable credentials as a radical journalist after *The Masses* passed into legend.[27]

Day's own writing for *The Masses* was confined to book reviews, where she showed her blend of radical social commitment and frankly personal concerns. Concluding a review about a female Irish revolutionary, she observed, "Perhaps the chief attraction of this book is that it makes revolution seem possible by making it so homelike."[28] Reconciling revolution-making with home-making was unfortunately not so simple for Dorothy Day herself. Feeling herself pulled between the new personal freedoms she enjoyed and the home and family she wanted, she could only conclude that the "woman question" was an enormous complication that made female radicals inferior to men.[29]

Although Day thoroughly enjoyed *The Masses*, her career there was brought to an abrupt end by World War I. Fighting a war to "make the world safe for democracy," the government noticed that *The Masses* was printing sarcastic, witty, effective antiwar propaganda. The Post Office refused to handle the August 1917 issue, and thereafter the magazine battled the censors until it was finally suppressed by the Justice Department in November. Meanwhile the magazine's editors, writers, and artists were disbanded by the war; some entered military service, while others were imprisoned for draft resistance or joined the radical underground that grew up in the United States and Mexico, especially after the Bolshevik Revolution in November. The kind of high-spirited rebellion represented by *The Masses* seemed increasingly impossible. Dorothy Day and others were particularly shaken by the "suicide" of *Masses* artist Hugo Gellert's younger brother. The death, which took place in a military guardhouse, was widely believed in radical circles to have been a murder. Although those radicals who remained for the famous *Masses* trial in April 1918 put up a spirited defense, most were privately dispirited. Day's testimony as a hostile witness about articles and cartoons she had selected did little to advance the government's case.[30]

Like the radical movement, Dorothy Day's life fell apart after the war. For the next decade she struggled, with little success, to find both personal happiness and a meaningful role in life. At first she was drawn deeper into the bohemian life of Greenwich Village, relishing its intellectual excitement and disregard of conventional pieties. Starting in December she worked part-time for Max and Crystal Eastman's *Liberator*, the successor of *The Masses* that was then printing John Reed's reports from revolutionary Russia. But she spent more time at the Provincetown Players' theater on MacDougal Street and in hangouts like the Hell Hole, a Third Street saloon frequented by a colorful collection of theater people, writers, artists, and radicals, such as Eugene O'Neill, Agnes Boulton, Maxwell Bodenheim, Terry Carlin, Hypolite Havel, and George and Ira Granich (Mike Gold). Malcolm Cowley later wrote in *Exile's Return* that "the gangsters admired Dorothy Day because she could drink them under the table."[31]

It was during long evenings at the Hell Hole that Day developed an attraction for Eugene O'Neill. She was one of the rare people who could pull O'Neill out of his night-long bouts of despondency, and the two saw a good deal of one another in the winter of 1917–18. Nothing came of the relationship, but O'Neill, like others, recognized Day as a strong and attractive character.[32] Her gift for friendship, along with her strong will, personal sensitivity, and striking looks earned her a fine reputation among New York intellectuals of the time. "She was highly respected by all the old *Masses* crowd," said one. "All the people who knew her respected her. She had a 'force' about her, and everyone agreed that what distinguished Dorothy was the intensity of her 'seeking'."[33]

The underside of bohemian life soon drove Day to try to change the course her life was taking. Distressed by the seeming disorder in her own life, and especially by witnessing the heroin death of one of the Hell Hole denizens, she left the Village in April 1918 to begin training as a nurse in a Brooklyn hospital. She found the disciplined regimen and sense of social service satisfying, but felt she was not cut out to be a nurse. "Before the year was up I became restless and began rushing over to New York on my half days off, looking for intellectual stimulus. After all, I felt that nursing was not my vocation, and that my real work was writing and propaganda." [34]

But it was personal tragedy rather than work that dominated the next few years of Day's life. At the hospital she met and fell in love with Lionel Moise, a hard-drinking roughhouse newspaperman who had once worked with Ernest Hemingway on the *Kansas City Star*. Although she had previously been cautious about sexual involvements, Day moved in with Moise in November 1918, and for the next year they carried on a stormy love affair. The following spring she learned she was pregnant. Aware that Moise would leave her if she had a child, she decided to have an abortion. After delaying for some months she obtained the abortion in September 1919, only to discover that Moise had abandoned her anyhow. [35] According to her autobiographical novel she returned from the abortionist to discover a note from him that said:

> After all, you are only one of God knows how many millions of women who go through the same thing. . . . In thinking it over this is as good a time as any to split up. I should probably detect subconscious resentments in your attitudes toward me which would build up serious counter-resentments in me. . . . It is best, in fact, if you forget me. [36]

A few months later Day married Barkeley Tober, an unstable forty-two-year-old literary promoter with a history of quick marriages. Tober and Day sailed to Europe in the summer of 1920, perhaps intending to join the growing colony of American expatriates on the continent. They spent time in London and Paris, but the marriage began coming apart almost immediately. Day ended up on the Italian island of Capri, living through a time of "heartbreak" and working on an autobiographical novel. In the summer of 1921 she returned to the United States and dissolved the marriage with Tober. [37] Shortly thereafter she moved to Chicago in an attempt to resume the relationship with Moise, who was living there. Day evidently saw him for a time, but he had other female interests and nothing came of it. She stayed on in Chicago for two years, leading a rather aimless existence. She worked at various free-lance jobs, and had another stint with the now-Communist *Liberator*, which had moved to Chicago under Robert Minor. Her evenings were spent writing stories, plays, and another novel.[38]

Finding experiences to write about had ceased to be a problem for Dorothy Day. She had been arrested and imprisoned with suffrage marchers in Washington in 1917 and joined them in a hunger strike (her own protest was not for suffrage, since as a radical she did not believe in voting, but against "political arrests"). In Chicago in 1923 she was swept up in a police raid on the headquarters of the Industrial Workers of the World and jailed again, this time with local prostitutes. "It was a strange and unforgettable experience," she recalled, "but one which I would not have done without."[39] In the fall of 1923 she moved to New Orleans and went to work for the *New Orleans Item*, where a feature assignment led her to work as a taxi dancer to report on the girls' lives.[40]

While she was in New Orleans her novel *The Eleventh Virgin* was published. Heavily autobiographical, it described her increasingly difficult struggle to find personal order and meaning amid the apparent chaos of the radical movement and bohemian life. Her character ("June") admits that she is unable to subordinate personal feelings and goals to abstract social commitments.

> There were afternoons when she walked the streets, or took bus rides, watching the women shopping on Fifth Avenue, looking at the homes of all those people who accepted permanency as the undercurrent of their lives. Those women were buying things to take home to their husbands—to their babies probably. Why couldn't she too have a home, a husband, and babies? . . . . She envied and hated them for the peace they could have, a peace which was denied her.[41]

The novel concluded with her abortion and abandonment by Moise ("Dick"). Putting that traumatic event "down on paper" may have been therapeutic for her, although she never again mentioned it in her writing. Other painful experiences of that period, such as an apparent suicide attempt that occurred some time during her affair with Moise, were not described even in *The Eleventh Virgin*, and remained unknown outside a close circle of Day's friends.[42]

The novel itself was undistinguished, but it did raise some important issues. Dismissed by one later critic as simply an example of the general disillusionment among American radicals in the era of normalcy, it can also be seen as Day's highly personal response to dilemmas shared by many modern female activists.[43] And it was a sign of the strength of Day's own convictions that, even though she expressed disenchantment with bohemian morality and her own life in the movement, she never retreated from her radical social critique. Unlike the bolder feminists she knew, she never came to see the woman-family question as a social and not simply a personal problem. But she frankly recognized the great dilemmas of reconciling personal happiness with serious social commitment, an issue few radicals of the time acknowledged.

The novel did not resolve the questions it raised, but it did take care of Day's financial future for a time. Shortly after publication, the movie rights to *The Eleventh Virgin* were bought by a Hollywood studio for $5,000, enabling Day to quit work and return to New York, where she bought a cottage on Staten Island. She kept up friendship with intellectuals in New York: Malcolm Cowley and his wife, Peggy Baird; Kenneth and Lily Batterham Burke; Allen and Caroline Gordon Tate; Hart Crane; and John Dos Passos. She wrote serials for a newspaper syndicate and occasional pieces for *The New Masses*, but much of her time was spent reading novels and exploring the beach. In 1925 she began living with Forster Batterham, a southern-born biologist and anarchist and the brother of her friend Lily Burke. On March 3, 1927 Day gave birth to a daughter, Tamar Teresa. Day, who had apparently doubted her ability to have children since the abortion, was overjoyed. Typically, she carefully recorded the childbirth experience and sent off an article about it to *The New Masses*. It appeared in the June 1928 issue and was praised by Communists and radicals in the United States and abroad. What most of them did not know was that by the time the article appeared both the baby and the mother had been baptized into the Roman Catholic Church.[44]

II

Most of what is known about Dorothy Day's conversion to Catholicism comes from her own accounts. Clearly, the roots of her religious orientation were set in her early childhood. Indeed, her natural piety was so strong as to suggest that her youthful atheism was the aberration of her life. In the first years after her undergraduate rebellion, she seemed to have made a successful break with religion, but it was not long before she found herself drawn to it, particularly in moments of loneliness or crisis. After being imprisoned and going without food for six days in the Washington hunger strike, she found comfort in the Bible: "I read it with the sense of coming back to something of my childhood that I had lost. My heart swelled with joy and thankfulness for Psalms." In the following years Day often "felt a need to pray," and began going to church on occasion, a practice that puzzled her radical friends. She returned to the religious novelists Tolstoy, Dostoevski, and Huysmans, whose books *The Oblate* and *The Cathedral* particularly drew her to Catholicism. When she heard Eugene O'Neill recite Francis Thompson's poem "The Hound of Heaven" in the Hell Hole, she became "fascinated" by the image of divine pursuit of the soul.[45]

But if Day's natural religiosity ran deep, so did her cultivated critique of much of American Christianity. A decade of experience had only deepened her conviction that the radical movement was morally superior to the churches on the great contemporary issues of social justice. "The Marxists, the IWW's, who looked on religion as the opiate of the people, were the ones who were eager to sacrifice themselves, thus doing without the good things of the world which they were fighting to obtain for their brothers."[46] Rather than strengthening man for involvement in the world, religion seemed to confirm him in his weakness and self-centeredness. Because she herself was especially drawn to religion for comfort in times of personal distress, she was deeply suspicious of its capacity to provide an emotional shelter from the storms of life. "I would not go to God in defeat and sorrow," she said. "I did not want to depend on Him."[47]

The psychiatrist Robert Coles has speculated that Day's conversion was intimately connected, on a psychological level at least, with just such an imminent personal defeat: the crisis in her relationship with Batterham at the time of their daughter's birth. Batterham, "a naturalist, an atheist, a pessimist," was unprepared for the pregnancy. There were conflicts because "Forster did not believe in bringing children into such a world as we lived in. He still was obsessed by the war. His fear of responsibility, his dislike of control of others, his extreme individualism made him feel that he of all men should not be a father."[48] Coles writes:

> Is it really all that surprising to find at this moment heightened religious and philosophical concerns in a sensitive, socially conscious, introspective woman, a thoughtful writer and political observer, a seeker and a bit of a wanderer, an outgoing yet in some crucial sense lonely woman, aware that (so far as a father for her child goes) she might soon be alone? Indeed it is hard not to dwell on the psychological significance of Dorothy Day's conversion. . . . The Church will be a mother and a father to this new and anxious mother, soon to be forsaken by Forster; the Church will give this somewhat rebellious and anarchic spirit (well, of course, it is minds we are talking about) a home at last, a home in which, finally, she will really feel at home, and therefore able to offer one to her daughter.[49]

Yet as disturbed as Batterham was by the pregnancy and birth, the question of ending the relationship did not arise until Day had the child baptized in July 1927, four months *after* Tamar was born. According to Day, the ferocity of Batterham's reaction came as a shock: "I had not even suspected this hatred until I had the child baptized; then it flared forth in an intense bitterness." It was then that Batterham began disappearing from their Staten Island home for periods of time—periods that increased in frequency and length after the August executions of Sacco and Vanzetti reinforced Batterham's misanthropy. It was, therefore, Day's religious inclination that precipitated the crisis with her lover, rather than the other way around. Further evidence for this view comes from Day's long hesitation before finally joining the Church herself. "I lived with this bitterness and sickened under it for a year," she wrote four years later. "I was sick with the struggle to keep human love and the love of God. I can say truthfully that I gave up human love when it was at its strongest and tenderest because I had experienced the overwhelming conviction that I could not live longer without God."[50]

The heavy price she had to pay for conversion, the loss of her lover and the father of her child, may have helped reassure Day that turning to the Church was not an act of weakness. Certainly she searched herself deeply to make sure that religion was not merely a psychological placebo.

> When I walked to the village for the mail, I found myself praying again, holding in my pocket the rosary that Mary Gordon gave me. Maybe I did not say it correctly, but I kept on saying it because it made me happy.
>
> Then I thought suddenly, scornfully, "Here you are in a stupor of content, like a cow. . . . Prayer with you is the opiate. . . ."
>
> "But," I reasoned with myself, "I am praying because I am happy, not because I am unhappy." And encouraged that I was praying because I wanted to thank Him, I went on praying. No matter how dull the day, how long the walk seemed, if I felt sluggish at the beginning of the walk, the words I had been saying insinuated themselves into my heart before I had finished, so that on the trip back I neither prayed nor thought, but was filled with exultation.[51]

It was not in despair, but in great joy, especially at the birth of her child, that Day gave free rein to her powerful religious instincts.[52] She now interpreted her long struggle over religion in light of Pascal's epigram, "Thou wouldst not seek Him if thou hadst not already found

Him." She gave herself over completely to religious reading—St. Augustine's *Confessions*, *The Imitation of Christ*, William James's *Varieties of Religious Experience*. It was the last that introduced her to the tradition of the saints. Passing over James's skepticism, Day became captivated by feminine models like Teresa of Avila. Her comments on that saint were replete with personal meaning: "She was a mystic and a practical woman, a recluse and a traveler. She liked to read novels when she was a young girl, and she wore a bright red dress when she entered the convent. Once . . . when she was crossing over a stream, she was thrown from her donkey. The story goes that the Lord said to her, 'That is how I treat my friends,' and she replied, 'That is why You have so few of them.'" Her reading removed any lingering doubts that she could remain religious outside the Church. She felt she had "to associate myself with others in loving and praising God." Yet when she finally took the step and was baptized in a small Staten Island church on December 28, 1927, it was only with "misery" at resolving her spiritual crisis by losing her lover. "I had no particular joy in partaking of the three sacraments, Baptism, Penance, Holy Eucharist. I proceeded grimly, coldly, making acts of faith, with no consolation whatever. One part of my mind stood at one side and kept saying, 'What are you doing? Are you sure of yourself? What kind of affectation is this? Are you trying to induce emotion, induce faith?' I felt like a hypocrite when I got down on my knees." [53]

III

Part of Day's remaining anxiety came from questions about how joining the Church would affect her life. The conversion settled some of the issues that had dominated her youth, but left others unresolved. It ended her long spiritual struggle but gave little indication where her new religious identity would take her. She was now a mother and could thus partly satisfy the side of herself that had always longed for love, domesticity, and order in daily existence. Yet the conversion had left her without a husband, making her family life a reminder of her unconventional past. She was now free to define her own life and career; yet that act of womanly self-assertion would take place not in the familiar avant-garde sector of American society, but among people who held extremely traditional views on questions of woman's place. Finally, Day's conversion had been for her an act of personal honesty and love for mankind that grew out of her social commitments; yet she was now cut off from the old ways of fulfilling her vocation as an intellectual and a radical.

Applying the term *intellectual* to Dorothy Day may seem curious because so many writers have stressed her emotionalism, simplicity, and lack of analytical ability. The Catholic historian David J. O'Brien is only one of many who have observed that she "lacked powers of constructive thought and precise analysis." Day herself admitted her limitations when it came to complex theoretical ideas. She "could not understand Marx," she once said. Pascal she found equally opaque. Even her friends were sometimes beyond her; she recalled one conversation among Burke, Cowley, and Dos Passos "which stood out especially in my memory because I could not understand a word of it." Although failure to comprehend Kenneth Burke could hardly be considered evidence of a weak mind, there is little to contradict Day's modest assessment of her ability to think and reason abstractly.[54]

But abstract thought is only one of the functions of the mind. Richard Hofstadter once said that "*intellect* is the critical, creative, and contemplative side of mind," (italics mine) and he went on to define an intellectual as a person in whom the "piety" and "playfulness" of the intellect are combined.[55] By this definition—a definition that would rule out a good many brilliant thinkers—one can make a case for calling Dorothy Day an intellectual, though hardly a typical one. Knowledge, critical thought, and reflection can be applied, not only to theoretical analysis, but to seeking an understanding of human events and lives, to the world of social and personal relationships, conflicts, and aspirations. For this sort of intellectual task the crucial ingredient is not ratiocination (though some conceptual ability is probably necessary) but a special kind of perception—the ability to sympathize, to "feel with," to see into other persons' situations and understand their lives. This "critical, creative, and contemplative" quality we recognize as the particular gift of the novelist and dramatist, though it also distinguishes the best historians and journalists.

The young Dorothy Day had developed a generous measure of just such a talent. An engaging conversationalist and careful listener, she had an extremely quick mind and retentive memory that served her well as a writer. She was also a working journalist, and like a few others in that field, she managed to combine an interest in hard facts and social institutions with a thoughtful sensitivity to the hidden meanings and subtle implications of human situations. Her strong reliance on fiction and drama as primary guides to the moral and spiritual universe accustomed her to looking at people with the attentive eye of the artist. She agreed with her friend Malcolm Cowley that "the purpose of literature is to lead us deeper into life," but she was also able to see in everyday life the stuff of the greatest literature. It was no accident that her tastes ran strongly toward Russian writers, whose combination of grand historical realism, intense emotionality, religious awe, and great interest in character, especially extreme types, conformed to her own sensibility. In her writings before and after her conversion, she alluded frequently to Tolstoy, Artzybasheff, Figner, Gorky, Chekhov, Turgenev, and especially Dostoevski, whose works she regarded as religiously and psychologically unsurpassed. She knew *The Brothers Karamazov* cover to cover and used it as an endless source of quotations and insights into religion and character. She also drew frequently on Dostoevski's other major novels as well as his lesser-known works, such as *A Friend of the Family*, *The Raw Youth*, and *The Honest Thief*.[56]

These intellectual concerns added depth to Day's writing, which was of notably uneven quality. Except when she did straight reporting, she wrote in a chatty, informal style that verged on stream of consciousness. In longer works the digressions and free associations often became distracting, and her lack of formal training showed up in rough syntax. But despite these flaws, Day could be a formidable writer. A keen observer of herself and others, she knew how to combine reporting and reflection into vignettes and commentaries that were penetrating yet completely down to earth. She had an eye for physical details but also a knack for getting to the heart of a matter, whether social, personal, or religious. While her tone invited intimacy, it never presumed upon the reader or condescended to him; thus she appealed to both a popular and a discriminating audience. The bulk of her work was ephemeral, but the best of it showed signs of literary merit.

If young Dorothy Day can thus be called an intellectual, it is also quite clear that her temperament and outlook differed considerably from those of most intellectuals. She always sought out the company of writers and artists and admired their work, but she frequently complained of something lacking in their attitudes toward life. Although she loved her intellectual friends, she felt they often substituted glibness and pseudo-sophistication for deeper moral and spiritual insight. "This exaltation of the articulate may obscure everything that we know," she said.[57] She rebelled at the notion of an intellectual elite cut off from ordinary human concerns or social problems, and considered religious and social ideas too important to be left to a few experts. If ordinary people were not exposed to the best thought available in their society, she believed, they would be open to crude prejudice. While Day's own coversion had certainly been deeply emotional, her religiosity had an important intellectual dimension as well. As she made her way "from Union Square to Rome," she began to look for ways to use her intellectual and journalistic talents in service of the new faith.

Day also sought to fulfill her calling as a radical. Converting to Catholicism did not mean repudiating her radical past, but rescuing from it all that was valuable and applying it to new purposes. "The convert wants to relate his faith to all his past experiences, all he has learned, all he has done," she said.[58] From Day's radical past she retained above all her love for the poor and downtrodden of society. Unlike some of her fellow radicals, Day genuinely liked ordinary people as individuals and not simply as part of a category, the "workers" or the "masses." She saw herself clearly as an American radical activist in the tradition that stretched back through Greenwich Village to the IWW, Debs, and the nineteenth century, but it was her own feeling for common people and their struggles, and not any social theory, that inspired her commitment.

But if the roots of Day's continuing radicalism were nonideological, the content was obviously derived from the American radical movement rather than simple personal sentiment or folk belief. Except on matters of religion and sexuality, her most cherished convictions faithfully reflected the ideals of American radicalism as they had developed at that time. Some of these principles were common property of the whole American experience, but were pressed with millennial urgency by the radical movement: personal liberty, greater social and economic equality, hostility to political coercion, and the general utopian sense of expanding human possibilities in an endlessly open future. Others belonged more specifically to the thought and experience of Day's own generation: a drive for a greater unity of life and art, an attempt to close the gap between private and public morality, a hostility to corporate capitalism and all its "bourgeois" works, and an inclination, at once visionary and practical, to start turning utopian dreams of greater social equality into realities, not in some distant future but immediately.

And if there was about all this a deadly serious commitment and anger at social evils, Day also kept something of the prewar American radical movement's sense that working for ideals was interesting and adventuresome, and that a life of social commitment, while sometimes dreary and unrewarding, could also be great fun. The fracturing of the movement after World War I, and the sometimes tragic personal experiences of those like Day who had participated in it, destroyed the innocence of that earlier American radicalism. Those who retained their radical commitments were forced to develop a far more sober and realistic outlook on life. But many of them, including Dorothy Day, never lost that older American belief that tragedy is not the final word in any human drama.

Though Day brought this radical heritage with her into the Church, she was at a complete loss about what to do with it. As a Catholic she was suddenly cut off from her closest friends and her old forms of commitment. "I wonder how many people realize the loneliness of the convert," she said. "[Conversion] meant giving up a whole society of friends and fellow workers. It was such a betrayal, they thought. One who had yearned to walk in the footsteps of a Mother Jones and an Emma Goldman had turned her back on the entire radical movement and sought shelter in that great, corrupt Holy Roman Catholic Church. . . ."[59] She wanted to remain a radical but could see no way to do so.

During the first four years after her conversion, the major continuity from her past appeared to be not social commitment, but her continued vocational uncertainty and rather aimless drifting. She stayed on for a time in New York, working at several odd jobs, then in August 1929, signed on as a Hollywood scriptwriter. But she disliked that work and after a few months left for Mexico, where she lived in a poor section of Mexico City with her daughter.

From Mexico she began submitting occasional articles to the Catholic journals *Commonweal* and *America*. Mexico was rife with political and religious controversy at the time, but Day concentrated on simple accounts of daily life among the country's poor.[60] In the summer of 1930 she returned to the United States. With the Great Depression settling over the country, she witnessed poverty nearly as severe as Mexico's. "On the fringes, by the rivers, on almost every vacant lot there was a Hooverville, where the homeless huddled in front of their fires."[61] She took a job with the New York Public Library, but journalistic assignments and a new novel took up most of her time. *Commonweal* and *America* were interested in the sudden upsurge of social action in the country, and saw in Day someone well qualified to report on such matters. She began covering rent strikes, Communist meetings, intellectuals' conferences, and activities of the unemployed.[62]

For a time she preserved the posture of noninvolvement. But the past life and experience she wanted to relate to her new faith was not primarily that of a reporter, but that of a committed advocate of social change. In December 1932 she was in Washington to cover a Communist hunger march that had been long delayed by injunctions:

> On a bright sunny day the ragged horde paraded three thousand strong through the tree-flanked streets of Washington. I stood on the curb and watched them, joy and pride in the courage of this band of men and women mounting in my heart, and with it a bitterness, too, that since I was now a Catholic, with fundamental differences, I could not be out there with them. . . .
> When the demonstration was over and I had finished writing

my story I went to the national shrine at Catholic University on the feast of the Immaculate Conception. There I offered up a special prayer, a prayer which came with tears and anguish, that some way would open up for me to use what talents I possessed for my fellow workers, for the poor.[63]

On her return to New York, she met Peter Maurin, an itinerant French peasant and social agitator, who urged her to start a Catholic newspaper for the unemployed. There were plenty of obstacles, but the first issue of the *Catholic Worker* was ready for May Day.

Dorothy Day had spent her youth exploring the seemingly conflicting demands of family, religion, social concern, and vocation. Now, at age thirty-five, she believed she had found her life's work in the public attempt to bring together Catholic faith and social concern in a paper for the poor. But certain as she was of her chosen role, the prospects of success for such a venture lay only partly within her control. What would it mean for a former Greenwich Village radical, and a woman at that, to carry on her radical agitation within the specific context of the Roman Catholic Church in America? Dorothy Day had been converted to the universal spiritual values of the Catholic faith. She now entered a unique branch of Catholicism, one quite unlike anything that had ever existed in the Church's history. Day had found her own way to reconcile faith and social radicalism, but how that might translate into public activity would depend on the much larger conditions of society and history that existed in the United States. Dorothy Day's personal search was over. The arena of her struggle was now no longer herself, but her Church and her society.

CHAPTER TWO

Religion and Social Thought: The American Context

The wedding of faith and social action derives from venerable religious traditions and has taken many forms in the past. Dorothy Day's Catholic Worker movement is historically significant as the first major expression of radical social criticism in American Catholicism. The Catholic Worker came on the scene just as Catholicism and Catholic social thought were assuming a distinctive place in American culture. The movement brought together some rare ingredients and blended them into something quite new, but it developed the mix within an existing context of American religious social thought. A consideration of Protestant and Catholic social ideas from 1870 to 1930 provides a framework for interpreting an American movement professing both orthodox Catholicism and social radicalism.

I

In the half-century before the Great Depression, American religion had confronted the unprecedented social conditions of industrialization and urbanization. Although they faced many of the same problems, Protestant and Catholic thinkers approached them from different vantage points and emerged with alternative prescriptions for social betterment. The roots of these differences, which appeared with particular clarity among the more extreme social critics in Protestantism and Catholicism, lay in divergent historical experiences in America, in disparate ideas about social reform, and, ultimately, in different religious outlooks.

25

Much of the variation between Protestant and Catholic social thought can be explained by observing that during the critical formative era of the industrial transformation, Protestantism was confidently at home in American culture and Catholicism was not. In 1927 the French visitor André Siegfried wrote that "Protestantism has been America's national religion, and to ignore that fact is to view the country from a false angle."[1] Most Americans were Protestant by cultural heritage if not by strict church membership, and from the seventeenth-century Puritan settlements to the nineteenth-century evangelical empire, Protestantism achieved an extraordinary identification with the life of the nation.[2] In the preindustrial centuries Protestantism had both shaped American society and been shaped by it; thus, it has often been difficult even for historians to tell which was cause and which was effect. Nineteenth-century church historians like Robert Baird, Daniel Dorchester, and Leonard Woolsey Brown may have exaggerated the direct influence of religion on American history, but they were not far wrong in seeing American Protestantism as "the religious expression of the whole national experience."[3] The Protestant churches, while still carrying a religious inheritance from the larger biblical and Christian worlds, had become so thoroughly identified with the American way of life by the mid-nineteenth century that the theological distinctions between the righteous and the unconverted, between the church and the world, were more and more difficult to maintain.

This was perhaps the major significance of the "New Theology" of the 1870s and 1880s formulated by Horace Bushnell and spread by popular preachers like Henry Ward Beecher and Phillips Brooks. Their "liberal" interpretations of the classical Christian doctrines were less a concession to new intellectual attacks on orthodoxy than a simple recognition that Protestant evangelism now operated in a culture where the boundaries between the "religious" and the "secular" were no longer clear. As Brooks said, "I do not know how a man can be an American, even if he is not a Christian, and not catch something of God's purpose for this great land. . . . The spirit of the world feels the things the church means, and tries to do them in another way."[4] This kind of accommodation between church and culture posed troubling religious questions, but the fact that the New Theology aroused so little intellectual opposition at the time and was widely hailed as another example of American Protestantism's successful adaptation to an evolving American society demonstrates how smooth was the fit between Protestantism and its cultural environment.[5] Even when Protestants in the early industrial era began to feel apprehensive about their country's future, they could derive hope from a contemplation of its past.[6]

To Catholics, America taught a different history lesson. While Protestantism came over on the decks of the *Mayflower* in the seventeenth century, Catholicism arrived in steerage in the nineteenth. (The exception was the tiny colonial elite, mostly in Maryland and Pennsylvania, whose experiences were alien to industrial-era Catholic immigrants.) Protestants laid the foundation of a new nation, while Catholics came as strangers to an established and often hostile culture. Catholics might struggle for economic and political success in America, but they could not easily erase the non-American cultural associations of their religion. A poor British Protestant immigrant arriving in, say, 1910 probably felt more culturally at ease in the United States than even a third- or fourth-generation Irish Catholic. Anti-Catholicism only became violent when it was linked to antiforeign nativism, but the fact that anti-Catholicism remained a significant factor long after the bulk of the Catholic population had ceased to be foreign suggests that it was the strangeness of the religion itself that aroused native (i.e., Protestant) concern.[7] That is why such episodes as the American Protective Association agitation of the 1890s, the Ku Klux Klan revival of the 1920s, and the anti-Catholicism during the 1928 Smith campaign were so painfully humiliating for Catholics, even though they were mild compared with the violent outbursts of the early nineteenth century: They suggested that Catholics were destined to remain cultural outsiders in America simply by virtue of their religion, which they could never abandon.[8]

The consequence of this situation was that much of Catholic thought was preoccupied with the relationship of Catholicism to American culture—a question that did not exist in the same way for Protestantism. Besides the problem of defending themselves against bigotry, Catholics had genuine difficulties relating their inherited religious practices and cultural ideals to a society that granted those ideals little value. This problem provided the context for the great struggle between Catholic "conservatives" and "liberals" in the late nineteenth century. The central issue was not social thought or theology, though both entered into it; instead the disagreement was about the prospects of reconciling the essentials of the Catholic religion with American civilization, which apparently rested on non-Catholic principles. Liberals like Bishop John Ireland and the Paulist fathers worked aggressively to "Americanize" the Church and to assure Protestants that it presented no threat to the dominant culture; conservatives like Bishop Bernard McQuaid and the Jesuits retained a hostile, defensive attitude toward a culture they regarded as inherently antithetical to Catholicism.[9] This controversy, heightened and complicated by ethnic rivalries, the parochial school question, and the meddling of some European Catholics, culminated in the bitter

"Americanism" crisis of 1895–1900. Pope Leo XIII's encyclicals *Longinqua Oceani* (1895) and *Testem Benevolentiae* (1899), while acknowledging the practical necessity of adjusting the Church to American institutions, warned sharply that "it would be very erroneous to draw the conclusion that in America is to be sought the type of the most desirable status of the Church, or that it could be universally lawful for state and church to be, as in America, dissevered and divorced."[10]

Although liberals like Ireland and Isaac Hecker promoted an almost uncritical enthusiasm for America and its culture, they have rightly been credited with raising the crucial question of how the ancient religious traditions of Catholicism should be related to a society born and raised in an age of liberty, democracy, and individualism. However, with that discussion largely suppressed within the intellectual sphere, the Church proceeded to make its way in American society without much systematic thought about what it was doing. Although the tremendous task of absorbing another vast wave of newcomers from southern and eastern Europe was not without strain, the adjustment of the "immigrant Church" to the external forms of American society proceeded with remarkable dispatch in the early twentieth century. Catholics might live somewhat apart from their countrymen in urban neighborhoods and social life, but they readily adopted most conventional American attitudes and practices. With the Church functioning as a halfway house for Americanization, neither the extreme defensiveness of the older conservatives nor the aggressive programs of the liberals seemed viable or necessary.

This acculturation without ideas undoubtedly eased the gradual acceptance of Catholics into American life, for it conformed to reigning secular notions about the place of religion in society as well as to the general nonideological bent of American culture. If Catholicism could come to be viewed primarily in sociological terms, as simply another denomination in the pluralistic American stew, rather than as a culturally powerful religious worldview, then it could be much more readily incorporated into the mainstream.

To say that Catholic acculturation occurred without ideas, however, does not mean that it entirely lacked an intellectual posture. On the contrary, there were a number of Catholic intellectuals in the early twentieth century who labored mightily to develop a cultural perspective appropriate to the American Church. But as historian William Halsey has brilliantly argued, they almost unanimously settled on a curiously defensive formula that combined outmoded forms of native American "innocence" with a mélange of Catholic "certainties" from past ages. "Untouched by postwar disillusionment," Halsey says, "Catholics set out as 'providential hosts' to defend the values and promises of American idealism which seemed threatened by various forms of irrationalism: probability in scientific thought, the subconscious in psychology, skepticism in literature, and relativism in law and morality." [11] While this outlook could at times score critical points against the disturbing new elements of post–World War I American life, its real effect was to keep Catholics from creative engagement with the living culture of their country.

The advantage of this formula, while it lasted, was that it helped spare America the kind of severe conflicts over religiously based issues that plagued many European nations in the modern era. By buying up a wholesale lot of shares in the American dream, Catholics acquired an attractively ready-made set of moral and social ideals, a buoyant communal spirit, and the growing toleration and even respect of most of their non-Catholic neighbors. The cost was an effective abandonment of the essential Catholic tenet that religion should shape culture rather than culture shaping religion.

History formed the cultural perspectives of Protestantism and Catholicism in America; it also affected their economic and social positions. Having first possessed the continent, Protestants naturally assumed a command of its institutions and wealth as their inherited birthright. To an American alive between 1870 and 1930, the association of the Protestant churches with a higher status would have seemed an obvious and immutable feature of American life. Throughout this period northern mainline Protestantism was solidly middle or upper class. An 1888 survey in Pittsburgh, for example, showed that 60 percent of Protestants in the city were "capitalists, professional men, lawyers, teachers," while less than 10 percent belonged to the working class. [12] In 1875 a denominational editorialist observed characteristically that "most of the readers of this paper are undoubtedly, compared with the mass of the community, in comfortable circumstances." [13] And when another commentator asserted in 1883 that "church members average much more moral, intelligent, and wealthy than non-church members as the natural result of church training," it was obvious that he had Protestants in mind. [14] Standard histories sometimes leave the impression that this situation somehow altered when Protestantism moved toward a new social awareness after 1890, but this was not the case. After several decades of Social Gospel preaching, institutional churches, and urban missions, the social makeup of mainline Protestantism outside the South was basically unchanged. While other forms of Protestantism, especially the new Pentecostal and holiness churches, attracted a large lower-class following in this period, such movements did not significantly alter the overall pattern of Protestant relations with major social institutions. A 1919 report of the Federal Council of Churches stated that although union leaders had become more friendly to the churches than formerly, the mainline denominations still attracted almost no working-class members. In urban America, Protestantism remained, the *Christian Century* lamented in 1920, "a bourgeois church in a proletarian world."[15]

Even if not all Protestants were well off, then the well-off were mainly Protestant. Until well into the twentieth century the upper levels of academic, business, and political life in America retained a Protestant character. In the universities the administrations, as well as the culturally important history and literature departments, bore a clear Protestant stamp. In business, industrialists like John D. Rockefeller, Cornelius Vanderbilt, Leland Stanford, Daniel Drew, Jay Cooke, and John P. Crozer were identifiably Protestant and contributed substantially to churches and seminaries. Protestants also held sway in public life. Between 1865 and 1933 all but four cabinet members were Protestant, and the presidents of the period were more than conventional churchgoers. Garfield was an ordained minister of the Disciples of Christ, Hayes an active Congregationalist layman. In the election of 1896 voters could choose between two active, pious evangelicals, Bryan and McKinley. And it is impossible to understand Theodore Roosevelt and Woodrow Wilson without taking into account the pervasive influence of a moralizing Protestantism on their personalities, rhetoric, and worldview.

Catholicism in America enjoyed no such social advantages. Although Catholics suffered no legal disabilities after the colonial era (the last state restrictions were removed in the 1840s), Catholicism in the early industrial era was a religion of the working and lower-middle classes. Although the "famine Irish" certainly arrived in desperate condition, recent historical studies have indicated that the image of most nineteenth-century Catholics as desperately poverty-stricken is overdrawn. By the 1870s many urban Catholics had risen into the categories of skilled labor, small tradesmen, and municipal employees rather than unskilled labor.[16] Yet if it is well to keep in mind that for Catholics "Lowell was a damn sight better than County Cork"—or later, Lvov or the Mezzogiorno—it remains a fact that during the early industrial era, most Catholics were nearer the bottom than the top of America's social and economic ladder. Furthermore, it appears that after initial gains Catholics found themselves locked for several decades on a kind of plateau; as late as 1940 two-thirds of the Catholics in one religious survey were described as lower class, rather than middle or upper class. Only in the 1940s and 1950s did the majority of American Catholics make dramatic improvements in social status.[17]

If Catholics made only slow progress into the middle ranks of society, they found it even more difficult to reach the top. Catholics pointed proudly to their co-religionists who had held high office in America—Charles Carroll, signer of the Declaration of Independence; Roger Taney, chief justice of the Supreme Court—but these were exceptions. Although Catholics were the largest American denomination after 1850, and made up about one-sixth of the population, they held only 1 percent of federal judgeships; by 1925 the figure had risen to only 4 percent.[18] Catholics were also underrepresented in Congress, and it was not until Al Smith became governor of New York and a Democratic presidential contender that a Catholic attained truly national political stature. A similar situation prevailed in business and education: Individual Catholics achieved prominence, but in nothing like their proportion of the population.[19] Efforts of intellectuals like John Lancaster Spaulding to promote Catholic higher learning, notably in the Catholic University of America, met with much disappointment.[20]

Whether Catholic social marginality in this period was caused primarily by Protestant hostility or was simply a natural consequence of Catholics' immigrant background is difficult to say. As usual in such circumstances, prejudice tended to keep the group in low status, and low status tended to reinforce prejudice. In any case, the implications of these differences for the social thought of both Protestants and Catholics were great. Because most Protestants entered the industrial age in relatively secure economic circumstances, they did not experience so directly the severe social dislocations attendant on the process. The problems of urban crowding, poverty, unemployment, and labor strife generally appeared from outside, and below, their own social situations. Because such problems seemed threatening to the society they knew, the initial reaction of the Protestant churches was almost universally negative. Before they could respond positively to industrial conditions, comfortable Protestants first had to discover a harsher world beyond their normal experience. Only then could they fashion a sympathetic response based on moral and religious sympathy rather than self-interest.[21]

The Social Gospel appeared as an articulate and definable movement precisely because it caused some Protestants to break with the historical experience and accepted interests of the Protestant community as a whole. The conversion experiences of the Social Gospel's most representative figures, men raised to the security and status of the Protestant ministry, typically involved some kind of eye-opening encounter with the alien lower-class world. For instance, as pastor of First Congregational Church in Columbus, Washington Gladden discovered that during the violent Hocking Coal Strike of 1884, his congregation included the principal coal company officials but none of the workers. His sympathy for the miners developed as he explored the reasons for this situation.[22] Walter Rauschenbusch underwent a similar intense conversion to "the social passion" during his ministry in the Hell's Kitchen district of New York, and his experience was later repeated by men like Charles Stelzle, Harry Ward, A. J. Muste, and Reinhold Niebuhr, who, like the Social Gospel pioneers, had grown up in secure Protestant communities.[23]

The rise of the Social Gospel generally meant a break by prominent Protestant spokesmen with economic orthodoxy and the older Protestant tradition of benevolent charity and social service perpetuated by conservative "social Christians" like Minot Savage and Joseph Cook, and the conservative evangelical denominations like the Salvation Army.[24] But despite this difference, the thought of the early Social Gospel leaders reflected their origins in the middle-class Protestant community and their ambivalence about abandoning the moral foundations of nineteenth-century individualism. In their optimistic assumptions about material and social progress, their emphasis on individual moral attitudes rather than power as the key to social change, and their description of the emerging Christian world order—the Kingdom of God—as a state of paternally ordered brotherhood among men, they reflected the cultural ideals and benign social harmony that prevailed within their homogeneous Protestant communities. Thus, Gladden's social preachments and reform activities remained largely in keeping with the benevolent social outlook of his well-off Ohio parishioners. In a typical sermon, he observed that "philanthropy, the principle of compassion and kindness, has been largely organized into the social life of the nation. The defective and dependent classes are now wards of the state. A considerable part of the life of civilized society is controlled by the Christian principle, and we have come to a day when it does not seem quixotic to believe that all social relations are to be Christianized."[25]

The second generation of Social Gospel leaders like Walter Rauschenbusch who came into prominence after 1900 were more critical than Gladden of the existing order, and more inclined to recognize the stubborn persistence of sin in the form of individual and collective selfishness. But Rauschenbusch too identified desired social change with the Kingdom of God already immanent in Protestant church life: "The Church has the greatest possible interest in a just and even distribution of wealth. The best community for church support at present is a comfortable middle class neighborhood. A social system which would make moderate wealth approximately universal would be the best soil for robust churches." [26]

Of course this close tie between the Social Gospel and the powerful Protestant community in some ways represented the movement's strength. It meant that the Social Gospel could sometimes affect society in substantial ways. At a time when the ministry still had considerable moral sway, critical comments from a Gladden or a Rauschenbusch about powerful industrialists, for instance, were not simply rhetorical gestures. Yet the tie to the community of power also tended to tame the ideas of the Social Gospel and confine its audience to those Americans who shared a particular experience and vocabulary. For all their genuine innovation in some areas, the first two generations of Social Gospel leaders remained fundamentally bound by the conventional symbols and values of their Victorian churchly heritage. [27]

The Social Gospel was transformed when the church itself became a significant problem for the most sophisticated Protestant social thought. Later Social Gospel leaders, while they often shared the background and ideals of their predecessors, were no longer able to simply identify the Gospel with the churches. Perhaps because they saw how little the Social Gospel had affected the Protestant community and American society as a whole, perhaps because they were more often editors, seminarians, and full-time activists than parish ministers, newer leaders began to locate the meaning of the Gospel and the Kingdom outside the churches. As the problems of class and power came to the forefront of social thought, the next generation of Social Gospel activists like A. J. Muste, Norman Thomas, Harry Ward, and Reinhold Niebuhr leveled class-conscious criticisms at the community that had bred them. Paul Tillich, a product of German social Protestantism who emigrated to the United States, stated the dilemma in 1931: "The proletarian situation . . . is the point at which history itself has posed the question to Protestantism, whether it will identify itself with the traditional forms in which it has been realized, or whether it will accept a challenge that calls into question a large part of its present day life and thought. The Protestant judgment becomes concrete, actual, and urgent in its application to the class situation of today." [28]

Protestant social thought deepened by contradicting Protestant experience; Catholic social thought emerged only slowly out of the depths of Catholic experience. For American Catholicism, unlike European, the problems of industrialization appeared not as external challenges to an established ethos, but as integral elements of the common life. The Catholic Church in this country did not have to discover urban social problems or the distress of working-class life; these conditions formed the basis of its own existence. "The Catholic Church is emphatically the workingman's church," lamented one Protestant minister in 1887. "She rears her edifices in the midst of the densest populations, provides them with many seats and has the seats filled."[29] The problem for Protestantism was how to reach a lower class with whom it had little in common; for Catholicism, it was to keep abreast of the pressing demands from a working-class membership eager for its ministrations. American Catholicism's encounter with industrialization, therefore, was more institutional and practical than intellectual or moral, more an unconscious necessity than a conscious choice. Its leaders were not a minority of articulate prophets challenging accepted beliefs, but numerous clergy and lay persons who seldom understood or proclaimed their activities as a distinctively religious response to industrialization.[30] Many Catholics, therefore, had a long experience in coping with social problems before they began to reflect on them.

The religious ideal of disinterested charity retained a place in American Catholicism, but it was effectively merged with a practical ethic of communal self-help. Catholic groups like the St. Vincent de Paul Society and the Sisters of Mercy helped establish a vast network of Catholic charitable institutions, but because the constituency of these agencies was so largely drawn from the distressed Catholic population itself, they tended to express communal solidarity—"taking care of our own"—as much as charitable benevolence. This impulse was strengthened by the widespread fear—and often fact—of Protestant proselytizing in orphanages, industrial schools, youth homes, and other institutions. In 1899 an agent of the Catholic Home Bureau wrote, "Experience has shown us that in the city of New York alone hundreds of children of Catholic parentage are every year placed in non-Catholic institutions . . . where their faith must almost inevitably be lost."[31] In the 1860s, decades before the creation of more-publicized Protestant institutional churches and settlement houses, a few Catholic parishes like St. James's and St. Stephen's in New York established elaborate social services for their tenement-dwelling parishioners. At St. Stephen's Father Edward McGlynn supervised activities that included day care, recreation, employment counseling; by 1900 the church was visited by more than ten thousand people a day.[32] Few Catholic parishes were able or willing to provide such services, but many were home to forms of self-help organized by the immigrant Catholics themselves. Parish benevolent unions, mutual aid societies, burial societies, and similar forms of primitive social security flourished during the late nineteenth and early twentieth centuries, and many of them were eventually combined into national associations like the Irish Catholic Benevolent Union and the German Catholic Central Verein.[33] Like the rudimentary social services provided by urban political machines, these resources were inadequate to cope with really hard times, but they did provide some cushions against the vicissitudes of industrial life.

The history of the American Catholic hierarchy's involvement with the labor movement also illustrates how circumstance induced Catholic support for social reform even when there was little intellectual basis for such a position. In the 1880s numbers of Catholic laborers joined the Knights of Labor, the semisecret order that had earlier been condemned by the Catholic Church in Canada. In 1887 Cardinal James Gibbons, the leader of the American hierarchy, interceded with Rome to prevent a complete condemnation of the Knights. He thereby won for the American Church a lasting reputation for sympathy to the working-man. In some respects Gibbons's historical reputation as a "friend of labor" is undeserved. His arguments against condemnation of the Knights showed little real sympathy for organized labor. The cardinal had a genuine pastoral sympathy for the workers' plight, but he was also very concerned that American Catholic workers would abandon the Church if it prohibited their legitimate efforts at self-improvement. Although more optimistic and tolerant about social matters than their adversaries, the Catholic liberals like Gibbons and Bishop John Ireland held no advanced ideas on matters of social class and social justice. Gibbons believed that distinctions in wealth and status between employers and workers were "a law of life established by an overruling Providence"; he saw Mormonism, divorce, "a vicious system of education, the desecration of the Sabbath, and a dilatory system of justice" as the central moral issues facing American society.[34] Despite their political battles and polemical exchanges, early Catholic conservatives and liberals differed more in temperament and in their attitudes toward American culture than in fundamental social views.

Nevertheless, the fact that the best-known leaders of the American Church were tolerant of labor organization meant that the American Church took a generally progressive stance on industrial issues. Limited evidence suggests that most parish priests, as well, at least accepted and sometimes encouraged their working-class constituency's efforts at organization. In the anthracite fields, for example, parish priests held services for strikers at the time of the violent Lattimer incident in 1897, even though they disapproved of worker violence. Compared to the average Protestant minister, observed economist Richard Ely, the Catholic priest had no difficulty being fair to labor. "It is not a difference of good will so much as a difference of knowledge. The Catholic reveals an acquaintance with the movements of the masses—the Protestant ignorance."[35] At times priests even led such movements, as Father Edward McGlynn did in backing Henry George's campaign for mayor of New York in 1887.[36]

The Church's toleration of working-class movements was contingent on their remaining explicitly anti-socialist and religiously neutral. After 1900 those conditions were increasingly assured in the American labor movement by the presence of Catholics themselves. Although the strategy of the American Federation of Labor was worked out independently, Catholics found it especially congenial. It is significant that the issue of socialism within the AFL was not resolved until the Progressive Era, when the swelling Catholic membership insured the AFL's future. By 1918 Catholics made up a majority of the organization, dominated the Executive Board, and held the presidencies of fifty internationals. While a few conservative bishops and priests saw dangers in the "mixed" AFL and occasionally fostered Catholic "dual unions" in Socialist union strongholds like Buffalo and St. Louis, the majority of Catholic leaders saw no reason for such a religiously divisive strategy when they could achieve their ends just as well within the AFL.[37]

The principal promoter of this alliance between the Church and conservative labor was Father Peter Dietz, who coordinated political activity among Catholic unionists through his Militia of Christ for Social Service, which functioned as an anti-Socialist caucus within the AFL. Dietz was also influential in other Catholic groups concerned with social reform, such as the Social Service Commission of the American Federation of Catholic Charities and the Central Verein, the distinctive organization that emerged from within the tightly knit German Catholic community. Under Dietz's direction, the 1911 convention of the Verein urged that "Catholic workingmen join trade unions whenever possible," but it warned that should the Socialists come to power in the AFL, then "all Catholics . . . would have to leave the Federation."[38] Such a test never came, even though most Catholic workers failed to join unions before the 1930s. Dietz proved that in America the Church could successfully combat Socialism without provoking the kind of mass defections from the faith and general ideological warfare it experienced in Europe. The price was Catholic acquiescence in the narrow job concerns and intellectual barrenness of the Gompers tradition.

The other major source of Catholic social thought in the prewar period was Father John A. Ryan. In contrast to Dietz's close ties to Catholic workers and union leaders, Ryan's career more nearly resembled that of most Protestant reformers. Although he grew up in a rural Minnesota infected with the Populist and Georgist heresies, Ryan's concerns were more those of a middle-class intellectual and social critic than of a mass-based political strategist like Dietz. Through his membership on numerous reform boards and committees (where he was usually the only Catholic representative), Ryan provided a link between the Catholic community and American Progressivism, which was not often sensitive to Catholic interests or concerns. Ryan's dual perspective as a spokesman for the particular interests of the Catholic community and a reformer concerned with the general social welfare was evident in his innovative use of Catholic natural law theory to promote social-justice reforms that were especially beneficial to the Catholic working class. His Catholic University doctoral dissertation, published in 1907 as *The Living Wage*, was a careful scholastic demonstration of the case for a minimum wage.[39]

From his position on the Catholic University faculty and through his extensive writings, Ryan also pushed the hierarchy into greater social concern. His efforts culminated in 1919 when he drew up the "Bishops' Program of Social Reconstruction" and succeeded in getting it adopted by the National Catholic War Council (later National Catholic Welfare Conference), the national organization of the hierarchy. This document, which called for minimum wage laws, collective bargaining legislation, social insurance, public housing, and worker participation in the ownership and management of industry, received considerable attention, and was greeted with anger by employer spokesmen like the National Civic Federation's Ralph Easley, who concluded that the bishops had been "duped by near Bolsheviks."[40] Easley's suspicions that the hierarchy's commitment to such a sweeping reform agenda was not wholehearted proved correct, for in the face of criticism and the growing conservative mood of the country, the bishops rapidly backed away from the program. It remained on the record as a statement of "ideals," but no effort was made to implement it. Even Ryan's NCWC Social Action Department, which reflected the liberal bent of the Bishops' Program, spent most of its time in the 1920s defending Catholic group interests rather than backing broad social reforms. Nevertheless, even the purely formal approval of the American hierarchy for the Bishops' Program indicates how the Church's experience in the United States inclined it to look favorably upon much of American liberalism's social-justice agenda, even though it could not approve of its intellectual underpinnings.

The similarity between the Catholic Social Action Department and the social service commissions of the Protestant denominations in the Federal Council of Churches suggests a certain common logic in institutional Christianity's response to industrialism in the United

States. But the differences of history, status, and thought that lay behind these organizations and their work made the lines of development merely parallel, not identical. Catholicism's immigrant background and distance from the dominant culture kept it apart from most of the Social Gospel and Progressive movements and left its social thought relatively underdeveloped and isolated from the American mainstream. A few activists like John Ryan admired the liberal tradition and tried to ally the Church with it, but they enjoyed little success before 1930. While Catholics could sometimes be enlisted in support of particular Progressive reforms—for example, regulation of urban housing—their involvement lacked the quality of moral passion and disinterested idealism that characterized much of middle-class Protestantism's support for social justice. Catholic commitment to social betterment was more obviously self-interested, more deeply rooted in the lives of the urban masses, more instinctively practical, and less intellectually developed than most of the Social Gospel. Catholics responding to industrialism did not "stand at Armageddon and battle for the Lord"; they coped in a confused, eclectic fashion with the demands of communal survival and upward mobility in America. This heritage spared American Catholicism much of the sentimentality, grand social preachment, and pious moralizing that later Protestant and secular reformers in the Social Gospel and Progressive traditions had to contend with. At the same time Catholics were more vulnerable to parochialism, anti-intellectualism, and the twists and turns of history. The career of Al Smith, which embraced both a simple, unreflective dedication to a better life for the urban masses he represented and a parochial suspicion of more-comprehensive reform proposals, suggests something of the strength and weakness of the Catholic experience in America.

The lack of any left- or right-wing opposition also indicates the immaturity of Catholic social thought. In America the characteristic function of both serious intellectual conservatism and radicalism has not been to shape social policy, but to deepen the reflections of the country's dominant liberal intellectual tradition. The Protestant Social Gospel quickly provoked a critique from both sides which helped define the movement and enrich its analysis. On the Right, the fundamentalist and conservative evangelical opposition to the Social Gospel and the Federal Council helped precipitate the "two-party system" that has characterized American Protestantism ever since. The most-thoughtful conservative opponents of the Social Gospel successfully demonstrated that it constituted a significant change of religious worldview—something Protestant liberals were slow to acknowledge.[41]

On the Left, a small but vocal radical wing prodded the Social Gospel toward stronger dissent and strengthened liberalism's acceptability among Protestants by making the liberals seem moderate and responsible. The most important early Protestant radical was George D. Herron, a Congregationalist minister and Professor of Applied Christianity at Grinnell College whose religious intensity and appeals for a "Christian socialist America" brought him sudden national attention in the mid-1890s. In a number of books—*The New Redemption*, *The Christian Society*, *The Christian State*—and on lecture platforms before large audiences, Herron called for "the restitution of stolen goods and an end to the accumulation of wealth through oppression, extortion, and economic atheism."[42]

Herron's meteoric career ended in an adultery scandal in 1905, but his radical vision of the social implications of Christianity was carried on by J. Stitt Wilson's Social Crusade and the Christian Socialist Fellowship. Organized in 1906, the Fellowship tried "to permeate churches, denominations, and other religious institutions with the social message of Jesus, showing that socialism is the necesary economic expression of the Christian life," and also to "strengthen the ethical and religious teaching within the Socialist Party."[43] Adding a religious dimension to the American Socialist Party might have been an easier assignment than converting the Protestant churches from capitalism, but neither goal was achieved. Among prominent Social Gospel leaders, only Walter Rauschenbusch was willing to call himself a "Christian socialist," and then of a "peculiar genus" uncommitted to any group or party of that label. Nevertheless, a strain of radical dissent clearly ran through American Protestantism's encounter with the industrial age.[44]

By contrast American Catholicism spawned little significant dissent before 1930. What passed for "conservatism" before that time was more an attitude of immigrant defensiveness than a fully developed social viewpoint. The Catholic militance of the nineteenth-century Jesuits and of bishops like McQuaid and Corrigan contained the germ of a social ideology, but not until Frederick Kenkel and the German Catholic *Wanderer* of the 1920s can one find anything like an American version of Catholic social conservatism. Although the eccentric Kenkel offered some telling criticisms of American industrial society, his ideas, like most forms of European-derived Catholic conservatism, were unable to take root in American soil.[45]

Intellectual radicalism had even less of a chance in early American Catholicism than conservatism. Only a few isolated Catholics identified themselves with radical ideas or movements. In the mid-nineteenth century T. Wharton Collens, a New Orleans judge and self-styled "Catholic communist and labor reformer" called for a cooperative commonwealth on the order of More's *Utopia*.[46] Individual Irish Catholics who professed radicalism were particularly attracted to Georgism or other land reform proposals. In 1909 a Catholic Socialist Society briefly reared its head in Chicago, and the next year some Polish Catholics came out openly for the Socialist ticket in Milwaukee. Two Catholic priests became well-known radicals. Father Thomas McGrady of Kentucky won an enthusiastic response from some Catholic workers when he declared that "American Socialism is entirely compatible with religion," and "violence is no more to be attributed to Socialism than the savage cruelty of a Torquemada is to be imputed to Catholicism." Father Thomas Haggerty promoted syndicalist unionism among his congregations in Chicago and Dallas and in 1905 became one of the founders of the Industrial Workers of the World. Neither Haggerty nor McGrady found much of a Catholic audience, however, and both soon left the Church.[47] Catholicism in general was hard ground for radical social dissent in this period, and the American Church, concerned about respectability as well as orthodoxy, seemed particularly well insulated against such tendencies.

The absence of any developed tradition of conservative or radical social thought within the Church often made it easier to say what Catholics were against than what they were for. Catholics were undoubtedly sincere, for example, in rejecting Socialism on religious grounds, but the obvious popularity of anti-Socialism in America tempted Catholics to stress that point rather than to develop their own perspectives. Catholics' disinclination to question basic social arrangements was also strongly encouraged by non-Catholic American conservatives who saw in the Church a political godsend for the established order. Mark Hanna, for example, stated that the only two safeguards against "anarchy" in the United States were the Supreme Court and the Catholic Church. William Howard Taft told a group of bishops that he considered Catholicism "the bulwark against socialism and anarchy in this country."[48] And as already noted, conservatives in the labor movement found the Church a valuable ally. By 1900 American Catholicism was already attracting ex-Socialist converts who seemed to value the Catholic religion primarily as an ideological weapon against social change.

Before 1930, then, the enormous social and intellectual implications of the large Catholic presence in America were only dimly recognized. Catholics had hardly begun to understand and interpret their own experience or consider it in the light of their richer universal traditions, much less speak thoughtfully about the condition of American society at large. This situation was about to change. The Church was becoming socially more at home in America and less fearful of criticizing the country's institutions. By 1930 new journals like *America* and *Commonweal* were examining matters of politics, culture, and morals with an increasing self-awareness. Most important, a few Catholics were again beginning to reflect on the deeper meanings of their religion's presence in America. Up to that time the Catholic religion had been largely an object of the nation's history. The mature development of American Catholic social thought would have to come not only from the community's own social experience, but from its reflection on the relations between Catholicism's universal traditions and American culture, and ultimately from Catholicism's distinctive religious evolution in this country.

II

Religion exists among men in history and society, yet it derives its singular importance in human affairs from its representation of mythical truths beyond time and social existence. Yet because religions themselves have histories, there is always a temptation to reduce religion to its social and historical dimensions and ignore its other qualities.[49] Furthermore, the complex interplay between religion and society often makes it extremely difficult to determine whether a particular historical development is due to a religious movement that altered society or to a social change that altered religion. This is perhaps more true of the religion of the West, Christianity, which has been especially alert to these matters because its fundamental myths themselves have a historical and social location. In its spectacular career across centuries, civilizations, and continents, Christianity has commonly supported dominant social and cultural arrangements. But on occasion it has turned sharply critical of society. This critical impulse has frequently taken the form of evangelical or millennial movements. Some of these have been short-term phenomena of rather limited historical significance, but others have instigated or advanced movements with tremendous social consequences.

The major impetus to social criticism throughout historical Christianity has come from particular interpretations of the Christian Gospel. Emerging from an environment of intense religious and ethical ferment, the Gospels have conveyed to later generations of Christians, in Ernst Troeltsch's classic statement, "a purity of intention and a greatly intensified reverence for moral commands based on the self-sacrificing love of God for his creatures." A "radical Gospel ethic" of this sort, where religious ideals of selflessness and poverty infuse social life, received special impetus from the Sermon on the Mount (Matthew 5–7), certain other sayings and parables of Jesus, and the apparent communism of primitive Christian communities described in Acts 5. The presence of such urgent social teachings in Christianity's most sacred writings and early history provided a permanent wellspring of potential social criticism. But as Troeltsch's great study also argued, the radical Gospel contained certain ambiguities and difficulties that made it a problematic guide for actual Christian social movements. The most important, he contended, was that grounding a communal social ethic in religion introduces a "sociological principle of authority" into any comprehensive value system based on it. Especially because the Gospel ethic presents such an elevated ideal of human social relations, "the security of the authority as its essential source will be a permanent task of the whole structure."[50]

Early Christianity developed other types of social thought less demanding than the radical Gospel. From St. Paul, St. Augustine, and others, later Christian thinkers derived social attitudes more appropriate to a universal religion.[51] Neverthless, while medieval Catholicism often invested existing social arrangements with religious sanction, it also continually produced dissenting movements with radical Gospel overtones that offered alternative views of Christianity's social implications. Of such movements Troeltsch says:

> In general the following are their characteristic features: lay Christianity, personal achievement in ethics and religion, the radical fellowship of love, indifference toward the authority of the state and the ruling classes, dislike of technical law and of the oath, the separation of religious life from the economic struggle by means of the ideal of poverty and frugality, or occasionally in a charity which becomes communism, the directness of personal religious relationship, criticism of official theologians, the appeal to the New Testament and the, Primitive Church.[52]

Most such movements were suppressed if they moved beyond quietist withdrawal to overt challenge of existing social arrangements. Nevertheless, their influence on the religious and social ideals of Western culture was considerable, and groups like the Brethren of the Common Life helped undermine the religious foundations of medieval church and society.

With the Reformation the advocacy of radical Gospel ideas for lay society passed almost entirely to Protestantism. Especially in the more radical wing of the Reformation, but also from within Calvinist and other traditions, radical Gospel notions provided a ready source of biblically inspired social thought and experiment that cropped up in widely scattered times and circumstances. The very presence of groups like the Moravians, Mennonites, and Quakers, even if they provided no direct challenge to the social order, offered a continuing testimony to the alternative social possibilities of religion. And sometimes, as in the Shaker, Oneida, and Mormon movements in early nineteenth-century America, millennial religion created impressive communal departures from prevailing social values.[53]

While the radical Gospel remained an active, if subordinate, tendency within Protestantism from the Reformation through the nineteenth century, it virtually disappeared in post-Tridentine Catholicism. Whereas medieval Catholicism's social conservatism had been continually counterpointed by radical Gospel opposition, later Catholicism seldom offered coherent alternatives to the status quo. Moreover, because Catholicism was strongest in lands where urban, capitalist, and democratic developments occurred more slowly, its social-ethical outlook was naturally linked to more traditional institutions and ideas. Even more fateful was the French Revolution, which appeared to fix a gulf between the Church and a whole complex of modern social ideas. In the nineteenth century it was commonly believed by most social thinkers of all persuasions that the "Catholic" values of order, hierarchy, and authority were irrevocably opposed to liberty, democracy, and social reform. Dissent from this dogmatic polarity did come from Catholic liberals like John Newman, Charles de Montalembert, Wilhelm von Ketteler, and Frédéric Ozanam, who resisted the Church's alliance with social reaction. But these liberals suffered a great defeat when Pius IX's *Syllabus of Errors* (1864) affirmed that it was "false to teach that the Roman pontiff can and ought to reconcile himself with progress, liberalism, and modern civilization."[54]

III

Just as European Catholicism enjoyed some advantages by allying itself with antimodern social conservatism, American Protestantism initially benefited by its symbiotic entanglement with early-modern social forms. In a New World where religion carried few traces of its earlier social authority, any sense of acute ethical tension between religion and society was difficult to sustain. Calvinism provided much of the original spiritual energy for American culture, but as the society evolved beyond its simpler early-modern forms, religion withdrew to a position of prosperous but subordinate partnership. By the mid-nineteenth century the American churches had acquiesced in a tacit social contract whereby religion addressed itself to the "personal, familial, and leisured sectors of life while the public dimensions—political, social, economic, cultural—were to become autonomous or pass under the control of other kinds of tutelage."[55] Accordingly, when American evangelical religion periodically "revived," its ethical-social consequences involved primarily personal morality or sumptuary legislation and seldom reached the dominant social arrangements. In the early republic evangelical Protestantism had sometimes sparked significant social criticism, especially in the great assault on slavery. (The sectional and premodern character of the peculiar institution made it an attractive target for northern Protestants. By contrast, Southern evangelicalism produced few significant antislavery movements.)[56] But after the Civil War, with reform energies spent and the basic relationship of religion and society apparently worked out, the major phases of the urban-industrial transformation could proceed with remarkably little institutional religious protest under the shrewd and soothing guidance of preachers like Dwight L. Moody and Henry Ward Beecher. True, the urban working classes were permanently lost to the churches, but even many American workers, in contrast to the European proletariat, appear to have held to a kind of unchurched Protestantism.[57]

While American Protestantism worked through its transition to modernism, however, it was also faced with a deep inner turmoil among its intellectuals. As developments like urbanization, Darwinism, and higher biblical criticism required wrenching adjustments in the relations of religion and culture, thoughtful Protestants were faced with an increasingly acute disparity between their Calvinist-evangelical heritage, which made religion a dominant force in both personal consciousness and social life, and the new American situation in which private religion passively accommodated secular change. Some resolved the tension by simply abandoning religion altogether. In the 1870s, for example, Episcopal clergyman William Graham Sumner decided to "put religious belief in a drawer and lock it up." Years later, he reported, he opened the drawer and found it empty.[58] Others, like William James and Josiah Royce, following along paths already traced by the Transcendentalists, made their way into one of the forms of philosophical idealism or pragmatism that served as halfway houses for American intellectuals as they withdrew from Protestantism.[59] In the same period a number of prominent New England Brahmin intellectuals with a Puritan heritage, such as Percival Lowell, Henry Adams, George Cabot Lodge, Charles Eliot Norton, G. Stanley Hall, and Van Wyck Brooks, began highly personal quests for spiritual meaning that led them to various forms of medievalism, orientalism, and "aesthetic Catholicism"—though not, significantly, to the Roman Church itself.[60]

It is in this religious and intellectual context, more than in the purely social setting of urbanization and industrialization, that the greatest significance of the Social Gospel lies. The concern of Protestant intellectuals for the moral regeneration of the new American industrial society was significant, especially in a country where common religious ideals and moral language were still shared by much of the population. But the Social Gospel would not have aroused such powerful religious energies if it had not also suggested a major new response to the crisis of faith. Despite the attention given its social performance, the Social Gospel was not primarily a moral or political movement but a religious awakening that simultaneously carried social meaning. In theological terms, the Social Gospelers were "evangelical liberals" who sought to retain for Protestantism its world-transforming power in the modern cultural climate. Where they differed from other purveyors of liberal theology was in their conviction that the central meaning of Christianity lay in a unified religious-social vision. As Walter Rauschenbusch stated, "religion and ethics are inseparable." Social ethics did not *replace* religion; it connected and fused with faith. Accordingly, they intended not to abandon key religious doctrines but to give them new importance and power. The central Protestant theological categories of sin, salvation, and most important, the Kingdom of God, would, they believed, be revived and strengthened in the new context. In the older Calvinist-evangelical tradition, the redeemed sinner had a mission to save the world; now the process of salvation itself was understood in social terms—as divine power acting to redeem society. "Does not the Kingdom of God consist simply of this—that God's will shall be done on earth as it is now in heaven?" asked Rauschenbusch. "You have the authority of the Lord Jesus Christ in it. . . . The Kingdom of God is a social conception."[61]

Although their fundamentalist opponents charged them with diluting or abandoning religion, it is clear that the Social Gospel intellectuals wanted to revive and strengthen it. The appalling distance between their vision of the Kingdom and American urban-industrial reality stimulated their religious-social imaginations. But for the ultimate justification of their case, they relied, in good evangelical-Protestant fashion, on Jesus and the Gospels. By drawing on one strand of the new biblical criticism, represented by Ernst Renan and Albrecht Ritschl, that stressed ethical idealism and the social teachings of the historical Jesus, the Social Gospelers could claim they were recovering the original Gospel message from a mass of theological distortions. This emphasis on the pre-Easter teachings of Jesus about ethics and the Kingdom thus ignored the difficulties in interpreting the Gospels—documents of the post-Easter church—and swept aside contrary biblical scholarship, such as Albert Schweitzer's interpretation of Jesus as an eschatological prophet.[62]

Thus, while neither transcendent spirituality nor truly critical biblical scholarship loomed large in the American Social Gospel movement, the theological undergirdings of its evangelical-social message were clear and intellectually respectable. In the stream of historical Christianity, the movement represented a resurgence in the modern American context of the old radical Gospel tradition that had always laid a heavy social burden on the faith. As in the primitive Church, the medieval dissenting movements, and the radical Reformation, religious and social passion tended to go hand in hand. A more intense religiosity implied a radical social vision, and vice versa. Thus, Gladden's mild social criticism fit easily with his optimistic religious liberalism that saw the Kingdom already immanent in American society, while Herron's fierce denunciations of the existing order flowed directly from his passionate commitment to the Gospel *kerygma*. Once the basic vision was attained, religious fervor spurred more sweeping social commitments, as a typical statement by prominent economist and Social Gospel leader Richard Ely illustrates:

> Christ calls upon us to choose between him and the world, and he wants no half-hearted followers. Remember the message unto the Laodiceans: "I know thy works, that thou art neither cold nor hot: I would thou wert cold or hot. So then because thou art lukewarm, I will spew thee out of my mouth." Some say we cannot maintain ourselves in the industrial world if we attempt to carry into it Christian principles. Very well, then, change the world until Christians can live in it; and in the meanwhile let me remind the reader . . . that there was a time when men and women could not be Christians and keep their heads on their shoulders, and that then they died cheerfully as Christians.[63]

This merging of religious and social vision, whether moderate or radical, was the source of the Social Gospel's strength. By restoring a public and critical element to a Protestantism that was in danger of becoming peripheral to American culture and society, the Social Gospel put the question of the meaning of the Christian Gospel in the industrial age back on the intellectual agenda. The claim that the spirit of the Social Gospel lay behind most of the reform energies of the Progressive Era may go too far (there were strong new secular reform visions also at work), but the Social Gospel's deep impact on modern American reform and social thought cannot be denied. Even when they held to no religious affiliation, American reformers often approached their task with an unmistakably evangelical zeal. The liberalism of the 1930s, while far more secular than Progressivism, retained elements of quasi-religious uplift that connected it with its predecessor. As one historian has said of the New Dealers, "With an assumed air of worldly aplomb, or a carefully cultivated cynicism, many of them tried to hide their idealism and moralism behind their frequent sneers at Puritanism, by self-conscious boozing, or like Harry Hopkins, by conspicuous larks at the races."[64]

Ironically, even as the Social Gospel succeeded in affecting the tone of American reform, it failed in its more fundamental religious purposes. Rather than ending the religious crisis by ushering the Kingdom of God into modern American society, as the early social prophets had hoped, the Social Gospel further revealed the weakness of Protestantism in contemporary culture.

Superficially, the religious problems of the Social Gospel appeared to be related to the changing times. Arising during the social crisis of the 1880s and 1890s, the Social Gospel reached its pinnacle during the optimistic Progressive Era, only to disintegrate during the 1920s. A dramatic sign of the movement's decline was the collapse in 1919 of the Interchurch World Movement, a massive cooperative venture of the churches that fell victim to postwar disillusionment.[65] America in the 1920s became almost completely indifferent to the Social Gospel's blend of religious intensity and social reform. Protestant intellectual reformers, who had enjoyed some national eminence and influence during the Progressive Era, found themselves increasingly marginal to a secular world whose values were shaped at the intellectual level by "cultured despisers" of religion like H. L. Mencken, and at the mass level by a new popular media culture that insulted religion mainly by ignoring it. Thrown back into the posture of a "prophetic" minority rather than harbingers of the coming Kingdom, the heirs of the Social Gospel were also forced to cope with divisive issues of organization, tactics, and fundamentalist counterattack that had been papered over by earlier successes—issues that did not readily yield to evangelical solutions.[66]

But the altered social context alone does not account for the Social Gospel's decline. More serious were the movement's own intellectual weaknesses, which diminished its value as a source of religious renewal in American Protestantism. The clearest sign of declension was the inability to hold together strong religious conviction, passionate social commitment, and intellectual depth in the same personalities. In the early Social Gospel religious intensity and social involvement were synergetic; by the 1920s they were in tension. The most socially engaged ministers tended to lose interest in religious questions, while the more faithful Protestants paid less attention to social reform. Some later Social Gospel leaders like Norman Thomas, A. J. Muste, Harold Rotzel, Cedric Long, Paul Blanshard, and Albert Coyle eventually left the church, while clerical activists like Kirby Page and Howard Williams who remained often appeared committed to Protestantism primarily because it offered a base for their political and lobbying efforts. Instead of politics being dissolved into the Kingdom of God, it appeared that the Kingdom was being dissolved into politics.

Perhaps the most telling attack on the Social Gospel came from within the religious world itself. Theology had never been a strong point of the American Social Gospel, and after 1920 religious scholars eroded whatever theological foundations the movement had. Drawing in part on European theological trends, seminary critics began to point out how ill-founded were Social Gospel understandings of faith, revelation, sin, and salvation.[67] Biblical scholars and historians, while frequently sympathetic with Social Gospel motives, criticized the movement's inconsistent approach to religious authority: It tended to appeal to biblical and traditional sources only where convenient. In 1928 a scholar sympathetic to the Social Gospel, Shailer Mathews, conceded a fundamental point in his book *Jesus on Social Institutions* when he showed that Jesus' understanding of the Kingdom of God bore little resemblance to the Social Gospel use of the term. Mathews tried to maintain that Jesus' ethical teachings still provided an adequate base for social religion, but Social Gospel leaders could not easily answer critics who asked why modern society should be judged by such an ethic.[68]

As the Social Gospel disintegrated in the 1920s, American Protestant thought fragmented in several directions. The immediate inheritors of the moderate Social Gospel, represented by Charles Clayton Morrisson of the *Christian Century*, continued to preach social reform, but as they shied away from the bold religious imperatives of the original social passion, their voices grew "baffled and tired."[69] Those who tried to preserve a strong link between evangelical passion and social radicalism, like Harry Ward and the Methodist Social Service Commission, did so only by ignoring the issues raised by the best Protestant thinkers. Committed to an intense but naive religious politics, such men sometimes became unwitting tools of the authoritarian Left during the fierce political wars of the 1930s.[70] The finest Protestant thought of the period came from H. Richard Niebuhr, who sought to preserve a central place for religion by rescuing it from both the "culture-religion" of the masses and the "un-Christian moral idealism" of politically engaged Protestant clerics.[71] The German emigré theologian Paul Tillich criticized the Social Gospel for failing to go far enough in casting off the church's outmoded patterns of life and thought; only by a radically faithful assertion of the antinomian "Protestant principle," he said, could Western culture free itself for new religious insight.[72] Finally, the end of the 1920s saw the emergence of Reinhold Niebuhr, who developed the major new approach to the problem of religion and politics that was eventually set out in *Moral Man and Immoral Society* (1932) and *An Interpretation of Christian Social Ethics* (1935).

IV

The agonizing dilemmas faced by Protestantism as it entered the modern world were felt only remotely by Catholics. Catholic intellectuals in Europe and America were aware of the new religious difficulties, but they tended to see the modern spiritual crisis as affecting others, not themselves. Several factors account for Catholicism's ability to keep pressing religious questions at arm's length. First, Catholics in Europe and America lived at a greater cultural distance from modern intellectual developments. The nineteenth-century assault on orthodox Christianity came primarily from Protestant sources, and the intimate Protestant connections of such critics as Hegel, F. C. Baur, Ritschl, Nietzsche, Kierkegaard, Schopenhauer, and Emerson made it easy for Catholics to dismiss the crisis as simply the natural culmination of Protestant religious rebellion and declension. Serious religious questioning was even rarer in intellectually underdeveloped American Catholicism than in the European Church. Even so tolerant an American Catholic intellectual as Isaac Hecker held that Protestant-induced subjectivism had caused modern religious and philosophical confusion, and considered Catholicism immune to such dangers.[73] In Europe a few Catholic intellectuals tried to keep up a dialogue with modern thought, but in America Catholics observed Protestant and secular intellectual struggles from a safe distance.

Catholicism also escaped the modernist crisis because it seemed more religiously secure from the front lines of the intellectual attack. In particular, higher biblical criticism was less threatening to a religion that placed much less emphasis on the authority of "The Word." As Troeltsch stated, "Catholic orthodoxy has found salvation . . . essentially in worship and mystical devotion, i.e., in the non-dogmatic elements of religion."[74] Part of the explanation for the "riddle" of Catholicism's self-contained religious system, Jaroslav Pelikan has said, is that "the liturgy of the Church was peculiarly its own. . . . Here the Church celebrates the action of God to which it owes its existence, an action beyond that through which God created the world and made culture possible. . . . Identity plus universality is the ideal of catholicity, and the liturgy of the church is Catholicity in action."[75]

Thus, while Catholicism would also become intellectually vulnerable to modernism in the long run, in the late nineteenth and early twentieth centuries it was far less subject to the kind of internal turmoil that eroded Protestantism's religious strength in dealing with contemporary culture. While Protestantism's typical modern situation was institutional adaptation but inner disarray, Catholicism was embattled without, but united within by an extraordinary religious confidence and élan. This unity was more impressive from outside than from within, for Catholics often minimized their internal differences and conflicts in order to preserve the appearance of unity and changeless certainty.[76] Yet Catholics in the critical period of 1870 to 1940 did agree on fundamental matters, and one was that Catholicism was a comprehensive religious worldview and not a mixed tradition to be adapted to individual taste. Accordingly, the proper course for a critical or doubtful Catholic intellectual was not to wrestle with the troubling issues in public, but to remain silent or leave the Church.[77]

The fact that Catholicism everywhere confronted modern social problems from this religious perspective was more important for its social thought than was its historical location outside the main currents of industrialization. For Catholics, social thought was presumed to be a corollary of unquestioned religious axioms, and the purpose of the Church's social action was not worldly betterment for its own sake, but that men might be led by progressive stages to a higher truth. "Nothing is more useful than to look at the world as it really is," stated Leo XIII, "and at the same time to seek elsewhere for the final solace of its troubles."[78]

In Europe Catholic social thought developed through the application of traditional scholasticism to modern circumstances. Leo XIII, the first pope to establish a Catholic social program that was not simply reactionary, was also the patron of the Thomist revival in Catholic theology. In good neo-Thomist fashion, Catholic social thinkers typically began with the immutable truths of divine revelation and natural law (e.g., the inherent dignity and rationality of man made in the image of God), proceeded to the general virtues required of man in natural society (commutative and distributive justice), and finally deduced specific social policies (e.g., social insurance or a minimum wage). This system admirably served the needs of a modern but specifically Catholic social thought. On the one hand it clearly distinguished social questions from the core of faith and dogma, thus subordinating ethics to theology. Yet it also lent the weight of religious authority to the Church's social views by presenting them as *necessary corollaries* of belief, nor "merely" ethical or pragmatic responses to social need.

This imposing intellectual system guided European Catholicism through its extraordinary passage from a premodern social world to a new industrial age. On the continent the Church at first appeared hopelessly mortgaged to the upper classes, and in France and Italy it engaged in a number of futile battles that reinforced its reactionary image. But beginning with Leo XIII's *Rerum Novarum*, the popes' pronouncements on social questions sanctioned a more progressive Catholic posture in the modern world. European Catholics threw themselves into social Catholic movements, which were spurred by growing defections from the Church. These movements demonstrated that it was possible to derive the most disparate social ideas from the same ideological core. German Catholics, for example, organized the corporatist, pragmatically conservative Center Party to represent their interests. French Catholicism exploded in fiercely ideological movements of both Left and Right like the Sillon and the Action Française. English Catholics divided between the nostalgic distributism of Hilaire Belloc and G. K. Chesterton and the labor reformism of the Christian Social Guild. And Austrian Catholics promoted what amounted to an authoritarian, anti-Semitic clerical state.[79]

Despite these serious social differences, European Catholic social thought in the early twentieth century was inspired and united by the overriding necessity of preserving some kind of Christian presence in an increasingly indifferent or hostile cultural atmosphere. By attacking both the Church's faith and its social stance, secular liberalism, Marxism, and Fascism roused Catholicism and often led it to rely on Catholic political parties for protection and power. Under these circumstances European Catholic intellectual life enjoyed a renaissance led by figures like Charles Péguy, Jacques Maritain, Christopher Dawson, Josef Pieper, and Romano Guardini.[80] Their work established a strong intellectual tradition in European Catholicism, but as agencies of Catholic social concern and religious renewal European Catholic political parties had serious weaknesses. Whatever their intent, their practical effect was to narrow the Catholic witness to a largely self-serving political program— a condition that mocked the universalist claims of Catholic theology and natural law social theory.[81] With "social Catholicism" largely institutionalized in the "Christian" parties and communities, only a few independent Catholic thinkers and activists like Emmanuel Mounier, Georges Bernanos, and Joseph Cardijn tried to develop radically alternative Catholic social approaches prior to World War II.

The American atmosphere was different. Catholicism in the United States did have to contend somewhat with the image of the Church as reactionary historical force, but this reputation was far easier to live down in a country where the Catholic Church had never relied on pre-modern monarchs, aristocrats, and peasants, and where there were no contemporary Catholics seeking to preserve a state Church or restore some *ancien régime*. After 1820 or so, the American Church's social base was among urban, industrial wage earners. This turned out to be a remarkably secure foundation, for not only were the Catholic masses deeply committed to their religion, they were immune to most of the hostile social ideologies that threatened the faith. The American cultural environment was too Protestant and secular for conservative Catholic taste, and native American anti-Catholicism was a persistent irritation. But on the whole, the United States provided a more salutary social environment for Catholicism's passage into the modern world than Europe. In particular, American economic and political life—including the unions and major political parties—were religiously neutral and open to Catholic participation. American Catholics recognized that they stood a better chance of advancement within general American institutions than in separate labor organizations or parties that would be accused of sectarian un-Americanism. (Only in elementary education, closer to the processes of primary religious formation, did the American Church take the controversial path of institutional separatism.) The fact that American Catholicism got, so to speak, a free ride not only into the postfeudal world of liberal democracy, but into the modern urban industrial context as well, helps explain why Catholics here were more inclined to follow "practical" strategies for betterment than ideological or political movements derived from religion. When *Rerum Novarum* originally appeared in the United States, for example, it stirred nothing like the interest that it did in Europe; its main appeal to American Catholics was its anti-Socialism.[82]

The American intellectual environment also affected the development of Catholic social thought. There were strong incentives for American Catholic thinkers to abandon the usual modes of Catholic discourse. While some Catholic apologists tried to deal in strict scholastic categories, most writers on social questions realized that American culture, rooted in Protestant and Enlightenment assumptions, was unprepared to listen to arguments drawn simply from Thomist natural law. Someone like John Ryan was quite capable of arguing for reform from specifically Catholic premises, as he did in his doctoral thesis and his book *Distributive Justice* (1916), which provided what might be called the scholastic proof for Progressivism. But except before certain Catholic audiences, he generally refrained from appealing for social change on any but the most general religious grounds.[83]

Thus, intellectual circumstances combined with the notably nonideological character of the American Catholic experience to inhibit much religious reflection about American society by the Catholic community. The American Church generally refrained from making social teachings strong corollaries of religious commitment, as was done in Europe. Although some Catholic intellectuals retained strong memories of their religion's historic role in shaping society, they generally acquiesced in the modern American confinement of religion to certain fairly narrow spheres of life. Popular Catholicism similarly adapted to American religious tastes, even developing forms of "Catholic revivalism" that imitated the methods of America's pervasive evangelical religion and fostered similar kinds of intensely private piety.[84] The result was that even though there existed a coterie of Catholic social activists in this country, and an institutional expression of Catholic social concern in the Social Action Department of the National Catholic Welfare Conference, these had far less impact on either the Church or American society than social Catholicism in Europe or the Social Gospel in America. Americans grew accustomed to the social pronouncements of the liberal Protestant ministry and the Federal Council of Churches, but American Catholic social teaching, such as it was, remained little known and poorly understood even by Catholics. While Catholicism was in fact involved in many kinds of social concern, it appeared to many American Catholics and non-Catholics alike to be, like fundamentalist Protestantism, a religion largely without social consequences outside the realms of personal and sexual morality.[85]

It is interesting to ask whether a more comprehensive Catholic social outlook would have developed at all in this country without the Great Depression. Certainly the economic collapse hastened the development of more mature and thoughtful social perspectives among American Catholics. Catholic social thought never influenced the mass of Catholics, but after 1930 a growing minority within the Church began to look to their religion for a serious critique of American institutions and social values. For the first time European Catholic social thought was examined for its possible relevance to the United States. When Pius XI issued the encyclical *Quadragesimo Anno* in 1931, it was received with enthusiasm by American Catholics, in contrast to the indifference that had greeted *Rerum Novarum*.[86] Journals like *America, Commonweal, Cath-*

olic World, and *Catholic Mind* were filled with social commentary, much of it attempting to relate religion and social life. Ater 1930 American Catholic thinkers might disagree about particular economic and political programs, but they were almost unanimous in rejecting the notion of a Catholicism without social consequences.

One indication of the new vigor and maturity of Catholic social thought in the 1930s was that it produced, for the first time, significant dissenting movements of the Right and Left. Catholic dissent was generally prevented by both American and Catholic constraints from moving in the directions of neofeudalism, Socialism, or laissez-faire conservatism. Yet Catholic social criticism still took provocative ideological forms. On the Right, the major figure was Father Charles Coughlin, who concocted an unstable blend of populist monetary nostrums and corporatist Austrian social Catholicism and anti-Semitism.[87]

On the Left the major voice was the *Catholic Worker*, the first significant expression of Catholic radicalism in the United States. Although American religion had known many social movements, no one in 1933 could have guessed what form an American Catholic radicalism would take. The past provided few clues as to what would happen to radical social thought in Catholic hands, or to Catholicism in radical hands. American Catholicism in some ways provided a fertile ground for social criticism: The Catholic experience in the United States had occurred partly outside the dominant culture and values; American Catholic history had been deeply engaged with the lives of the less privileged; and the Church possessed a formidable intellectual tradition that could be applied to social questions. Yet American Catholicism also contained contrary tendencies that inhibited radical social movements: a patriotic inclination to celebrate American society; a fear of criticism arising from marginal social status and the general Catholic respect for authority; and the indifference and even hostility to intellectual values ingrained in American folk Catholicism.

Some hints about the future direction of any Catholic radicalism could be derived from the experience of modern Protestant dissent. Protestant social engagement demonstrated that religious thought in the United States could speak to large numbers of Americans and become engaged in the most pressing contemporary concerns. Protestant activists had further shown how tensions could arise between the demands of social prophecy and the largely conservative social function of the local churches in the United States. Their experience also suggested that American religious radicalism, like all forms of American radical dissent, was more likely to be successful in raising new issues than in altering institutions or changing fundamental American beliefs.

Most of all, the past suggested that the most crucial issues for any Catholic radical movement would not be social at all, but religious. The Social Gospel arose at a time of deep religious turmoil in American Protestantism, and it was immediately faced with the most difficult questions about the relation of religion and society in America— questions that touched directly on the meaning of religion itself. The passage of several decades had heightened rather than diminished the urgency of those questions, and the lack of satisfactory answers made the Social Gospel an inconclusive model for those seeking to combine religious and social concern. Roman Catholicism in 1933 was struggling to find its proper stance toward the new industrial world, but it did not yet feel itself part of the Western religious crisis, with all its uncertainty and doubt. American Catholicism, still preoccupied with institutional adjustment to American life, clung to its precious certitudes and scorned modern doubt as a sign of weakness. Much of the interest in a radical Catholic movement would lie in seeing what variation the quite different social perspectives of Catholicism would introduce into the rich stream of American social criticism. But a more provocative question in the long run might be how such a movement would perform as American Catholicism experienced within itself the religious tremors of modernity.

CHAPTER THREE

A Penny Paper

I

Peter Maurin's appearance on Dorothy Day's doorstep in December 1932, was a stroke of perfect timing. Still in an emotional state after her return from the Washington hunger march, Day was prepared for some sign that would point her at last toward a meaningful life's work. For Day and her followers, Peter Maurin himself was the answer to her tearful prayer in Washington, and their providential meeting betokened the Catholic Worker's singular mission.

At the time, however, the shabby visitor on Day's doorstep did not seem like much of a revelation. Only the hospitality of her sister-in-law persuaded Dorothy to give Maurin a hearing, and only after several weeks of listening to his persistent propaganda did she begin to see how Maurin's mission might fit with her own. Her eagerness to find a new direction for her life had not entirely erased her skepticism about ideologues and prophets. "I certainly did not realize at first that I had my answer in Peter Maurin," she later said. "I was thirty-five years old and I had met plenty of radicals in my time, and plenty of crackpots, too; people who had blueprints to change the social order were a dime a dozen around Union Square."[1]

It would have been easy indeed to mistake Peter Maurin for a Union Square "crackpot." The Frenchman was already fifty-four years old in 1932, with few visible achievements to his credit. The first of twenty-two children of a Languedoc peasant, Maurin had been educated by the Christian Brothers near his village. The order took notice of him, and he was sent for further study to Paris where, after military service, he became involved in the burgeoning social activism that characterized French Catholicism at the turn of the century. At first an enthusiast of Marc Sangnier's *Sillon*, a liberalizing republican Catholic movement founded in 1901, Maurin became increasingly disillusioned by the movement's politicization and drifted away from the Church. He emigrated to Canada in 1909 and entered the United States two years later. For the next decade he drifted about as a manual laborer and occasional teacher of French. Sometime in the mid-1920s his earlier interest in religion and its social implications returned, and he began to devote himself to reading and copying from Catholic literature, composing his own succinct verses on social themes and engaging in a kind of nonstop propaganda for social Catholicism that he called "clarification of thought."[2]

Although the Depression created a bull market for social agitation, this itinerant peasant seemed unlikely to reach an audience beyond a few Union Square regulars. To all external appearances, he was simply another eccentric. Even after he made his mark at the Catholic Worker, Maurin was frequently mistaken by the uninitiated for a vagrant; Catholic groups shooing a "bum" from the door suddenly discovered that he was their invited guest speaker. Although Dorothy Day once pointed out that Maurin "gave no impression of carelessness, for he invariably wore a felt hat (not too wide-brimmed), a shirt (rough-dried), a tie, and sturdy shoes" and "was not at all the bearded, sandaled, hatless fanatic," the French peasant was certainly indifferent to both convention and comfort. He slept wherever he found a spot, ate one bowl of soup a day, and either gave away the little he earned or spent it to print pamphlets containing his verses, which he also gave away. These pamphlets were Maurin's best hope as an agitator, for his speeches, shouted at close range in an almost incomprehensible, thick French accent, were largely ineffective and, indeed, often somewhat comic. Although he possessed a sincere manner and an unfailingly kind disposition, Maurin's tireless monologues seldom persuaded listeners. His chief asset was his dogged devotion to his task. According to one of the many stories told about him, when Maurin was staying in a Chicago flophouse, a prostitute knocked on his door and asked if he wanted "to have a good time." "Come in, come in," he called, and then proceeded to lecture her at length on the meaning of "a good time" from his Catholic point of view.[3]

In 1932 Maurin was working at a Catholic boys' camp in upstate New York and visiting New York City on weekends to read in the public library and propagandize in Union Square. Apparently seeking some more effective way to spread his message, Maurin sought out George Shuster, an editor of *Commonweal*. Although impressed by Maurin's familiarity with the literature of Catholic social thought, Shuster realized *Commonweal* was not the place for Maurin and suggested he look up their contributor, Dorothy Day.[4]

As soon as he met her, Maurin pronounced Day a new St. Catherine of Siena and proceeded to try and win her over to his cause. It was no easy task. Though she later professed to find it "amazing how little we understood each other at first," it is more remarkable that they were able to communicate at all. For all her emotional intensity, Day was a woman of keen judgment and vigorous common sense, not at all disposed to be swept up in eccentricity, even—or especially—under the banner of religion. Though Maurin became a daily visitor to her apartment in early 1933, she quickly wearied of his shouted sermons, most of which she found unintelligible.

> In my subconscious I was probably tired of his constant conversation. Sitting there thinking of the past weeks, I had to face the fact that Peter was hard to listen to. I would tune in some concert and beg him to be still. He would be obedient for a time, but soon he would look at my forbidding face, and seeing no yielding there, he would go over to the gentler Tessa. Pulling a chair closer to hers and leaning almost on the arm he would begin to talk.[5]

Fortunately for Maurin, he finally came up with the one suggestion calculated to win a hearing from his new acquaintance: Day should start a Catholic newspaper for the unemployed. Given Dorothy's background, this was a logical suggestion, and she might well have come to it on her own; but the fact that it originated elsewhere gave it the force of prophetic injunction for her. Maurin's earnest appeal to her own abilities and perhaps unacknowledged ambitions made her immediately revise her estimate of him, even though his limitations as a partner in the proposed journalistic venture soon became apparent.

> I could see the need for such a paper as Peter described, but how were we going to start it? Peter did not pretend to be practical along these lines. "I enunciate the principles," he declared grandly. "But where do we get the money?" I asked, clinging to the "we."[6]

Maurin's theory of fund-raising was to follow the practice of the saints and pray for the money. He did propose one scheme involving a well-off priest on the Upper West Side; but the good father's supposed interest in a Catholic paper turned out to be a figment of Maurin's eager imagination. This bit of wishful fantasy, which delayed the *Catholic Worker*'s inaugural for several months, at first angered the practical-minded Day, but it brought home to her exactly the kind of partner she had in Maurin.

All the real work—the fund raising, reporting, circulation—would be hers; Maurin's role would be the more comfortable one of "theorist."

Even on that basis the collaboration got off to a bad start. When he read the proofs for the first issue of the *Catholic Worker*, with its stories on strikes, race relations, labor schools, and housing, Maurin declared that "everybody's paper is nobody's paper" and immediately left the city. Not only did he want the paper to be called the *Catholic Radical* or the *Catholic Agronomist* rather than the proletarian-sounding *Catholic Worker*, but he apparently expected it to contain nothing but his own little versed "essays." Realizing that Day's paper was his only hope of reaching a wider audience, Maurin returned shortly after May Day, but the second issue of the *Catholic Worker* made it plain that he did not endorse everything in the paper. "Peter Maurin has his program, which is embodied in his contribution this month," said an editorial. "Because his program is specific and definite, he thinks it is better to withdraw his name from the editorial board and continue with the paper as a contributor."[7]

Maurin's basic "program" consisted of three "points" that he set out in his "Easy Essays."

We need round-table discussions
To keep trained minds from becoming academic.
We need round-table discussions
To keep untrained minds from being superficial.

We need Houses of Hospitality
To give to the rich the opportunity to serve the poor.
We need Houses of Hospitality
To bring social justice back to Catholic institutions.

The unemployed need food.
They can raise that
In an agronomic university.
The unemployed need to acquire skill.
They can do that in an agronomic university.[8]

Although Day immediately dismissed some of the "specific and definite" parts of Maurin's proposal, such as his notion that the Houses of Hospitality be exclusively male, she did accept this "Three-Point Program," along with the newspaper, as the blueprint for what soon became the Catholic Worker movement. After his initial discontent, Maurin accepted Day's complete direction of the paper and the movement. Because he was incapable of implementing his proposals and, indeed, cared little for the practical consequences of his grand ideas, the Frenchman quickly became the elder guru of the Catholic Worker, the co-founder who set forth the theoretical ideals that Dorothy Day and everyone else tried to live out. It was an entirely congenial role for Maurin, who had probably never expected even this degree of success. He happily spent the last decade of his active life, from 1933 to 1943, traveling about the country, speaking to interested audiences about the Catholic Worker, contributing more of his "Easy Essays" to the paper, and returning to the New York House of Hospitality and Catholic Worker farm where he was honored by those in the movement.

The nature and relative importance of Maurin's contribution to the movement was a matter of discussion during his lifetime and has remained a source of conflicting interpretations among those who have written about the Catholic Worker. For some early Catholic Workers Maurin, rather than Day, was the dominant force in the movement. John Curran and Arthur Sheehan, Maurin's first biographer, "idolized" him.[9] To Julia Porcelli, Maurin was "a poet, an agitator, the gentle, strong voice of truth, of the Holy Spirit."[10] Others, like John Cogley and Joseph Zarella, were more skeptical. Maurin was "supposed to be learned in a special, insightful way," Cogley observed, but in fact "his intellectual genius was clearly exaggerated." Maurin was "obviously uncomfortable in the feigned role of leadership," and helpless unless the questions were "abstractly philosophical or sweepingly historical."[11] John Cort, also a prominent worker during the thirties, expressed the frustrations some felt with Maurin's version of "Round-Table Discussions":

> From long practice on the debating fields of Union Square and Columbus Circle Peter had learned not to breathe between sentences. And if by chance he did stop to breathe he held up a finger to indicate that there was more to come. And if by some act of reckless bravado some one were to ignore his finger and interrupt before he was ready to yield the floor, he made a face that, like Medusa, was calculated to turn the visitor to stone.

Cort also stressed, however, that "if you got him alone Peter was a gentle, lovable soul who would give you his last pair of pants. And he never had more than one. It was an article of faith. 'The coat that hangs in your closet belongs to the poor,' he used to say."[12]

In moments of candor, Dorothy Day also recognized Maurin's failings. "I was sure of Peter—sure that he was a saint and a great teacher—although to be perfectly honest, I wondered if I really liked Peter sometimes. He was twenty years older than I, he spoke with an accent so thick it was hard to penetrate to the thought beneath, he had a one-track mind, and he did not bathe."[13] Although she devoted her life to a social movement based on Maurin's Three Points, as well as to the newspaper he first proposed to her, she did not hesitate to alter or reject his other ideas when they went contrary to her own. Usually she tried to maintain modestly that this was only because Maurin possessed an excess of the virtues of selflessness, purity, and zeal. "He always expected so much in the way of results that I often felt called on to put a damper on him," she said.[14] But the real reason she suppressed some of Maurin's notions was that she knew they would harm the Catholic Worker. Maurin, for example, exhibited a mild anticlericalism of a sort not uncommon among European, and especially French, Catholic social activists. Day made sure no hint of this got into the *Catholic Worker*. "I do indeed keep out some of his stuff which attacks the bishops," she told one correspondent. "I just don't think it's politic. There are quite a number of priests who think Peter just quaint when he verbally attacks the clergy, but who would hold up their hands in horror if we printed the stuff."[15] The *Catholic Worker* also ignored Maurin's opposition to unions and his suggestions for *ex post facto* punishment of moneylenders.

Dorothy Day herself promoted the fiction that the Catholic Worker was simply an attempt to realize Peter Maurin's "Idea." But it was her common sense and awareness of American social and cultural realities that enabled her to distinguish between the kind of religious idealism that could inspire a viable social movement in this country and fantastic notions that would merely look ridiculous. Among Maurin's schemes that she kept well under wraps were his plans to interview one hundred "traditionalist European exiles" and send the results to newspaper columnists, to broadcast recorded Easy Essays from street loudspeakers, and to send out teams of "Troubadours for Christ" who would travel about the country, singing the praises of God and the rebuilding of the social order.[16] It is not surprising that Day sometimes grew nervous about Maurin's extended speaking trips. "Don't talk to me about any more of Peter's ideas," she told a Nova Scotian priest who wrote after hearing one of Maurin's talks. "He keeps us so busy working out the ideas he has already given us that when he springs a new one I almost go crazy."[17]

If Maurin's actual contributions to the Catholic Worker were not as great as Day and others maintained, they were nonetheless real. Besides his idea for the paper, each of his Three Points was incorporated into the life of the movement. The "Round-Table Discussions" became shorthand for the Catholic Worker's intellectual emphasis, the Houses of Hospitality formed its model of Christian life and service, and the agronomic universities or farming communes—by far the most troublesome point—represented its utopian social ideal. Although the specific social ideology of the Easy Essays, discussed in the next chapter, found only a limited following even within the movement, some of these disarmingly simple verses attracted readers' attention and provided shorthand summaries of key Catholic Worker ideas. Two of the most famous, frequently reprinted, expressed the movement's purpose in a nutshell:

Blowing the Dynamite

If the Catholic Church
is not today
the dominant social dynamic force
it is because Catholic scholars
have failed to blow the dynamite
of the Church.
Catholic scholars have taken the dynamite
of the Church,
have wrapped it up
in nice phraseology
placed it in an hermetic container
and sat on the lid.
It is about time
to blow the lid off
so the Catholic Church
may again become
the dominant social dynamic force.

What the Catholic Worker Believes

The Catholic Worker believes
in the gentle personalism
of traditional Catholicism.
The Catholic Worker believes
in the personal obligation
of looking after
the needs of our brother.
The Catholic Worker believes
in the daily practice
of the Works of Mercy.
The Catholic Worker believes
in Houses of Hospitality
for the immediate relief
of those who are in need.
The Catholic Worker believes
in the establishment
of Farming Communes

where each one works
according to his ability
and gets
according to his need.
The Catholic Worker believes
in creating a new society
within the shell of the old
with the philosophy of the new,
which is not a new philosophy
but a very old philosophy
a philosophy so old
that it looks like new.[18]

Maurin was also the first to bring to Day's attention the rich resources of European Catholic social thought that became so important to the Catholic Worker. Some of this material was already reaching American Catholics through religious and academic channels, but it was unclear what use could be made of it in this country. Details aside, Maurin's encyclopedic reading and references to European Catholic activists suggested to Day the untapped potential of Catholic social theory. Especially in the early days when the movement had not yet developed its own intellectual traditions, Maurin served as an invaluable walking bibliography of Catholic social thought. Furthermore, as a former participant in European Catholic movements, Maurin represented a personal as well as intellectual link to the thinkers he constantly cited, and so encouraged Day and others to look across the Atlantic for continuing inspiration, as well as practical models.

Yet Maurin's real significance for the Catholic Worker was more personal and symbolic than programmatic or intellectual, and it developed only as Day elaborated the Maurin legend in the *Catholic Worker* and elsewhere. The Maurin that others came to know was in large part Dorothy Day's image and interpretation of him. Day's belief that Maurin came in answer to her prayer symbolized the religious character of the Catholic Worker and Day's personal vocation. Maurin's peasant and European origins complemented Day's status as a middle-class American convert. As a man who lived for "ideas" and was familiar with influential Catholic social theorists, Maurin covered what seemed a weak point in Day's own background. Making Maurin the "co-founder" of the movement gave Day confidence in a risky undertaking, enabling her to feel some support as she assumed a position of leadership. "It is very hard indeed, being in command, with such a sense of responsibility," she wrote to a priest friend in 1934. "I don't think ever in my life I have had anyone to lean on." [19]

Maurin was not much help in lifting this burden, and may even have contributed to it; but he was a necessary symbolic helpmate for Day. Indeed, the fact that Maurin was able to serve as a purely theoretical partner for Day may have increased his attractiveness for her. Such a partnership could cover her ambivalence about her own assumption of leadership, an ambivalence partly rooted in her views of her sex. "Man proposes and woman disposes," Maurin told her early in their acquaintance, and despite her occasional bristling at such masculine presumption, Day accepted in principle such a sexual ordering of roles. Her own life, she believed, had taught that women could not and should not escape the cultural implications of gender—even in striving for social change. "I am quite ready to concede that men are the single-minded, the pure of heart in these movements," she asserted in her autobiography. "Women by their very nature are more materialistic, thinking of the home, the children, and all things needful to them." Women could work and assume responsibility in certain areas, but they should ultimately defer to men. [20]

It was therefore personally comforting to Day, as well as strategically useful to her as a woman leading a social movement in the sexually conservative Catholic Church, to be able to point to the male cofounder of the movement and to emphasize that she was merely carrying out Maurin's program. There was more than a little dissimulation in this claim, for Day could hardly avoid noticing that Maurin's success depended on her far more than hers depended on Maurin. She was quite sincere in her professions of feminine deference, but she had also ingeniously constructed a situation that allowed her to pay homage to masculine supremacy in theory without being constrained by it in practice.

Yet, ultimately, Maurin's most important function for Day was that he provided her—and through her the Catholic Worker movement—with a personal symbol of traditional Catholic spirituality. As a peasant with roots in French Catholicism going back fifteen hundred years, Maurin represented a direct link to what seemed to Day a richer and purer Catholicism than she saw around her in the United States. Because he advocated and lived a life of absolute poverty and generosity based on Catholic ideals, Maurin expressed perfectly Day's most deeply held beliefs about religion and society. His humble appearance and openhearted simplicity brought to mind the saints she knew so well from her studies and suggested that sainthood was a present as well as a past reality. "Peter was the poor man of his day," she said. "He was another St.

Francis, in modern times." Looking at him, she thought "how much he looked like the picture of St. John Bosco, the Italian peasant." She compared his itinerant travels to those of St. Benedict Joseph Labre, another penniless holy man. In Day's religious assessment of the matter, Maurin's guilelessness and indifference to worldly standards were the greatest virtues. "He had the simplicity of an Alyosha, a Prince Mishkin," she wrote after his death. "Peter accepted gratefully what people offered, finding plenty of work to do, always taking the least place and serving others." [21] For Day, Maurin was like the Russian *starets*, or "holy fool," the eternal religious innocent whose attitude of open abandonment toward life expressed the deepest spiritual values. [22] Although Peter Maurin has a place in the intellectual history of the Catholic Worker as the author of the Easy Essays and as the movement's first bridge to European Catholic social thought, he made his real contribution as a religious archetype and symbol.

II

Dorothy Day began a newspaper—the *Catholic Worker*—to advocate social change, but she quickly found herself at the head of a social movement—the Catholic Worker—that tried to show the way to the ideals the paper defended. The movement followed in the wake of the paper, and the paper publicized the movement, so that the two soon became entirely dependent on one another. It was a pattern familiar in other social movements, including the *Sillon* that Peter Maurin had known in France.

The enormous success of the *Catholic Worker* paved the way for the movement. Despite some initial hostility on the streets (two of the four sellers that first May Day gave up and went home), the new paper quickly caught on, gaining the attention even of those who disagreed with it. Dwight Macdonald has described the initial reaction of some skeptical New Yorkers:

> Volume One, Number One of the *Catholic Worker* hit Union Square on May Day, 1933, with an ambiguous thud. The Marxian natives couldn't classify this political chimera: its foreparts were anarchistic but its hind parts were attached to the Church of Rome. . . . Fourteenth Street cafeteria savants who could distinguish at the drop of a coffee spoon between Manejsky and Mayakovsky, Dan and Deniken, Malenkov, Mertov, Miliukov, Muralov, and Muranov were stumped by Maurin (Peter). Their conclusion, reasonable enough on the premises, was that the

Catholic Worker was either a Trojan horse rigged up by the Vatican to betray the oft-betrayed proletariat or, more charitably, an "adventure" by "confused idealists. . . ."[23]

Street sales and word of mouth spread the first news of the *Catholic Worker*, but Day used other techniques to gain support as well. She mailed copies of the paper to editors, book reviewers, academics, prominent bishops and priests, and heads of Catholic organizations, asking all for their comments. Many wrote back with encouragement, and they included sufficient contributions to assure a second issue and to prompt Day to rent the barber shop below her East Fifteenth Street apartment as an office headquarters. Equally important, two young Catholic women with journalistic experience showed up to help put out the June issue. Eileen Corrigan and Dorothy Weston were the first of a staff of volunteer editors that expanded along with the paper's circulation.

The *Catholic Worker*'s growth was phenomenal by any standard. Day's original $57.00 paid for 2,500 copies of the first issue. In November 1933, 20,000 copies were printed and sold. A year and a half later, in March 1935, circulation was up to 65,000. The increase continued throughout the 1930s: 100,000 by the end of 1936, 150,000 in 1938, 185,000 by the end of 1940, on the eve of World War II.[24] These figures include copies sent in bulk orders to Catholic parishes and organizations, but the *Catholic Worker* was frequently passed from hand to hand, so the figures are probably a rough index to actual readership.

The original decision to sell the paper for one cent (twenty-five cents a year by subscription) was made offhand, but it was typical of Day's talent for a kind of ingenuous public relations. She quickly recognized the promotional as well as the ideological value of the penny price, which became a *Catholic Worker* trademark through the years. The existence of a price meant that the *Catholic Worker* sold by subscription or on streetcorners like a normal publication (although a one-year subscription often stretched into ten, given the vagaries of the *Worker*'s direct-mail operation). But the nominal cost and the fact that the editors received no compensation underscored the paper's hostility to the capitalist profit motive.[25]

The *Catholic Worker*'s original format also highlighted its intention of engaging the Catholic religious tradition with urgent problems of the day. Day cleverly designed the paper to appeal to a diverse constituency that included the alienated poor and unemployed, religious leaders, and lay Catholics concerned about the social implications of their faith. Much about the paper suggested its distinctively proletarian appeal: its name, the tabloid size, and the two brawny workmen on the masthead (one black, one white, at the suggestion of a reader). At the same time, the book reviews, the quality of writing, and the frequent references to Church history and teaching reflected the paper's intellectual intentions. The goal, in Peter Maurin's phrase, was to "bring the workers to the scholars and the scholars to the workers."[26]

In its first years much of the *Catholic Worker* was given over to current events. The paper reported on wage reductions, strikes, evictions, racial incidents, and the like. A typical early issue (May 1935) included reports on efforts to organize food relief for displaced sharecroppers; poor mothers in need of child care; the Scottsboro case; a farm labor strike; a utility stockholders' meeting; and the conditions of life for slum children.[27]

But in the *Catholic Worker*, news always took second place to analysis and advocacy—Peter Maurin's "clarification of thought." Although the paper looked like a tabloid throwaway, it was really a journal of opinion. Especially after the late thirties, most of the news that appeared concerned social problems or ideas of direct concern to Catholic Workers or Catholicism in general. But it was the other features that came to dominate the paper and convey its essential message: book reviews (which gradually grew longer); quotations from church fathers, saints, popes, theologians, and Catholic writers; editorials and commentary from Day and other movement writers and fellow travelers; and Peter Maurin's Easy Essays. Some articles swelled to three thousand words or more, but since the paper carried no advertising, it regularly crammed several such lengthy pieces into its eight, or sometimes twelve, tabloid pages. An especially effective visual feature was added in 1934 when Ade Bethune, a young Belgian immigrant artist, began contributing her drawings and calligraphy to the paper. Her simple, bold portrayals of Christian symbols, and of Christ and the saints as laborers (St. Joseph the Carpenter, St. Isidore the Farmer, and so on), created appealing images and lent an iconographic quality to the *Catholic Worker*. "Dorothy taught me to use the missal, and to draw the things that would take part in the Church's cycle," Bethune said. "I used the saints because these were authentic, historic people. I found that much more interesting."[28] The *Catholic Worker*'s artistic tradition was continued after 1950 by Fritz Eichenberg, a woodcut artist who added people and scenes from the Catholic Worker movement itself to the paper's frequently reprinted collection of drawings.

The artwork and the quotations from the popes and other authorities gave the *Catholic Worker* the desired air of connection with universal Catholic tradition. But while vigorously asserting its essential loyalty to, and continuity with, historic Catholic orthodoxy, the *Catholic Worker* also worked to develop its own distinctive intellectual viewpoint. Starting with Day's American radical experience and bits of European social Catholicism she picked up from Maurin, the *Catholic Worker* eventually drew on a wide range of sources to construct a coherent and enduring radical Catholic ideology. Day was quite sure of her own radical beliefs, but she was also aware that they needed firmer intellectual underpinnings if they were to have an impact. Over the years, therefore, the *Catholic Worker* reached out wherever it could to find support and elaboration of its fundamental outlook. While retaining its deceptively simple appeals and commentary on current affairs, the paper built up an increasingly sophisticated intellectual tradition that constituted a permanent resource of the movement.

Since there was little precedent for American Catholic radicalism, the *Catholic Worker* initially turned to Europe to find an intellectual patrimony. The first channel for European ideas was, of course, Maurin himself. Maurin based much of the legitimacy of his own social program on European writers. He frequently cited them in his Easy Essays, and hand-copied extensive passages from those he most admired. For many early Workers Maurin's lists of "Books to Read" were an important feature of the *Catholic Worker*.

Although the host of names on these lists added a glow of intellectual prestige and historical precedent to the *Catholic Worker*, only a few of Maurin's favorite writers had much direct influence on the paper or movement. But ideas from three European sources—one French, one English, one Russian—did tangibly affect the *Catholic Worker* outlook and shape the movement's enduring character.

The foremost influence came from Emmanuel Mounier's *L'Esprit*. Founded in 1932, *L'Esprit* was home in the thirties and forties to a group of French intellectuals who tried to engage religion with the great social and moral issues of the day. Trained in philosophy, Mounier tried to construct a politically relevant synthesis of both Catholic and secular critiques of "bourgeois civilization" and thus provide "a new historical ideal" for Western man. As spelled out in *L'Esprit*, this "philosophy of action," which Mounier called personalism, outlined a broad but definable alternative to the reigning French intellectual fashions of Marxism and existentialism, with which it kept up a running dialogue. Although not well known in North America, personalism directly influenced many of the prominent post-World War II French intellectuals, including Raymond Aron, Paul Ricouer, Jacques Ellul, Denis de Rougement, and Daniel Henri-Rops. Ellul, for example, called it "more essential in my view than Sartrean existentialism."[29] Although personalism as a philosophy was often deliberately vague, a recent historian's summary of its leading ideas suggests something of its flavor:

> Committed to the primacy of the person as a free and spiritual being, personalism denied all attempts to reduce the human being to any immanent order of society, politics, and history. Committed to the person as an embodied and communal being, personalism equally denies all doctrines that deny man's temporality and historicity in the name of a transcendent order. In its metaphysical impulse, personalism thus aspires to be a new realism by recognizing equally man's spiritual and material nature. In its spiritual inspiration, personalism affirms that man's freedom is fundamental, but that it is realized only amidst other men in their social and historical conditions. In its ethical and political aspirations, personalism seeks to affirm the unities between thought and action, person and community, community and historical situation.[30]

Unlike his older friend and mentor Jacques Maritain, who upheld similar principles on the lofty plane of philosophy, Mounier plunged *L'Esprit* into the messy affairs of French political and social life, since he believed that the "moral and material revolution" needed to bring about a "new civilization" demanded clear social commitments by religious intellectuals. Accordingly, *L'Esprit* became for Mounier and his associates not simply a journal, but a cause, "an identity and a destiny."[31]

It was this quality of commitment to a new religious civilization, along with bits of the philosophical vocabulary of personalism, that the *Catholic Worker* borrowed from *L'Esprit*. Maurin had immediately recognized in Mounier a kindred spirit, and one who drew on many of the same French sources for his critique: Proudhon, Bloy, Péguy, Maritain. The *Catholic Worker* editors lacked the easy familiarity with weighty philosophical abstractions of the French Catholic movement, but they drew freely on Mounier's essential language and outlook. The *Catholic Worker* followed *L'Esprit*'s fortunes closely during the thirties. Maurin translated items from the journal for reprinting and persuaded St. John's Abbey of Collegeville, Minnesota, to bring out an English translation of Mounier's book *The Personalist Manifesto*.[32] Both the *Catholic Worker* and *L'Esprit* used the rhetoric of "revolution" to describe radical social changes that would preserve traditional values, and Day adopted Mounier's slogan of "the primacy of the spiritual" in all social action and transformation. Like *L'Esprit*, the *Catholic Worker* plunged into the rough-and-tumble of contemporary social thought and action. Although operating in a very different setting, the American movement developed similar social notions. Indeed, the most recent historian of Mounier and *L'Esprit* has shown how the French Catholic intellectuals were led toward some of the anarchism and nonstatist radicalism that also held sway at the *Catholic Worker.*[33]

Of course there were differences as well. Unlike the *Catholic Worker*, *L'Esprit* never appealed to a popular audience. The French movement operated in an environment where relations between religion and the established traditions of social thought were far more hostile than in the United States. *L'Esprit* also developed complex connections with various philosophical currents such as Marxism and existentialism that barely existed in the United States. In the postwar years, many at the *Catholic Worker* came to believe that Mounier had weakened his distinctively Catholic stance through too close a cooperation with French Communists and other "progressives." Still, in 1952 *Catholic Worker* editor Michael Harrington argued that *L'Esprit* was "probably the most important Christian review of our time," and that Mounier's major thesis, "that we as Catholics must face our age forwardly, making use of what is good in its techniques for liberation of the whole man, the person, is one of the greatest contributions to Catholic thought."[34]

While *L'Esprit* thrived on visionary Gallic abstractions pointing Catholics to the future, the second European influence on the *Catholic Worker*, distributism, was a homier Anglo-Saxon movement looking to the past. As propounded by the prominent English Catholics Hilaire Belloc, G. K. Chesterton, Eric Gill, and Father Vincent McNabb, distributism was one of the anti-capitalist, anti-industrialist, and antistatist doctrines that flourished everywhere in the thirties. Instead of the "corrupt" modern order, distributists favored a decentralized economy of property-owning artisans, farmers, and shopkeepers. Since some of these notions accorded well with Peter Maurin's romantic "Green Revolution," distributism found a place in early *Catholic Worker* propaganda.[35] While its more nostalgic tenets were only one of the ingredients in the *Catholic Worker*'s ideological stew, the English movement was essential in pointing Day and others toward what became enduring concerns of the group: the spiritual nature of work, the oppressively large scale of modern society, the necessary connection of property and responsibility, and the quality of everyday life. One of the distributists, sculptor Eric Gill, became a particular friend of the movement by stressing such principles as well as pacifism, and his ideas exerted considerable influence on the paper over the years.[36]

Of course the distributists were not the only ones to raise these issues. Similar notions were common in the American radical and anarchist traditions that Day had known well before 1933. But distributism provided a specifically Catholic perspective on industrial problems and reinforced the *Catholic Worker*'s essential conviction that much of the alienation of modern society resulted from "the horrible separation of religion and life, religion and work."[37] Ironically, while distributism faded in its homeland after World War II, the *Catholic Worker* kept it alive by stripping it of its quaint English dress and putting it in a rougher outfit of American radicalism. While postwar Catholic Workers sometimes looked askance at distributism's reactionary overtones, Day insisted that there was still value in a "living distributism" which "needs to be constantly re-written, re-assessed, with the wisdom and clear-sightedness of a Chesterton who, by his paradoxes, made us see our problems in the light of faith."[38]

A third diffuse but powerful intellectual influence on the *Catholic Worker* came from two Russians: the novelist Fyodor Dostoevski and the religious philosopher Nicholas Berdyaev. Through Dorothy Day's constant stress on their central importance to the movement, they became, as Catholic Worker historian William Miller has shown, continuing vital sources of "the Catholic Worker idea."[39]

It was typical of Day's capacity for intuitive intellectual invention that she was able to make Dostoevski, the great reactionary Russian novelist, into one of the ideological pillars of her American Catholic radical movement, rather than a more obvious candidate like Tolstoy. This inversion was achieved by no complicated analysis, but simply by appropriating Dostoevski's central moral and spiritual themes in such a way as to slough off the more specific social ideas (including anti-Catholicism and anti-Americanism) to which he attached them.

By making advances in social and material well-being the polar opposite of the highest Christian spirituality, as in his legend of the Grand Inquisitor, Dostoevski "set bread against freedom," and suggested that all forms of committed social idealism constituted a Christian heresy: the attempt to set up a heavenly kingdom on earth, which was also one of the temptations of Christ. Day and the Catholic Workers, however, believed that the great Dostoevskian themes—selfless Christian love, spiritual and moral freedom, the virtue of living for ideas, the perpetual inner struggle with evil, and the special religious significance of the poor—that all these were compatible with an active commitment to social justice, and even to a social utopia, so long as it was clear that the sources and goal of all such activity was not within the human self or society but transcendent. Through selfless "love in action" Christian idealists could work to improve society without sacrificing individual liberty or putting the "bourgeois" values of purely material progress and self-advancement ahead of spiritual ones. Day believed that such a commitment could even reinforce rather than weaken that most troubling of Christian and Dostoevskian ideas, the spiritual value of suffering, because, in her favorite line from *The Brothers Karamazov*, "love in action is a harsh and dreadful thing compared to love in dreams." Faith was the necessary foundation of "personalist" Christian freedom, but that freedom was fully realized only in taking up the task of love and responsibility for the world. The *Catholic Worker* frequently quoted Dostoevski's phrase, "Hell is not to love any more," and it saw, like the Russian novelist, that there had always been a strong connection in Christian thought between love and suffering.

The *Catholic Worker*'s social idealism, therefore, rested not on a soft or sentimental view of mankind, nor on any expectation of realizing the eschatological kingdom of heaven on earth through social improvement. Rather, it depended on a thoroughly religious understanding of human nature and Christian life in the world. For Dorothy Day and the *Catholic Worker*, the spiritual intensity and suffering that Dostoevski associated with a purely transcendent religiosity and reactionary social order were made part of a movement concerned with the tangible goals of earthly peace and social justice. The *Catholic Worker* had a positive view of human nature and human possibilities, especially when touched by "grace." But unlike many progressive or liberationist movements in America, the movement possessed a core of hard moral and religious teaching that balanced its hopeful vision of social betterment.

The Russian Orthodox philosopher Berdyaev was also frequently cited in the *Catholic Worker* for his understanding of the connection between Christian freedom and social transformation. Peter Maurin put Berdyaev's *The Bourgeois Mind* high on his reading lists, and Day was much taken with his essay *Dostoevski*. For Berdyaev, as for the *Catholic Worker*, it was the bourgeois corruption of true social ideals, a corruption shared by such mistaken anti-bourgeois movements as Marxism, that created the apparent contradiction in modern society between transcendent spirituality and an improved social order. In the 1930s no one at the *Catholic Worker* claimed to understand the complex philosophical system that lay behind Berdyaev's arguments, but they grasped the essential point that Christian idealism was of great practical value in an excessively anxious and materialistic civilization.

Although no other individual writers shaped the movement's vision in such a clear fashion, the *Catholic Worker* quickly established a channel of communication with the intellectual currents of European Catholicism that grew broader and deeper over the years. The writers of the contemporary Catholic renaissance—Maritain, Dawson, Guardini,

Pieper, Chesterton, Mauriac, Bernanos—were always reviewed and quoted in the *Catholic Worker*, even when their work did not directly pertain to social problems. The paper thus promoted a general Catholic consciousness in its readers that complemented its treatment of the gritty conditions in American factories and slums. The activities of European Catholic activists were also followed closely in the *Catholic Worker*, especially those of Luigi Sturzo, Abbé Pierre, Lanza del Vasto, and Danilo Dolci, and others who worked directly on behalf of workers and the poor.

Important as its European connections were, the *Catholic Worker* could not have survived solely on a diet of imported Catholic thought. In order to make a mark in this country, the paper had to discover a workable synthesis of Catholic and American social and intellectual traditions. That process began with Day's own creative use of Maurin and his message. At first through Day's own experimental example, and then in the propaganda and activities of the movement, the *Catholic Worker* gradually developed a new style of intellectual radicalism that was both thoroughly Catholic and recognizably American.

In addition to the paper itself, the Round-Table Discussions at the newspaper office—House of Hospitality in New York were the most visible sign of the Worker's commitment to an intellectually well-founded American Catholic radicalism. Beginning at Fifteenth Street in 1933, and continuing at more than half a dozen CW headquarters down to the present, leading intellectuals, activists, and religious figures have come every week to lecture and discuss the contemporary questions debated in the paper. Day described the first session:

> Not only the store where the sessions were being held was crowded, but the kitchen and hall. Carlton J. H. Hayes began our series of lectures. . . . The audience was made up of unemployed men and women, plumbers, mechanics, steam fitters, sign painters, students from New York colleges, and Catholic Worker readers in general.[40]

Hayes on "Nationalism," James Vaughn on "Scholastic Philosophy," Wilfrid Parsons on "Social Welfare and the State," Parker T. Moon on "Peace"—these lectures started a tradition that over the years brought many of the best minds in American and international Catholicism to the slum headquarters of the *Catholic Worker* for such open-ended encounters. There writers, artists, and students could rub elbows and sip coffee with *Catholic Worker* activists and "guests," to their mutual benefit. The "clarification of thought" that Peter Maurin proclaimed as the goal of these exchanges seldom occurred. They were, said one Worker, "lively affairs, often marked by long monomaniacal comments by the participants." But the effects of these regular sessions went beyond the evening to enhance the spirit of open and thoughtful inquiry around the paper and the movement and to spread word of Day's singular enterprise in intellectual circles. Jacques Maritain, who came in 1934, was only one of many visitors who left behind glowing reviews. "It seemed as if I had found again in the Catholic Worker a little of the atmosphere of Péguy's office in the Rue de la Sorbonne. So much good will, such generosity, such courage!"[41] By its easy informality and simple hospitality toward all kinds of visitors, the *Catholic Worker* invited its numerous readers and others to drop in and see how the editors were living out the principles they advocated. "Never was there such a paper as the *Catholic Worker*," Day observed. "Do the readers of *Commonweal*, *America*, *Nation*, the *New Republic* come to spend weeks, and by the hundreds at that?"[42]

For many young Catholic intellectuals in the thirties, the Catholic Worker seemed like another, livelier kind of Catholic university that introduced them to unsuspected worlds of thought and challenged them to integrate ideas and experience. A few were introduced to the movement on campuses where the *Catholic Worker* was sold or where Dorothy Day came to speak. Cy Echele of St. Louis University said, "We all became steeped in the literature of the Catholic intellectual and literary revival in Europe represented by Chesterton, Dawson, and Maritain. We developed the germ of a Catholic consciousness. The false shades of modernism were lifted from our eyes, and we saw again the saints, the great lovers of God, as the finest exemplars upon which to fashion ourselves." Reading the *Catholic Worker* sparked this new religious commitment in Echele, Donald Gallagher, and other young intellectuals at the Jesuit school, and they were soon running a House of Hospitality, hawking the paper outside factories and churches, and carrying on an energetic debate with "capitalists, Marxists, political Catholics, bingo Catholics, anti-Communists, and Jew baiters."[43]

But in the thirties the Catholic Worker more often took the place of formal education. College was beyond the means of many intelligent young Catholics of the working and lower middle classes whose families were struggling through the Depression. The Catholic Worker offered an opportunity for intellectual growth and personal development they could find nowhere else. Garry Wills's comment that Day's movement provided a "way station for troubled young men" is correct if it is recognized that a good deal of the trouble came from the inner conflict many lower-income Catholics felt in those days between their commitments to religion and the urgent social needs of the day, between the often stifling anti-intellectualism of much American Catholic folk culture and their own awakening interest in critical ideas.[44] The history of the Catholic Worker is filled with the Irish, Italian, and east European names of young people who found the movement a doorway to a richer Catholic tradition than they had known in their parishes and neighborhoods. The Catholic Worker encouraged them to develop their talents in the service of the Church, and after a few years in the movement many went on to become Catholic writers, organizers, and lay social activists.

Dwight Macdonald was not entirely correct, then, when he said of the Catholic Worker that "by 1930 . . . Catholicism began to produce middle class intellectuals as full of reforming zeal as their Protestant counterparts a century before. As long as the majority of Catholics were proletarians the hierarchy could, if it liked, deal with them in an authoritarian way and dragoon them into a conservative social pattern, but as the laity became richer and better educated, there was an increasing ferment of liberalism in the old bottles of the Church."[45] Until 1950 or so, most Catholics were not middle class, and certainly not rich. The background of many of the prominent early Catholic Workers—John Cogley, James O'Gara, James Rogan, William Gauchat, Julia Porcelli, Ed Willock, Arthur Sheehan, Joseph Zarella, Stanley Vishnewski, Ed Marciniak, for example—was lower or lower-middle class. "There were few—I mean *few*—who gave up jobs to go to the Worker," said Zarella. "There were a lot of college dropouts, there were ex-seminarians, there were people who had no employment in the first place that had talent."[46] In its formative years as a radical movement, therefore, the Catholic Worker had much more of the flavor of the immigrant enclave, the day labor agency, and the parish hall than of upwardly mobile middle-class Catholicism. Many of those who came to intellectual maturity in the Catholic Worker, unlike those in such Protestant reform movements as the Social Gospel, did not have to travel far to discover the problems of industrialization and poverty in America.

III

The intellectual history of the *Catholic Worker* must be viewed from two angles: the central place of Dorothy Day and the equally important contributions of the many others who elaborated and refined her vision. One of the secrets of Day's success was her capacity to recognize the talents of others and to assimilate their ideas into the movement, much as rings accumulate around the core of a tree. In their attention to Day and Maurin, journalists and others have often overlooked the crucial contributions of Day's many other associates to the *Catholic Worker's* intellectual tradition.

Of course from one perspective the preoccupation with Dorothy Day is entirely justified. As Dwight Macdonald observed, "The only recent American institutions that fit Emerson's generalization [that 'an institution is the lengthened shadow of one man'] are J. Edgar Hoover's FBI and Dorothy Day's Catholic Workers."[47] As with Hoover, Day's longevity alone accounted for some of her singular influence. But more important was her steadfast adherence to a single vision of what the movement should be. Others were better at developing the fine points of a Catholic radical social theory, but Dorothy Day provided the still point around which the *Catholic Worker* revolved.

Day was first of all important to the *Catholic Worker* as a journalist and editor. The radical intentions and Skid Road environment of the *Catholic Worker* never interfered with her professional commitment to making the paper a first-rate journalistic effort. Much as she disdained "bourgeois" values of the social or commercial sort, Day's great capacity for hard work and her single-minded devotion to the success of her enterprise paid off in the high quality of writing and editing that consistently marked the *Catholic Worker*, especially after its early days.

During the thirties Day edited the paper herself, except when she was away on trips. After 1940 she increasingly relied on a succession of managing editors for the selection of material and day-to-day supervision of the operation. Still, she always kept abreast of the *Catholic Worker's* content, soliciting articles and screening material for anything that violated her understanding of what the *Catholic Worker* stood for. In 1952, for example, she blocked an article by editor Tom Sullivan that endorsed Adlai Stevenson for president.[48] Another editor recalled that "she probably hit some kind of height or depth of editorial *chutzpah* when she took out a paragraph of something Mike Harrington had written and inserted a paragraph she thought was better under his name."[49] The editors constantly debated issues, and differing views frequently found their way into print, but the major outlines of editorial policy were clearly set by Day.

She also contributed to the *Catholic Worker* as a reporter and columnist. Her old talent for descriptive and partisan journalism was put to especially good use in the thirties, when she covered some of the dramatic conflicts of the Depression, as well as the unspectacular daily lives and sufferings of the people she met in the slums and elsewhere. In her vivid personal style, she wrote about such things as evictions, the maritime strikes, New York's Municipal Lodging Houses, and the

Republic Steel massacre. In 1936 a series of reports on Arkansas share-croppers showed that she had lost none of her touch as a muckraker:

> It wasn't until late afternoon that we reached the worst place of all, just outside Parkin, Arkansas. There drawn up along the road was a tent colony which houses 108 people, four infants among them, and God knows how many children.
>
> The little girls giggled and laughed with their arms around each other while we talked to this evicted crowd of sharecroppers. It was seventeen above. Only one of them had a sweater, and the heels and toes of all of them were coming out of their shoes. Their giggles started them coughing and woke one of the babies who cried fretfully, weakly. . . .
>
> So while surveys are being made and written the Southern Tenant Farmers Union carries on, organizing the sharecroppers. They have had a hard struggle in the past, and the future looks dark. But combined with faith and charity they have hope, and the terror that walks by day and by night in Arkansas does not daunt them.

These reports, which appeared in both the *Catholic Worker* and *America*, drew the attention of Eleanor Roosevelt, as well as the local landowners and the governor of the state who denounced "this Catholic woman who makes fat salaries off the misery of the people."[50]

Day also gave *Catholic Worker* readers some of the decade's best coverage of the labor movement. The paper's working-class sympathies helped it develop inside sources for the coverage of unions, strikes, and labor issues. Day knew many national labor figures, and interviewed union heads like Philip Murray, John Lewis, John Brophy, Harry Bridges, Joseph Curran, and others. One story on pro-labor priest Father Stephen Kazincy described his speech to a group of steel workers at Braddock, Pennsylvania: "With his snow white hair he stood broad and straight in the broiling sun, head held high, as he told the men, 'Do not let the Carnegie Steel Company crush you.'" Day was one of only two reporters permitted by the workers to enter the auto plants during the General Motors sit-down strikes. The same event brought her close to Frank Murphy, the Catholic governor of Michigan, whom she encouraged in his pro-labor stand.[51]

In later years Day gave up most of her muckraking and investigative reporting in favor of her column, but she retained a sharp reporter's eye for the significant detail and the revealing quote. When her travels took her to places like the New York Women's House of Detention, Communist Cuba, Rome, or the California vineyards, she provided informative reports as well as personal reactions. The tradition of partisan muckraking Day established never entirely disappeared from the *Catholic Worker*, which periodically dug into such little-covered events as the dislocation of the poor by urban renewal, the plight of migrant sugar workers in Louisiana, Indian water rights, and the exploitation of Bowery men by day labor agencies.

Besides direct reporting Day could also produce substantive background pieces on important issues that could stand comparison to the best conventional journalism. In May 1954, for example, she wrote a lengthy "sketch" (about thirty-five hundred words) on the problem of Vietnam. Having read "half a dozen books" in researching the article, Day went into the entire question of Western involvement in Indochina, using as a touchstone a nineteenth-century Catholic missionary, Theophane Venard, who had opposed French political and economic imperialism and admired Buddhist culture and religion. She cited Venard's plea that "the Annamese have a civilization equal to our own in Europe," and followed a description of the current French war and the situation of Catholics in the country with a warning against American intervention.[52] Even apart from whatever confirmation it gave to their prior convictions, such articles made the *Catholic Worker* a valuable source of offbeat information for its subscribers.

Day's real forte, however, was her personal column, originally called "Day By Day," and changed to "On Pilgrimage" in 1946. There she could give full rein to her personal style, what Macdonald called "an odd composite of Pascal's *Pensées* and Eleanor Roosevelt's 'My Day.'" The column's folksiness appealed to readers who might not care for the more abstract writers elsewhere in the paper. Bus rides, speeches, meals, visitors, wars, books, saints, deaths, weather, noises, smells, children—all appeared jumbled together in the chatty paragraphs of "On Pilgrimage." A further personal touch came from Day's constant emphasis of her role as mother, and later as grandmother and great-grandmother. Sometimes this led to an engaging blend of domesticity and propaganda:

> The children of the house were bending engrossed over a toy catalogue the other day figuring up what they would like to have for Christmas. "It's no use looking at it," one of them was saying. "It is only for rich children, this catalogue. A toy train costs fifteen dollars!"
>
> "When I grow up I'm going to be rich," five year old Freddy said. "Rich!" said seven year old Teresa. "Don't you know it's bourgeois to be rich?"
>
> I would have liked to tell her that it is also bourgeois to have

the acquisitive spirit and to want so much for Christmas, but I didn't have the heart, so I sat down with them to look at the catalogue.[53]

Day's personal touch was imitated by other writers in the *Catholic Worker*. Regular columns reported on life in the New York House of Hospitality and the farm, while other reports came from Catholic Worker groups around the country. Such items ran the danger of making the *Catholic Worker* a house organ devoted to the movement's internal concerns and, thus, inaccessible to outsiders. Yet the paper's human ambience was also an effective way to overcome the bifurcation between great issues and mundane existence that often occurs in social or political movements. For Dorothy Day, a social revolution would be worthwhile only if it was also homelike. By making the themes of community and domesticity that had always been important to her part of the fabric of Catholic Worker life, she made its radical Christian idealism seem homey as well. Such personalism helped insure that the *Catholic Worker's* brand of revolutionism would never push aside the individual in favor of the mass, the immediate human need in favor of the abstract and impersonal cause.

One result of this approach was that year after year the *Catholic Worker* provided detailed and often moving reports on the seldom-seen underside of American society. From its close observation of daily life among the poor, the paper drew regular portraits of individual "workers" that were remarkable for their unsentimental appreciation of ordinary lives.

Albert Brady is dead. Late lord of the kitchen, and heir of his own magnificent dreams, he succumbed to the abrasion of daily reality. Broken in body, a hunchback, he cherished a mental picture of himself as a strong, self-sufficient, silent power, a man, not always a cripple, able to cope with the best. Fawning to authority and domineering to the weak, he could only live by lying to himself, for the truth was too bitter to accept.

When we consider his life, what we know of it, we can only pray for this friendly, little, queer, unhappy man. He used to talk to me often for hours at a time: truth, fantasy, vague statements, obvious lies, waved away at a question, following one another in a mysterious whisper. He loved to get one behind a closed door, and with an air of mystery, expound upon an obvious commonplace. He lived in a world of make-believe, and cooked abominable food.[54]

It was Day's own ability to join matters great and ordinary that inspired this kind of writing in the *Catholic Worker*. In print, as in person, she conveyed a kind of keen attentiveness to simple forms that enriched and ennobled them—what Erik Erikson called "the capacity to find infinite meanings in finite things."[55] This capacity allowed her and the paper's other writers to find significant subjects amidst the often bleak surroundings of America's urban wastelands, and their observant personal accounts of society's outcasts, as much as anything else, explained the movement's concern for the poor.

Day was not, however, just a good-natured *mater familias*. Anyone who mistook her disarming simplicity and earthiness for naiveté was likely to be quickly disabused. Especially when she was dismissed or patronized as a well-meaning but sentimental do-gooder unaware of the complexities or evil of the world, Day could quickly show her tougher, saltier side. Her tongue and pen could both be sharp, and she knew how to use them to good effect. After she once wrote a biting piece on longshore boss Joseph Ryan in the *Catholic Worker*, he snapped at a young Catholic Worker, "You go tell Dorothy Day she's no lady."

Those who tangled with her in public or private had reason to agree. Beneath her unassuming demeanor stood a strong-willed woman whose varied life had left her no stranger to all-out personal and ideological conflict. One Catholic Worker who knew her well said, "She's not all sugar, see. She's tough, she's smart, she's stubborn, she doesn't listen well all the time, and she holds grudges."[56] Another old associate noted that "Dorothy could also be rather sarcastic at times and she had a cutting edge to her tongue. . . . She had a habit, in those early days, of cutting people down if they were ornery or proved to be too disagreeable. This was a fault she freely acknowledged and prayed to overcome. But Dorothy was not the sort of person to suffer fools to provoke her—that is, not strong, healthy fools."[57]

Day usually repented her personal piques and clashes with individuals in the movement. But her deep well of charity and toleration reached their limit when she encountered what she saw as clear denials of Christian values. "If the situation is as reported," she wrote to one welfare agency supervisor concerning a payment denied to a poor parent, "then God have mercy on your soul."[58] To a writer who complained about her lack of concern for "the poor kids in Korea," she replied, "If it refers to our soldiers the phrase is maudlin, and I don't think it means the children being killed by our bombs."[59] In 1937, she spoke before a Catholic sodality where the well-dressed ladies in attendance denounced unions and talked of sterilization for those on welfare:

> We are told to keep, and we always try, a just attitude toward
> the rich. But as I thought of our breakfast line, our crowded
> house with people sleeping on the floor, when I thought of the
> cold tenement apartments around us, and the gaunt faces of the
> men who come to us for help, it became impossible not to hate,
> with a hearty and strong anger, the injustices of this world.
>
> St. Thomas says that anger is not a sin, provided there go not
> with it an undue desire for revenge. We want no violent revolu-
> tion. We want the brotherhood of men. But when we meet
> people who deny Christ in his poor, we feel, "Here are atheists
> indeed."[60]

Equally passionate was her column on the dropping of the atomic bomb:

> Mr. Truman was jubilant. True Man. What a strange name,
> come to think of it. . . . He went from table to table on the
> cruiser which was bringing him home from the Big Three Con-
> ference, telling the great news. *Jubilate Deo.* We have killed
> 318,000 Japanese.[61]

Day was obviously a complex individual: visionary and hard-
headed, pious and worldly-wise, overflowing with Christian *agape* and a
shrewd and determined public dissenter. In trying to understand what
held together her unique social vision, some have looked for clues in her
personality. Certainly it is hard to ignore the force of her character. It was
widely agreed that her charismatic "presence" and inner strength inspired deep admiration and commitment from people inside and outside
the Catholic Worker. "Dorothy always conducted herself with an air of
quiet dignity," observed longtime Catholic Worker Stanley Vishnewski.
"But beneath the softness was a strength of character and an iron will
that enabled her to keep the movement going in spite of all the adverse
criticism and vicious slanderings that were hurled against her."[62] For all
the words written about her, by herself and others, the truly private Day
was not readily accessible to others. In the 1930s her looks were sometimes compared with those of the actress Greta Garbo, and there was
something like the Garbo mystique about her person as well. Even to
many who knew her well, she seemed complex, elusive, a bit removed.
Individuals could see in her the most diverse traits. H. A. Reinhold
commented on what he thought was a "grim" undertone in her life,
while John Cort discovered joy at the core of her personality: "It was a
quality of humor deeper than you get from a comedian, a laughter that
seemed to reach down to the secret places of the soul, promising at any
moment to explain the mysteries of life and existence."[63] Vishnewski

said, "One also got the impression that Dorothy was a person who had been hurt and rebuffed many times by people that she had loved and trusted, and that in spite of it all she wanted to keep on loving and trusting them, but was a bit fearful of how her offers of friendship would be received."[64] Significantly, she chose for the title of her autobiography a line from the English nun Mary Ward: "We women especially are victims of the long loneliness." Whatever the complex forces that shaped Day's inner self, she effectively molded them into a powerful public presence. And this achievement, there is little doubt, was intimately connected with religion.

IV

Day's meeting with Maurin and her successful founding of the Catholic Worker gave a new scope to her religion. As late as November 1932, she still felt the strain of being cut off from her old radical associations, yet she was still unable to establish comfortable relationships with her fellow believers. "I am among people, yet I am in a desert place," she wrote. "St. Francis de Sales speaks of spiritual friendships but I have not known these. Bonds of duty tie me now to these people, but I feel lonely in their presence."[65] Her new status as a Catholic social leader ended her isolation as well as her fear that in converting to Catholicism, she had abandoned her commitment to social justice.

Even in the years when Day had gone without religion she had brought the intensity of religious devotion to her radical involvements. Now that she had satisfactorily united her two passions, she found unsuspected reserves of confidence and strength. Looking back, she felt that her whole earlier life had been a preparation for the Catholic Worker, and she looked to religion for further sustenance in the difficult work ahead. "I just have to go lean on the altar rail and drop the burdens there," she wrote to a friend in 1934. "I mean the burdens of all the things left undone or half done or remembered too late."[66]

Finding in Maurin someone whose simple love of the poor also rested on a religious foundation ended whatever lingering doubts Day still had that Christianity was incompatible with a radically activist sympathy with the lower classes. There might be difficulties in working out a theory of social class and social change within the Catholic context, but on the fundamental point that Catholic faith and radical social action were compatible, Day no longer held reservations. "Meekness" was indeed a Christian virtue, she explained, but its application had been misunderstood. "We were ready to 'endure wrongs patiently' for ourselves—

this is one of the spiritual works of mercy. But we were not going to be meek for others, enduring *their* wrongs patiently."[67] When accused of "class war tactics" in the founding of the *Catholic Worker*, Day responded with the quip of another convert, St. Augustine, that "the bottle always smells of the liquor it once held."[68]

Day began the *Catholic Worker* as an attempt to express her faith in social action. Although wholeheartedly devoted to social causes, she never strayed from an insistence that religion was at the heart of the movement. "The center of our thoughts is not social justice but religion itself," she wrote shortly after the paper was founded. It was Day's special function as leader of the movement to emphasize that principle and instill it in others.

The religion that Dorothy Day made the core of her movement was mystical, liturgical, sacramental, ecclesiastical, and unswervingly orthodox. Her commitment to Catholicism was closely attuned to the models she found in the early saints of the Church, whose spiritual illumination came through asceticism and prayer. "Anatole France introduced me to the Desert Fathers in *Thais*," she commented in the early days of the CW, "and even in that satire the beauty of these saints shone through." Her attraction to the Catholic mystical tradition was also evident in her comments on Thomas Sugrue's controversial book, *A Catholic Speaks His Mind on America's Religious Conflict*. Passing lightly over matters of Protestant-Catholic and Catholic-state relations, Day stressed the importance of Sugrue's mystical understanding of the faith, which drew on Plotinus, Dionysius the Pseudo-Areopagite, John of the Cross, and Teresa of Avila. "'They are the heart of Catholicism; they are its mystical core,'" she quoted approvingly. "'After I had found them and studied them, I would not have left the Church under any persuasion.'"[69]

The basis of Day's orthodox Catholicism lay not only in the affinities she found with the tradition of the saints and mystics, but in the Church's custody of the sacraments. For Day, the Eucharist in particular was the foundation of spiritual life, connecting the spiritual and material. She rejoiced in the use of bread and other common elements in Catholic ritual. "I loved all the physical aspects of the Church," she said. "They showed that man was body and soul, and could learn through his senses. The sacramentals which attuned one to accept the sacraments with intensified faith also delighted me. It was easy to accept the teaching that all water had become holy since Christ was baptized in the Jordan."[70] Day had begun attending daily Mass before starting the *Catholic Worker*, and she continued the practice throughout her life. "The Eucharist is the center of liturgical worship for her," reported one friend.

"All liturgy is first of all concerned with bringing us the body and blood of Christ."[71]

Happily for Day and the *Catholic Worker*, the view of the Eucharist as a vital center of Christian life and community was encouraged by an influential group of theologians and liturgical reformers who began to have an impact on American Catholicism in the 1930s. Foremost among these was Father Virgil Michel, the eminent Benedictine who began the American liturgical movement at St. John's Abbey and College in Collegeville, Minnesota, and spread it through his journal, *Orate Fratres*.[72] Michel's liturgical and sacramental theology included a strong emphasis on social action and community, and he and Day immediately recognized one another as allies. In the pages of *Orate Fratres* and throughout the Catholic community, Michel vigorously promoted the Catholic Worker as one of the most vital movements in the Church and denounced the "dirt" that was circulating among Catholics about Day's radical past. For her part, Day saw in Michel's work the best religious foundation for her work. "We feel that it is very necessary to connect the liturgical movement with the social justice movement," she wrote in 1933. "Each one gives vitality to the other."[73]

Day corresponded extensively with Michel, Alcuin Deutsch, Gerald Ellard, and other liturgicalists in the early years of the movement. The *Catholic Worker* reflected her effort, as she said, "to see that every number of the paper gives liturgy its proper place."[74] Not only did the *Catholic Worker* contain specific discussions of the meaning of the Mass, but sacramental notions were integrated with seemingly secular concerns. An editorial on the National Recovery Act, for instance, could turn to the doctrine of man expressed in the Eucharistic Prayer: "Oh, God, Who in creating human nature didst marvelously ennoble it, and hast still more marvelously renewed it, grant that by the mystery of this bread and wine we may be made partakers of his divinity who vouchsafed to become partakers of our humanity."[75] Michel himself wrote for the *Catholic Worker* and spoke at Worker Houses. After his visit to New York in 1934, Day and others in the movement adopted other liturgical practices as well, such as the singing of Prime and Compline mornings and evenings—although participation in such worship was entirely voluntary in Worker Houses.

Besides the emphasis on an active sacramental and prayer life, the key idea the *Catholic Worker* took from the liturgical movement was the doctrine of the Mystical Body of Christ. Contemporary theologians like Michel were increasingly propounding the ancient doctrine concerning the Church's relationship to Christ through the sacraments as a model for the real relations among men in society. Using the orthodox formula that "Christ is the Head and we are the members of the Mystical Body," the *Catholic Worker* developed the theme that such a relationship implied a radical reconstruction of human society. "The illnesses of hate, injustice, disunion, prejudice, class war, greed, nationalism, and war weaken this Mystical Body," the *Catholic Worker* declared, "just as the prayers and sacrifices of countless of the faithful strengthen it." In protest against some social evil, Day frequently quoted the lament of Clement of Alexandria: "Why do the Members of Christ tear one another? Why do we rise up against our own Body?"[76]

Also consistent with the *Catholic Worker*'s religious radicalism was the doctrinal interpretation, promoted by Michel and others and later to be endorsed by Vatican Council II, that the Church is not an exclusive club by which a favored few gain salvation—"no salvation outside the Church"—but rather the visible sign of a divine presence already immanent in all men, though in some unconsciously. Thus, Day could repeatedly stress the ethical implications of St. Thomas's view that all men are "members or potential members" of the Body of Christ and that devotion to Christ demands service to those in whom He dwells: "Now it is with the voices of our contemporaries that He speaks," she wrote. "It is with the eyes of store clerks, factory workers, and children that He gazes, with the hands of office workers, slum dwellers, and suburban housewives that He works."[77] For Day and her followers, the radical social consequences of this religious insight were inescapable.

Day's immediate grasp and creative use of these Catholic doctrines showed her awareness that the *Catholic Worker* had to rest on the firmest possible religious foundation. But she encountered a personal problem in integrating her own piety with the high intellectual traditions of the Church. Although sure of her faith, she had to develop from reading and experience a spirituality more attuned to her own sense of the meaning of life "in Christ." As in her social thought, she had a clear view of essential directions, but looked for help in working out the particulars.

Part of her difficulty in developing a fully satisfactory Catholic outlook came from her old ambivalence about intellectuals and intellectual approaches to life. Ideas always played a vital part in her religious life, and she recognized from her reading the wisdom and authority of the theologians and scholars of the Church from St. Augustine onward. Yet her own temperament consistently pointed her away from these great religious teachers toward more ordinary models of religious life—those saints whose main contributions had been love, piety, and moral action rather than thought.

Day was well aware that Catholicism contained such models. Even before her conversion she had been attracted by St. Francis and the Desert Fathers. Her taste for directness and emotionality in religion found special satisfaction in *The Imitation of Christ* of Thomas à Kempis, the classic of late medieval spirituality that stressed feeling, sincerity, and humility against the more intellectual virtues. Yet for many years after her conversion, she had failed to find anyone in American Catholicism who could evoke the full power of this tradition in a modern setting for a person of her temperament. Her attempts to move beyond the ordinary level of religious understanding of a devout Catholic lay person were frustrating. Several attempts at weekend retreats at local convents repelled her. "I endured it for two days and could not wait to get out on the streets where I could breathe, walk freely," she said. "Probably I was suffering from what I came to call the 'spiritual bends.'"[78]

But in 1939 Day finally discovered what she had been looking for. Her friend Maisie Ward told her of attending a retreat for the poor given by a French Canadian priest, Abbé Seay. Day was at first unimpressed by notes she read from the retreat, and in any case, the language barrier prevented her participation. But a year later she met Pacifique Roy, a Josephite priest from Quebec who represented the same movement. Roy's simple but fervent exposition of the Gospel paradoxes struck just the right note with Day. "Father Roy talked to us of nature and the supernatural, how God became man that man might become God, how we were under the obligation of putting off the old man and putting on Christ," she reported. "We had to aim at perfection; we had to be guided by the folly of the Cross."[79] The inspiration was like that she had received from Maurin. "As Peter always dealt with the things of this world, so Father Roy always dealt with the things of the next, but the two were interwoven; time and eternity were one."[80]

Roy directed Day to John J. Hugo and Louis Farina, two Pittsburgh priests who were actually conducting "the retreat" as they had learned it from its founder, Onesimus Lacouture, a French Canadian Jesuit. Beginning in 1940 and throughout the war years, Day and other Catholic Workers attended Hugo's retreats, first in Pittsburgh and then at the Catholic Worker farm. For Day these retreats—which consisted of a week of absolute silence, meditation, and spiritual exercises—were a liberating spiritual experience. "This was what I was looking for in the way of an explanation of the Christian life," she rejoiced. "Though still I saw through a glass darkly, I saw things as a whole for the first time with a delight, a joy, an excitement which is hard to describe. This is what I expected when I became a Catholic."[81] Because Hugo had brought about this liberation, and because his own radical Gospel perfectionism coincided with the Catholic Worker's social commitments, particularly its controversial wartime pacifism, Hugo became for several years a dominant intellectual influence on the *Catholic Worker*.

Yet as with most intense religious movements, "the retreat" was a cause of controversy as well as celebration among the Catholic Workers. Especially as the initial effects wore off, some who had "made" the retreat seemed to become lost and confused. One Worker said that "a lot of people got sort of fouled up, and there were many people who were very strong supporters of the retreat who later turned against it and became very bitter."[82] With its ascetic rigor and radical Gospel perfectionism the retreat inevitably raised issues of spiritual elitism and Jansenism. In its Canadian home base, the founder of the movement, Lacouture, and two of his associates, Leseuer and Seay, were dispatched to remote outposts by Church authorities after it became evident that wealthy young people who heard them were relinquishing their status to take up social service.[83] In the United States, controversy over Hugo's retreats broke out in theological journals, and he was eventually refused ecclesiastical permission to give them. Even within the Catholic Worker movement, the retreat caused for a time "a sort of division between those who had made the retreat and those who had not. It was as though they lived in two spiritual worlds." While Ade Bethune and others spoke out against Hugo's attacks on "the world" and his assertion that "the best thing to do with the best of things is to give them up" as contrary to a proper Catholic view of the goodness and beauty of natural things, others continued to hold the retreat in high esteem.[84]

The effects of the retreat on Dorothy Day were more complex. Someone as religiously adept as Day was better able to interpret and balance the paradoxical Gospel formulations concerning "the way of the Cross." Although it led her temporarily into some bewildering theological thickets, the retreat was her first direct encounter with the sort of radically inward Christianity she had known only from books, and the effect was exhilarating. The intensity and sense of total commitment evoked by the retreat were welcome, as was the strong support it gave from within Catholic tradition to the Catholic Worker's ethical applications of the radical Gospel. Both Roy and Hugo preached the doctrine of the Mystical Body, attacked society's individualism and materialism, and urged radical action to end race and class discrimination and war. The retreats also came at a time of crisis and decline for the movement, so that the traumatic experiences of division, loss, and failure could suddenly be seen in light of Gospel paradoxes as the "stripping of natural desire" and "taking up the Cross." Although Day was sidetracked for a time by some of the sumptuary moralist preachings that accompanied the retreat—such as attacks on cigarettes and cosmetics—she was eventually able to sort out these peripheral elements from the valuable core of the experience.

Some of Day's friends and followers believed that the retreat marked "the great spiritual *metanoia* of Dorothy's life." They professed to see her a different person before and after—the political activist and journalist transformed into the religious teacher and writer. After the retreat, one said, "Dorothy became a deeply spiritual woman."[85] Although a change was evident, such sharp dichotomies overstate the case. The pre-retreat Day had always stressed "the primacy of the spiritual" in her writing and work, just as the post-retreat Day continued to be a busy social activist.

The difference was one of emphasis rather than a complete turn of direction, and might best be described as a new stage of religious growth. This change is symbolized by Day's altered view of "the two Teresas"—St. Teresa of Avila and St. Thérèse of Lisieux, both among her longtime favorites. In 1944, after several years of the retreats, Day took a "leave of absence" as editor of the *Catholic Worker*—her only break from the job in forty-seven years. During months of solitude at an isolated spot on Long Island, she followed a rigorous schedule of worship, prayer, and meditative reading. At first she suffered "an agony of boredom" in the routine. But gradually she began to gain what she considered new religious insight and described it in terms of her revised assessment of the two Teresas. Before, the Spanish Teresa had been her preferred religious model. She was religiously intense but also bright, gay, intelligent, attractive, and a successful writer and activist. But now Day was more drawn to the French Thérèse, a passive teenager who had suffered a debilitating illness and died in obscurity without accomplishing anything of consequence in the world. "I could see clearly the difference between the two Teresas," she wrote, "and I came to the conclusion that St. Thérèse of Lisieux's was the loftier vocation, the harder and more intense life." While Teresa of Avila knew that "prayer overflows into action," Thérèse of Lisieux was proof that silence and inactivity were the sources of all right action. "From that year I spent away from my work I began to understand the greatness of the Little Flower," she wrote. "By doing nothing she did everything. She let loose powers, consolations, and streams of faith, hope, and love that will never cease to flow."[86]

Day's choice of Thérèse of Lisieux also indicated a recognition that her own religiosity required deep emotional as well as intellectual sustenance. Although she felt at home with intellectuals and clung to her vocation as a journalist and activist, she was ultimately drawn to the outwardly uninspiring Little Flower who, as Robert Coles has noted, was a tremendously popular devotional figure with "no following among intellectuals within or without the Church."[87] Day repeatedly defended the sort of piety inspired by Thérèse and Thomas à Kempis against intellectual attack and eventually wrote a hagiography of the Little Flower precisely because, Day said, she was regarded as so "ordinary" by all but "simple folk."[88]

Day recognized the importance of following her particular spiritual tastes, but she never tried to inflict them on others. "Men being so diverse in temperament, they are bound to differ about these matters," she observed. "There will always be those who worship . . . in calm objective prayer, and those who cry out from their own need. . . . These attitudes were all reflected in the controversy over Father Lacouture's and Father Hugo's retreat." Observing her own "avidity" during the Mass, Day placed herself among those who need a strong "subjective" element in religion and are inclined to follow the "little way" of suffering. "I must in humility be conscious of my needs, of my hunger and thirst, and trust only to grow in strength and sense of worship."[89]

Similarly, Day discovered signs of the divine presence among human beings not primarily in truth or goodness, but in the gentle deviancy of holy fools like her favorite literary characters, Prince Mishkin and Don Quixote. In such personalities, an apparent simplicity and irrationality concealed a spiritual genius that confounded ordinary society, yet in some way saved it and preserved its sanity. She found the essence of religion, she said, in "the wild, the mystical, the holy," qualities that transcended even goodness and compassion without excluding them. "There are always fools and conventionals among us in our various Catholic Worker Houses across the country," she wrote, "and while I sympathize with the conventionals and know that they are the backbone of the movement who keep things going, still I rejoice that we have an abundance of fools. I am sure Peter Maurin was thought to be such a fool by many who knew him."[90]

But if Day's spirituality was distinctive and personal, it was firmly anchored by her objective commitment to Catholic Christianity. However intense her inner religiosity, she insisted on the complete authority of the Church in matters of faith and doctrine. She always distinguished, however, between the Church's religious essence and its sometimes dubious social, economic, and political entanglements. It was because the Catholic Church taught the eternal truths of salvation that it was to be revered and obeyed, and for no other reason.

I loved the Church for Christ made visible, not for itself, because
it was so often a scandal to me. Romano Guardini said that the
Church is the Cross on which Christ was crucified. I knew that
one could not separate Christ from his Cross, and that one must
live in the Church in a state of permanent dissatisfaction. . . .

   The scandal of businesslike priests, of collective wealth, the
lack of a sense of responsibility for the poor, the worker, the
Negro, the Mexican . . . and even the oppression of these made
me feel often that the Church was more like Cain than like Abel.
And yet the priests were the custodians of the Sacraments,
bringing Christ to men, enabling us to put on Christ and to
achieve more nearly in the world a sense of peace and unity. . . .
We can never root out the tares without rooting out the wheat
also.[91]

Thus, whatever her disagreements with Church authorities or
fellow Catholics, Day could never consider disobedience or separation
because that would be presuming to "separate the wheat from the tares."
Breaking with the Church because of its faults would constitute "un-
faithfulness not to the error but to Christ." "It is impossible to understand Dorothy without understanding her great love for the Church,"
one friend said. "She loves it so much she feels she can criticize it as an
institution. She believes it is the Body of Christ—that it is what Christ
left us, and that it is our bond of unity."[92]

   This critical but fervent loyalty to Catholicism underlay not
only Day's religious life but the outlook of the *Catholic Worker* as well.
The paper was emphatically devoted to the Catholic faith and stressed
the authority of the Church's bishops, doctrines, teachings, and living
traditions. But the *Catholic Worker* and its related social movement were
also entirely lay ventures, with no official sponsorship, and thus subject
to no religious discipline except in the matters of "faith and morals"
recognized by all Catholics. In declaring its fundamental faithfulness to
the Church, the *Catholic Worker* also asserted its freedom to speak openly
and critically on all other matters. "When I started the *Catholic Worker* I
asked no permissions, expected no recognitions," Day said. "Of course
there have been plenty of criticisms and complaints to the Chancery
Office ever since." Although she was requested to come to the New York
Chancery on at least four or five occasions, Day's confidence that Church
authorities would maintain the distinction between spiritual and other
matters as scrupulously as she did proved to be well placed. "The only
assistance I have from my spiritual director is in confession. He does not

agree with us on the Spanish question, on the CIO, on our tactics," she said. "But he has never tried to direct the course of the paper in the confessional. He was approved by the Cardinal as our spiritual director, that is all." [93] Even though the hierarchy of the New York diocese during Day's tenure—Hayes, McIntyre, Spellman—was considered archconservative, there was never a serious move against the paper. When Hayes died in 1938, the Chancery even listed among his accomplishments "the birth of the Catholic Worker movement, which he encouraged by wise counsel and generous assistance, and resisted every effort to interfere with its efficiency." [94]

For Day, the indivisibility of the Church as a spiritual community freed Catholics, and especially lay persons, for greater action in the world. Catholics might disagree over fundamental social questions, but they remained united "at the altar." About one monsignor who attacked the *Catholic Worker* as subversive, she said, "I loved him because he epitomized to me the great diversity and liberty in the Church." [95] Although she could be very critical in private of the failings of churchmen, Day generally avoided or downplayed direct criticism of clergy in the *Catholic Worker*. Although this reticence was considered a weakness by some, especially in later years when general Catholic inhibitions against such criticism broke down, Day held to the view that Catholic religious owed obedience to their superiors and that lay persons should concentrate on positive social action rather than on attacking the Church and its leaders. When a group of activist Catholics in Los Angeles wrote her complaining of opposition from the hierarchy there, she replied:

> We must follow where the spirit leads. So go ahead, and don't look for support or approval. And don't always be looking for blame, either, or see opposition where perhaps there is none. It is judging the motives of others. Excuse my didactic tone, but I do have long experience. I beg you to save your energies to fight the gigantic injustices of our times, and not the Church in the shape of its Cardinal Archbishop there. It is a temptation of the devil to divert our energies, discourage us, sadden us, and neutralize all we would like to do. [96]

This stance put Day in the position of being able to appeal to churchmen on their own ground, to criticize Catholic practice in the name of shared religious ideals. Where she believed a principle was at stake, she did not hesitate to oppose the hierarchy. One of the most notable conflicts occurred in 1949, when the *Catholic Worker* and the movement began supporting a strike of gravediggers against Cardinal

Spellman's diocesan cemetery. A letter she wrote to Spellman after he had issued a strong attack on the strikers shows Day's subtle blend of criticism and faithful loyalty to the Church:

> This is so far your only statement, which has certainly not been a fair statement to the workers, and has been aimed at alienating any sympathy from them. I am sure you did not intend it in this way, and that you have been misinformed. I am writing to you because this strike, though small, is a terribly significant one in a way.
>
> It is not just the issue of wages and hours, as I can see from the conversations our Catholic Workers have with them. It is a question of their dignity as men.
>
> You are a prince of the Church, and a great man in the eyes of the world, and your opponents are all little men, hard working day laborers filled with grievances. They want to talk to you, and, oh, I do beg you so with all my heart to go to them. . . . It is easier for the great to give in than the poor.[97]

Although Day was thus willing to use her "Catholic freedom" to criticize bishops and priests where necessary, she never wavered in her conviction that, ultimately, the Church was to be obeyed when it spoke with its full religious authority. This was the meaning of her controversial declaration that "if Cardinal Spellman ordered me to close down the *Catholic Worker* tomorrow, I would."[98] Being a Catholic meant, finally, accepting religious limits on freedom. Day consistently refused to accept the distinction, traditional with most American Protestants and increasingly popular among Catholics after Vatican II, between loyalty to the Gospel or to Christian ideals and loyalty to the flawed Church and its leaders. When one of her young editors protested that this kind of subordination might violate his own conception of the right, she retorted, "If you want to edit the *Quaker Worker* you've come to the wrong place."[99]

Such a traditional Catholic view of community and authority ran against powerful strains of American libertarianism and individualism that the *Catholic Worker* upheld in the social sphere. Almost all the traditions of American social action and dissent, like the country's dominant evangelical religiosity, rested on ideas of the final moral autonomy of the individual.

Day's stance, on the other hand, was that of the pre-Reformation Catholic reformer who appealed to the Christian Church from within to be truer to itself, but was unable to imagine religious or moral life at all without the institution. Her religious vision was completely tolerant and ecumenical, without a trace of triumphalism, but it rested on the conviction that the Catholic Church could finally distinguish correct spiritual values. This faith was obviously a great source of personal strength. How it would be implemented by her followers in the actual circumstances of American society was another matter.

CHAPTER FOUR

A Radical Catholic Movement

I

The radical Gospel has long been honored as an ethical ideal. What distinguishes radical Gospel movements is their attempt to make this ideal the foundation of a functioning social order. The history of such Christian efforts shows a persistent tension between two goals: to preserve the integrity of the Gospel ideal as understood by the group, and to witness the utopian vision to the larger society. In the initial stages of enthusiasm and expansion these goals can appear compatible, but in the long run they are difficult to reconcile. Efforts directed at maintaining the group's own hold on the ideal tend to turn it inward toward sectarian withdrawal, while attempts to present the ideal to others become entangled in social and moral complexity, thus eroding the purity of the original vision.[1]

Beginning almost inadvertently out of the publication of the *Catholic Worker*, the Catholic Worker movement became one of the first Roman Catholic efforts since the Reformation to advocate a thoroughgoing radical Gospel perfectionism in social life. Amidst the unusual social circumstances of the Great Depression, the Worker established numerous communities and gained a small but firm foothold within American Catholicism. A series of conflicts toward the end of the thirties presented the movement with the typical dilemmas of radical Gospel utopianism. Although it was forced into some intellectual and social isolation, it held to a path that enabled it to avoid sectarianism and remain relevant to the larger society.

The Catholic Worker's birth was unexpected. Day's journalistic undertaking to discuss social problems had involved no particular plan of action to solve them. But shortly after the first issue of the paper appeared, Peter Maurin began bringing two hungry transients, "Dolan and

95

Egan," to Day's apartment to be fed. At first Day was annoyed by the intrusion. "All the while Peter was in the country I was visited by the pair of them," she reported. "They always announced themselves before I opened the door: 'Dolan and Egan here again.' It got so that my personal friends, knowing how exasperated I was becoming at having my time taken up, used to call out upon arriving, 'Dolan and Egan here again.'" [2]

However unwelcome at first, Dolan and Egan had found the right place. Day soon came to realize that an editorial commitment to the needy was not enough; the *Catholic Worker* would have to practice what it preached. Maurin turned up with more transients in tow, and the editorial staff found themselves serving soup when they were not putting out the paper. "Anyone who came in was invited to the meal being served in the kitchen," Day said. "When the room would not hold all of us we ate in shifts." [3]

In offering food and then beds to the unemployed, Day and the others found themselves implementing willy-nilly the second point of Maurin's program, the Houses of Hospitality. Although there were precedents in the old IWW headquarters that Day had known in the radical movement and in the hospices run by the French *Sillon*, the Catholic Worker House of Hospitality developed into a unique American urban institution. The Houses became newspaper offices, volunteer centers, soup kitchens, boarding houses, schools, places of worship, and the centers of a far-flung social movement—what one visitor called "revolutionary headquarters." All these activities sprang up almost overnight at the New York House of Hospitality—named St. Joseph's after the Catholic Worker's patron saint.

The barber shop below Day's East Side apartment was quickly outgrown, and a second place on Charles Street also proved too small to accommodate the growing movement. In the spring of 1936 the Workers moved to a large double tenement on Mott Street, near Chinatown. Two large stores on the ground floor became dining rooms, editorial offices, a print shop, and clothing rooms. Two floors of apartments for men and one floor for women were home to approximately one hundred and fifty Catholic Worker staff and "guests." By 1938 the soup lines at Mott Street were feeding an estimated twelve hundred people mornings and evenings. [4]

As the major institutional expression of "the Catholic Worker idea" advocated in the paper, the Houses of Hospitality were a highly complex blend of ideal and necessity, order and chaos, liberty and authority. Their basic social forms and round of activities reflected the religious idealism that gave them birth as well as the ambiguities and compromises that attended the effort to live out a radical Gospel ideal.

Even the most casual of the many visitors who passed through the Houses could tell that the Catholic Workers were committed Christians doing good works in the slums. More difficult to discern was the distinctive approach—really a social theory—that the Catholic Worker used to link its interpretation of the radical Gospel to its mission and practical life as a social movement.

As Day came to interpret it for her followers, Maurin's radical Gospel personalism meant, above all, making "Christian love" the foundation of social existence. True love required, first of all, taking responsibility for one's self, then developing "love in action" in service to one's immediate neighbors, and then transforming society at large through the power of this love. It also implied a commitment to satisfying and socially useful labor, a rejection of all forms of violence and coercion, and a personal detachment from material goods through the practice of "voluntary poverty." Day and her followers devoted themselves to these principles, and the attempt to realize them shaped the movement's distinctive character.

The ideals of free association and voluntary cooperation based on Christian love were thought to be exemplified in the movement's own founding and history. The Catholic Worker, Day liked to say, was "an organism rather than an organization" because it grew "spontaneously" in response to need rather than according to any plan. Though this account of Catholic Worker origins understated the founders' strong influence on the group as well as that of its important intellectual models, it was true that the Workers cultivated an anti-bureaucratic formlessness and a deliberate lack of planning that was the bane of those who looked for structure and regularity. "This is a movement, not a business," Day stressed in the *Catholic Worker*, and the attempt to maintain the fluid openness implied by the metaphor of "movement" was one of the distinguishing marks of the Workers' version of the radical Gospel.

Each individual who came to a House of Hospitality was understood to be acting on his own responsibility, and to be engaged in discovering for himself the full implications of the Christian Gospel. There was no procedure for becoming a Catholic Worker. The successive choices of coming to a House of Hospitality, starting in the work, and eventually taking up residence were seen as carrying their own levels of commitment. Nor did the movement establish a program of indoctrination or training in its special way of life. Rather, each person was assumed to be carrying on his own search for a more authentic Catholic existence and a deeper understanding of the meaning of the Gospel. While trying to transform society, therefore, a Catholic Worker was engaged in transforming himself as well. "The communitarian revolution is basically a personal revolution," said Peter Maurin. "It always starts with *I*, not with *they*."[5]

Catholic Worker communities were, thus, never thought of as ordinary social institutions. They were understood to be spiritual centers, the imperfect external expressions of the interior lives of those who inhabited them. In practical terms, this meant that each Catholic Worker House of Hospitality constituted itself as a free anarchist commune held together only by shared commitment, religion, friendship, experience, and the spiritual leadership of Day and Maurin. There were no constitutions, officers, elections, or meetings. Workers and their "guests" shared whatever space was available in the Houses of Hospitality, which were usually large, rented multistory buildings, tenements, or storefronts in the slums. Meals were prepared in a common kitchen. Where possible, regular residents ate communally with others who came for food.

Despite the theory of a purely internal consent, the practice of "voluntary poverty" in fact served as the tangible outer sign of the Workers' individual and collective adherence to the radical Gospel. Although reinforced by no vows or formal constraints, their low standard of living was a cohesive source of identity and discipline. Following Charles Péguy, the Workers defined poverty as "a state of simple sufficiency of food, clothing, shelter, and other goods, with nothing superfluous." This state was to be clearly distinguished from "destitution," the involuntary poverty of the down-and-out.

The actual condition of Worker Houses in different cities at different times ranged from moderately comfortable to atrocious. The inspections and condemnations by city officials that occurred on occasion during the movement's history were often politically motivated, but there was seldom any difficulty in finding very real violations of building or boarding house codes. Inside, plain walls and used furniture gave most Worker Houses a drab appearance, relieved only by simple religious art. A minimal cleanliness was usually maintained, but housekeeping was seldom a high priority.[6]

Food was a central concern of the Catholic Worker. Providing regular meals for all who came was a major activity of all Houses of Hospitality. Coffee, bread, and soup were the staples everywhere, with more varied fare when donations or funds permitted. Some Worker Houses followed the old IWW practice of maintaining a perpetual pot of soup or stew, to which anyone could contribute ingredients. The act of sharing food, full of religious and social meaning, was at the very heart of the Catholic Worker idea. "Meals are so important," Day often said. "The disciples knew Christ in the breaking of bread. We know Christ in each other in the breaking of bread. It is the closest we ever come to each other, sitting down and eating together." [7]

Houses of Hospitality also distributed secondhand clothes, and Catholic Workers, including Dorothy Day, often dressed in donated clothing, which became a kind of shabby uniform. Workers received no salaries; they were entirely dependent on the movement for sustenance. In most Houses there was a fund for incidental and personal expenses like medical care and travel. In New York and elsewhere there were occasionally experiments where Workers took part-time jobs and turned income over to the movement, but these arrangements were eventually dropped in most cases because regular wages, even when given over to the cause, were held to be inimical to the principle of poverty. "It is simpler just to be poor," explained Day to one critic who urged the movement to become self-supporting. "It is simpler to beg. The thing is not to hold onto anything." [8]

The movement depended on donations to cover rent, utilities, food, and the cost of putting out the paper. When contributions fell short, the Workers pleaded with creditors, reduced expenses, sent out emergency appeals for food and clothing, and prayed to St. Joseph. Since the movement believed that the vows of poverty of many Catholic religious had been rendered meaningless by the collective wealth of their orders, the Workers took care that the group as a whole should not accumulate assets beyond the bare minimum. The movement, as well as its individual adherents, was to remain in a constant state of "precarity," which was described as "the opposite of security." Rare surpluses were given away, and the Catholic Worker refused to incorporate as a tax-exempt charity. "Some of our organization-minded friends point out that we lose many possible bequests because the Catholic Worker, not being a legal entity, cannot inherit anything," Day reported. "This we do not regret. It is better that we remain poor and dependent on the small contributions of those who can send us a dollar now and then." [9]

According to Catholic Worker theory, voluntary poverty conferred both religious and practical benefits. Poverty, Workers said, was a "mysterious thing, a thing of the spirit." Citing the Church fathers and St. Thomas, they insisted that living without attachment to material goods "opens a new way of seeing the world and the things of the world" and "removes the obstacles that stand in the way of spiritual perfection." [10] But poverty was also of immense practical benefit to a movement trying to serve and change society. "Once we begin not to worry about what kind of house we are living in, what kind of clothes we are wearing," Day explained, "we have time, which is priceless, to remember that we are our brother's keeper, and that we must not only care for his needs as far as we are immediately able, but try to build a better world." [11]

The inner effects of this mild asceticism on individuals are of course difficult to assess, but its consequences for the movement as a whole are easier to see. The invitation to live a morally exacting existence in accord with radical Gospel ideals attracted many highly motivated persons to the movement. Poverty created an immediate sense of identification with the downtrodden that greatly intensified radical commitment, while the sense of sharp departure from the whole cluster of American values surrounding abundance and consumption constituted a significant critique of American society. The group's indifference to material considerations also made it less vulnerable to distraction and compromise.

There were other less beneficial consequences of the practice. The extraordinary pressures of living without means in the slums took a heavy toll on the group, especially on those members who had been attracted by romantic or sentimental motives. Instead of eliminating material concern, the general deprivation sometimes resulted in an acute awareness of the minor differences that remained. Individual possession of space, clothing, bedding, personal effects, and so on, could become a source of tension and conflict. "We hold on to our books, radios, our tools such as typewriters, and instead of rejoicing when they are taken from us, we lament," the *Catholic Worker* reported. [12] A variation on this competition over small material things was a more subtle kind of spiritual competition in selflessness, an attitude that could also erode the theoretical benefits of poverty. Overall, the shared sacrifices and struggles of poverty greatly strengthened the movement's sense of distinctive identity and mission, but at a high price to many "weaker" individuals. The turnover rate among new Workers was high, although once "seasoned," most of the volunteers learned to cope with the singular problems of the Catholic Worker way of life. Veteran Catholic Workers learned what kind of newcomers would adapt to "the work." "One soon became skilled at judging how long people would stay with us," one said. "Usually if a person came who was a bit indifferent or even skeptical of the work then we could count on having him or her stay with us for a reasonable period of time. But if they arrived full of enthusiasm and gushing about our beautiful way of life then it was a foregone conclusion they would not last long." [13]

Whatever problems it caused in practice, voluntary poverty was at least a clearly definable and visible ideal with a strong basis in Catholic and radical Gospel tradition. But the Worker's communal principle of purely voluntary cooperation and free use—from each according to his ability, to each according to his need—was more ambiguous, less clearly rooted in Catholic or radical Gospel tradition, and more productive of conflict in actual communities. The ideal that each individual should assume responsibility for necessary labor proved difficult to uphold in practice. The clash between the ideals of freedom and personal responsibility and the reality of differential effort and contribution to the community inevitably caused disputes. In the typical Catholic Worker House the primary tasks of cooking, serving the breadlines, and getting out the paper were usually accomplished without great difficulty, but other chores sometimes became matters of conflict. "In the real world of Mott Street," John Cort reported, "you could throw good examples at some people forever and they would just bounce off them like peanuts off a tank." Nevertheless, he noted, "sometimes good example did work, and the other times, if nothing else, it gave you a glow of self-righteousness that could sustain you for days."[14] Although most Catholic Workers displayed extreme dedication by ordinary standards, their inevitable shortcomings could easily cause demoralization or escalate into major crises because they appeared to threaten the movement's perfectionist ideals. That so much difficult work was accomplished under this system argued against the cynics, some within the movement itself, who said it was impossible and bound to fail. That it was done at a price proved the difficulties of utopia.

Similar difficulties plagued the attempt to live without rules or authority. Day did control the *Catholic Worker* directly through the editors, and she usually named someone to be in charge of the House and the kitchen. But according to the anarchist ideal, all leadership was to be "functional" rather than "coercive." "With rules things might run a little more smoothly *on the surface*," the *Catholic Worker* said in response to a critic of the apparent disorder in a House of Hospitality. "But in the Catholic Worker community more people do get housed and fed because there is no red tape and so-called efficiency."[15]

One of the barriers to efficiency was the incredible social diversity within the Houses of Hospitality. Because of the movement's broad appeal and open-door policy, the population included all types: teachers and journalists, religious and ex-seminarians, students and unattached intellectuals, refugees, clerical workers, salesgirls, skilled and unskilled industrial workers, migrant day laborers, and the very poorest denizens of Skid Road. With the numerous fellow travelers and weekend volunteers also on hand, the Houses always contained a richly variegated social mix. "A more motley group would be hard to invent," one Worker observed. "[It was] a constant procession of men and women, rich and poor, young and old, notable and humble. . . ." At meals, he noted "an eminent French philosopher or a Brazilian prelate might be seated beside a Bowery alcoholic or a *non compos mentis* woman who was persuaded that the drinking water was poisoned."[16] It was difficult to sort the Catholic Workers into standard social categories, partly because many had complex backgrounds or unclear prospects. Many unemployed workers and student dropouts, for example, concealed their own real need for the House of Hospitality under the attractive guise of joining a social movement to aid others. The impulse to serve was genuine, one noted, but "they came also to *be* served, although they never recognized this."[17]

It was the desperately poor who received the most attention in the Houses of Hospitality. The central importance of serving the hungry and homeless in Catholic Worker thought and practice was explained by Peter Maurin. In earlier centuries of Christianity, Maurin contended, the poor had been fed and clothed by Christians, and these actions had shaped the values of the whole social order. The fact that the poor were now largely ignored or handed over to the state was proof that modern society had become "pagan." Establishing Houses of Hospitality was the first step toward restoring Christian civilization. In a public letter to the American bishops meeting at the Conference of Catholic Charities in New York in 1933, Maurin explained in Easy Essay form why he believed that "hospitality, like everything else, must now be idealized":

> We need Houses of Hospitality
> to give to the rich
> the opportunity to serve the poor.
> We need Houses of Hospitality
> to bring the bishops to the people
> and the people to the bishops.
> We need Houses of Hospitality
> to bring back to institutions
> the technique of institutions.
> We need Houses of Hospitality
> to show what idealism looks like
> when it is practiced.[18]

Only Christians following the perfectionist social ethic of the radical Gospel could undermine the value system underlying capitalism and other secular ideologies, Maurin believed. The key to destroying the "business ethic" of modern society was for Christians to begin immediately to feed the hungry, clothe the naked, and shelter the homeless at a personal cost to themselves. The world would only become better, he said, if people "stopped trying to become better off," and "nobody would be poor if everybody tried to be poorest."[19]

In aiding the poor, therefore, the Catholic Workers insisted that they were not performing acts of charity or social service, but engaging in a "personalist revolution" by giving proper treatment to people who were, in the eyes of God, fully the equals of those who served them. For Maurin, it was actually the poor, as "ambassadors of God," who were doing the favor:

Ambassadors of God

People who are in need
and are not afraid to beg
give to people not in need
the occasion to do good
for goodness' sake.
Modern society
calls the beggar
bum and panhandler
and gives him the bum's rush.
The Greeks used to say
that people in need
are the ambassadors of the gods.
We read in the Gospel:
"As long as you did it
to one of the least
of my brothers,
you did it to me."
While modern society
calls the beggars
bums and panhandlers,
they are in fact
the Ambassadors of God.
To be God's Ambassador
is something
to be proud of.[20]

The Catholic Worker tried to realize this ideal by treating the poor with as much dignity and respect as possible. "Hospitality is derived from the Latin word for guest," the *Catholic Worker* said, "and it expresses a relationship between equal men: host and guest."[21] Along with bread, soup, and beds, therefore, the Catholic Worker offered those who came to them a measure of compassion, dignity, and even respect. The first result was often surprise. "It was a new twist to Bowery bums and tramps to learn that they were 'Ambassadors of God,'" Stanley Vishnewski reported. "All types of eccentric characters made their way to the Catholic Worker, and they were all welcome. The Catholic Worker strongly believed in the saying that Christ comes in the guise of the poor, the stranger."[22]

This radical openness greatly affected life in the movement. During the thirties, most of those who came to Worker Houses for help were discouraged but employable. After the Depression, however, the majority were not so much unemployed but unemployable. "Almost all the men at the House and in the lines now are old or crippled or slightly deranged or a bit unbalanced or hopelessly maladjusted," a Chicago Catholic Worker reported in 1941.[23] Over the years this continued to be the case, as Catholic Worker Houses took in and fed alcoholics, drug addicts, unmarried mothers, abandoned teenagers and elderly, the eccentric, the lazy, the chronically ill, the depressed, the deformed, and the decrepit. Yet the Workers struggled to avoid any patronizing sense of impersonal charity or social service given by superiors to those below. "Personalism" meant trying to prevent treating others bureaucratically or impersonally. "The big danger is that the human elements get buried," one Worker said. "Men and women become 'cases' instead of people, weird abstractions stripped of personality and self. It is easy to forget that they are men, each with his own private passions, feelings, drives, capacities, virtues, and sins. It is easy to forget that men are men when they seem to have been stripped of manhood itself."[24] Derogatory terms like *bums* and *derelicts* never appeared in the *Catholic Worker* and were supposed to be avoided even in conversation in the Houses; the proper terms were *guests* or *fellow workers* or simply *the men and women*.

Maintaining such attitudes was not easy under the circumstances. Although some of those helped by the movement responded with good grace, others did not. "We soon learned that one must never expect gratitude from the poor," said one Worker. "We learned (and it was painful) that if you gave the poor man your coat he was just as likely to hit you on the head and steal your pants."[25] The poor are poor "in everything," another noted, "including kindness, gratitude, and charity," and they "can be as greedy as the rich. . . . It is no easy job, this being for the poor. Men are men, and human nature is what it is. You run into deceit and rank ingratitude. You expect it, of course, and yet it never comes that it doesn't bring disappointment and discouragement."[26] Yet the Catholic Worker continued to insist that this "natural" behavior was not the whole story and should not determine the response. "You can look at all the people in the Houses and see them as pretty rotten," Day said. "That, of course, is one way we should look at things, to see men as dust. But from the standpoint of the supernatural they are a little lower than the angels, and we could only keep that attitude toward them. When we are in love with people we see all the best that is in them, and understand very clearly their failures and lapses. But the love continues strong and works wonders." [27]

The "supernatural attitude" also meant straining resources to the limit and refusing to impose on the "guests" in any way. Since the demand for basic necessities was almost always greater than could be met, the Workers had little trouble maintaining their ideal of voluntary poverty and, indeed, often found themselves slipping into the "destitution" they decried. When funds were pinched, hard choices had to be made. "Balanced on the scale of values, it seems better that all of us sacrifice some comfort for the common good," a Chicago Worker argued. "Everyone takes less so everyone can have something. Everyone lives in a crowded condition so no one has to sleep on the streets. Everyone does without butter and desserts so no one has to miss a meal. That is one phase of what we mean when we speak of voluntary poverty." [28] In accord with this principle, Workers often lived with extreme overcrowding. "We still use every inch of the three houses we occupy for sleeping," wrote the director of the Martin de Porres House of Hospitality in Cleveland to the New York headquarters. "That is, every room but the kitchens, which are left to the rats at night. The legend is that Blessed Martin sends mice and rats as messengers that he is answering one's prayers. The House is divided into two schools of thought on the matter—one for relentless battle, the other for live and let live with the 'messengers.'" [29] In Baltimore the House of Hospitality held over two hundred, half of whom slept on the floor because there were only ninety beds. No toilets or showers worked; residents could only wash in sinks and could not clean clothes or bathe. [30]

Such conditions were considered admirable in a House of Hospitality—a sign that it was practicing the movement's ideals. When one or two Houses established restrictions so that they could provide better living conditions for those they served, they ran into criticism from Dorothy Day. "The Philadelphia House is not good," she told another Worker group. "They fix it up so beautifully but they make room for only 25 or so and their breadlines are short. Some even admit that they don't want anybody in the House who can't contribute somehow to it." [31] Although frequently criticized for its policies, the Catholic Worker refused to distinguish between the "deserving" and "undeserving" poor, or to establish moral, religious, or labor conditions for its assistance. Once restrictions began to be imposed, Day argued, there would be no end to the process. "Who are we to judge what has brought them to such a pass?" she asked, and quoted St. Clement: "'By pretending to test who will receive the benefit and who will not you may possibly neglect some who are beloved of God.'"[32]

Although the movement adhered to this open-handed policy to a remarkable degree, even the Catholic Workers discovered that there had to be limits to freedom and pure Christian love in their circumstances. After years of "painful experience," the Workers prudently decided they could not cope with people "who were obviously sex deviates or who used dope." They also discovered that they could not deal with "killer drunks or obviously dangerous psychotics. . . . People of this nature were a problem to the community as well as a hazard to themselves."[33] Most Worker Houses were also forced to develop a few common-sense rules: Meals were served only at regular times; doors were locked after a certain time at night; and fighting, gambling, and drinking were prohibited on the premises. Since a substantial number of "guests" at any given time were likely to be alcoholics, liquor was a perpetual problem. Striking a balance between "concern" for the chronic drinker and restraint of his habit proved difficult. Sometimes Workers, including Day, would explode at incorrigible behavior; at other times they would simply "love, hope, and pray" until an incident passed. Occasional attempts to establish stiffer regulations for community governance ran into opposition from Day. In general, she argued, it was better to "suffer some disorder" than to impose order by force.[34]

Despite its failure to live up to a pure radical Gospel ideal, the Catholic Worker's generous policies enabled it to perform a unique function in the center of America's cities. Its willingness to take almost all comers with no questions asked often made the House of Hospitality the last refuge for those rejected elsewhere. While the mass desperation of the thirties never returned, the Workers continued to receive those who somehow fell through the cracks and crevasses of the modern American welfare state. Sometimes agencies themselves would appeal to the Worker:

> There are yards of red tape holding back many a person from getting assistance. More than once the telephone has rung here and at the end of the wire was a worker for the Relief Administration. We have a man or woman here, she will say, who hasn't had anything to eat since yesterday morning. The person is destitute, and we just don't know what to do. The person won't be eligible for state assistance for another six months, and we have no way of helping him right now. Can we send him over to you?[35]

Even through the affluent fifties and sixties such incidents were commonplace. Police, hospitals, welfare departments, mental institutions, juvenile agencies, halfway houses—all might end up sending the Catholic Worker those unfortunates who had exhausted emergency aid and somehow failed to meet "eligibility requirements." Such practices led Day and other Workers to complain frequently that other institutions, including "Holy Mother the State" and the Christian churches, were not doing enough for the really poor of American society. Although its actual welfare assistance was only a drop in the bucket, the Catholic Worker's generous policy provided an effective critique of the larger society's treatment of its most vulnerable members.

Some Catholic Worker guests recognized the benefits of the Houses of Hospitality. "The men will hop a freight and ride for miles to a city where there is a House of Hospitality," the *Catholic Worker* reported. "They would rather sleep on the floor of the Catholic Worker than take what the 'mission stiffs' have to give them." In the Frederick Wiseman documentary film *Welfare*, an indigent stymied by the bureaucracy of a public welfare office finally draws himself up and announces that he will go, instead, to the Catholic Worker.[36] In the supportive atmosphere of the Houses of Hospitality, some down-and-outers slowly recovered their spirits and dignity and returned to useful activity. Although there was no pressure to do so, many such individuals stayed on to become stalwart Catholic Workers. In fact, a good deal of the movement's work—cooking, serving, cleaning, farming, mailing the paper, hawking it on street corners—was done by Workers who had first come for a handout. A few of these persons ended up writing for the *Catholic Worker*.[37]

Such success stories were gratifying and seemed to justify the Worker's approach. Yet the movement could hardly make a case for its method on practical grounds because it continually attracted more marginal characters who undermined its perilous stability. Knowing that the Workers professed radical Gospel ideals, some guests delighted in testing them. "Three sayings are on their lips, and they fling them at you triumphantly to stop criticism," Day reported. "'There but for the grace of God go I,' one drug addict reminded me as she fell into the room. 'Let him that is without sin cast the first stone,' said Jennie as she lurched upstairs one morning after a night on the Bowery. 'Seventy times seven, Dorothy—remember, seventy times seven,' Bill used to cry after me down the street."

The Catholic Worker's utopian social doctrines also gave it a dangerous attraction for dreamers, misfits, and oddball social critics of all sorts, especially religious ones. "There are followers of seemingly every lost cause and believers in every path to world brotherhood," Day reported. "Hardest to deal with are those who have gone entirely 'off the deep end' and whose poor brains have collapsed completely. They will follow you around for hours laying out some fantastic panacea for the social order. There are always a few of these in our midst." [38] Religious quirks were also in evidence, since the Catholic Worker functioned as a kind of halfway house for dropouts from Catholic institutions and orders. "Sometimes it seemed that the CW had the rejects of every religious order in the country," Vishnewski said. [39]

Considering the Workers' own diverse backgrounds and the percentage of injured souls sheltered by the Houses, it is not surprising that the movement had trouble holding to its radical Gospel ethics and anarchist social principles. It took considerable dedication for more conventional persons to persevere in the work. "Living with the poor and deranged for 24 hours a day proved to be a terrific strain," one said. Those who stayed for any length of time had to maintain a healthy sense of perspective and often developed a subtle sense of humor about the whole enterprise. "The Catholic Worker consists of saints and martyrs," observed Stanley Vishnewski, "and the martyrs are those who have to live with the saints." [40]

Although the movement paid a high price in terms of realizing its utopian social principles, the Catholic Worker's service to the poor contributed to maintaining its identity and religious élan. Like voluntary poverty, the daily practice of the "works of mercy" provided a powerful communal discipline and a check against abstracting or sentimentalizing religious ideals. "Being on this coffee line . . . keeps me from getting too far into loving the human race and forgetting the ones close by," one Worker said. "If this is not done then all the love we talk about tends toward Norman Vincent Peale or Bishop Sheen." [41] For the Workers, serving individual needs was not a deflection from their mission or a case of "putting band-aids on cancer," but, as Maurin contended, a deliberate strategy for undermining the ideological foundations of capitalism. Even in their ideal Christian society, the Workers expected the need for such service to continue because Christ had promised, "The poor you have always with you." "That is a saying that has griped many for nineteen hundred years," Day commented. "The Marxists use it with sneers, pointing out that Christianity preaches pie in the sky, and the rich use it to excuse themselves from aiding the poor." But for the Catholic Worker, she said, it was not a barrier to radical social action—only a guarantee that there would always be opportunities to practice the Gospel. "This class structure is of our making, not His," she contended. "There will always be His poor, but there need not be so many." [42]

For all their failings, the Houses of Hospitality kept alive the Catholic Worker vision of a future Christian society. While Worker communities sometimes seemed to be living hells, at other times they offered "an unforgettable vision of paradise, with all living in love and unity." [43] "The Worker provided for . . . many of us a signal and very special experience of Christian community, and of community pure and simple," one Worker recalled. For those who lived, worked, and wrote in them, the Houses of Hospitality were an ongoing experiment in radical Gospel Christianity and the perfect matrix for the development of an American Catholic radicalism.

II

The principles worked out by Day and her associates in the New York House of Hospitality became the model for similar ventures in other cities. The Catholic Worker spread rapidly to become a truly national movement in the thirties. As soon as the *Catholic Worker* editors began reporting on their own experiences in New York, they were bombarded with requests from Catholics elsewhere asking how they could join the effort. In response, the editors compiled lists of readers in various areas and put them in touch with each other. Day and Maurin soon received invitations to come and speak in these locations, and these visits typically led to the formation of Catholic Worker groups and eventually to the opening of Houses of Hospitality. The first Houses outside New York appeared in Boston and St. Louis in 1934; in 1935 Houses opened in Chicago, Cleveland, and Washington, D.C., and in 1936 more than a dozen were established. By 1941 there were thirty-two Houses of Hospitality in twenty-seven cities, with an additional dozen or so Catholic Worker "cells" that functioned in some lesser way. [44]

Most Catholic Worker groups followed a similar pattern of development. Readers of the *Catholic Worker* would meet informally in homes or church basements and invite Day or Maurin to come and speak. Following the talk, which often attracted a substantial audience, those most interested would begin reading Catholic social literature and discussing the most pressing needs of their community. Day insisted that new Worker groups engage in this period of study and reflection before embarking on "the work" because she had learned that those who went through such a process of intellectual preparation were more unified and clear about their commitment. After a public appeal for funds in Catholic papers or churches, the Workers would obtain a tenement, flat, or storefront and open a House of Hospitality named in honor of one of the saints. On the recommendation of the group, Day would name one person as director of the House and, in effect, leader of the local Worker movement. Each group was responsible for its own fundraising, which was usually carried on through a local *Catholic Worker*, which could be anything from a mimeographed sheet to a substantial publication.[45]

Beyond these common elements, the Worker groups varied considerably. Some consisted of only a handful of people; others grew to substantial size and involved hundreds of part-time volunteers in addition to the full-time Workers committed to the movement. In the thirties the St. Louis House fed 2,700 people daily and distributed an additional 700 meals in the neighborhood. The Detroit Workers served 600 people a day through a wide range of activities. In some cities, such as Pittsburgh, Chicago, Seattle, and Milwaukee, the Workers were encouraged by Church officials and local priests, who helped them develop close ties with other Catholic groups: parishes, colleges, seminaries, labor groups, youth groups, bookstores, and so on. In other places, like Los Angeles, Boston, and Philadelphia, the movement met indifference or hostility from the official Church and other Catholic institutions.[46]

Because they operated autonomously, each Worker group developed its own character and interests. Some were intensely intellectual; others showed little interest in that side of the movement. Some were deeply involved in labor organizing, rent strikes, and similar forms of direct social action; others concentrated on the works of mercy and liturgical concerns. Some Houses, like those in Cleveland and Detroit, developed a strong core of stable Workers who carried the movement through three or four decades. Others experienced rapid turnovers in leadership, with little continuity from one group to another.

Although they were thus free to develop along somewhat different lines, the Worker groups all depended on the leadership of Dorothy Day. As co-founder and editor of the *Catholic Worker*, Day held the movement together through her spiritual and practical direction. Beyond naming the House directors, Day tried to avoid direct involvement in the local groups' affairs or internal problems. When the head of the Cleveland House wrote her about some difficulties, she replied, "We can't give you advice—you will have to work it out yourself."[47] What Day did offer each House was encouragement and personal assurance that they were not alone in their efforts. "Until these problems and sufferings begin the work is really not getting underway," she wrote the Buffalo House. "Don't blame the situation you have in Buffalo on the lack of leadership. When you are feeling especially bad you ought to take time off to visit a few of the other Houses."[48] To local leaders discouraged by petty bickering among the Workers, she pointed out that there were precedents for the problem. "I often think that our Lord must have been terribly bored with the disciples, humanly speaking," she wrote. "Certainly he wasn't picking out brilliant accomplished pleasing personalities with whom to live. Isn't it in today's Gospel where the mother of James and John wanted the best place for her two sons? So even the relatives were hanging around to see what they could get out of the situation. He certainly had to get away from them every now and then and do a lot of praying."[49]

In the pressure-cooker atmosphere of the Houses of Hospitality, quarrels easily arose over personalities, policies, leadership, money, ideology, religion. Many disputes were resolved or endured for the sake of the movement and its ideals, but others led to bitter feuds that hindered the work. "You do not fully know the extent of the vicious whispering campaign carried on against her," said one letter writer to Day about a local leader. "Please forgive me, Dorothy, but you and you alone can put a stop to this wrangling."[50] The Boston House in particular was a snake pit of acrimony for many years, with factions maneuvering for control and plotting to expel one another. "As usual Boston is causing you annoyance," a Worker from that city told Day. "It is not possible to reason out our problems."[51]

While the *Catholic Worker* alluded to such problems in a general way, readers of the paper were largely uninformed about dissension in the movement. A report from Boston for the *Catholic Worker* announced: "New faces are always joining us. New thoughts, new ideas, and to those with eyes to see new wonders in the visible manifestation of the Mystical Body of Christ in action." But a private letter to Day painted a different picture: "Things are deader than a door nail here in Boston. The CW group is in sore need of a shot in the arm."[52]

The necessary "shot in the arm" for the scattered Worker groups often came from Day's personal visits. As head of the movement, she kept up a busy round of travels, always by bus, that included the Houses of Hospitality.[53] The Workers valued these visits not only because Day's public appearances attracted local attention to the movement, but because she was often able to revive morale and quell discontent. She told a meeting of St. Louis Workers not to "be discouraged at your seeming lack of results. This is a propaganda movement and you cannot expect quick and tangible results."[54] "Whatever you said or didn't say, did or didn't do Tuesday night was perfect," wrote a leader of the Buffalo House after a visit. "The ruffled waters were calmed."[55] After another trip a

Worker reported, "With Dorothy's two visits . . . spirit has picked up considerably. Her inspiration and advice give courage to those who work here to care for Christ's poor."[56]

Day's personal charisma was not always able to achieve such positive results, but it was, along with the ideas propounded in the *Catholic Worker*, the necessary unifying force in a movement that was otherwise uncoordinated. Day's visits and the frequent hitchhiking from House to House by other Workers were part of an extensive communications network that involved *Catholic Worker* readers, activists, and fellow travelers. The result was a nationwide Catholic social movement that reflected Day's American radical values of freedom and local autonomy. St. Joseph's House in New York was the keystone of the movement, and developments there inevitably reverberated through all the Houses. But New York was not the Catholic Worker, and the movement's deep moorings in numerous American Catholic communities gave it a grass-roots resiliency it never lost. Even during periods when Houses in a given area ceased to operate, Workers often kept up with the movement and each other. With this nucleus of support it was easier for others to start up the work again. Thus, local Catholic Worker communities and new Houses of Hospitality continued to spring up spontaneously in the decades to come.

The movement's national character enabled it to establish enduring ties with other American Catholic movements and institutions. While some of these became evident in intellectual influences on the *Catholic Worker*, other ties were direct and personal. Local Catholic Worker groups, for example, had close connections with, among others, St. John's Abbey and College in Collegeville, Minnesota, the center of the liturgical movement; the Young Christian Workers, St. Benet's Bookstore, Mundelein Seminary, and numerous other groups and movements in Chicago; the Grailville Catholic women's community near Cincinnati; the Catholic Rural Life movement headquartered in Des Moines, Iowa; Graham Carey's liturgical art center in Newport, Rhode Island; Catholic labor schools and groups in Pittsburgh, Philadelphia, and other places; and many Catholic colleges and seminaries such as Notre Dame, Catholic University, Gonzaga, Marquette, St. Louis, Seattle, and so on. The itineraries of Day's speaking trips from the thirties through the fifties define a sort of intellectual-political geography of American Catholicism in those years, for the Catholic institutions and communities she frequented were often centers of ferment, if not at the time then in later years. Of course, only a minority of Catholics in such places who heard Day supported the Catholic Worker's viewpoint, but the exposure itself helped prepare the way for other sorts of Catholic social criticism.

III

Although the Catholic Worker's own social theories shaped much of its inner life, the movement was also affected by the context in which it developed—i.e., by Catholic and American life in the Great Depression. In the early thirties the Catholic Worker seemed at first just another of the proliferating Catholic social agencies of the time, and part of what might be called the "American Catholic consensus" about the Depression.

From the time of the crash until about 1935, most Catholic spokesmen held a common view of the problem and its solutions. The Depression, they contended, indicated that the time had come for the U.S. to replace the acquisitive capitalist system based on the individualistic "Protestant ethic" with a new social order founded on the eternally valid principles of natural law.[57] Most Catholic leaders combined their rejection of Marxian socialism with strong calls for action by government to aid the Depression's victims, foster recovery, and overhaul the American economic structure.[58] After Pius XI's timely encyclical *Quadragesimo Anno* appeared in 1931, most Catholic reformers followed Rome in advocating some kind of organization of both workers and employers aligned in "vocational group orders" to protect "the helpless working man" and promote "the common good."[59]

After 1932 this consensus found concrete political expression in the nearly unanimous support Catholic opinion leaders gave to Franklin Roosevelt and the New Deal. Average Catholics undoubtedly backed the early New Deal out of simple self-interest, but the strong endorsement of FDR's programs by the articulate Catholic leadership gave a communal quality to Catholic political behavior. The diverse Catholic leaders who initially backed Roosevelt included Cardinals Patrick Hayes and William O'Connell; reformers John Ryan and Francis Haas; the editors of *Commonweal*, *America*, the *Boston Pilot*, and the *Brooklyn Tablet*, and even the maverick Father Coughlin.[60]

Roosevelt won favor with these leaders not only because he opened his administration to the Catholic minority in new ways—for example, by increasing fourfold the number of Catholic judicial appointees as compared to the 1920s—but because his reforms seemed to follow the broad outlines of the "Catholic consensus." From 1933 to 1935 American Catholics gave their imprimatur to such measures as the National Recovery Act, which they purported to see as a form of the "vocational group order" advocated by Pius XI. This rather facile identification of Catholic and New Deal goals was encouraged by Roosevelt. During the campaign of 1932 he called *Quadragesimo Anno* "one of the greatest documents of modern times," and he and his advisors made similar references before Catholic audiences at every opportunity. The New Deal, said Secretary of Agriculture Henry Wallace, was only "traversing ground in detail which has been described in more general terms in certain of the Papal encyclicals."[61]

In the early thirties, with American Catholicism and American society in such a reforming mood, a group calling itself the Catholic Worker seemed to most observers a part of the broader Catholic response to the Depression rather than a unique new phenomenon of religious radicalism. *Commonweal* called the Workers "a new and vital group" dedicated to "opposing Communism and atheism by fighting for social justice for the working man."[62] *America* said that the Workers "seemed from the beginning to voice the unspoken thoughts of millions."[63] Worried about growing Communist influence in the country, *Catholic World* also fervently hoped the movement would become the means by which Catholic social theory would "influence the multitudes," while the Knights of Columbus magazine called the Worker "useful and deserving of success."[64] The *Brooklyn Tablet*, too, was pleased to see in the *Catholic Worker* a publication that would "counteract the influence of the radical sheets."[65]

Similarly, most non-Catholics who took notice of the movement in the thirties saw it as another instance of the Catholic Church's general effort to fortify its working-class constituency against radical appeals during hard times. The *American Mercury* said that "nothing is more significant of the attempt to re-fortify the Church, to win back wavering proletarians seduced by famine and Communism, than the emergence of the Catholic Worker." Noting the Worker's "odd" blend of Catholic piety and class-conscious radicalism, the *Mercury* discerned behind the movement "the hand of the conservative Church," and declared it "an open secret that Day carries on her work at the behest of the Cardinal."[66] Similarly, the Communist *Daily Worker* saw in the movement's sympathy for the underdog a "front" for Rome's "secret program of fascism."[67]

In the unusual atmosphere of the early thirties, then, the Catholic Worker appeared at first to belong within the wide circle of American Catholic opinion. Close readers of the *Catholic Worker*, or those who came to visit its slum headquarters, were aware that the movement's dissent cut much deeper. But the fact that the Catholic Worker was regarded for a time as an authentic, if unconventional, churchly movement helped it take hold within American Catholicism and attract loyal Catholic recruits. The Worker's success in stirring social concern among Catholics during the thirties, however, partially masked its distinctiveness. The movement was not, as first appeared, simply another Depression phenomenon, but the means whereby the unsettling perspectives of the radical Gospel first found their way into American Catholicism.

To see how far the Catholic Worker diverged from the mainstream of American Catholic social thought, it is only necessary to examine Peter Maurin's Easy Essays. From his extensive reading in contemporary Catholic social literature, Maurin had produced a blend of perfectionist Christian ethics and romantic Catholic agrarianism that he called "the Green Revolution." At the heart of Maurin's propaganda was a familiar Catholic complaint against modern society, particularly the irreligious worldview fostered by capitalism. "Everything has been secularized," Maurin wrote. "We have divorced religion from education; we have divorced religion from politics; we have divorced religion from business." [68]

This secularization had destroyed the Church's social influence, Maurin asserted, and with it the necessary religious foundation of society. The lack of spiritual values accounted for the whole host of modern evils. Capitalism with its system of mass production for profit was simply the most pervasive form of dehumanization which prevented men from seeing themselves and others as precious beings made in the image of God. "Mechanized labor is never creative labor," Maurin insisted. "The industrial revolution did not improve things; it made them worse." [69]

Maurin blamed the capitalists and bankers "who made the dollar sign the standard of value" for this state of affairs, but he pinned primary responsibility on Christians who had abandoned their ideals in order to compromise with "Mammon." [70] Once Christ had driven the money changers out of the Temple, Maurin said, but today "nobody dares to drive the money lenders out of the Temple because the money lenders have the mortgage on the Temple." Once the poor had been fed and clothed by Christians at a personal sacrifice, and society had said of them, "See how they love each other." Now the poor were handed over to the state, and society said about Christians, "See how they pass the buck." [71]

The immediate response to the crisis of capitalism was for Christians to establish Houses of Hospitality in the centers of modern social decay, the urban slums. But Maurin's long-range solution to social problems lay elsewhere—on the land. The goal of the "Green Revolution" was to develop self-sufficient "agrarian communes" or "agronomic universities" where urban refugees could take up farming and craft production. A combination of private dwellings and gardens with communal ownership of livestock, tools, land, and buildings would provide a decent living on four hours of work a day, Maurin contended, with the remaining time to be given over to the pursuit of religion and learning.[72]

The romantic medievalism of Maurin's Easy Essays is apparent. The harsh polemics against the modern world, the hostility to capitalists and bankers, the backward yearning for a simple society held together by the Catholic Church, and the rejection of cities, factories, and technology in favor of a small-scale village and handicraft existence—all these put Maurin in company with typical nostalgic forms of social Catholicism. Indeed, historian Anthony Novitsky has argued that it is a mistake to consider Maurin a radical because some of his fundamental ideas derived from right-wing French social Catholicism. Although Maurin did belong to the *Sillon*, a liberal and modernizing movement, he apparently also had come in contact with the *Cercles Catholiques*, a reactionary movement led by Albert de Mun. With his peasant origins, Maurin was easily susceptible to the more nostalgic strains of Catholic social thought. In the literature he recommended to the readers of the *Catholic Worker*, for example, Maurin consistently favored writers with a romantic or medievalist cast of mind: Vincent McNabb, William Cobden, G. K. Chesterton, Eric Gill, A. J. Penty.[73]

Maurin cheerfully admitted the backward direction of his thought. The "new society" the Catholic Worker wanted, he said, was based on "a very old philosophy, a philosophy so old it looks like new." Many people contend we cannot go back, Maurin acknowledged, but "neither can we go ahead, for we are parked in a blind alley, and when people are parked in a blind alley the only thing they can do is go back." Significantly, Maurin's ideal society was early medieval Ireland where, he liked to point out, a simply organized population of peasants, priests, scholars, and artists had created a beautiful and flourishing culture without cities, merchants, or manufactures.[74]

Despite these important considerations, it is probably a mistake to label Maurin simply a reactionary. His program did fit into the Catholic medievalist mold on several points, but equally significant was its complete lack of certain elements that usually had a part in right-wing European Catholic programs: order, hierarchy, authority, militarism, anti-Semitism. The absence of the last item is especially significant, since Maurin so strongly disliked moneylenders and usury; despite these antipathies, Maurin was something of a philo-Semite.[75] A comparison of Maurin's program with other American Catholic corporatists of the time, such as Edward Koch and Frederick Kenkel, shows how much closer Maurin was to the modern values of toleration, personal freedom, social equality, and pluralism.[76] Maurin's description of his own program

as "personalism," and his attraction to Emmanuel Mounier, who was
certainly not a simple reactionary, also suggests the difficulty of placing
Maurin on the right. Besides Mounier and his favorite medievalists,
Maurin drew on a number of modern European social thinkers who resist
easy ideological classification, such as Péguy, Proudhon, Kropotkin,
Tawney, and Maritain.

In endorsing these writers Maurin steered well clear of intellectual controversy. He took what he found agreeable and simply ignored
the points where these theorists disagreed with each other or with him.
The truth is that the French peasant was not an original social thinker,
and it was an error to try to extract any coherent social theory from his
Essays.

What truly moved Maurin, and what Day recognized in him,
was his deep feeling for the lack of spiritual humanism in the modern
world. Complaints about the dehumanizing loss of transcendence in
modern societies had become common during the last two centuries.
Such indictments were less clearly defined in America, where some religious and idealist sensibilities had managed to survive amidst the growing secularity of advanced industrial society. But the Depression, with its
apparent disclosure of fundamental defects in American civilization, was
a propitious time for presenting a radical critique of the society's lack of
spiritual foundations. Whatever its weakness in offering specific social
prescriptions, Maurin's essentially religious intuition provided a sturdy
basis for continuing rejection of the status quo. Mistakes, confusion, and
disappointment may have attended some of the Catholic Worker's efforts
to alleviate immediate social problems. But there could be no mistake
concerning Day's and Maurin's deeper conviction of the spiritual defi-
ciency of modern society, a conviction that transcended immediate circumstances and conventional political categories. Unlike those in the
Catholic consensus of the early thirties, or many other dissenters in this
country before and since, the two spiritual radicals would not be easily
returned to the American mainstream.

IV

Day and the Catholic Workers understood themselves to be carrying out the mission of the Church, the Gospels, and the saintly
Maurin. But they had also made service to others in their immediate
circumstances the foundation of their existence as a "personalist" radical
Gospel community. A movement whose central premise was the supreme social relevance of religion could hardly begin by turning its back

on the most pressing social issues of the time. Acting in the American tradition of experimental utopianism, the Catholic Workers tried to show the importance of their radical ideas by putting them to work here and now.

Accordingly, it was Day, the American radical, who brushed aside the Frenchman Maurin's distaste for industrial proletarianism in general and the American labor movement in particular. Maurin contended that "organized labor preys into the hands of the capitalist by treating labor not as a gift but as a commodity, selling it as another commodity at the highest price." One of his slogans was "strikes don't strike me," and he urged discontented workers to "fire the bosses," presumably by walking away from their jobs.[77]

Day agreed with this regard for work itself as a sanctified activity, but believed that the mass movement toward unionization reflected an equally sacred instinct for dignity and social justice that could not be ignored. Furthermore, the whole heroic history of modern American radicalism had been bound up with the labor cause, and Day could not imagine a social movement ignoring it. "Both unions and strikes and the fight for better wages would remain my immediate concern," she said.[78] The Catholic Worker stood for more than unions, but it would have to stand at least for that.

While the *Catholic Worker* propagandized for the labor cause, the Workers quickly moved beyond rhetorical backing for unionization. Their first important involvement was a 1934 New York department store strike, where Workers joined surprised strikers on picket lines with signs saying, "Unionization Is Favored by the Pope" and "The Catholic Church Backs a Living Wage." A number of Workers were arrested during the strike for violating an injunction, but their actions were credited with bringing the stores' management to the bargaining table.[79]

Numerous other labor actions followed. Workers picketed, organized consumer boycotts, and occasionally served as third-party mediators. Their greatest involvement came in the New York maritime strike of 1936/37, when a special CW headquarters was set up near the docks to provide shelter and meals to hundreds of striking seamen—an action that led several of the seamen to join the movement permanently.[80] Outside New York, Catholic Workers helped organize stonecutters, fishermen, printers, tenant farmers, and workers in the steel, auto, textile, meat, and brewery industries. Although their participation in most of these efforts was small in relation to the work force, the Workers' tireless zeal and effective propaganda use of the Catholic name meant that their help, like that of the Communists, was valuable to organizing efforts in ways that could not be measured in numbers.[81]

Equally important was the movement's part in encouraging active clerical support for union efforts. A few pro-labor priests like Father James Cox of Pittsburgh and Father John Boland of New York had already gained notice for their union activities before 1932. But many more priests were drawn into involvement by the example of the Catholic Worker. A short-lived Catholic Worker Labor School in New York, partially modeled on A. J. Muste's Brookwood, provided assistance for Catholics entering the labor field. It was followed by many similar Catholic institutions, usually sponsored by Catholic colleges or by the Association of Catholic Trade Unionists. Some priests who began their labor activity with the Catholic Worker, like Carl Hensler and Charles Owen Rice of Pittsburgh and Jerome Drolet of New Orleans, contributed substantially to CIO success among Catholics in their areas and later gained national reputations.[82]

The Workers' labor activities drew criticism. Some priests warned parishioners against the movement; employers sometimes took out anti-CW ads; and each publicized strike involvement cost the *Catholic Worker* some cancelled subscriptions. Yet without its labor actions, the Catholic Worker would not have achieved the prominence it did. Its backing for labor gained the movement a reputation for serious activism, brought numerous volunteers to the various Worker groups, and led to the founding of new Houses of Hospitality, which were often strongly labor oriented. And the cancelled subscriptions were more than offset by new readers who looked to the *Catholic Worker* to make labor news as well as report it.

Besides slighting Maurin's views on labor, the Workers were also more tolerant than he of government involvement in the economy. The Frenchman absolutely rejected anything that smacked of state intervention, even when it was specifically directed to aiding the Depression's victims. He was, for example, completely hostile to the New Deal. Politicians could never lead the way to a better society, he said, because they were forced to follow the popular course. "While the people stand in back of the President," he wrote, "the President stands in back of the people, and people and President go around in a circle, getting nowhere."[83]

Day's anarchist suspicion of politics in general and the large national state in particular was nearly as strong as Maurin's, but she accepted the argument that as long as the state existed, it had an obligation to act for the common good in economic matters, especially by relieving suffering in an emergency. While critical of the National Recovery Act's "bias" toward business and against labor, she initially took the position in the *Catholic Worker* that NRA was a positive step toward overcoming the environment of competitive individualism and replacing it with something more cooperative. Similarly, she argued that workers were primarily responsible for organizing themselves, but that government could legitimately protect their "human rights" from being trampled.[84]

On the matter of relief, the Workers constantly stressed the necessity of personal obligation to the poor, and of not abdicating responsibility to the state. But they recognized the inadequacy of private relief efforts and knew that government was the only answer for many. In New York and other cities, while straining their own resources beyond the limit, Workers often tried to help the unemployed get whatever assistance they could from Home Relief and other agencies.

It was these factors—the support for labor, parts of the New Deal, and the bishops' social statements—that made the Catholic Worker appear part of the Catholic consensus of the early thirties. Except for the Houses of Hospitality, which were known more as soup kitchens than as radical communities, the more distinctive tenets of the Worker's religious radicalism made relatively little impression on those who did not read the paper or know the movement firsthand. Among Catholic college students in the thirties, Abigail Quigley McCarthy recalled, the Catholic Worker was known more as a Catholic form of social and labor work than as a unique movement of religious social criticism.[85] Perhaps the high point of the Catholic Worker's participation in this Catholic version of the Popular Front came in 1935, when Dorothy Day joined 130 other prominent Catholics as a signer of *Organized Social Justice*, the National Catholic Welfare Conference's widely publicized document denouncing the Supreme Court's *Schechter* decision and arguing the Catholic case for a further program of extensive social reform.[86]

But the Catholic Worker's cooperative efforts to attain real social goals eventually yielded to the task of sustaining the movement's own perfectionist ideals and mission. Even when they were being most practically relevant to the issues and social needs of the Depression, the Workers took care that their own community should function only according to its radical religious principles, without consideration of external factors. At first this posed little difficulty, as the movement spread rapidly without serious strain. The group's remarkable growth and its members' Christian élan fed on one another, while the social atmosphere in the nation and the Catholic Church favored such a venture. For a brief time, the Catholic Worker enjoyed the best of both worlds—the purity of its principles and a growing influence on others. But as the full implications of its radical Gospel commitment became clearer, and especially as times changed, the Catholic Worker clashed more sharply with its surrounding society.

V

From 1935 to 1937 the Worker encountered a series of external and internal challenges that clarified the movement's purposes and determined more clearly its place in American Catholicism. Externally, the disintegration of the "Catholic consensus" and a growing awareness of the Catholic Worker's radical ideology brought opposition and isolation. Internally, the Workers had to deal with those in the movement who were reluctant to accept the quasi-sectarian implications of its Christian utopian course.

In 1935/36 the broad social consensus among American Catholic spokesmen broke up. The first serious disagreement among Catholic opinion makers came over the proposed Child Labor Amendment to the Constitution. Lacking only eight states for ratification in 1935, the amendment had support from nearly all elements of the New Deal coalition. But opponents succeeded in characterizing it as a threat to parental prerogatives in child rearing—an issue of particular concern to Catholics. Most of the Catholic hierarchy, the diocesan press, and journals like *America* and *Catholic World* began attacking the amendment; only a few liberal bishops, social reformers, and liberal publications like *Commonweal* and the *Catholic Worker* stood against the tide. When Catholic Worker Dorothy Weston delivered a passionate radio appeal for the amendment in New York, the movement came under attack from the *Brooklyn Tablet* as well as many Catholics in the city.[87] Monsignor Patrick Scanlan, the archdiocesan censor, wrote Day asking "the names of priests who are interested and sympathetic with the work you are doing," so that one of them might "review any theologically objectional material." Day suggested the name of her confessor, Father Richard McSorley, and he was appointed "editorial advisor" to the paper. When Scanlan told McSorley to tone down the paper's support for the amendment, Day protested that the issue was not dogmatic. "The stand we take is also the stand taken by Monsignor John Ryan," she told Scanlan. "It is, after all, a matter of opinion."[88] The Chancery let the issue drop, and McSorley quietly discontinued the advisory position, but the incident indicated that the Catholic Worker's political disagreements with prominent churchmen would soon be out in the open.

In the wake of the child labor controversy came a cluster of disagreements between Catholic conservatives and liberals over the direction of the New Deal, the rise of militant CIO unionism, and anti-Communism at home and abroad. Most respectable Catholic spokesmen deplored the increasingly scurrilous character of the Coughlinite movement, but some of Coughlin's belligerence rubbed off on broader segments of Catholic opinion. Publications like *America*, *Catholic World*, and *Our Sunday Visitor* gradually replaced their concern for the national well-being of the country with parochial defensiveness and jeremiads about the dire trends in the liberal government and society. The earlier contentions that the dangers of Socialism and Communism could best be countered by positive programs of social reform were replaced by a crusading and largely negative anti-Communism, especially after Pius XI's militant anti-Communist encyclical *Divini Redemptoris* appeared in 1937. Catholic bishops and journalists revived the habit—partially abandoned since 1929—of warning that the nation was on the road to Socialist decay. Sounding the alarm at their annual meeting in 1938, the American bishops declared that "the spread of subversive teaching and the audacity of subversive action present a real danger."[89]

Catholic voices who resisted these trends found themselves an increasingly embattled minority in the Church. Respected Catholic intellectuals like George M. Shuster of *Commonweal* were shunned, while the slum-based *Catholic Worker*, once tolerated as an attempt to steal the Communists' thunder, was criticized for its naive or dangerous flirtation with left-wing views. The Workers' practice of picketing and attending meetings with Communists came under strong public attacks at Catholic sodalities and communion breakfasts. Dorothy Day replied that even though Communism was wrong, one could not give up support for good causes simply because the Communists also favored them. "The Communist often more truly loves his brother, the poor and oppressed, than many so-called Christians," she said.[90] The *Catholic Worker* deplored the apparent effort by some Catholics to line up anti-Communism, patriotism, and Christianity in opposition to social reform. "When workers see red," declared Peter Maurin, "it is useless to wave the red, white, and blue."[91]

The increasing ideological divergence among Catholics came to a head during the Spanish Civil War. The sensitivity of the American Catholic elites to foreign policy questions had already become apparent in flare-ups over Mexico and the recognition of Russia. When the Spanish revolt occurred, the American Catholic leadership rushed to give fervent and almost unanimous support to the Franco movement, which was, they assured their fellow Americans, "liberal, democratic, and in the tradition of the American Revolution."[92] Despite evidence from some polls that the mass of Catholics was rather evenly divided on the issue, only a handful of Catholic publications dared to criticize the rebel cause. When *Commonweal* finally came out in favor of the republic, it lost one-quarter of its circulation, and Shuster was denounced as a traitor to the faith. The *Catholic Worker*'s appeal for neutrality and reconciliation also made it an outcast from the broad mainstream of articulate opinion in the American Church.[93]

By 1937, then, the Catholic Worker's radical views on prominent issues were leaving it isolated from all but the most liberal sectors of the American Church. In a series of critical articles in *America* in 1936/37, the aristocratic Jesuit John LaFarge summed up the objections being made to the Catholic Worker. LaFarge had been one of the CW's earliest backers, had taught at its labor school, and had promoted its interracial involvements, but now he felt that the movement had turned from the spirit of Christian charity to dangerously naive political involvements. It was all right for the Catholic Worker to speak out for social justice in particular cases, LaFarge said, "but when it broadens its scope and goes into the task of declaring a complete plan of integral Catholicism . . . a stricter intellectual accounting is demanded." The Worker was trying to interpret Catholic teaching so as to justify its own extreme views on matters of industrialism, international relations, and the state, he charged. While the individual Catholic lay person was, of course, free to disagree with the hierarchy on social or economic matters, the Catholic Worker had become something quite different. "There is a vast difference between the two cases of a free-lance layman and a widespread movement" bearing the Catholic name, LaFarge said. The Catholic Worker did not in any sense represent American Catholicism, and it was rightly losing whatever influence it might have had on the Church.[94]

While these developments were highlighting the Worker's lonely standing within American Catholicism, a number of internal conflicts undermined its social effectiveness. Idealistic, anarchist, and anti-authoritarian groups face their severest test when their principles are violated from within. Since the Catholic Worker put no restrictions on membership, it was bound to attract persons who did not share all of its personalist, utopian views. In December 1934, Day wrote privately to a friend that she did not know how to deal with a Worker named Patrick Clare who was actively promoting anti-Semitism in the name of the movement. All "friendly tactics of persuasion" had been tried and failed, she said, "so aside from bopping him on the head and so disposing of him, I can think of nothing further to do."[95]

Clare disappeared before he could be the cause of any nonpersonalist action, but a more serious organized challenge soon appeared in the form of the Campion Propaganda Committee. Led by a Worker named Thomas Coddington, the Campionites operated as a kind of caucus within the New York and Boston Houses. Assuming that the Catholic Worker's fusion of intense piety and social concern required a zealous assault on the status quo, the Campionites took the lead in some of the militant demonstrations that brought publicity to the Worker in 1934/35. Specializing in direct street-corner confrontations with pro-Nazis, scabs, and anti-Catholics, the Campionite demonstrators on several occasions incited angry abuse and minor physical assaults on the Workers.[96]

Day at first vacillated about these developments. She was impressed by the Campionites' commitment, and especially by the fact that they refused to strike back when attacked. The passive acceptance of blows showed sincere belief in Gospel ethics, she believed, "and it is a good thing to be struck sometimes, since it helps us meditate on the passion of Our Lord."[97] By mid-1935, however, with the number of incidents increasing, Day recognized that the Campionites were provoking violence, despite their formal nonviolence. Furthermore, Coddington was pressing her to make the movement more "effective" by limiting the soup-line operation, expanding fundraising in Catholic parishes, and removing some of the "bums, deadbeats, and freeloaders" among the Workers in order to improve the morale of the group. In its general outlines, this blueprint was designed to push the Catholic Worker closer to the model of the militant lay "Catholic Action" groups that were then meeting with some success in Europe and Quebec.

Although the threat to the Catholic Worker's character had become clear, the dilemma was how to meet it without damaging the movement's principles. Peter Maurin's advice was simply to walk away from the paper and the House of Hospitality and start over. But Day told him she was "not ready to give up." Relying instead on a combination of persuasion and subtle pressure, she moved to counter the Campionites. She reemphasized the centrality of the service to the poor in the movement and dropped all mention of Campionite demonstrations in the *Catholic Worker*. After some futile plotting to oust Day and take over the paper, Coddington and his followers left in the winter of 1936 to set up their own movement and journal.[98]

The Campionite affair indicated how vulnerable the little group of Christian idealists was to internal political maneuvering, especially when they engaged themselves in volatile public questions. Not surprisingly, the Workers' labor involvements also generated conflict. The passage of the Wagner Act and the formation of the CIO in 1935 put industrial unionism high on the American social agenda and convinced many activists that a major transformation of the country's institutions was at hand. "The CIO will determine the future of the labor movement," declared John Cort in the *Catholic Worker*, "and the labor movement will determine the future of America." Because Catholics formed a large proportion of the labor force in such key industries as steel, rubber, and autos, some Catholics saw a great future for a Catholic alliance with labor. Since "the American labor movement has never had a philosophy of labor," argued one labor priest close to the Catholic Worker, it was Catholicism's historic mission to move American labor beyond Gompers-style bread-and-butter unionism.[99]

The Catholic Worker seemed a likely spearhead for this task. By the late thirties, the movement was enjoying considerable success in its support of industrial unionism. The 1936 "Catholic Worker Stand on Strikes," widely reprinted as a pamphlet and circulated to Catholic workers, made a persuasive case for standing side by side with labor and especially the new CIO. "The Catholic Worker does not believe that unions as they exist today in the United States are the ideal solution for social problems," the Worker statement said, "but they are the only efficient weapon which workers have to defend their rights as individuals."[100] The *Catholic Worker* praised the effective use of the sit-down tactic in the automobile industry as a superb example of nonviolent social change. In several cities, notably Pittsburgh, Chicago, Detroit, and Seattle, Catholic Worker groups were closely linked with the local labor movement. It was appropriate that a group of Catholic Workers and Catholic unionists chose the New York House of Hospitality as the place to form a new "Association of Catholic Trade Unionists" in 1937. With its goal of spreading religious and democratic principles within the labor movement, the ACTU expanded rapidly in the years before the war.[101]

But as soon as Day saw that the Catholic Worker's labor involvement was having less effect on labor than on the movement itself, she turned to reemphasizing the Worker's utopian ideology. From the standpoint of religion, she said, Maurin was quite right that unions failed by treating labor as a "commodity" rather than a "gift of God." In her speeches Day began underscoring the Catholic Worker's own distinctive reasons for backing the labor cause. "Again and again we have helped workers on strike regardless of all talk about whether the strike was just or unjust," she said. "We have always done this for two reasons. First, it is never wrong to perform the Works of Mercy. Second, because in a time of industrial warfare it is easy to get in touch with the workers by meetings and distribution of literature; it is a time when they are struggling and thinking."[102] Like some other independent reformers who aided labor, the Catholic Worker was unwilling to subordinate its own social ideals to the aims of the unions. Rather, the Worker would continue to discuss the labor question in the language of religious idealism. "The Catholic Worker, as the name implies, *is* directed to the worker," Day explained. "But we use the word in its broadest sense, meaning those who work with hand or brain, those who do physical, mental, or spiritual work, and primarily the poor, the dispossessed, the exploited."[103]

In holding to a perfectionist rather than a practical course on labor and other issues, Day received strong support from Paul Hanley Furfey, a Sulpician sociologist who became one of the Catholic Worker's foremost defenders and interpreters. Furfey came across the *Catholic Worker* in 1934 while teaching at Catholic University, and was immediately converted to its vision of a religiously based social radicalism.[104] Furfey conducted retreats for the Workers and helped start a House of Hospitality in Washington, D.C., but his real contribution to the movement was intellectual. In articles for the *Catholic Worker* and then in his book *Fire on the Earth* (1936), Furfey developed a theologically informed social theory that, in effect, justified the Catholic Worker's radical Gospel perfectionism as the best basis for social reconstruction. Day and other Workers endorsed the book as an expression of the movement's principles, and it stood for several decades as the clearest theoretical rationale for an American Catholic radicalism.

Fire on the Earth was a fervent radical Gospel manifesto from a Catholic perspective. Criticizing what he saw as the weak, compromising versions of Catholic social thought prevalent in the American Church, Furfey called for Catholics to recover the authentic Gospel ideal as presented in "the precept and example of Our Divine Lord and the saints." Catholic social thought and behavior, Furfey said, had become too bound to notions of natural law that established a minimum standard of Christian social ethics. But the Church had never intended that the rational natural law standards should become the whole sum and substance of Catholic social teaching. Insofar as they advocated and practiced only the barest standards of decency defined by the Church, Catholics became indistinguishable from the secular world, and their social action was "unidealistic, lacking in spiritual enthusiasm, more or less worldly in its ideals."[105]

What was needed was a "supernatural sociology," based frankly on the truths of Revelation and the power of Grace, that would "try to realize the ideal." Such a social ethic would "view society, not so much in the light of reason, as in the light of eternity." It would willingly follow radical Gospel principles—the "counsels of perfection" in Catholic terms—in order to bring explicitly Christian principles into social life and point man toward his eternal destiny. While there was nothing inherently wrong in working through institutions and legislation to improve society, Furfey argued, there were definite moral limits to any liberal program of reform through state action or institutional adjustment:

> The state can make us share our goods with the poor. It can do this by taxation and by the distribution of money to relieve the unemployed and the indigent. But the state cannot make us love the poor. The state can make us admit Negro children to our schools, but it cannot make us accept the Negro wholeheart- edly as a member of the Mystical Body. The state can restrain selfish competition, but it cannot root out avarice from our hearts.[106]

That laws could not change hearts was a commonplace, but Furfey stressed that Christianity possessed a positive and effective means of social change. Only "personalist action," defined as generous social behavior "performed by a person as a member of the Mystical Body rather than as a member of the state" could transform society and bring it more in accord with "the true mind of the Church."[107]

While Furfey's plan for "supernatural sociology" could easily suggest some neo-medievalist Catholic social order, he tried to avoid any coercive implications of his vision. He insisted that the change to a Christian social order could only come about voluntarily, through win- ning others to Gospel principles, and that freedom must be a primary value in a religious society. Nevertheless, the question of how social institutions in a pluralist society like the United States could be "Chris- tian" in any meaningful sense went largely unanswered in Furfey's treatise.

But whatever its difficulties as a comprehensive social theory, Furfey's call for Catholics to practice the admittedly "extreme" ideals of the Gospel, rather than to adopt practical or politically effective strat- egies, provided an attractive rationale for the Catholic Worker's outlook. Although Furfey maintained that all Catholics, and not merely a few aberrant saints, were capable of taking the ideal path, he also advocated Catholic "non-participation" in all morally compromised social institu- tions and the establishment of explicitly Christian communities as mod- els for society. In practice this meant, as the Catholic Workers recog- nized, a special role for the minority of Christians willing to live free of most institutional constraints in order to witness the Gospel to society.[108]

The Catholic Worker's labor involvements had given it a small measure of social influence in the thirties. The fact that it was ready to surrender that influence in order to adhere to the radical Gospel, as

Furfey urged, indicated clearly which side Day and the majority of workers would take in the inevitable conflict between power and ethical purity. Others who believed that Christian ideals must somehow find firmer points of contact with the actual patterns of American social life gradually found their views unrepresented in the *Catholic Worker*. By the late thirties many of them had begun to leave the movement. John Cort and the New York ACTU group broke their ties with the Worker in 1938. In other cities like Chicago and Pittsburgh, however, pro-union Workers remained in charge of local Houses of Hospitality, thus creating a fissure in the national movement that was not resolved until the eve of World War II.[109]

The third internal development that defined the movement's character in the thirties was the attempt by some Workers to begin implementing the theoretical heart of Maurin's program—the agrarian communes. Although the *Catholic Worker* held up the farm communes as the ultimate solution to the social crisis, and Maurin never tired of spinning out his plans for village utopias, neither he nor Day had done anything serious about them in the movement's early days. Day saw plenty of urgent work at hand in the urban Houses and the labor movement, and she had a city girl's doubts about the value of rural life. Maurin himself seemed to prefer propagandizing in New York. As far as seeing anything tangible come of his dreams, he would apparently have been content with a one-acre vegetable garden the Workers had planted on Staten Island.[110]

But in a personalist movement this kind of gap between theory and practice was intolerable. Taking Maurin at his word, a number of young Workers began insisting that the movement go "back to the land" at once. Although Day was skeptical, she was unwilling to drop another key point in Maurin's utopian critique and to continue advocating social ideals without testing them. The agrarians in the movement were right, she admitted; the *Catholic Worker* could hardly "write about farming communes unless we had one."[111]

A more practical consideration also figured into the rural experiment: the problem of families in the movement. A few married couples had joined the Catholic Worker early on, and soon there were numerous marriages among young Workers across the country. Some couples left the work immediately or when children came along, but others stayed on. Efforts were made to accommodate the families, but problems soon arose, as one Worker described:

> Single persons under the influence of a powerful religious motive can live happily in a communal society where everything is shared in common. . . . But we soon learned that marriage and

our attempts at communal living were incompatible, for no matter how devoted to the work, the moment they married their relationship gradually and imperceptibly and then frankly and strongly veered away from the community to take care of their own. Women changed, began demanding that their husbands devote more time to the welfare of the children, and complaining about the loafing of the other men. Singles resented what they thought were extra benefits for the families.

This fact, that the family seeks its own because it is a natural community, is the fundamental reason why a complete plan of communal living was bound to fail.[112]

By 1936 the problem of families had become a major issue in the movement. Some Workers proposed excluding couples, or at least those with children, and turning the movement into a Catholic "secular institute," the term for an avowed lay religious order. This was the path eventually taken by Baroness Catherine de Hueck's Friendship House, the Catholic interracial movement that started as an offshoot of the Catholic Worker. But Day and others insisted that the Worker must remain an unrestricted social movement without a specially defined "religious" character and mission. The farming idea suggested a way out of the dilemma, since Maurin had specifically emphasized the role of families in his utopian scheme. In April 1936 the *Catholic Worker* announced that through the generosity of a reader the group had acquired a twenty-eight–acre farm near Easton, Pennsylvania, about seventy miles from New York. In response to readers who criticized the move as an escape from urban problems, the paper noted "the difficulty families have in living with other people." The farm, it said, would be the first step in "a community of families living in separate establishments, and given the exclusive use of a parcel of land."[113]

Soon a number of the more enthusiastic agrarians, led by Joseph Zarella, Paul Toner, and James Montague, took up residence on the place and began repairing buildings, putting in vegetables, and tending a few chickens, cows, and hogs. The following year an adjacent plot of forty acres was added to the farm. Three families moved into the large common house, where single Workers and guests also resided, but this was to be a temporary arrangement. Construction was begun on separate family dwellings located on three-acre plots that were given to the families under a fifty-year lease arrangement.[114]

Within a few years about a dozen other Catholic Worker farms were established in connection with Worker communities in Boston, Pittsburgh, Minneapolis, Detroit, Cleveland, Chicago, St. Louis, and San Francisco. Each of these independent ventures had a distinctive history, and some exerted considerable influence on Catholics in their areas. St. Benedict's Farm in Massachusetts became an important Catholic art and liturgical center; Our Lady of the Wayside Farm in Ohio took in the retarded; St. Isidore's Farm in Minnesota was part of the same movement as Eugene and Abigail McCarthy's St. Anne's Farm which, like the Worker experiments, took inspiration from Monsignor Luigi Ligutti's Catholic Rural Life Conference. A few of the midwestern farms where Workers acquired decent land and had a little farming experience survived through World War II and beyond. Most, however, failed to provide even a subsistence living and exacted a hard toll on those who tried to keep them going. [115]

Lack of sufficient land, capital, and farming experience was not the only reason for the failure of the rural experiments. Catholic Worker farms deliberately invited failure by following the movement's radical Gospel commitments to openness, toleration, and personal sacrifice for others. Those Workers who supposed that the movement was seriously trying to establish viable rural communities were perpetually frustrated. Whenever modest gains seemed in view, they were undercut by the practice of opening the farms to all comers. At Easton, slum children, Bowery "guests," students, rural life advocates, and *Catholic Worker* readers in general arrived in a constant stream that consumed the community's limited resources and created an atmosphere more like a combination fresh-air camp, alcoholic recovery center, and lay retreat house than a working farm. Some visitors did contribute to the community, but most preferred "scholarly" discussions of the theory of the "Green Revolution."

Therefore, to an even greater extent than the urban Houses, the farms bred a running controversy over slacking, called in CW terms "the conflict between workers and scholars." Periodic proposals from the more serious agrarians to restrict visitors and impose some order on the community were blocked by Dorothy Day and the majority of Workers who insisted that the farms, too, must be "an experiment in man's freedom and what it implied." [116] The refusal to coerce anyone meant that Catholic Worker farms regularly sheltered such recalcitrant residents as Maurice O'Connell, who made a practice of abusing visitors and stealing tools to finance his drinking. In her notebook Day wondered "what to do about M's having six pairs of shoes, a dozen suits of underwear, when others go without." The answer was that "God had chosen Maurice" to teach the Workers that their "faith in these ideas" of liberty and voluntary cooperation must be "tried as though by fire." "The only true influence we have on people is through supernatural love," Day wrote. "This sanctity, not an obnoxious piety, so affects others that they can be saved by it. Even though we *seem* to increase the delinquency of others, and we have been many a time charged with it, we can do for others, through God's grace, what no law enforcement can do, what no common sense can achieve." [117]

These sentiments were incompatible with the idea of viable farming communities. The Easton experiment ended bitterly at the end of World War II when two of the original families demanded that they be deeded more land and began conducting "raids" on the main farm house, then being used as a retreat center. In 1946 the Catholic Worker finally granted most of the land to the families and sold the rest. Although they admitted that this failure showed there was a "contradiction" between "the two ideas of performing the works of mercy at a personal sacrifice and saving to provide for one's own," the Workers felt that there was more "glory" in "suffering for a cause" than in making a living as farmers. "Often the practice of the works of mercy distracted the Green Revolutionists from the soil," wrote William Gauchat, an Ohio Catholic Worker, in 1953. "God bless them. It is better to try to be a Christian than a successful soil engineer." [118]

Although the move to the land failed as a social experiment, it left a permanent stamp on the Catholic Worker. Exposure to nature and relative solitude had salutary effects on hard-pressed Workers and some of their Skid Road guests. The New York Catholic Worker, therefore, continued to maintain farms within easy distance of the city, at Newburgh, Staten Island, and Tivoli, New York. Other Catholic Worker farms followed suit. Relieved of their impossible assignment as agrarian utopias, these "Houses of Hospitality on the Land" served admirably as retreat centers, halfway houses, and suppliers of vegetables to the urban Houses. Only in the 1960s did a new batch of communal Catholic Worker farms spring up, inspired by Maurin's original vision. [119]

Although the farms could not solve the family problem, the effort made in that direction probably saved the Catholic Worker from taking on a strictly celibate and formally religious character. Most of the urban workers remained single, but couples had been made to feel welcome, and efforts to make room for them in the work continued. A few Houses were run by couples; others experimented with maintaining nearby apartments for families. Many Worker families became strong fellow travelers and often devoted weekends or summers to the work. In this way some Catholic Worker children were raised with their parents' commitments, which led to the phenomenon of second- and third-generation Catholic Workers.

More important were the intellectual consequences of the rural efforts. The fact that the Workers had acted on Maurin's decentralist vision, however unsuccessfully, kept their social criticism pointed in that direction. Their own efforts to "solve" problems like the spiritual emptiness of factory labor, worker alienation, technological unemployment, and the inhuman scale of social institutions amounted to little, but the issues themselves remained surprisingly pertinent long after the farm experiments failed. Through the years, the *Catholic Worker* printed lively discussions of ways to remedy the centralization, bureaucratization, and mass impersonalization that, the Workers generally agreed, afflicted modern industrial America.[120]

A strain of unabashedly romantic agrarianism remained at the Catholic Worker. It drew strength not only from the continuing appeal of medievalist nostalgia for a few Catholics, but from the curiously similar note of pastoralism in American culture, an element that was particularly strong in the native brand of radical libertarianism and anarchism. In the forties and fifties, medievalism was kept alive at the Worker by distributists like David Hennessey, Dorothy Day's son-in-law, who still cherished the legacy of Chesterton, McNabb, and Gill. Closer relations between the Catholic Worker and indigenous anti-industrialism were fostered by Ammon Hennacy and others who tried to show that the Worker stood in the old American libertarian-decentralist tradition of Jefferson, Thoreau, Benjamin Tucker, Scott Nearing, and Ralph Borsodi.[121]

While the more extreme forms of backward-looking social thought suggested sectarian withdrawal, the decentralist emphasis at the Catholic Worker also took more moderate and realistic directions. From the thirties on, the Catholic Worker maintained intellectual affinities with social critics who saw many of the same problems as the romantic agrarians, but suggested less drastic solutions. Lewis Mumford's consistent warnings about urban mass society, centralized bureaucratic power, and the abuse of technology caused his works to be favorably reviewed and quoted in the *Catholic Worker* in the thirties and after. The movement publicized the similar concerns of Jacques Maritain and Martin Buber in the forties and fifties, and Thomas Merton, Jacques Ellul, Paul Goodman, and E. F. Schumacher in the sixties. (Much of Schumacher's work was first published in this country in the *Catholic Worker*.) The spectacular revival of American decentralism and anarchism in the 1960s, including even a new wave of experimental communities reminiscent of the 1830s and 1840s, made the Catholic Worker's concerns seem more pertinent than at any time since the thirties.[122]

Although the movement maintained a broader agenda, the Catholic Worker's communitarian experiments also put it in close touch with a host of modern intentional communities, especially those based on religion. Perhaps the most important of these connections in the

United States was with Clarence Jordan's interracial Koinonia Community near Plains, Georgia. In the fifties many Catholic Workers, including Dorothy Day, spent time at Koinonia while it was living under a virtual state of siege from the Ku Klux Klan. This commitment not only led the Catholic Workers deeper into the civil rights movement in the South, but also became an important experiment in religious coopera tion between Roman Catholics and conservative evangelical Protestants, black and white.[123]

Although there was less direct cooperation, the Catholic Worker also established important intellectual and personal ties with numerous religious, pacifist, and nonviolent communities around the world, including Lanzo del Vasto's Community of the Ark in France, the Simon Community in Britain, kibbutzim in Israel, various communities of the Grail, an international Catholic women's movement, and Indian ashrams following the teachings of Gandhi and Vinoba Bhave. The *Catholic Worker* publicized such idealistic ventures, and visitor exchanges with these distant communities often gave an international and ecumenical flavor to life at Catholic Worker Houses and farms. Vietnamese Buddhists visited the Catholic Worker farm in 1954, for example, thus establishing connections that bore fruit in later years. Although these intentional communities varied considerably in background and purpose, most of them shared with the Catholic Worker some vision of a new world order based less on high technology and power politics and more on a discovered inner harmony of nature, man, and God.[124]

Thus, the final significance of the Catholic Worker's rural ventures was that they established clearly the movement's view of the proper relation of religion and social change. As in the other internal controversies the Workers faced during the thirties, the governing consideration was always which path would best testify to their religiously grounded radical Gospel ideals. The contradictions between the movement's attempt to practice those ideals and its professed aims of altering society were consistently resolved in favor of the religious witness. The Catholic Worker did not seek isolation and political irrelevance, but it was willing to accept both as the price of its central vision.

VI

By 1940 Dorothy Day and her followers had succeeded in creating the first significant movement of Catholic radicalism in the United States. Although the *Catholic Worker* enjoyed a surprisingly wide readership for a time, the movement itself, like most radical and intellectual efforts at social change, was hardly felt at all by the masses. As John Cogley later said, "The 70,000 persons who, in the thirties and forties, lined up outside the Servite Church in Chicago every Friday for the Novena to Our Sorrowful Mother were undoubtedly more typical of the Catholic millions than the ardent supporters of the Catholic Worker or the elite devotees of the liturgical movement. While the 'litniks' were eager to relate the Church to the broader needs of the time, the novena-goers were more likely to be found desperately praying for a boyfriend, a salary increase, or the happy outcome of a lawsuit." [125]

Given the outlook of most American Catholics, the surprising thing about the Catholic Worker is not that it remained small, but that it grew even to the extent that it did without official Church backing. American Catholicism in the early twentieth century was generally regarded as a tightly run operation in which nothing happened without hierarchical direction. The image of a smooth clerical monolith partially concealed the considerable internal conflict within the ethnically diverse American Church. But it was true that independent lay initiatives were almost unheard of in an era when the accepted role of lay Catholics was to "pray, pay, and obey." The mere existence of an obviously independent Catholic movement indicated that there were greater possibilities for innovation and diversity in the Church than most people believed. It was probably no accident that it took a convert and a Frenchman to launch such a venture in the American Church, but the strong chords they struck among younger Catholics and intellectuals suggested that there was a good deal of ferment below the smooth surfaces of Catholic America. Although the first response to the Catholic Worker was conditioned by the distinctive circumstances of the thirties, the deeper excitements and loyalties sparked by the Worker phenomenon reflected a more widespread concern among thoughtful Catholics with the place their religion ought to have in American civilization. As Cogley noted, even when the Catholic Worker was enjoying some success in the thirties, it was less important for its immediate accomplishments than because "seeds of change were being planted. In the long run, the leaders of the social movements had far more influence on the future of the Church than the pillars of the Catholic establishment." [126]

Although the Catholic Worker was thus a significant sign of things to come in American Catholicism, the movement's singular approach to the problem of relating religion, culture, and politics made it of intrinsic interest as well. Something of the Catholic Worker's distinctive approach to these questions can be seen by comparing it with the parallel movement in American Protestantism, the radical wing of the

Social Gospel. Of course there were similarities in the basic concern of both movements to relate the Christian message to modern society, and in the particular issues each encountered in its pursuit of social change. But what stands out are differences in the two movements' constituencies and relations to the institutional church, in their outlooks on American society, and in their interpretation of the best way to relate Christianity to politics and social change.

In contrast to the Social Gospel, the Catholic Worker was entirely a lay affair, and it made no direct attempt to affect the Church's official positions on social questions. Except for Richard T. Ely early in its history, the important leaders of the Social Gospel were clergymen: Gladden, Herron, Bliss, Rauschenbusch, Ward, Niebuhr, Muste. Some lay persons did play a part in the movement, but for the most part they acted in supporting roles or behind the scenes. In the Catholic Worker these roles were reversed: lay persons ran the show, while priests, nuns, and seminarians appeared only as advisors or fellow travelers. Despite Dorothy Day's high regard for the religious prerogatives of the priesthood and her stated willingness to stop the movement if the hierarchy ordered, the Catholic Worker was noteworthy because it simply went its own way without regard to either clerical interference or confrontation.

That such a movement should take root in Catholicism rather than Protestantism is somewhat surprising, since the Reformation tradition had placed a greater emphasis on the idea of the church as the "people of God" and "the priesthood of all believers." Yet whatever religious motivations Protestant lay persons carried into modern worldly affairs tended to be stripped of their specifically religious character. As an example of lay initiative, the Catholic Worker stood out because it carried deep religious concerns directly into the social arena without official backing or guidance. Of course clerical leadership gave the Social Gospel an immediate visibility and intellectual depth, and was instrumental in altering the official social stands of the Protestant church bodies. But particularly during the twenties and thirties, as the politics of pulpit and pew moved in opposite directions and the churches lost more of their cultural influence, the Social Gospel ministers often found themselves in the position of "officers without troops." Some Social Gospel ministers accepted the penalties of the prophetic role, but others experienced increasing difficulties in reconciling their clerical and political beliefs; it was partly this problem that led men like Norman Thomas and A. J. Muste out of the church and into full-time political leadership. [127]

A social-political movement of Catholic lay persons, however, occupied no readily discernible niche in American culture. Although such a movement could have little immediate effect on official Church

positions, it was correspondingly freer to take radical stands on controverted issues without calculating institutional consequences. While the
Workers remained religiously loyal to the most clerical and hierarchical
of American ecclesiastical establishments, their spontaneous local voluntarism gave them affinities with the anti-institutionalism of America's
evangelical and congregational religious heritage. Even though neither
the paper nor the movement affected large numbers, the Catholic Worker
had an elemental appeal that attracted seamen, carpenters, housewives,
and former Bowery residents as well as intellectuals, artists, and social
activists.

The Catholic Worker also differed from the Social Gospel in the
way it related to American culture. Even in its more radical forms, the
Social Gospel had trouble overcoming the strong identification that existed between Protestantism and the prevalent values and institutions of
the United States. As Protestant leaders became more critical of American society, they often found that their most difficult task was to find
ways of "freeing" a religious heritage and language that was deeply entangled with existing American culture. [128]

For a Catholic radical movement, as for Catholic social thought
in general, this problem took a somewhat different form. Although Catholicism had successfully migrated to the United States and had func-
tionally adapted itself to American folk culture, the higher intellectual
and spiritual traditions of Catholicism were still largely unassimilated in
America. A Catholic movement that drew on these traditions found
them rich and untapped resources for religious and social reconstruction,
but it also faced the difficult task of translating essentially foreign ideas
into a quite different social setting. In trying to follow the Catholic
traditions of sainthood as well as the radical Gospel, and in reviving
styles of thought and piety associated more with the Franciscans, Thomas
à Kempis, and the Brethren of the Common Life than with modern
religious institutions, the Catholic Worker introduced into American
culture religious-social ideals little known in the United States.

If the Workers had confined themselves to mere imitation of
traditional models of Catholic sainthood and social action, the movement would rank as only a minor religious curiosity. But Day and the
Catholic Workers intuitively recognized that the American setting offered a great opportunity for a vital reinterpretation of Catholic tradition. Traditional Catholic piety and religious social activity, for all its
spiritual and ethical power, had tended to remain rather passive in trying
to correct the institutional forces implicated in human suffering. In the
Catholic Worker, Day in effect wed the older Christian spiritual tradition to the world-transforming activism and optimism of American cul-

ture that she had absorbed so deeply during her early life in the radical movement. In its emphases on humility, poverty, and contemplative Catholic spirituality, the Catholic Worker looked like something from a bygone age—and certainly a time before 1776. But in its social activism, egalitarianism, and concern for individual liberty, it obviously revealed its American provenance. Indeed, at times the movement resembled nothing so much as a Catholic version of the American tradition of perfectionist utopianism and religious radicalism that went back to the early nineteenth century and before.[129] Of course a movement that was, first and foremost, Roman Catholic could not fully conform to earlier notions of what it might mean to be American; but if the fusion of Catholicism and Americanism in the Catholic Worker was sometimes awkward and incomplete, it accurately reflected the state of relations between Catholicism and American culture as a whole.

A religious social movement has significance not only for the few who adhere to it, but in the effects it has on the far greater number outside. For most religious social movements, the issue of preserving the integrity of their own vision versus affecting the larger society has taken the form of a debate about the proper relationship of religion and politics. Here, too, one can detect differences between the Social Gospel and the Catholic Worker.

By the 1930s the Social Gospel tradition had become deeply committed to politics. Although radical ministers disagreed about exactly where to draw the line between religion and political action, most of them held that Christians betrayed their faith if they remained aloof from political struggle in all its dimensions. In the twenties, Social Gospel leaders like A. J. Muste, Sherwood Eddy, Kirby Page, and J. B. Mathews threw themselves headlong into politics, casting aside the inhibitions that had generally kept the early Social Gospel leaders out of the political arena. Muste's return to the church in 1938 only strengthened his insistence that Christians should be involved in "economic, political, and cultural struggles," and he dismissed religious social movements or communities that tried to avoid politics. Such groups, he said, were "primarily outlets for certain types of intellectuals and disoriented middle class people, which are therefore inherently incapable of expansion beyond very narrow limits."[130] Reinhold Niebuhr also argued strongly for Christian involvement in politics. In *Moral Man and Immoral Society* he posed the ethical dilemmas of social idealism in stark terms and tried to show that Christians' responsibility for life in this world implied a necessary acceptance of political means—means which often eroded the kind of moral purity envisioned by the radical Gospel.[131] In his later works, such as *Christianity and Power Politics* and *The Nature and Destiny of*

Man, Niebuhr made a great effort to preserve "transcendent" religious meanings from a total absorption in politics. But for Protestant intellectuals who followed in Niebuhr's path, such as John C. Bennett, author of the influential *Christian Realism* (1940), the area of intersection between religion and politics remained large.[132]

In contrast to this newer emphasis on the imperative of Christian involvement in power politics, the Catholic Worker remained closer to the classical position that religion as such belonged to a sphere separate from politics, and that the most authentic kind of Christian life meant rejecting power. The Worker's traditionalism on this point is suggested by the fact that it never attempted a theological reconstruction to take account of modern circumstances, but simply drew on the existing body of Catholic social teachings and elaborated such basic Catholic doctrines as the Mystical Body of Christ.

Of course such caution is not at all surprising in a group of American Catholic lay persons in the 1930s, even given their social radicalism. Within its still-secure intellectual bastions, pre−Vatican II Catholicism firmly resisted any theological accommodation to modernism, even as the Church struggled to adjust itself to modern social conditions. The papal social encyclicals, which rigorously upheld traditional doctrine while reaching out to the new social aspirations of the age, conveyed this attitude perfectly.

But the Catholic Worker's religious traditionalism was more than an acceptance of necessary constraints. Instead, the movement enthusiastically embraced the orthodox tradition as the fount and strength of its radical social attitudes and actions. Although the movement itself never established doctrinal requirements for participation, and Catholic Workers engaged in the popular American Catholic pastime of gossiping and grumbling about the Church and its leaders, there was no doubt that a firm religious commitment was the most pronounced trait of Day and Maurin's followers. "One wanted this. One wanted that," observed a Worker about the movement's early days. "It was the word Catholic that united us all. I doubt very much if we would have fought and struggled for a mere political or philosophical ideal."[133] And speaking of the 1950s, another said, "There was a great deal of religious seriousness about the Catholic Worker. There was a great loyalty to the Christian Church, and a great love for it, even in the acerbity of the barbs and jokes and debates that took place."[134]

In some ways this approach resembles that of the earlier Social Gospel leaders, also deeply pious men who attempted to make the Gospel and the Kingdom the center of their social criticism and action. Unfortunately, their movement coincided with a profound religious crisis within Protestantism itself—a crisis that was inextricably bound up with controversy over the nature and authority of Scripture and revelation, the contemporary significance of Jesus' words and life, and the meaning of terms like *the Kingdom of God*. Once these fundamentals were controverted, the task of making them the center of a unified religious social movement became infinitely complicated. Later figures like Niebuhr, Muste, and Bennett tried to assert in new ways the primacy of religious commitment for effective social action. Their views found resonance within segments of the Protestant and intellectual communities, but proved difficult to translate to the wider public culture. Not until Martin Luther King did American Protestantism find a leader who could effectively evoke an obviously transcendent spiritual vision as the foundation for a movement of social renewal, and King's religious roots lay only partly in the Social Gospel.

The Catholic Worker's approach to the issue of religion and politics followed more the lines of the theory of "integral Catholicism" that was widely accepted among Catholic intellectuals in the twenties and thirties. In contrast to the popular evangelical Protestant idea that religion should not be entangled with politics because religion ought to be concerned primarily with the higher goal of personal salvation, integral Catholicism reflected the somewhat different Catholic understanding of the proper relationship of religion and civilization. Religion was, indeed, concerned with ultimate truth, and therefore higher than politics, art, and culture, went the integral Catholic argument, but when religion was vital, it so deeply affected those areas of life that all united in testifying to the religious foundations of the whole civilization. In the twenties and thirties, this kind of thinking was strongly endorsed by many American Catholic intellectuals and educators, who began what a recent historian has called a "search for unity" of religion and culture. A typical statement of the Catholic College Association in 1933 said that "Catholicism is not a creed, a code, or a cult. Catholicism must be seen as a culture." In 1928 the president of the American Catholic Historical Association stated that Catholics' faith enabled them to see "even as in a glass darkly, the magnificent unity of life, the stupendously intricate weave of the warp and woof of human existence."[135]

Unfortunately, given the minority situation of Catholics in American society and the sterile posture of "American innocence" in which Catholic intellectuals chose to define their cultural vision, most of the heralded efforts to develop "a synthesis of religion and life" took the form of expanding the churchly sphere to other areas from whch it had been excluded. Despite the lofty rhetoric, the practical effect of most of these endeavors was to extend the subculture of the "Catholic ghetto," as

American Catholics proliferated societies of Catholic artists, philosophers, historians, firemen, librarians, teachers, doctors, lawyers, and so
on. As efforts of minority self-assertion against a still-prejudiced society,
these groups made good sense. But as attempts to realize the theory of
integral Catholicism, they were self-defeating—unless one accepted the
triumphalist notion that all America would eventually become a "Catholic country."

The Catholic Worker can be seen as representing a different
approach to the same integralist theory. Catholicism's spiritual values
were to spread not through overt political or institutionally religious
means, but by slowly reaching into the consciousness of the people and
altering their way of life. Following a long Catholic tradition, the Catholic Worker believed that the practice of the Gospel counsels of perfection
by even a small minority of Christians could have such a transforming
effect on society. Then a spiritual view of life would begin to pervade the
entire society, so that every feature of civilization—and not simply the
formally "religious" ones—would point to the unifying principles behind it.

In one sense, then, the Catholic Worker conformed quite nicely
to the prevalent mentality of pre-Vatican II American Catholicism. The
movement's integralism gave it an appeal to even a few Catholic intellectuals who did not share its social radicalism, while some of its committed
backers, like Paul Hanley Furfey, could even try to connect it with integralist social theories that called into question the value of American
pluralism.[136] Since it was also unhesitatingly loyal to the Roman church,
the Catholic Worker even shared many of the folkways of the American
Catholic ghetto. At least up to the early sixties, the most minor events in
Catholicism were followed with great interest, and the movement was
"very concerned with the personalities and subjects then dominant in the
Catholic world."[137]

But if the Catholic Worker's integralism could be superficially
matched up with triumphalist or sectarian Catholic visions of society, its
deeper currents ran in quite the opposite direction. Although the Worker
operated from distinctively Catholic religious premises, the movement's
entire outlook tended to erode, rather than confirm, the isolation of
pre-Vatican II American Catholicism. As a convert from the dominant
culture, Day recognized, better than those within the Catholic ghetto,
which values of the American Church belonged more to immigrant defensiveness and institutional aggrandizement and which to the enduring
religious tradition of catholic (as well as Catholic) Christianity. She also
knew in her bones what many Catholics had to struggle to understand:
that Catholic spiritual values could make headway in pluralist American

culture only if the Church as an ecclesiastical entity did not use pressure
to impose its views on the society. Accordingly, in the Catholic Worker
the radical Gospel "counsels of perfection" were combined with a kind of
ecumenicalism and spiritual openness, even toward honest secularity,
that was foreign to many varieties of integral Catholicism. The rigorous
practice of the works of mercy in Worker Houses indicated not only a
firm rejection of any conventional form of religiously inspired politics,
but a radically antitriumphalist approach to the spread of Catholic values
in America as well. A similar motive could be seen behind the movement's use of such distinctive Catholic practices as daily Mass, the little
hours of the liturgy, regular fasting, pilgrimages, the rosary, the Church
calendar, and so on. Their very presence signaled the capacity of an
integral Catholicism to extend over all of personal and social life, but
their completely voluntary use was testimony to the important American values of freedom and pluralism.

The Catholic Worker's unique approach depended on a combination of intense religious commitment and tolerance not easy to sustain. Until the 1960s, when Catholicism became more a part of the
general American religious culture, the primary threat to the Worker's
balancing act was probably a militant Catholic rigorism, not indifference. The group's strict principles and hostility to compromise could
easily have pushed it toward a complete sectarian isolation, or perhaps
more likely in the Catholic tradition, some kind of formal "religious"
status. Indeed, the movement's history in the thirties shows how the
firm rejection of political or ideological compromise isolated the Workers from the main currents of American society and forced them back on
their own resources.

What probably saved the Catholic Worker from a dead-end
journey into sectarianism and irrelevance were two factors: the leadership of Dorothy Day, and the group's willingness to risk complete failure
through its practice of the Catholic counsels of perfection. With her
experienced knowledge of American culture and politics, Day successfully steered the Workers away from sectarianism and kept them engaged with major contemporary problems and the dominant spiritual
tenor of American life. While vigorously endorsing integral Catholic
values and using them to criticize American society, Day also held the
Worker to principles of liberty and equality rooted in the nation's Protestant and Enlightenment heritage. The movement thus helped resume,
in a somewhat more critical fashion, the intellectual dialogue between
Catholicism and America begun by the nineteenth-century liberals.

By making their homes not in some isolated setting but in the
open sores of American urban civilization, the Workers constantly risked

failure but also maintained a responsible relationship with the whole Catholic Church and the larger society. The farming communes raised for a time the temptation of inward-looking retreat, but in choosing to practice the radical Gospel on behalf of society at large rather than to try to build their own utopia, the Workers preserved their greater religious vision at the expense of what in their eyes was a lesser one.

While the Worker's social responsibility could not be doubted, questions could be raised about the movement's sense of political responsibility. One of the cornerstones of the radical Gospel outlook was the distinction between religiously motivated social action and politics. Like some of the early adherents of the Social Gospel and other radical Gospel movements, the Workers did not see themselves acting as members of a polity. They generally refused to take political considerations into account, and said little about the proper relationship between the Gospel and the political values of proximate justice and democracy. When they marched in picket lines, demonstrated at embassies, organized unions, or helped integrate all-white facilities in the South, the Workers insisted that they were not engaging in politics but performing one of the works of mercy—"enlightening the ignorant."

What this meant, in fact, was that they did not seek power for themselves but for others. But the distinction was a subtle one, especially where intensely controverted issues of public policy were concerned. At the very least, the Catholic Worker seldom considered the problems, so eloquently defined in Niebuhr's *Moral Man and Immoral Society*, of entangling an essentially religious moral idealism with the inherent moral ambiguity and even evil of political life. The problem was heightened rather than resolved, Niebuhr argued, by pointing to the righteously disinterested motives of the religious personality.[138] The Workers were more careful than most in the Social Gospel to avoid simply politicizing, and hence debasing, religious symbols and language. But they did not ask whether, in trying to move society closer to radical Gospel ideals, they might also have to assume political responsibility for the consequences of their actions. Dorothy Day, for one, implicitly acknowledged the difficulty of the Worker's attitude, but argued that it had compensating virtues. "There is always a great need of idealists who uphold the ideal rather than the practical," she told a skeptical correspondent. "Without them men would not strive so high. Little by little it can be found that the ideal works and is practical, and then men are surprised."[139]

Thus, the Catholic Worker appealed not only to the long-standing values of Christian idealism, but to the very American belief that portions of the ideal, at least, might "work" in the unlovely social world. The Worker's ability to carry on amidst inevitable disappointments and failures rested partly on faith and partly on the intriguing connections it explored between the Christian Gospel's "freedom" to love and serve mankind and more modern ideas of freedom, including the native American traditions of libertarianism and anarchism. In terms of the Catholic Worker's place in American culture, this was an important linkage, for an essentially anarchist dislike of coercive political power could be found not only on the American radical fringe, but near the heart of the whole culture. If the Catholic Worker seemed largely to ignore the tragic dilemmas of power, it was hardly alone. Major elements of the American political tradition, going back to Jefferson, were also inclined to believe that human societies should be ordered by something other than coercive force.

As the thirties came to a close, this old American idealism was about to undergo another severe test. The question of power in its most violent form, war, was dividing religious intellectuals and Americans of all kinds. It was bound to affect the Catholic Worker as well.

CHAPTER FIVE

The Catholic Worker and Catholic Liberalism

I

Adhering to its radical Gospel perfectionism prevented the Catholic Worker from exercising much direct influence in American society. But the movement did significantly affect important segments of American Catholicism, especially as various new Catholic groups and publications spun off from it. Many individuals who started out with the Catholic Worker became prominent Catholic writers, social activists, and religious leaders, and through them, as well as by its own activities, the Worker played a critical role in American Catholic intellectual life. An examination of some of these figures shows both the powerful attraction of America's dominant liberal intellectual tradition for American Catholics and the Catholic Worker's gadfly relation to that liberal mainstream.

For some Catholic Worker intellectuals, the process of moving away from Worker-style radicalism occurred fairly easily and began as soon as they understood the full implications of the movement's uncompromising positions. In the depths of the Depression, many were attracted to radical ideas and activities more because moderate reform seemed inadequate to the crisis than because of any considered preference for an alternative social philosophy. Young people especially were drawn to the Catholic Worker because, like the Communists and some other radical groups, the Workers had new ideas and seemed to be "doing something" about the crisis. Houses of Hospitality, demonstrations, and labor organizing seemed both exciting and in keeping with broader currents of Catholic social teaching. But many of the same individuals readily moved toward the liberal center as the contours of the social problem changed, and as there emerged alternative ways to "do something" effective without requiring, as the Catholic Worker finally did, a sharp break with the inherited values of American liberal reform.

145

This essentially describes the intellectual trajectory of Richard Deverall and Norman McKenna's Christian Front, a journal and movement that represented the first instance of a turn to liberalism by former Workers. Like most of the other young Catholic Worker intellectuals of the 1930s, Deverall and McKenna were second- and third-generation immigrant Catholics who were shocked by the Depression's devastating effects and puzzled as to how to relate their personal religious faith to the obvious social imperatives of the time. Also like many others, Deverall and McKenna first learned that the Catholic Church had a "social program" of its own from the radio broadcasts of Father Coughlin. Although Coughlin's preachings were confusing and demagogic, he did make a seductive appeal to the injured sense of justice and religious pride of economically insecure Catholics. Deverall and McKenna might easily have drifted into the Coughlin camp had they not encountered a quite different kind of Catholic social action in the Catholic Worker.

Deverall and McKenna first came across the *Catholic Worker* on New York street corners in 1934. After reading the paper, they were immediately attracted to the movement and went to its Fifteenth Street headquarters to begin work. Their enthusiasm for direct action was dampened by Dorothy Day. Telling them that they were ignorant of Catholic social thought, she handed them a stack of books by classical and contemporary Catholic writers. After this crash course, the two became committed advocates of what they now saw as "the Catholic social tradition." Besides Chesterton, Belloc, Maritain, Franziskus Stratmann, and the modern papal encyclicals, they read "Gregory of Tours, the letters of St. Bernard, the philosophy of St. Antoninus, the great writings of Innocent III and Boniface VIII. We ransacked works on the Guilds, Aquinas, St. Francis, and other great Catholic thinkers."[1]

By 1935 Deverall and McKenna had completed their education and were active in the New York and New Jersey Houses of Hospitality. But their reading had awakened a thirst for broad social criticism. Seeing the *Catholic Worker* as primarily oriented to immediate problems, they recognized the need for a Catholic journal that would explore current social issues in more depth. Having secured the apparent endorsement of Peter Maurin for the journal they ambitiously proposed to model on Emmanuel Mounier's *L'Esprit*, they ran into objections from Dorothy Day, who called their project "premature" and blocked their planned use of Maurin's name.[2]

But Deverall and McKenna went ahead without the blessing of the Catholic Worker founders, and the first issue of their journal, the *Christian Front*, came out in Philadelphia in 1936. The magazine was clearly an offshoot of the *Catholic Worker*, and its program for "a complete reconstruction of the social order" initially rested on the Worker movement's radical interpretation of Catholic social theory. Quoting the medieval Catholic writers as well as the popes, the young journalists announced they would "aim always for the ideal" and "favor only those reforms which indicate a definite advance toward a Christian social order, opposing any palliatives which would perpetuate the present unreasonable system." They concluded their manifesto by posing stark alternatives. "We are not liberals. Let men make their choice: to stand for Christianity, or to stand for what is opposed to it—capitalism, Marxism, Fascism." [3]

In its first year the *Christian Front* lived up to its militant platform by denouncing capitalism in the most sweeping terms and printing articles by Catholic intellectuals already identified with the Catholic Worker. Father Virgil Michel, the Benedictine liturgical reformer and editor of *Orate Fratres*, said that capitalism was "an un-Christian system founded on greed, selfish egoism, and heartlessness" and urged its complete destruction. Paul Hanley Furfey wrote in favor of "Catholic extremism" and said that the traditional Catholic virtue of "prudence" consisted in "choosing the right means to reach a right end." From that perspective, he argued, the militant means of picketing, boycotts, and strikes were perfectly prudent ways to bring about the proper Catholic goal of transforming capitalist society and its values. [4] The journal's other articles and editorials breathed the same spirit of uncompromising disaffection with the economic system.

Yet by 1937 the *Christian Front* had begun to move away from Catholic Worker–style radicalism toward a more moderate brand of social criticism. Without the Catholic Worker's philosophical and practical grounding in an anarchist communitarianism, the *Christian Front* gradually drifted toward the sort of "palliatives" its editors had so recently denounced. Within a short time their fierce arraignment of capitalist reforms had been replaced by a growing appreciation of the liberal welfare state's "middle way" between laissez-faire and totalitarianism. [5]

For a time Deverall and McKenna's philosophical break with the Catholic Worker was partly obscured by their strong interest in the cooperative movement. Following its decentralist emphasis, the *Catholic Worker* had published some of the more comprehensive Catholic cooperative experiments, such as those sponsored by the Catholic Rural Life movement at Homestead, Iowa, and Antigonish, Nova Scotia. The *Christian Front* took up this cause as well, promoting a variety of cooperative efforts from producer coops to parish credit unions. But gradually a difference of emphasis became apparent. Unlike the *Catholic Worker*, the *Christian Front* did not call on such experiments to reject the profit system in order to certify that they were steps on the road away from competitive capitalism. It was sufficient that cooperatives work for the "common good" of the membership and make actual improvements in the well-being of the whole group. This followed the line of another advocate of cooperatives, Monsignor John Ryan, who began to take the place of more radical writers in the pages of *Christian Front*.[6]

The influence of Ryan, the most well known Catholic spokesman for the New Deal, indicated the journal's growing accommodation with liberal reform. But Ryan could not satisfy the young intellectuals' hunger for direct social action. It took a more inspiring reform movement, organized labor, to complete Deverall and McKenna's conversion to liberalism. While the *Catholic Worker* increasingly qualified its support for unions with perfectionist objections, the *Christian Front* saw the surging Committee for Industrial Organizations (CIO) as an awesome popular expression of Christian social principles that demanded commitment rather than carping from intellectuals. The "heroic" labor organizing struggles of the late thirties overcame any lingering doubts about the limitations of American industrial unionism, and the *Christian Front* came virtually to identify Catholic commitment to a just social order with the aims of the CIO.

As the great CIO organizing drives in steel, rubber, and autos got underway, the *Christian Front* focused its attention almost exclusively on the labor question. "As the issue stands now," said the editors, "those who attack the labor program of the CIO—labor leaders and capitalists—are attacking the workers specifically and social justice generally." Like the *Catholic Worker*, the *Christian Front* applauded the sit-down tactic. But while Dorothy Day emphasized its potential as a method of general social change, Deverall and McKenna stressed its essentially conservative character as a way of establishing a "property right" in jobs.[7]

By 1938 the *Christian Front* had established chapters of a Christian Front movement in several cities where the journal was circulated, including New York, Washington, Philadelphia, and Detroit. There were also chapters on college campuses, where they were often affiliated with the Newman Clubs. The principal activity of these groups was aiding labor, as the mostly young people spread union propaganda and lent assistance to strikes. Deverall and McKenna became acquainted with leading Catholics in the CIO, such as John Brophy and Philip Murray. The Catholic union officials' articles and speeches to Catholic audiences were printed in the *Christian Front*, which became an interpreter of the labor movement to the Catholic community. Although there were still occasional rhetorical complaints about the "un-

Christian" character of American society, religious themes gave way to programmatic discussions of labor tactics and the legislative proposals of union officials, liberal politicians, and the more socially active members of the Catholic hierarchy.[8]

In 1939 the journal changed its name to *Christian Social Action* because the original name was appropriated by Father Coughlin's anti-Semitic Christian Front. Like the Catholic Workers, the Christian Social Actionists opposed the still-powerful Coughlinite movement among Catholics in the major eastern cities, and they tried to show the new Christian Front's incompatibility with Christian teaching. A Coughlinite counterattack developed, and in Philadelphia right-wing publicist Elizabeth Dilling made things so uncomfortable that in July 1939, Deverall moved the magazine to Detroit, where Archbishop Edward Mooney's anti-Coughlin policies provided a more favorable climate. Although McKenna did not follow the journal to Detroit and soon left the group, the move gave *Christian Social Action* a few more years of life as a close ally of the strong Michigan chapter of the Association of Catholic Trade Unionists (ACTU). Mooney and the ACTU had been important in Detroit's labor environment, but by 1940 the great days of the CIO were over. Except for a brief flurry during the United Auto Workers' final victory over Henry Ford in 1941, *Christian Social Action* generally accepted labor's view that it was time to consolidate gains rather than break new ground.[9]

After flirting with pacifism for a time, the magazine folded in June 1942. Deverall subsequently went to work for Jay Lovestone's International Labor League, the overseas arm of the AFL-CIO that, with United States government aid, opposed Communist influence among the international working class. In 1953 Deverall wrote Day from Japan, "We run a magazine for the trade unions plugging the basic philosophy of the Popes and Sam Gompers. . . . It is you who got me into this crusading business and I can never thank you enough."[10]

That the nature of this "crusade" differed from that still carried on by the Catholic Worker was not acknowledged. For Deverall, as for many other Catholic labor priests and intellectuals of the time, the general acceptance of industrial unionism as a necessary protection for the worker was sufficient to close the gap between the Church and the prevailing social order. The alliance of Catholicism and Americanism—the popes and Sam Gompers—became simply another step in the effective assimilation of Catholics into American liberal institutions that had begun long before. As with earlier stages of the Americanization process, the very lack of any guiding ideology in such institutions was one of their attractions. Catholics who had already come to feel at home in other areas

of American society—neighborhoods, political parties, popular culture—could now also find a satisfactory harmony between their religion
and economic life.

II

The experience of the Christian Front illustrates how some
Catholic Workers could be drawn toward the dominant American tradition of liberal and labor reform. A more significant example of the same
tendency was the group of young intellectuals who gathered around the
Catholic Worker in Chicago. Their grasp of the Worker's religious personalism was deeper than Deverall's and McKenna's, and the break between Day and the group's leader, John Cogley, was more painful and
consequential for later Catholic intellectual history.

The Catholic Worker in Chicago began in 1936 with a small
band of committed readers led by Dr. Arthur Falls, a black Catholic
physician. Falls organized a House of Hospitality on Taylor Street that
was run by a brilliant local eccentric named John Bowers. Among the
young Catholics drawn to the Chicago Worker was Ed Marciniak, the
son of a Polish immigrant steelworker and grocer, who became an instant
convert to the movement after hearing Peter Maurin. "I discovered
through the Catholic Worker, through Dorothy Day and Peter Maurin, a
church I had never heard about, never knew existed," he recalled. "All of
a sudden there was this new world for me, a world of great intellectual
vitality. There were many of us, and we read avidly, every learned Catholic magazine we could locate. We raised every question, we challenged
every conceivable position, we subjected the Church to so much scrutiny
because we loved her so much. Sometimes our sessions would go from
Sunday afternoon right through to early Monday morning—one week,
Maritain; the next, perhaps, the steel strike." [11]

Dorothy Day visited Chicago in the spring of 1937 and concluded that the Taylor Street House was not doing enough to spread
Catholic Worker principles in the nation's second-largest city. At her
urging Marciniak and Alex Reser, an intellectually inclined German
Catholic railroad worker, opened a second House of Hospitality on Blue
Island Avenue, and there began the usual Catholic Worker story of soup
lines, unpaid bills, and fervent prayers and appeals for assistance. [12]

By the fall of 1937 St. Joseph's House had become the most
exciting center of Catholic Worker activity in Chicago. It attracted to the
movement a talented and highly articulate group of young Workers,

which included, besides Marciniak and Reser, Martin Paul, James O'Gara, Tom Sullivan, Catherine Reser, and Marie Antoinette de Roulet. But the most noteworthy recruit was John Cogley, a young unemployed Irishman whose organizational and literary abilities soon made him the leading figure in the Chicago movement.

The winter of 1937/38 was a particularly bitter one in Chicago, as severe cold, high unemployment, and a completely exhausted relief system caused widespread hardship. The city had already been rocked on Memorial Day by the bloody Republic Steel "massacre," in which striking workers were killed by police, and more labor violence threatened. The Catholic Workers were active in a number of strikes and organizing drives, but they also tried to assist the unemployed. By mid-winter, with temperatures dropping below zero, St. Joseph's House became the scene of a grim struggle to survive. "The old men slept on [cots]; the young ones found places on the floor, under beds and tables, and even on the wide display counter at the storefront window," Cogley recalled. "After the place was chock full, with men wedged in like cigarettes in a pack, it was heartbreaking to tell another hundred standing outside the door, shivering and pleading, that there was no more room and they would have to 'carry the banner' for the night. Inside, the house was heavy with the stench of unwashed bodies and filthy clothes; noisy with eerie, spoken nightmares and the sudden shouts of troubled sleep." When city health inspectors eventually came around and ordered the number of overnight guests cut from three hundred to forty, the Workers protested that there would be casualties from the cold. "Our job is inspecting lodging places," they were told. "We can't underwrite the health of every bum in Chicago." [13]

In order to publicize such official indifference to the plight of the poor and spread word of their own activities among local Catholics, the group began publishing a *Chicago Catholic Worker* in June 1938. Unlike the usually ephemeral sheets put out by other local Worker Houses as supplements to the *Catholic Worker*, the Chicago paper was a substantial effort. It followed the *Catholic Worker* format with its familiar masthead, penny price, and art work by Ade Bethune, but it was entirely independent in staff and editorial content. Calling itself "the only Catholic paper sold on the streets of Chicago," the *Chicago Catholic Worker* reached a circulation of 12,000, and it was, as the new York *Catholic Worker* ruefully admitted, "better written than ours." [14]

In its basic outlook the *Chicago Catholic Worker* followed Dorothy Day's radical interpretation of the meaning of the Christian life. "The fundamental truth, one constantly to be reiterated, is the fact of our supernatural solidarity," Cogley wrote in the second issue. "Men are, or should be, joined to the infinite God, not merely by knowing Him and loving Him, but by sharing His inmost life. In the Mystical Body one's personality is developed and completed in the very act of fulfilling one's obligation to the whole society. . . . It is through love, founded not on vague sentiments, but on these facts, that a better world shall be achieved." Like Day, Cogley was able to write about important religious questions without sentimentality or theological obfuscation. His attitude toward the Church was also like hers: Catholicism possessed a core of true spirituality, but it was constantly necessary to struggle with institutional failings in order to get at it.[15]

Like many who came to the Catholic Worker, Cogley developed a strong feeling for the social outcasts with whom he lived in the House of Hospitality. The poorest of the poor possessed "real strength" and "untouched nobility," he wrote, but also equally naked failings. "It is no easy job being for the poor," he admitted.[16] But Cogley was convinced that the Catholic Worker's method was the only one that could really deal with the human side of poverty.

> Here at the House of Hospitality the temptation to grow efficient and statistical, to run on a smoother basis, to borrow the techniques of social work, is ever with us. We try to resist the temptation. . . .
>
> The "social problem" is not a matter of paper and ink and tabulations and graphs. It is not something to get together and discuss coolly and dispassionately as you would the influence of the typewriter on Victorian commerce. The social problem is basically, essentially, a human problem that can only be really met humanly and dealt with warmly, intelligently, sympathetically, and interestedly, as man naturally deals with man.[17]

In matters of religion and poverty then, the Chicago Workers faithfully reflected the integral personalism of Day's movement. They were just as skeptical of politics and legislation as real solutions to social ills, just as insistent that social questions required personal commitment rather than abstract debate. "You hear our leaders saying that if we could just elect this man, change that law, or accept some pet scheme to modify our government everything would be all right," the paper editorialized. "But they refuse to be *realists*. Legislation and monetary reforms and such are very good and very necessary, but their influence is limited." It was only "personalist action" that, by its nature, "can spread its influence imperceptibly until the whole people has been changed."[18]

Yet for all its adherence to the central religious tenets of the Worker movement, differences of tone and emphasis began to appear in the Chicago group. The anarchist and "revolutionary" language common in the New York *Catholic Worker* seldom appeared in its Chicago counterpart. Although the Chicago paper also professed rejection of capitalism, its objections ran more to the philosophy and values of the system than to the particular matters of industries, markets, and profits that received specific condemnation from the New York group. The old Wobbly slogans, the slightly bohemian atmosphere, the European influences—none of these lesser features of the New York Worker movement met much favor among Catholic Workers in the midwestern city.[19]

As with the Christian Front, an important impetus toward moderation came from involvement with organized labor. From its early days the Chicago CW had close ties with the labor movement in the city. Marciniak was an intimate of Chicago Catholic union activists, and when he wrote about labor issues for the *Chicago Catholic Worker*, he avoided attacks on the factory and assembly line system, the wage contract, and the corporation as such. Although his tone was sometimes militant during the dangerous early days of labor struggle, the note of class conflict quickly faded as the unions won recognition. By 1941 Marciniak had accepted the argument of many liberal labor intellectuals that promoting class consciousness and conflict was inappropriate in America, with its great wealth and flexible social system. And James O'Gara argued that far from being plutocratic monsters, "the majority of employers are men of good will who would do their best to remedy social ills did they but know how to go about it."[20]

Another factor in moderating the *Chicago Catholic Worker*'s stance was the liberal atmosphere of official Catholicism in the city. In contrast to the generally conservative Hayes-Spellman-McIntyre regime in New York, the Chicago hierarchy under Cardinal George Mundelein and his auxiliary bishop, Bernard Sheil, strongly supported social reform during the Depression and tilted the Church toward labor. The *Chicago Catholic Worker* could happily quote Mundelein as saying, "Our place is with the workingman. We belong on the side of the poor. Too long have we been allied with the wrong side, victims of the unctuous flattery of despots who got the support they wanted by calling the Church the great bulwark against Communism, the impregnable tower of conservatism, the fortress of capitalism." Monsignor Reynold Hillenbrand's socially conscious seminary, the liberal Catholic School of Social Service that trained labor priests for the diocese, Father John Egan's community organizing—all these made Chicago the center of American Catholic liberalism in the thirties and forties.[21]

The Catholic Worker was naturally attracted to these activities, which were often socially innovative and intellectually exciting. Instead of focusing on its own distinctive ideas and actions, as the New York paper eventually did, the *Chicago Catholic Worker* reported on the work of Monsignor Hillenbrand and other clergy, the efforts of numerous Catholic labor organizers in the heavily industrial city, and the lively growth of such groups as the Catholic Youth Organization, the Association of Catholic Trade Unionists, and the Catholic Labor Theater. [22] The Chicago Catholic Worker was strongly backed in the diocese by a number of socially active clergy and academics at Mundelein Seminary and Quigley School, St. Viator's College, Loyola University, and *New World*, the official diocesan publication. Particularly important was Martin Carrabine, a charismatic Jesuit who headed CISCA (Chicago Inter-Student Catholic Action), to which a number of the Workers belonged. [23] The effect of such connections was to blur somewhat the distinctive radical Gospel emphasis of the Catholic Worker and to keep the Chicago group within the wide circle of progressive Catholicism in the city.

A significant effect of this was the Chicago group's gradual loss of interest in the decentralist emphasis of the Catholic Worker program, an emphasis which distinguished the Catholic Worker from most of the liberal American Catholicism of the time. In its early years the *Chicago Catholic Worker* had endorsed the need for decentralization. Ed Marciniak, for example, wrote that "man and his family were not intended by nature to inhabit squalid tenements, or even to live in apartment houses." Catherine Reser, Martin Paul, and even the thoroughly citified John Cogley urged a movement "back to the land." In November 1939, seeking funds for a rural settlement to be sponsored jointly with the Milwaukee Catholic Worker group, the *Chicago Catholic Worker* published "An Appeal for a Farm," but the project never got off the ground—or onto it—and thereafter the decentralist emphasis disappeared. The interest in utopian social thought and integral Catholic culture that accompanied Catholic Worker farming efforts elsewhere was little felt in Chicago. [24]

Although these differences on social and economic questions were plainly evident within the national Catholic Worker movement by 1940, it is unlikely that they alone would have been enough to cause a real split in the movement. Although Dorothy Day had made her own position clear, she allowed the different Worker groups to go their own way on such matters. The Houses with a strong labor emphasis generally ignored the decentralist and anarchist parts of the paper's program, but a common Catholic idealism, faith in Day's leadership, and the work among the poor still held the national movement together.

It was only when the issue of pacifism came to the fore that room for compromise disappeared. Although the Chicago Catholic Workers, like those elsewhere, had been aware of Dorothy Day's pacifist leanings from the beginning, the issue seemed remote in the thirties compared with the visible urgency of poverty, unemployment, and labor strife. The Chicago group paid little attention to the Spanish Civil War, an issue that received banner-headline treatment in the New York *Catholic Worker*. Even when war broke out in Europe in 1939, the *Chicago Catholic Worker* still saw foreign policy taking a back seat to social change at home.

The one issue that did attract interest was conscription. In 1939 when the issue was raised, Cogley strongly denounced the draft as an "immoral" violation of "Christian freedom." At the same time, his way of framing the argument suggested that he was wrestling with the deeper question of war itself. "One man can sincerely believe in the justice of war," he said. "Another man with just as much sincerity can deny that any need, duty, or even right to fight for the cause exists. Both have consciences, and no government has the right to act against the voice of conscience or to imprison those who exercise this fundamental right." Cogley did not say which man he was, but the statement appeared to point to the possibility of a "just war" waged by volunteers.[25]

For the most part, however, the *Chicago Catholic Worker* simply avoided discussing the impending war in any but the most general terms. When compared to the increasingly vocal pacifist resistance being advocated in the New York paper, this silence was correctly interpreted as opposition to pacifism. By early 1940 the issue was causing growing strain within the national Catholic Worker movement, with the New York and Chicago groups forming the two poles of opposition. As the New York *Catholic Worker* gave itself over more and more to antiwar propaganda, Catholic Worker groups in places like Seattle, Los Angeles, and Pittsburgh stopped selling it and, instead, began circulating the *Chicago Catholic Worker*, which stressed the hospitality and labor elements of the CW program. Although Cogley himself tried to keep the peace between some of the vehemently antipacifist groups and the New York House, it became ever more difficult to do so.

The whole controversy blew open in August 1940, when Dorothy Day suddenly sent a letter to all thirty Catholic Worker Houses. "We know that there are those who are members of Catholic Worker groups throughout the country who do not stand with us on this issue," the letter stated. "We have not been able to change their views through what we have written in the paper, by letters, or by personal conversation." Groups could continue to disagree with pacifism, she said, but they must distribute the New York *Catholic Worker*. Otherwise, they should "disassociate themselves from the Catholic Worker movement and not use the name of a movement with which they are in such fundamental disagreement."[26]

This ultimatum, apparently so contradictory to the open anarchist principles of the movement, came as a complete shock to Cogley and others in the Catholic Worker. He had believed that the disagreement could somehow be contained, but with that illusion gone, he announced that he was quitting the movement. Hearing of his intention from Marciniak, Day wrote asking him to delay any decision until he could come to the national Catholic Worker retreat scheduled at the Easton farm later that month. "You are bone of our bone and flesh of our flesh," she assured Cogley, "not a bone of contention." Hoping to find some way to stay in the movement, Cogley agreed to come to Easton.[27]

At the Maryfarm retreat, with over a hundred Workers gathered for a week of discussion, meditation, and worship, Day told Cogley that her letter had been "misunderstood" and that he and other nonpacifists were still welcome in the movement. Cogley spoke little, and by the end of the week Day thought that she had persuaded him to stay in the movement despite the disagreements. "When we separated it was with pain," she said. "We loved each other more truly than ever before, and we felt that sense of comradeship and Christian solidarity which will strengthen us for the work."

Cogley, however, had been more confused and distressed than comforted by all the *agape* that surrounded him at the retreat. A month after returning to Chicago he wrote Day:

> I never realized until I got home just how changed everything is—and how terribly vague and unsettled everything was left at the Retreat. I tried to tell the Resers just what was decided and discovered that I couldn't. I did tell them that your letter was generally misunderstood—but I couldn't tell them just what it did mean. Re-reading the letter it seems clear and direct enough. This present uncertainty is much more confusing than ever the letter was. Will you write when you get a chance and tell me just what the letter *did* mean if it did *not* mean what it seemed to say? Is there a "party line" or isn't there? Is the non-pacifist a welcome member of the movement or is he *tolerated* for sentimental or some other reason?[28]

Day did respond to this letter, and on October 10 Cogley wrote a reply indicating the Chicago group's final break with the movement.

Since you are a woman, I should let you get the last word in. I am not going to. "First you say my famous letter was perfectly clear, and then you write to ask me to clarify it once more. You are really quite impossible." I thought your letter was perfectly clear; you didn't. If you hadn't cast doubt on the clarity of what I thought—and others thought—was a very clear statement, I wouldn't have written. There wouldn't be any confusion.

Lord, I didn't write the letter. Emerson Hynes didn't write the letter. The Los Angeles group didn't write the letter. You did. And you must have realized when you wrote it that it would nestle like a bombshell in every Catholic Worker House and group throughout the country. If you write letters like that one (and you have all the right in the world, even the duty to write them) you must expect what will follow. That is one of the prices you pay for leadership, and it should—and probably does—make you feel good that you are not leading blind followers, but men and women with minds . . . and pens.

I don't think it is a question of our loving one another. We obviously do or we would tell each other to go to hell and call the whole thing off. . . . I got that into my head and heart a long time ago.

The only thing I resent about this whole matter is an attitude of toleration, of deliberate charity to another who is not able to go "the whole way." Disagreement is not handled on any intellectual plane. It would be much healthier to have a few healthy brawls (intellectual), even public brawls. It just doesn't seem right, normal, that so many people as at Easton should agree so perfectly and unanimously on such a highly controversial question unless some of them have not been thinking. Now I am not saying that all non-pacifists think. They don't. But pacifists—especially Catholic pacifists backing up their position on theological ground—have to justify their stand. People who are following the general trend of the Church aren't expected to be theologians and philosophers. Others who take a position which if not at variance is at least not parallel with the general trend must justify themselves theologically and philosophically.

And on this score I am very much to blame myself. I had a fine chance to start a controversy at the Retreat—and I failed. I felt so hopelessly outnumbered and was too much of a coward to begin the attack. . . .

I don't mean this observation as a condemnation of anyone. It is an attitude that has somehow creeped in, and it is the attitude that I don't like. The fear that if the question were thrown out openly bitterness and hostility might creep in. Nobody can criticize the fear of hurting others. You can criticize the fear that others would be hurt if everybody spoke freely. There is something cagy, something not quite honest about that, something foreign to the Catholic Worker.

We look forward to seeing you again, all of us. And don't take everything so seriously. I did, and look at the state I'm in. After this letter it seems unnecessary, but please give my love to everybody at Mott Street.[29]

The *Chicago Catholic Worker* came out a few more times until it was discontinued in June 1941. The House of Hospitality kept going until early 1942. But by that time Cogley, O'Gara, and most of the other nonpacifist Catholic Workers had gone into the army, while the pacifists had been scattered among conscientious objector camps and prisons.

Despite the obvious reluctance on both sides to make the break, this split in the Catholic Worker was inevitable. The issue of war was simply too important to gloss over, and the absolute pacifist stand, by its very nature, could not be compromised. The most unfortunate aspect of the controversy was that the disagreement was not publicly aired before the break. Despite Cogley's complaint about the lack of intellectual discussion of the issue, the *Chicago Catholic Worker* made very little effort to put forth a thoughtful case for the war based on Catholic intellectual tradition. The "dominant trend" in Catholicism was still to accept the legitimacy of war on the basis of authority, and there was as yet little incentive to subject the issue to intellectual scrutiny. The result was that the Catholic pacifists' arguments did not receive the intelligent criticism they deserved, and World War II left nothing like a Catholic counterpart to Reinhold Niebuhr's anguished justification of the Allied cause.

While it was the pacifist issue that finally divided the Catholic Worker, the split followed the lines of a general ideological fissure that had opened up on a whole range of issues: unions, class conflict, agrarianism, factories, technology, democracy, nationalism. On the one side were those who tended to see America, like all existing nation-states, as deeply flawed. Great merit might exist in the country's ideals, but its major institutions and functioning beliefs were fundamentally out of keeping with the Gospel ideal, or with anything that could be called truly Catholic or Christian. On the other side were those who saw grave problems in American society, but believed they could be alleviated through a combination of individual action and reform measures rooted in both Christian and American values.

This disagreement over issues coincided with a kind of temperamental difference that may have been equally important. Day and her strongest followers possessed the classic radical attitudes: adherence to a fixed set of ideas, a focus on ends rather than changing circumstances, and a willingness to endure political failure and to stand alone if necessary against society in order to witness to deeply held beliefs. Although they shared many values with the radicals, the liberal Catholic Workers tended to be somewhat more worldly, more attuned to the times, more conscious of how "taking a stand" might harm rather than help a cause. During the thirties while the Catholic Worker still fit in with the temper of the times, these differences had not been so important. But as the mood of the country changed and the Catholic Worker fell far out of step with the prevalent national mood, it became obvious that upholding radical principles would require radical personal qualities as well.

The most significant issue raised by the Catholic Worker split, however, concerned the proper relations of religion and politics. The Cogley-Day exchange revealed in a direct way a fundamental problem that afflicts Christian social movements, and for all their moral concern and good will, Day and Cogley could not avoid it. Day's unswerving adherence to the radical Gospel value of sacrificial love may have avoided political contamination, but only at the price of a certain moral rigidity and intellectual evasiveness. Cogley, on the other hand, adhered to the less distinctively Christian values of intellectual clarity and political realism, but at the price of breaking the circle of fellowship. Of course the two still shared a common faith and affirmed their "love" for one another, but a religious *agape* that could only "transcend" political division, not overcome it, could hardly witness to the power of Christian spirituality in the world. And if such conflict could not be avoided in a small group, how could Christian idealism—however valuable as a leaven in society—expect to transform a heterogeneous civilization? If the Catholic Workers' inability to answer such questions after the split was particularly painful, it was because they had tried far more than most professed Christians to engage their faith with the most serious problems of the world.

III

Another major center of Catholic Worker–inspired liberalism in the thirties and forties was the Association of Catholic Trade Unionists (ACTU), which encompassed such related groups as the Catholic Radical Alliance and the Catholic Labor Association. The founder and leading intellectual spokesman for the Catholic viewpoint represented by ACTU was John Cort. Finishing his senior year at Harvard and feeling "somewhat spiritually lonesome" because of his Catholicism, Cort joined the Catholic Worker after hearing Day speak in Boston in May 1936. "Dorothy convinced me that I could get more fun out of life on Mott Street, New York, than on Pinckney Street, Boston," he said later. When she invited him to come down to the farm in July, he immediately accepted.[30]

A brief stint at Easton convinced Cort that the farm commune, and the utopian "itch for martyrdom" it symbolized, did not represent the real strength and potential of the Catholic Worker. He appreciated more the House of Hospitality, where he became an effective leader and keen observer of the often comic tragedy of slum life. But much as he admired Day's and Maurin's religiously motivated service to the "undeserving poor," Cort found himself drawn to union halls rather than soup lines, to helping the large working class rather than the minority of permanent social victims.

Convinced that "labor was where the really hot action was," Cort spent his time writing fervently pro-CIO articles for the *Catholic Worker*, taking menial jobs in order to gain a better view of the workers' plight, and organizing Catholic Worker backing for a number of major strikes. The young Harvard graduate soon made himself thoroughly at home in the rough-and-tumble world of the longshore and garment industries, where unreconstructed employers, union toughs, Communists, gangsters, and labor priests waged battle for the allegiance of workers. At the same time Cort became a devoted student of the papal encyclicals, which he interpreted as a Catholic charter for the labor movement.[31]

In February 1937, Cort and ten other young Catholic union activists organized the Association of Catholic Trade Unionists at the Mott Street House of Hospitality. The Association was based on Pius XI's statement in *Quadragesimo Anno* that where Catholic workers belonged to religiously neutral labor organizations, "side by side with these unions must be Catholic associations which aim at giving their members moral and religious training." Although this language suggested that the organization should be a shelter for Catholics in a hostile religious environment, the genuine religious neutrality of American unions made such a function largely unnecessary. Instead, the ACTU functioned for the most part to add a specific Catholic sanction to the CIO. The organization used the papal encyclicals to persuade the Catholic working class that they had not only a right but a "duty" to join unions and to strike for "just cause."[32]

On one crucial point, however, the ACTU offered a distinctively Catholic critique of American unionism. The pope had urged "the setting up of guilds for the self-regulation of industry and producer cooperatives in which the worker shares as a partner in the ownership, management, or profits of the business in which he works." Much later, Cort came to accept Garry Wills's erudite argument in *Politics and Catholic Freedom* (1964) that the encyclicals did not support any specific program of American unionism. But in the thirties Cort's radical interpretation of *Quadragesimo Anno* was included in the ACTU Charter and became a focal point of ideological controversy for the group. By remaining even theoretically critical of pure bread-and-butter unionism, Cort and the ACTU made their work in the labor movement more difficult, while neither their theoretical critique nor their actions went far enough to satisfy their old friends in the Catholic Worker movement.[33]

During its heyday in the late thirties and early forties, the ACTU helped dispel the image of Catholics as a passive presence in American unionism. With chapters in most of the major eastern and midwestern cities, the "ACTists" became an effective propaganda and pressure group within several of the major industrial unions, notably the auto, steel, transport, and electrical workers. The national organization maintained its own legal department, published labor papers like Cort's *Labor Leader* in New York, and sponsored labor schools, often in cooperation with sympathetic Catholic clergy and educators. Like their parent Catholic Workers, the ACTists were especially effective in swinging Catholic moral prestige behind particular strikes, with the added advantage that ACTU operated from within labor's ranks. (All ACTU members had to belong to a union.) During a 1940 strike of Barbara Hutton's Woolworth stores, the Catholic picketers carried signs reading, "Babs gave $11,000,000 to charity, but 'the worker is not to receive as alms what is his due in justice'—Pius XI." From 1939 to 1949 the ACTU provided support for over three hundred strikes. Although most successful in cities like Chicago, Detroit, and Pittsburgh where they enjoyed backing from pro-labor members of the Catholic hierarchy, the lay persons in the ACTU undoubtedly played an important role in arousing American Catholic workers in general. In the 1939 Chrysler strike, for example, it was said that only fellow Catholics could have persuaded the Polish and Italian workers to join the CIO. "When the strike was won," commented Richard Rovere in *The Nation*, "there was little doubt that credit for reversing the trend belongs to the Catholic unionists. The stock of ACTU shot up."[34]

By 1941, with most of the major union recognition strikes won, the ACTists began to turn their attention to internal union politics. Their primary goal was to counteract the presumed influence of Communists and corrupt elements within the CIO. Although they functioned as an organized caucus within several unions, the ACTists were generally cautious about pushing their own candidates for union leadership, preferring to coalesce behind religiously neutral candidates. From 1946 to 1948, as Communism became a primary national concern, the ACTU sparked internal union revolts against such apparently pro-Communist union heads as Mike Quill of the Transport Workers and Julius Emspak of the Electrical Workers. Although at the time these actions were part of a much larger domestic campaign against Communism, it was often the Catholic union activists who, as Norman McKenna said, "provided the doctrinal oil for the anti-communist machines."[35]

All this, however, took Cort and the ACTU far from their Catholic Worker origins. The Catholic Worker initially backed the ACTU and publicized its union activities, but Cort's group began deemphasizing its utopian rhetoric just as the Catholic Worker was reaffirming the purity of its idealism. While Cort admitted that a truly "Christian democratic society" would require such things as redistribution of wealth and a worker share in management, he put aside these goals because, he said, any person in the United States who advocated them was viewed as a "crackpot." And in a sense, the ACTU leader concluded, "he *is* a crackpot, because he is going too fast."[36]

After 1940 the Catholic Worker became highly critical of the political direction being taken by the ACTU. "The goal should not be to get the Communists out and our own clique in," the *Catholic Worker* said. "It is all the workers we are trying to reach, and all the leaders, whether they are Communist or Catholic." The final break between the two groups came over ACTU's support for expanded weapons production, but that issue only pointed up how far apart the two groups had become. The Catholic Worker charged that the ACTU had trimmed the meaning of a Christian social reconstruction and thereby undermined its religious power. Instead of speaking directly to men's hearts, the ACTists had become tied to a narrow union ideology that ultimately promoted the very bourgeois materialist values that caused social injustice in the first place. While union workers' wages and living standards might improve, the Catholic Workers said, the "mindless" processes of mass production would continue to degrade millions of workers. During the forties and early fifties *Catholic Worker* writers like Ade Bethune drew on Benedictine works such as Etienne Borne and Francis Henry's *A Philosophy of Work* and Dom Rombert Sorg's *Holy Work* to reemphasize the fundamental Catholic idea, shared by Day and Maurin, that all work must be "a gift, a holy sacrifice, offered for the joy of building up brotherhood into the measure of the perfect man."[37] "La-

bor is a discipline imposed on all of us because of the Fall," wrote Dorothy Day. "But it is also a vocation . . . whereby man shares in God's
creative activity. . . . It is not the low pay and rough conditions of modern factory work but the lack of *responsibility* that is devastating. The
worker feels little relationship to the human and social consequences of
what he produces."[38] It was up to Christians to bring these perspectives
to American labor, the *Catholic Worker* said, but the ACTU had stopped
even trying. The Catholic Worker had to oppose both the ACTU and
present-day unions, Day said, because "we are not interested in increasing armaments jobs, going along with big business, and perpetuating
the *status quo*."[39]

Cort waged a vigorous counterattack against this kind of criticism in the ACTU journal *Labor Leader* and later in *Commonweal*, where
he was a regular contributor in the forties and fifties. The debate turned
not so much on the newer issue of organized labor's complicity with the
military and the state but on the old Depression question of modern
industrialism and technology. Against his radical critics, Cort argued
that the ACTU had always stood for more than just better wages and
hours. He agreed that the worker must be able to protect his "essential
dignity," and to have the "right to express and govern himself in matters
affecting his work." Cort grew lyrical about the possibilities that lay
ahead when "workers who are capable of creative effort once again become 'workers' in the true sense, and no longer the unthinking slaves of
machinery and stockholders. Then industrial democracy will reign not
only in each plant and company, but throughout the national economy."
A true "partnership" of labor and capital, as advocated by the popes, was
"only a question of time."[40]

What Cort denied was the Catholic Worker's contention that
mass industrialism and the wage contract were in any way inconsistent
with these objectives. The anarchist attack on mass production was
naive, utopian, and totally contrary to the best interests of the workers
and everyone else. Technological abundance was the basic prerequisite
for any social progress. "Mass production means that technique of producing things in large quantities through the use of machines which has
made it possible to distribute large quantities of the world's goods to a
large number of people," Cort said. "Greed and profiteering have frequently got in the way of a fair distribution, but that is another story."
Some giant corporations may be economically inefficient, he admitted,
and mass urban society leaves much to be desired, but the solution was
not to revert to some simpler economic order. Cort enjoyed tweaking the
nose of Catholic Worker heroes like Eric Gill, who had once sent a typed
letter to the movement saying that technological goods like typewriters

were fine as long as they were produced only by "responsible craftsmen."
"Okay, Mr. Gill," Cort said. "If industrialism as we have known it
stinks, how are you going to produce typewriters cheap enough so more
than a few men like yourself can buy them?" Since they cannot show how
the world's millions can be supported in any other way, Cort concluded,
the decentralists' sweeping attacks on the assembly line and the factory
as "contrary to the dignity of man" were "so much nonsense."[41]

Cort also rejected the Catholic Worker's attacks on the wage
system. The popes clearly endorsed such employment if the workers
were paid a "living wage," defined as a rate sufficient to support a family
and accumulate some property after a time. This, Cort argued, was precisely what American unions had enabled American workers to do. Although the workers might go farther and press for the security of an
annual salary, free collective bargaining had already brought them a
standard of material well-being unimaginable in the nineteenth century.

It was true that papal statements advocated "worker participation in the ownership, management, or profits of the enterprise," but
this goal should be approached not by the Catholic Worker's talk of
"non-violent revolution" against "capitalism," but by realistic steps toward cooperation between existing industry and labor. While Cort believed that major changes would come in the long run, the only presently
feasible instruments of cooperation were the "Industry Councils." Modeled on the labor-management committees established in most plants
during World War II, the Industry Council idea enjoyed some vogue in
the late forties and early fifties among labor-oriented intellectuals and
reformers. The ACTU pushed the councils on the basis of the encyclicals, and Cort continually expressed faith that "decent employers" and
"democratic union leaders" would sit down together and "work out common problems." In this way capitalism might be gradually transformed
into the humane and Christian economic order envisioned by the popes.
"If that is 'New Dealism,' if that is 'lacking in vision,' if that is 'class
collaboration,' okay."[42]

Cort also defended the liberal state against the Catholic Worker's
anarchist attack. The omnipotent Marxist or Fascist state threatens liberty, he said, and most functions should be performed by intermediate or
subsidiary institutions. Yet there is no absolute right to either liberty or
property, and when any individual or group violates the rights of others
or the common good, the state must intervene—a principle recognized
by Catholic philosophy from St. Thomas onward. "The value of the
Christian anarchist," Cort said, "is that he often focuses attention on St.
Peter's boundary—'We ought to obey God rather than men'—at times
when more timid souls hasten to excuse their disobedience to God by

their excessive fear of man. But this value should never blind us to the great good sense of Christ and St. Paul, who remind us that the Christian way, within the limitations of St. Peter's boundary, is a way of obedience and submission, even to an ungodly mammoth of a state like the Roman Empire."[43]

In a 1952 *Commonweal* article, "The Catholic Worker and the Workers," Cort summarized the Catholic liberal case against the Catholic Worker's radicalism. The essential problem with the Worker's personalism, he found, was that it prevented serious engagement with men in the world over the long term. The Worker had indeed helped some workers in the thirties with its open-armed generosity, but when the problem turned from a visible crisis of injustice where the Christian obligation to serve the poor was immediately applicable to the unglamorous work of patiently maintaining viable institutions, the Catholic Worker chose to leave the work to others. Where was "the decent worker" to go, Cort asked, when he needed legal help, education, organizational sustenance, and lobbying to protect him against unfair employers, corruptionists, and Communists? The ACTU's provision of these things over the years, although they were nowhere mentioned in Scripture, had been no less "works of mercy" than providing food and shelter. No wonder the Catholic Worker had long since lost touch with the real American working class, Cort said, and he blamed Peter Maurin for having led Day and her movement "deeper and deeper into the waters of contradiction and confusion." "Dorothy Day is a great woman and the mother of us all," he concluded. "And the Catholic Worker has taught us magnificent lessons about these same works of mercy, about love and the importance of poverty, about the primacy of the spiritual and the importance of faith. These things we should remember as long as we have the power to remember; these things we should cling to and imitate. But we have no obligation to cling to the theoretical confusions of the movement, the sloppy thinking, the silly posturings, and the more-radical-than-thou."[44]

Although it was muddied by the arcane debate over the correct interpretation of the encyclicals—where, as Wills showed, both sides were probably wrong—the disagreement between the Catholic Worker and the ACTU touched on some of the most basic unresolved issues of contemporary social thought and brought to them perspectives that were recognizably religious. The refusal of Catholic decentralists to fall in love with the factory and the assembly line simply because they produced more goods for an expanding economy struck at a fundamental weakness of twentieth-century American liberalism. Not all industrial labor was as dehumanizing as the Catholic radicals and other decentralist critics said. But rather than critically examine the actual historical effects of industrialism and technology on human society, liberals tended to promulgate the progressive "myth of the machine," as Lewis Mumford called the cult of efficiency and big technology. The radicals never answered Cort's question about cheap typewriters, but liberal writers seldom dealt adequately with the issues of individual and cultural alienation in mass industrial societies. Even American liberals who were acutely sensitive to problems of injustice usually did not explore the apparent contradiction between the obvious material successes of industrialism and an underlying cultural malaise that touched not only those on the bottom, but sometimes those who prospered under the system. While some questioning of this sort had gone on in the thirties, it tended to disappear with the return of prosperity after World War II. One could conclude that American liberals, like Americans generally, were often so impressed with the increase of national strength and the spread of material satisfactions that they overlooked less tangible requirements for human well-being.

Traditional Catholic social theory, whatever its other weaknesses, had a strong sense of exactly these issues. Cort, Cogley, and others reflected the authentic strengths of the American liberal tradition: its emphases on individual liberty, equal opportunity, practical accommodation to change, distrust of fanaticism and closed ideologies, and faith in human nature and the future of liberal society. But in the middle of the twentieth century those liberal values were challenged as never before, and liberalism had trouble constructing an effective response. Most distressing, perhaps, was the uneasy feeling that the American liberal tradition was somehow an inadequate response to the profound spiritual and social crises of the twentieth century. In the age of Auschwitz, Hiroshima, and the Gulag, the more thoughtful liberals recognized that they lacked a completely satisfactory foundation for their progressive values. Arthur Schlesinger, Jr., for example, observed, "The most important thing for the preservation of civilization is a belief in moral standards. That belief is really most solid when it is founded upon a fervent belief in a supernatural order. . . . I am impressed, for example, by the way the declining faith in the supernatural has been accompanied by the rise of the monstrous totalitarian creeds of the twentieth century."[45] The attempt, after World War II, of some secular American liberals like Schlesinger to root their cherished ideas in religious soil, such as Reinhold Niebuhr's neo-orthodox theology, testifies to the anxieties of those in the progressive tradition. But even with the injection of heavy doses of the new "Christian Realism," liberals found it difficult to sustain the drive for a firmer spiritual foundation for liberalism in an American culture that rested on so many liberal premises. During the 1950s many liberals concluded that America and its way of life already embodied the finest of the Western moral tradition and lost much of their metaphysical anxiety.

Two other examples of Catholic liberalism spawned by the Catholic Worker deserve mention. Both were related to the ACTU and followed its basic pattern of development. In Chicago, Catholic Worker alumnus Ed Marciniak headed a group called the Catholic Labor Association (later the Council on Working Life) that published a monthly journal, *Work*, from 1943 to 1960. The Catholic Labor Association performed many of the same functions as the ACTU, although unlike Cort's group, it admitted non-Catholic members. As an organizer and journalist, Marciniak further developed the combination, already evident in his Chicago Catholic Worker days, of a deep commitment to lay social Catholicism and institutional change with an instinct for reconciling conflict and restoring the consensus necessary for community action. Marciniak could be sharply critical of American capitalism, and he retained a deeper concern than most in the ACTU for such noneconomic problems as worker alienation and the loss of the sense of the sacred in American industrial society. On the questions of industrial production and the assembly line, *Work* placed itself somewhere between the Catholic Worker and the ACTU.[46]

But Marciniak also knew that most American workingmen simply wanted a minimum of social acceptance and reasonable economic security, and that American liberal capitalism could give them both. In the forties *Work* was still critical enough to say that "the industrial revolution's inventive genius has made man master of nature but a slave of the machines he has built" and to print moving first-person accounts by factory workers of both their obvious physical and more subtle psychological injuries. But like the contemporary movement of Young Christian Workers, the American counterpart of the European "JOCists" (*Jeunesse Ouvrière Chrétienne*), the Council on Working Life's solution was to promote a kind of evangelical élan and social solidarity among lay Christians in their existing occupations rather than tackle the difficult question of transforming the nature of the work itself. "Despite its drudgery," *Work* insisted, "there is joy and creativeness in manual work." Like Cort, Marciniak still considered himself a radical Christian reformer who favored "the widest possible distribution of property" and a worker share in management through agencies like the industry councils. But as the working class became more content in the prosperous fifties and industrial questions gradually lost their urgency, *Work* settled down to a calmer middle age in support of decent labor as well as racial and community causes.[47]

In Pittsburgh the Catholic Worker was originally represented by two priests, Charles Owen Rice and Carl Hensler, who ran an enormous House of Hospitality (one of the few officially backed by a diocese) and strongly supported the CIO. On labor questions the Catholic Radical Alliance, as the local Catholic Workers called their group, was at first extremely militant. They called for an immediate implementation of "the radical social program of the Labor Encyclicals" and sharply criticized the CIO for being "content to sell labor for a wage." Yet this ideology slipped away as Rice and Hensler became involved in the enormously difficult task of organizing workers and defending the CIO against charges of Communism and violence. Closely allied with the Catholic leadership of the United Steel Workers, Rice found the Catholic Worker's insistence on ethical and ideological purity increasingly irrelevant and led the group into the ACTU. The pacifism issue brought a final split with the Catholic Worker in 1940. As with Marciniak, Rice's and Hensler's reforming zeal was chastened by close dealings with ordinary Catholic laborers. Whatever their occasional militant outbursts, Rice noted, American workers were, in fact, deeply conservative—and more appreciative of American capitalism than their employers. Defending a steel strike against conservative critics, Rice wrote that "the steel worker is willing to strike because he *likes* the capitalistic system and wants to do his bit to save it by preventing management interests from gutting the economy and cutting their own throats as they did in the Depression." Like the ACTU and the Catholic Labor Alliance, the Pittsburgh group gradually lost much of their specific identity and sense of urgency. Rice remained a prominent social activist during the fifties and sixties, while receiving widespread recognition for his pioneering accomplishments.[48]

IV

The late forties and fifties were a transitional period for American Catholic liberalism. The practical accommodation of Catholics to American institutions was virtually complete. Catholic intellectuals, like Catholics in general, felt more secure and free to assert themselves in the larger society. The subculture of the Catholic ghetto still continued—indeed, in some ways it enjoyed a heyday—but it was becoming less preoccupied with its own more parochial concerns and more inclined to turn outward to the larger society.

For some Catholics and non-Catholics alike, the new Catholic assertiveness revived old fears about the basic incompatibility of the Roman Church and American liberal culture. Around 1950 a series of noisy public controversies—over Supreme Court decisions concerning public aid to Catholic schools, the sending of an American ambassador to the Vatican, and some harsh words between Cardinal Spellman and Eleanor Roosevelt—pitted the Church against American liberals, while Senator Joseph McCarthy's witch-hunting crusade against Communism was sometimes thought to be instigated primarily by Catholics. Reacting to what they saw as a growing Catholic threat, leading Protestant liberals formed Protestants and Other Americans United for Separation of Church and State, while Paul Blanshard made a public career out of warning that American Catholicism threatened the nation's liberties.[49]

This apparent polarization partly cloaked an accommodation between liberalism and Catholicism that, on a deeper level, was taking place in the fifties. Many younger Catholic intellectuals were political liberals who were eager to show that their Catholicism in no way contradicted American liberalism, but could actually strengthen it. In effect, these intellectuals were trying to pick up the old Catholic liberal dialogue that had been so abruptly cut off at the turn of the century.

Former Catholic Workers like John Cogley, James O'Gara, and John Cort played significant roles in this effort. When they returned from overseas military service in 1945, Cogley and O'Gara decided that there was a need for a new Catholic journal that would speak to the concerns of the younger generation of Catholic intellectuals who had grown up amidst Depression and war. But when they attempted to get financial backing for such a project, they found that the "real Catholic money" they approached wanted reassurances that they would "go easy" on political controversy, particularly the racial issue. The two young journalists therefore decided to begin more modestly with *Today*, a monthly published in Chicago by the liberal Chicago Inter-Student Catholic Action group. As editor of that little magazine, Cogley quickly assumed his role as the self-conscious leader of the postwar generation of liberal Catholic intellectuals. Directed at a student audience, *Today*'s thoughtful treatment of cultural and political issues signaled the readiness of younger Catholics to create a more mature Catholic culture in the United States. The journal published up-and-coming writers like O'Gara, Ade Bethune, Robert Reynolds, Abigail Quigley McCarthy, Ed Willock, and Joe Dever, while Cogley's editorials urged American Catholics to overcome the parochial and philistine elements in their past.[50]

In 1949 Cogley, then thirty-three years old, was named editor of *Commonweal*, where he was joined two years later by O'Gara. As editor and columnist for the leading lay Catholic journal, Cogley exercised a considerable influence on Catholic intellectual life in the 1950s. Loyal to the hierarchy and well within the bounds of the Catholic subculture, Cogley's *Commonweal* deviated, nevertheless, from what appeared to be the Catholic line on such issues as McCarthyism, movie censorship, and parochial education. It thus drew the wrath of Catholics for whom these were emotional issues. As the "pope of the *Commonweal* Catholics," Cogley was vehemently attacked by McCarthyites, including his own pastor and the Wisconsin senator himself, who said he was "doing a tremendous disservice to the Catholic Church and a great service to the Communist party."[51] In 1952 Cogley in turn wrote a widely reported anti-McCarthy speech for Chicago's Bishop Bernard Sheil, the only member of the Catholic hierarchy to publicly challenge McCarthy, and later led the Fund for the Republic's effective fight against blacklisting in the movie industry.[52]

Although deeply controversial in the overheated atmosphere of the time, *Commonweal*'s stands were, in fact, quite tame, and within a few years most were quietly accepted within the Catholic community. The relative ease of the transition on such issues as censorship and ecumenicalism suggests that *Commonweal* was not breaking new ground, but simply rediscovering in the mid-twentieth century what nineteenth-century Catholic liberals had loudly proclaimed—that the central elements of the American liberal tradition were completely compatible with Catholicism. Many conservative Catholics and secular liberals alike had trouble seeing how this could be so. But the American Catholic experience had created the fact of a Church in a liberal pluralist society, even if there was no theoretical justification for such a phenomenon. Thus, it was only a matter of time until theory caught up with the facts. In 1960 John Courtney Murray's *We Hold These Truths* finally supplied the necessary Catholic arguments for religious freedom and democratic pluralism at the most abstract philosophical and theological level.[53]

Philosophical liberalism on basic propositions did not of course imply political liberalism on contemporary issues. But most of the intellectuals who took the lead in resuming the dialogue between Catholicism and Americanism were political liberals as well. *Commonweal*'s liberal politics were for the most part bland and imitative of secular liberal opinion. But the very existence of such an organ challenged the common notion that Catholics were not somehow a part of the liberal tribe—even though Catholic voters had been an essential component of liberal political coalitions since the thirties. By the end of the fifties the idea that it was possible to be a good Catholic and a good liberal at the same time was no longer in question.

Although most *Commonweal* opinions were unexceptional, it maintained a few concerns that went beyond the conventional liberalism of the 1950s. And where this was so, it was often because of the continuing influence of the Catholic Worker on Cogley and his colleagues.

The relationship of the Catholic Worker to *Commonweal* was an old one. George Shuster of *Commonweal* had sent Peter Maurin to Dorothy Day in 1932, and Day continued to write for Shuster's journal after she started the *Catholic Worker*. Since both were part of the small lay Catholic intellectual movement, were socially conscious, and were located in New York, the two publications inevitably influenced one another. During the thirties, for example, the *Catholic Worker* picked up some of *Commonweal*'s cultural concerns, while articles in the *Catholic Worker* helped turn Shuster against the Spanish Civil War. For many Catholic intellectuals, the two mandatory stops on a visit to New York were at the *Commonweal* offices and the Catholic Worker House of Hospitality. Although the patrician origins and academic respectability of *Commonweal* set it apart from Day's slum-based paper, some Catholics saw the two as complementary in their concerns, especially after the connection was strengthened by the influx of former Catholic Workers into *Commonweal* in the fifties.[54]

Although Cogley had become more conservative over the years, his intellectual makeup retained a strain of radical disaffection with the American mainstream that he ascribed to his Catholic Worker background. His vigorous opposition to McCarthy, for instance, was strengthened by his own conviction of "the failure of anti-Communism." "When I was in daily contact with a long breadline in Chicago, and scurrying around to get food for it, I used to get disgusted when prominent Catholics met in swank hotels to condemn Communism," he wrote in 1950. "I used to know a lot of Communists in those days, and I knew what they were up to while Catholics sat around making speeches and passing resolutions."[55]

Throughout the generally complacent 1950s, Cogley retained an acute interest in the problem of poverty in America. The contrast between his earlier career and his more recent one prompted reflections on the ways in which national and personal prosperity could cause human distress to disappear from consciousness. "From this height [out *Commonweal*'s Manhattan office window] all below seems calm, orderly, prosperous," he observed. "But hidden in the shining city down there are pockets of poverty and despair all too easy to ignore and forget."[56]

Although Cogley continued to reject pacifism as firmly as he had in 1940, his attitude toward it differed from that of many liberal intellectuals in the 1950s. Cogley had come to believe that Dorothy Day's radical pacifism was invaluable because it "has made it impossible for non-pacifists like me to accept violence unthinkingly." Pacifists and non-pacifists always have "hard and difficult and embarrassing questions to ask one another," he said, and "the point, if there is one, is that we all see through a glass darkly. We are burdened with one another, and in the last analysis all are baffled by the evil in the world—evil on a scale greater than any generation before us has known." The witness of the pacifist, Cogley said, "bespeaks the doubt that might otherwise be silenced in the rest of us. And without that doubt we are all lost." Although *Commonweal* endorsed the major American policies of the Cold War and was willing to risk war to implement them, Cogley's "doubt" led him to campaign almost single-handedly against the arrest of the Catholic Workers and other pacifists for civil disobedience against air-raid drills and to advocate that the federal government permit individuals to designate that their tax money go to nonmilitary purposes only.[57]

In 1959 Cogley gave up his *Commonweal* column to go to work for the Kennedy campaign, where his specialty was the religious issue. Cogley's subtle grasp of both the intellectual and political dynamics of the Catholic question helped Kennedy defuse the issue early in the campaign. Since Kennedy himself exemplified the ignorance of most American Catholics on the intellectual problems of relating their religion and society, Cogley had to give him "instant theological training" before his decisive meeting with the Houston ministers. Kennedy's careful speech and well-prepared answers to the ministers' questions effectively removed religion as an issue in the campaign and ended one of the oldest taboos in American politics.[58]

The election of the first Catholic president and the convening of the Second Vatican council by Pope John XXIII made the early sixties a heady time for American Catholic liberals. Their perspectives and programs were suddenly being welcomed by the highest authorities in Church and state. In Rome, the rapid transformation of Catholicism astonished even the most progressive American Catholics. Besides accepting Murray's view of the Church-state question, Vatican II introduced sweeping changes in practically every area of Catholic life and thought. In Washington things were less dramatic but no less gratifying. Although religion played no particular role in the Kennedy administration, the administration was certainly open to Catholic liberal influence. It was, therefore, no accident that one of the major domestic innovations of the Kennedy-Johnson administration owed its origins to another former Catholic Worker, Michael Harrington.

Significant changes in national policy can seldom be traced to a single book, but such was the case with Michael Harrington's *The Other*

America (1962). Although the persistence of poverty in the affluent post-war era had been noticed by one or two economists, it was Harrington's passionate book, followed by Dwight Macdonald's compelling review of it in the *New Yorker*, that sparked first the widespread national discussion of the problem and then the Kennedy-Johnson administrations' "War on Poverty."

Few readers of *The Other America* were aware how much the book and its author had been influenced by the radical Catholic Worker movement. Harrington did refer briefly to his experiences at the New York House of Hospitality, and stated that "it was through Dorothy Day and the Catholic Worker movement that I first came into contact with the terrible reality of involuntary poverty and the magnificent ideal of voluntary poverty."[59] But Harrington carefully confined the book's discussion to the condition of the poor as an invisible minority, and avoided suggesting remedies, so that there were only hints that the author was a former Catholic radical and now a Marxian Socialist. While Harrington's migration from Catholic radicalism to Marxism theoretically distinguishes him from the other Catholic Worker liberals, his actual life's work suggests that he had much in common with them.

Harrington's biography was more typical of the young people who came to the Catholic Worker after World War II than of the earlier Depression generation. Born in St. Louis in 1928, he came of age in a middle class Irish Catholicism that was still deeply committed to the ideas and subculture of the American Catholic ghetto, but was becoming confident enough to assert itself in the larger world. Harrington received a thoroughly traditional Jesuit education in St. Louis and at Holy Cross College. Harrington later came to regard much of the theology and philosophy he learned as a "decadent" catechetical rationalism derived not from St. Thomas but from the Counter-Reformation polemicists. It was, he said, "the philosophical analogue of the daily experience of a closed Catholic world" in the United States. But through such teaching Harrington acquired not only a taste for sophisticated metaphysical theories but "the Jesuit inspiration of our adolescence that insisted so strenuously that a man must live his philosophy."[60]

For Harrington, as for an increasing number of educated young Catholics of the postwar era, the place to live out philosophy was outside the Catholic subculture. In 1948, Harrington went to Robert Hutchins's intellectually exciting University of Chicago for graduate work, and discovered there a world of unconventional life-styles and left-wing politics unknown within the Church. By the time he went to New York in 1949, Harrington was an aspiring poet, a social radical, and a devoted bohemian who plunged into the exotic life of Greenwich Village with all the wide-eyed enthusiasm of a young Catholic just arrived from the Midwest.[61]

But Harrington remained a Catholic, so he naturally drifted to the one place where the American radical tradition had fused with serious Catholic religion and thought. "All I knew of the Catholic Worker when I walked into its House of Hospitality on Chrystie Street just off New York's Skid Row (the Bowery) was that it was as far Left as you could go within the Church," Harrington recalled. Like other young Catholic Workers of the period, he found the Worker's combination of Catholic and radical intellectualism exciting and morally engaging. "Besides engaging in the corporeal works of mercy, we thought of ourselves as lay apostles at the center of a movement for Christian renewal," he said. "At mealtime, at the regular Friday night meetings, or at retreats or conferences at the (then) two Catholic Worker farms in New York state, we discussed the new developments in Catholic theology and philosophy. The talk was of Jean Danielou, Henri de Lubac, Yves Congar, Jacques Maritain, Gabriel Marcel, Romano Guardini. . . . And we debated non-Catholic thinkers in that gentle Catholic household: Marx, Engels, Dostoevsky, Kropotkin, Emma Goldman, and Freud."[62]

During the two years he lived at the Catholic Worker, from January 1951 to December 1952, Harrington was one of the movement's leading intellectual lights. Although radical activism was at a low ebb during the McCarthy period and the Korean War, the *Catholic Worker* enjoyed perhaps its greatest intellectual flowering in the early fifties. Along with Robert Ludlow, Irene Naughton, Edmund Egan, Tom Sullivan, Elizabeth Bartelme, Anthony Aratari, Roger O'Neil, John McKeon, Eileen Fantino, Mary Anne McCoy, Dick Donnelly, and others, Harrington explored the movement's Catholic anarchist-pacifist heritage in light of current social and intellectual developments. Harrington was, in Worker parlance, a scholar rather than a worker, who earned a considerable reputation for his provocative *Catholic Worker* articles and his patient, thoughtful letters to the movement's critics.[63]

Harrington's *Catholic Worker* contributions showed the two sides of his mental outlook. On the one hand there were highly abstract analyses of the most demanding philosophers and theologians of the day: Marcel, Maritain, Buber, Berdyaev, Mounier, Arendt. In these pieces Harrington displayed his talent for high-order metaphysical argument in the Jesuit mold. On the other hand he wrote down-to-earth reports and criticism of current events: prison conditions, Spanish worker life, steel strikes, birth control, poverty. In these he showed not only the typical Catholic Worker concern for commonplace events and people, but an uncommon eye for practical politics.[64]

The philosophical Harrington was an earnest religious seeker, still committed to Catholicism, but openly wrestling with the classic problems of belief and doubt that, as yet, troubled few American Catholics. Before coming to the Worker he had already passed through one religious crisis by reading Pascal and Kierkegaard—both at that time still on the Index of Forbidden Books. He therefore felt closest to what he saw as an Augustinian "existential" tradition within Catholicism, best represented in the contemporary Church by Gabriel Marcel. His review of Marcel's *Being and Having* was in part a plea that thinkers like Marcel ought not to fall within the papal condemnation of existentialism.

> But we do not *have* the important things. Do we *have* life at all in the sense of controlling it? Hardly. We cannot even think of *it* as external to us. It is in the realm of being, and being leads to Being, to God. This is not the concentration on the flux of existence, which the Pope condemns. It is the affirmation of Essence.[65]

Harrington's social commentary leaned in two opposite directions. At times he defended Catholic Worker utopianism in the movement's familiar language. "I hope we can conceive of ourselves in . . . the vocation of prophecy," he told one correspondent. "Short-sighted, perhaps, where the immediate problem is concerned, but visionary in the best sense where the transcendent values of Christ are concerned. It is a hard role to play, yet it is necessary that we have our pilgrims of the absolute. . . . For the great danger is that, in attempting to compromise, to soft-peddle, to mitigate our criticism, that we will lose sight of our ideal."[66] Yet Harrington's great interest in effective action and politics gradually led him to "soft-peddle" prophecy in order to deal with "the immediate problem." Unlike most *Catholic Worker* writers, Harrington looked eagerly for any small victories the movement might win and scrutinized the signs of the times for evidence that broader progressive "forces" were somehow on the upswing. Such signs could usually be found—a successful strike, church-state tension in Spain, a Supreme Court decision—but attaching such significance to passing events ran counter to the *Catholic Worker's* general indifference to temporal success.[67]

Harrington left the Catholic Worker not for political reasons but because he left the Catholic Church. Unable to make any longer his "leap of faith," he concluded that God was dead. Sophisticated mental gymnastics like his own might appeal to a certain sort of intellectual, he contended, but they could not "sustain a church or provide a basis for a culture." Anticipating discussions of the 1960s, Harrington said that

Catholic religious belief in America was upheld only by maintaining a closed institutional subculture, and that as those walls crumbled so would the Catholic faith.[68]

In Marxism Harrington found what seemed a better metaphysical system and a new intellectual community. He became a "Schachtmanite," one of the minuscule Socialist splinter groups in New York, and happily immersed himself in "talmudic" doctrinal disputes and "exegeses of the holy writ according to Karl Marx." In lengthy debates over such questions as whether, from a Marxist viewpoint, the Soviet Union was imperialist or only expansionist, Harrington was finally able to combine his philosophical tastes and his interest in detailed political analysis of current events. Even though the number of American Socialists in all the sects was tiny, Harrington, like other democratic leftists, used Marxism to develop a critical perspective on American society, to seek out various social forces that might stir change, and to commune with the international Socialist movement.[69]

But unlike many of his Marxist comrades Harrington was never an ideologue or sectarian. His bent for practical politics had not been satisfied at the utopian Catholic Worker, and he could not be content working within theoretically pure but politically irrelevant Socialist groups either. Like his friend and mentor Norman Thomas, Harrington developed Socialist rationales for cooperating with other "progressive" groups working for the causes of civil liberties, civil rights, organized labor, improved wages, and so on. Since there was no mass Socialist movement in America, it was simple to justify working with liberals for good causes as the best way to nudge them toward Socialism. But however compelling the argument for such cooperation, the political result was to make American democratic Socialism simply a slightly more daring version of the liberal wing of the Democratic Party. Especially on issues like civil rights, where the Democrats were morally vulnerable, shrewd independent political organizers like Harrington and Allard Lowenstein who operated outside party structures could help push liberal Democrats toward more forthright positions, as they did in demonstrations and meetings at the Democratic conventions of 1960 and 1964. But from a Socialist standpoint these were Pyrrhic victories, because the more the liberals took up such causes, the less reason there was for any group such as Blacks to look to Socialism as an alternative.

The fate of *The Other America* also illustrated this irony. In 1960 Harrington and his fellow Socialists refused to support the Democrats because they saw no difference between Kennedy and Nixon on civil rights. But as the civil rights movement began to arouse national concern, the Kennedy administration was forced to a greater awareness of the problem of Blacks, which were still largely defined in terms of legal segregation and discrimination. *The Other America* aroused the interest of economist Walter Heller and other Kennedy administration officials partly because it suggested that the problem of race was also a problem of poverty. In January 1964, after Lyndon Johnson committed the federal government to act on the issue, Harrington himself was called in by the administration as a consultant to help design the program. Although he told Johnson and antipoverty director R. Sargent Shriver that "the abolition of poverty would require a basic change in how resources are allocated," and wrote memos calling for "planned and massive social investments and therefore structural changes in the system," he also worked on the more limited and politically acceptable proposals that actually emerged as the War on Poverty. Seeing the administration's effort as progress toward his goals, Harrington campaigned hard for Johnson's election in 1964.[70]

Like his decision to keep mention of Socialism out of *The Other America*, such compromises were morally and politically defensible but ideologically hard to swallow.

> Once the government had determined to do something about poverty, should I simply have said that its efforts were inevitably going to be inadequate and that in the not-so-long run they might well benefit the rich more than the poor? That . . . would have been to turn my back on hungry, hopeless people who needed all the advocates they could get to push reform to its farthest limits.[71]

Harrington's conclusion was that such dilemmas were "endemic to the socialist movement itself. . . . Anyone who wants to change the system must still live within it and utilize its institutions, if only to transform them," he said. "So the Archimedean point on which every radical stands is a compromise. That is, I know, a necessity; it is also a contradiction."[72]

However, the fact that Marxian Socialism could not be a political force in America certainly heightened the contradiction. An American liberalism powerful and self-confident enough to welcome Marxian intellectuals into its inner councils was unlikely to alter its basic ideas or political appeals in the direction of Socialism. While Harrington argued that Socialists had to identify with the humane values of the liberals "in order to help them go beyond their present program," the historical reality was that practical American liberalism was considerably strengthened by its ability to accommodate the moral concerns of independent intellectuals like Harrington.

Like the other Catholic Worker liberals, Harrington brought from his Catholic Worker experience a special concern for society's poor and weak, a belief in the personal responsibility to work for social justice, and an awareness of the importance of basic ideas for society. Like them, too, he turned from the Worker's Christian utopianism to more practical and political modes of thought and action. The younger Harrington was more concerned than the others with finding his own metaphysical truth, and with linking his philosophy and his politics. He therefore turned from Catholicism to the alien doctrine of Marxism and practiced liberal politics in its name. In Marxism's intricate intellectual puzzles and international brotherhood he found a spiritual home; from its dissenting social perspectives he defined his role as a political gadfly; and from its intellectual interest to many Americans he developed a career as author and lecturer.

But it was indicative of the deep religious undercurrents in American life that America's leading Socialist in the mid-twentieth century was a figure far more easily understood in terms of Christianity and native American idealism than of Marxism. Harrington may have shed belief in God, but he had obviously been more affected by the teaching of his Catholic youth that "your life is in trust to something more important than yourself" and should be lived in service to others than by any dialectical metaphysics. In later years Harrington admitted that there was a "Pascalian cast to my Marxism," and called himself "an atheist fellow traveler of moderate Catholicism." Like his Socialist predecessors Norman Thomas and Eugene Debs, Harrington can be considered basically an American moral activist, using an imported political vocabulary to arouse national concern for serious social evils. And like them, the author of *The Other America* came to be admired by many of his countrymen not for his economic and social theories but for the sincere moral and personal commitment that inspired them.

By the end of 1965 the self-assurance of Catholic liberals was being eroded, replaced by a mood of doubt and criticism. With the War on Poverty being overshadowed by the Vietnam War, Harrington stopped advising officials and joined antiwar protests. The change was also very visible at *Commonweal*. In 1965 and 1966, as the editors suddenly awakened to the dangers of the nation's Vietnam involvement, the magazine's old dialogue with Catholic radicalism became more intense. Growing highly critical of many American foreign and domestic policies and even approving limited civil disobedience against the war, *Commonweal* underwent its own opening to the Left during the sixties. O'Gara and Skillin's *Commonweal* remained liberal at heart—it was much closer to Eugene McCarthy, one of its old contributors, than to Daniel Berrigan— but it looked with a new seriousness on the sort of Christian anarchism and pacifism that had long been represented by the Catholic Worker.[73]

These developments underscored what had already become apparent decades before: the primary intellectual importance of the Catholic Worker came not from any real social acceptance of its ideas, but in its special appeal to segments of the Catholic and intellectual worlds. Day and the Catholic Worker remained more or less on the fringes of American and Catholic life—more isolated in periods of apathy, less so in times of social concern—but many Catholic intellectuals understood that the movement's influence lay not in its numbers or even in its visibility to the world, but in its moral and spiritual integrity. Thus, even when it seemed outrageously wrong on particular matters, they paid attention to the Worker because they saw in it something authentically Christian and recognized the value of people who tried to live out their own ideals.

Respect for the Catholic Worker's absolutism increased over the years because Christian intellectuals were often acutely aware of the gap between their own theoretical commitments to promoting moral values in society and the difficulty of witnessing to the Gospel in a secular society that was skilled at taming religion and using it for its own purposes. Something of this concern appeared in a letter Ed Marciniak wrote to Father John Egan in 1954 as his Council on Working Life was preparing to move from its original spartan offices in a working-class district to sleek facilities on Chicago's Gold Coast: "It may be that what scares me is the fear of what Dorothy Day might say if she saw us comfortably settled along a stately parkway."[74]

Of course a healthy sense of failing to live up to Christian values could easily turn into mere guilt or a sentimental idealization of the Catholic Workers as pure witnesses to the Gospel. When John Cogley exclaimed on one occasion, "Dorothy Day is still in the slums, Thank God!" his gratitude for her commitment also suggested a certain willingness to leave the more difficult practice of religion to a few heroes.

Dorothy Day herself was sometimes hard on lukewarm Christianity, and she was especially disdainful of those who "prematurely canonized" her in order to celebrate Christian ideals they were unwilling to live out. There was no way, she believed, to avoid the personal cost of genuine religiosity. Yet Day's vision of the Gospel was broad enough to accept a diversity of Christian vocations. Some years after he had abandoned his own radicalism, Senator Eugene McCarthy encountered Day on a railroad platform and worried out loud, "I suppose you don't like me any more, Dorothy, now that I've gone into politics." "Nonsense," Day replied. "God puts people where He wants them." Certainly the Catholic liberals also tried to pursue the truth as they saw it. If their words and example seemed less demanding than the "harsh and dreadful love" of Dorothy Day and the Catholic Worker, they may also have been, like Dostoevski's Grand Inquisitor, more understanding of weak and imperfect humanity.

Reading the *Catholic Worker* in Union Square, circa 1937. By this time, it had a circulation of 110,000. Courtesy Marquette University Archives.

Dorothy Day in Seattle, on a speaking trip in 1942. Courtesy Marquette University Archives.

The Blessed Martin de Porres House of Hospitality, Harrisburg, Pa., which emphasized the interracial apostolate. Among its activities were day care centers for children. Courtesy Marquette University Archives.

A 1962 breadline in New York City. The Houses of Hospitality offered soup, bread, and coffee as basic fare. Photo by Vivian Cherry. Courtesy Marquette University Archives.

Inside the St. Joseph's House of Hospitality on Mott St., New York City. Notice the Ade Bethune mural, which depicts one of the Seven Works of Mercy, Visiting the Prisoner. Courtesy Marquette University Archives.

Reverend Charles O. Rice, left, helping an unidentified man unload furniture for the Pittsburgh House of Hospitality. Courtesy Marquette University Archives.

Helen Gott plowing at Maryfarm, Easton, Pa., sometime before World War II. Courtesy Marquette University Archives.

Peter Maurin at Maryfarm in 1941, eight years before his death. Courtesy Marquette University Archives.

Some residents of Maryfarm, Easton, Pa., in 1940. Third, fourth, and sixth from left (standing): Dorothy Day, Father Pacifique Roy, and Peter Maurin. Courtesy Marquette University Archives.

Dorothy Day, about 75, with an unidentified Catholic priest. Courtesy Marquette University Archives.

Ammon Hennacy, the ardent pacifist and Catholic convert who was "damn sure" the world could not change him. Courtesy Marquette University Archives.

Catholic Workers supporting the 1966 Farm Workers' Strike. This shows the last day of the march from Delano to Sacramento, California. Courtesy Marquette University Archives.

The second floor of St. Joseph's House of Hospitality on Chrystie St., New York City, awash with stacks of *Catholic Worker*s being prepared for mailing. Photo by William Carter. Courtesy Marquette University Archives.

CHAPTER SIX

The Catholic Worker and Peace

The peace witness within American Christianity was originally confined to a few small sects derived from the left wing of the Reformation: the Quakers, Mennonites, and Brethren. In the early twentieth century pacifism emerged from this sectarian base to make strong inroads in the mainline Protestant denominations. Among Roman Catholics, however, organized peace activity remained almost nonexistent in this country until the development of the substantial antiwar movement within American Catholicism during the 1960s. The Catholic Worker played an important role as the forerunner of this historic reaction in the Catholic Church and added new dimensions of Catholic thought and spirituality to postwar American pacifism.

Catholicism's long-standing resistance to antiwar sentiments had several causes: the Church's long historic entanglement with belligerent European political systems; its commitment to formalistic and hierarchical modes of thought that tended to justify established social practices like war; and the Counter-Reformation hostility to the Protestant and secular perfectionism that had produced most of the modern critique of organized collective violence. Such traditional factors counted for less in the transplanted Catholicism of America, but the eagerness of an immigrant Church to demonstrate loyalty to the nation made American Catholics even more immune to antiwar feelings based on religion. Even amidst the spread-eagle patriotism of the nineteenth century, Catholics developed a certain reputation for martial ardor. During the Civil War, for instance, the American flag flew conspicuously atop St. Patrick's Cathedral in New York, while inside Bishop John Hughes roused his immigrant flock to passionate heights of patriotism with militant sermons. During World War I Cardinal James Gibbons, the leader of the American hierarchy, told Catholics that "the primary

189

duty of a citizen now is loyalty to country. This loyalty is exhibited by
. . . an absolute and unreserved obedience to country, so that no ground
will be left after the ordeal is over upon which the enemies of the Church
might raise unfair charges." To Gibbons's dismay, there were a number
of Irish and German Catholic opponents of the war, but their opposition
was political rather than religious in character. In contrast to the visible
minority of Protestant ministers who refused to back the war on religious
grounds, only four Catholic conscientious objectors were recorded.[1]

Although it was generally believed by American Catholic
priests and draft boards that no "good Catholic" could ever oppose a call
to arms by "legitimate authority," orthodox Catholicism actually provided a strong basis for a religiously based antiwar stance in its teaching
of the "just war." The absolute pacifism of the primitive Christian
Church, like other features of the radical Gospel, had largely disappeared
from Catholicism after the Reformation, except in such traditional ves-
tiges as the prohibition on clerical arms bearing which was everywhere
observed in the West. The just war doctrine, however, had come down
intact to modern Catholicism as the Church's moral and intellectual
solution to the problem of how to reconcile the peacemaking Gospel of
Christ with the realities of human life.

The conversion of the Emperor Constantine marked the end of
pacifism as a distinctive sign of Christianity, but the strength of the
pacifist religious ideal became evident in the efforts of Christian writers
to preserve some of its elements. Picking up some hints from classical
writers, St. Augustine and other Church fathers redirected the original
Christian revulsion against war into a moral theory concerning when a
state might legitimately resort to arms. By emphasizing that the Gospel
required "not bodily actions but an inward disposition," St. Augustine
turned Christian moral attention away from the fact of war itself to the
moral intent and methods of warring states. In theory, at least, warfare
was thereby "civilized and spiritualized" by being confined within *mod-
eran inculpatae tutelae*—the limits imposed by a just defense. The Middle
Ages developed separate principles of *jus ad bellum* and *jus in bello*—the
proper moral causes of war and the proper moral methods of war—and
these in turn were elaborated by the late scholastics Vittoria and Suarez
in the sixteenth and seventeenth centuries. By the nineteenth century
these principles had been framed by Catholic moralists into sets of formal "just war requirements." A typical statement from the *Catholic Encyclopedia* of 1912 specified that a state could only go to war if its inner
disposition was defensive rather than aggressive, if its safety and honor
were genuinely threatened, and if the necessary means of violence were
kept in proper balance to the legitimate ends of the war—the so-called
principle of proportionality. There were also principles for the proper

conduct of war: no wanton violence, no vengeance or maltreatment of wounded or imprisoned enemies, no injury to innocent noncombatants, and so on.[2]

Such attempts to formulate an "ethic of war" were always problematic in Western history. The Church's periodic efforts to give substance to its moral theories were often undermined by unyielding belligerents and by the Church's own blemished record of military involvement, especially in crusades against infidels and heretics. Yet the belief that there ought to be some sort of moral limits on Western man's frequent bloodlettings, and the fact that states did often fight for limited aims with limited military means in ways that seemed to fit the just war requirements, meant that the Augustinian tradition was never entirely discarded. Especially in the twentieth century, as the Catholic Church's influence on international affairs became almost exclusively moral rather than political, the popes and other Catholic spokesmen found the just war tradition useful in trying to restrain the new forms of barbarism that accompanied modern war.

Twentieth-century American Catholics therefore had available to them an estimable body of moral teaching on the problem of war that they could attempt to apply to contemporary circumstances. The evolving Catholic antiwar movement in this country, which in many of its externals closely resembled its Protestant and secular counterparts, developed a distinctive intellectual history partly because of its intimate dialogue with the imposing heritage of the just war theory.

I

When the Catholic Worker was founded in 1933, there was no organized Catholic antiwar movement in the United States. In Europe World War I had produced the German Catholic Friedensbund and the French Ligue pour la Paix, mass-membership Catholic groups which attempted to reconcile old enemies and prevent future conflict. Associated with these organizations was a small but influential group of intellectuals and theologians who urged the Church to declare herself unequivocally against war. The best known were Father Johannes Ude of Graz University and the German Dominican Franziskus Stratmann, whose antiwar writings were later cited by American Catholic pacifists.[3]

In this country, however, the only Catholic peace activity came from the semiofficial Catholic Association for International Peace, which had been organized in 1927 as an agency of the Bishops' National Catholic Welfare Conference by a group of prominent clerics and lay persons, including John LaFarge, Vincent Ferrer, George Shuster, John Ryan, Raymond McGowan, and Carlton Hayes. Unlike the Friedensbund and the European Catholic peace agitators, however, the leaders of the CAIP disdained mass organization and antiwar action, preferring instead the more genteel peace activities prevalent in America and elsewhere before World War I. The CAIP confined itself to lobbying for American participation in the League of Nations and the World Court and advocating "peace education" and "international cooperation and arbitration" in Catholic circles, while it carefully avoided any taint of association with the more strident and political antiwar elements in the National Council for the Prevention of War. Like many other established peace groups in the interwar years, the CAIP moved easily from support of international organization and cooperation to advocacy of collective security against powers hostile to America. By 1937 it had largely turned to promoting the cause of Anglo-American cooperation among American Catholics. Naturally, the CAIP endorsed World War II, and its strong support in later years for the Cold War, the Korean War, and the Vietnam War, as well as its close ties to the Department of Defense and the Georgetown University Foreign Service School meant that its subsequent labors for peace seldom departed from official definitions and policies.[4]

In contrast to the CAIP's cautious and eminently respectable peace activity, the Catholic Worker's pacifism was at first a simple corollary of its Gospel-based social radicalism. Critics later charged that pacifism was a late innovation in the movement, but the evidence indicates that opposition to war was a definite though minor theme of CW publicity from the beginning, even though few activist energies went in that direction. In October 1933, a group of Catholic Workers attended a U.S. Congress Against War meeting as "representatives of Catholic pacifism." Within a year the *Catholic Worker* had attacked nationalism, the arms race, and imperialism, as well as German anti-Semitism and Mexican government persecution of Catholics. Stratmann's works, particularly *The Church and War*, were favorably reviewed and quoted in the *Catholic Worker*. The movement's emphasis on nonviolence was occasionally attacked by Catholics who cited the Church's "official position" on war and by leftists who saw in the Worker's general opposition to violence the proof of its bourgeois sentimentality and class betrayal.[5]

When Mussolini invaded Ethiopia in 1935 the *Catholic Worker* antagonized its Italian readers by criticizing the aggression, though it conceded that Italian imperialism was no worse—only later—than its British and French counterparts. The Italians' bitterness was, however, merely a preview of the storm that broke the next year when the *Catholic Worker*, *Commonweal*, and the diocesan *Buffalo Echo* became the only

Catholic voices to oppose Franco's cause in Spain—the closest thing Catholicism has known to a crusade in modern times. Under banner headlines like "Rebels Did Not Exhaust Peaceful Means; Both Sides Fight Like Savages," the *Catholic Worker* printed articles on the conflict by prominent European Catholics including Stratmann, Emmanuel Mounier, Jacques Maritain, and Alfredo Mendizabel, whose neutrality or opposition to Franco was little known to U.S. Catholics.[6]

The sharp debates provoked by the movement's stand in the Spanish conflict led, in 1937, to the first active organization of Catholic Worker pacifism. A group of CW pacifists led by William Callahan formed "Pax," modeling it on a similar group already active in England. Working out of the New York House of Hospitality, the group organized chapters among Catholic Workers and their sympathizers around the country, thereby setting off the first of the disagreements over pacifism that eventually split the movement. Callahan's Pax enrolled about two hundred members who agreed to the vague goal of removing "the cause of war in themselves and society." Awareness of this initial organized Catholic peace effort did not extend much beyond the little circle of Catholic radicals, and Pax had no observable impact on the Catholic community at large. But the group successfully prompted the *Catholic Worker*'s further discussion of events in Europe and the prospects of war, a discussion which revealed the weak intellectual position of Catholic pacifists at that time.

As with other of the movement's positions, Catholic Worker pacifism derived at bottom from Dorothy Day's simple personal commitment. Her association with the pacifists in World War I, her hatred of class violence against and by workers, and her acceptance of the radical Gospel injunctions against force, all contributed to her opposition to war. At the time of the Spanish Civil War, she wrote up a "Catholic Worker Stand on Force," which said, "As long as men trust to force, only a more savage and brutal force will overcome the enemy. We must thus use his own weapons, and we must be sure our own force is more bestial than his. . . . Therefore we cannot sit back and say, 'Human nature being what it is, you cannot overcome an adversary by love.'" But as usual, too, Day found followers in her movement who could elaborate these basic convictions in an attempt to develop a Catholic case against war. The first *Catholic Worker* writers on the subject, William Callahan, Arthur Sheehan, and Paul Hanley Furfey, developed a defense of the movement's position that combined the radical Gospel pacifism of the early Church, a legalistic application of the just war theory, and some of the crude economic determinism of the 1930s that blamed war on businessmen and arms merchants. Furfey was the writer who most clearly based the antiwar case on the Gospel counsels of perfection. "The Prince of Peace would rather that we suffer injury than protect our national rights by violence," he contended. Critically examining the Church's history of tolerating and even endorsing war, he urged abandonment of the "Constantinian compromise" with the warmaking state and a return to the eschatological pacifist vision of the early saints and church fathers.[7]

Other *Catholic Worker* writers found in the just war theory alone a sufficient basis for a modern Catholic rejection of war. Whether wars had ever been just was moot, argued Arthur Sheehan and other Catholic Workers in the late thirties; it was now clear that warfare could not be waged according to the traditional criteria, particularly those concerning pure intentions and the protection of noncombatants. Detailed evidence from the Spanish Civil War and other recent conflicts was submitted to show that no matter how much theoretical right lay with one side or the other—and both sides in modern war typically asserted the complete justice of their cause—the vast destructiveness of technological weaponry guaranteed that no side could pursue even self-defense without perpetrating a greater moral evil—a violation of the just war principle of proportionality.[8]

Before the Workers were forced to clarify their stand by the approach of actual war, even the absolute nonresisters in the movement used such applications of the well-established just war teaching to gain a hearing for their views within the Church at large.

In the years before World War II, the Catholic Worker made a concerted effort to build an effective Catholic peace constituency. Rather than attempting to witness to the Church at large, the Catholic Worker pacifists could easily have chosen to stress only the individual Christian's personal opposition to participation in violence—the traditional "conscientious objection" of the historic Protestant peace churches. Yet the Catholic Worker, influenced by both the Catholic and radical dislike for purely personal or internal solutions to moral problems, tended to subordinate the matter of individual abstention from war to the larger question of stopping war itself.

Therefore, as the war issue became salient in American politics in 1938 and 1939, the movement's energies and propaganda were increasingly directed to arousing public opposition to belligerency. The Catholic Worker publicized the occasional papal statements urging negotiation among the powers. It brought noted European antiwar Catholics like Eric Gill to the United States to oppose war preparations. Day's speaking tours, too, focused increasingly on the danger of war. She warned audiences from the Sisters of the Sacred Heart to U.S. Naval cadets of the harm another great war would do to the cause of religion, and urged them to "work and pray for peace." When the European war did break out in September 1939, some Workers tried to organize a "Non-Participation League" to boycott war related products and jobs. The League was notably ineffective, because even the Catholic Worker's best friends in the working class were not willing to sacrifice hard-won economic positions for abstract moral goals. But it did attract attention and win some support from two members of the hierarchy, James Duffy of Buffalo and James McNicholas of Cincinnati, who opposed American war preparations and called for "a mighty league of Catholic objectors" to the impending conflict.[9]

During 1939 and 1940 the proposed Selective Service Act provided the most politically and religiously attractive focal point for Catholic antiwar sentiment. "To fight war we must fight conscription," Day stated. The *Catholic Worker* noted that Catholic theorists of various political persuasions had generally opposed peacetime conscription because, as an innovation of the French Revolution, it supposedly epitomized the modern secular state's "Rousseauist" tendency to assume absolute control over its citizens' lives. In an exhaustive series of articles in the *Catholic Worker* in 1940, Monsignor Barry O'Toole of Catholic University, a former member of the CW-related Catholic Radical Alliance in Pittsburgh, developed with scholastic thoroughness the objections of Catholic moral theology to a permanent system of conscription. Selective Service could never be endorsed by Catholics, O'Toole argued, because "the citizen cannot be forced to be free by his government, whether in the form of a totalitarian party or the liberalistic majority." Quoting Aquinas, Vittoria, and Franziskus Stratmann, among others, O'Toole put Selective Service to the test of the just war teaching and concluded that no war in which men were forced to fight against their will could pass the traditional criteria. Although O'Toole artfully sidestepped any suggestion of absolute pacifism, he seemed well aware that, under modern conditions, opposing all war fought by conscripts would mean opposing all war.[10]

In July 1940 the Catholic Worker joined a number of peace groups in carrying the anticonscription message to Congress, which was then considering the proposed Selective Service Act. O'Toole, Day, and Joseph Zarella, a young draft-age Catholic Worker, testified before a House Military Affairs Committee that conscription was contrary to the teachings of the Church fathers and the popes and that some young Catholics could not conscientiously enter the Armed Services under compulsion. Even while urging defeat of the bill, however, the Catholic Worker representatives asked that it include liberal provisions for individual conscientious objection, so that COs besides those from the "historic peace churches"—Quakers, Brethren, and Mennonites—could be recognized.[11]

This dual emphasis in the Workers' testimony reflected the basic tension in the aims of politically conscious pacifists at that time. Pacifists wanted to influence public opinion in order to prevent war; yet they also wanted to protect their own vulnerable position in case war actually came. The request for the safety valve of conscientious objection represented, in effect, the beginning of these pacifists' wartime retreat from politics. Their decision was realistic, for the passage of the Burke-Wadsworth Selective Service Act in August 1940 signaled the effective end of pacifist political efforts to stop the drift toward war. With the rest of society about to embark on the course they regarded as morally wrong, the pacifists had to stop trying to influence others and turn inward to shield their own convictions and serve their own constituency.

But even while they muted their public propaganda and looked to protect their own constituency, some radical pacifists like the Catholic Workers were determined that their recognition of the fact of war would not be taken for quietist acquiescence and that their personal actions would still witness their beliefs to the larger society. Uncertain how pacifists would be treated under the new law, Day wrote, "We will expect our Catholic Workers to oppose, alone and singlehandedly if necessary . . . the militaristic system and its propaganda." Acknowledging that the movement's work would be jeopardized by its stand, she nevertheless asked "how we can sacrifice our principles or remain silent in the face of this gigantic error."[12]

The most immediate impact of the impending war on the Catholic Worker occurred not outside but within. Day's continued opposition to the draft and American war preparations split the movement and altered its emphasis. In 1939 and 1940 the thirty or so Worker Houses were torn by debate over pacifism and the draft, specifically over the radical antiwar propaganda appearing in the New York *Catholic Worker*. The Detroit, Cleveland, and Boston Catholic Workers supported Day's stand; Chicago, Seattle, and Los Angeles were opposed. Milwaukee, Pittsburgh, and others were divided. In several places, such as Buffalo and St. Louis, a precarious truce was maintained only by forbidding all discussion of the issue.[13]

In this tense atmosphere, Day's August 1940 open letter to all Catholic Workers asserting the centrality of pacifism to the movement was bound to have a shattering impact. Although she tried to soften the edict by demanding only distribution of the New York paper and not complete conformity on the question, her ultimatum "nestled like a bomb" in every Catholic Worker group and House in the country, as John Cogley said. Dozens of Workers, including prominent local leaders like Cogley, H. A. Reinhold, Jerome Drolet, and Emerson Hynes were dismayed by what they saw as the straitjacketing of a broad social move ment by a narrow stand on a single issue. Reinhold, the director of the Seattle House, asked Day "if you can take the name of the whole movement, which stands for more things than conscription [*sic*], and tag it on this one issue, throwing out all those who do not agree with you." Nor did the irony of a display of power by pacifists escape their opponents' notice. They accused Day of adopting "dictator methods" and laying down "party lines" to purge dissenters.[14]

Day was shaken by the reaction and tried to deny that she had used her authority to impose a doctrinal orthodoxy on the movement. But she remained adamant on the point of distribution of the paper. The pacifist-oriented Easton Retreat for Catholic Workers in August 1940, and the subsequent departure of Cogley and others from the movement, indicated that the dissidents would be tolerated only as a silent minority.

Several of the nonpacifist Houses of Hospitality closed immediately after the crisis. A few tried to operate for a time within Day's restrictions. Others dropped the names Catholic Worker and House of Hospitality while carrying on the work much as before. But after Pearl Harbor the number of Houses dropped rapidly, and the *Catholic Worker* lost over 100,000 in circulation. By the end of 1942 only sixteen Houses remained in operation. By January 1945, just ten were left. It is difficult to say precisely how many Houses closed because of the split over pacifism, and how many because of the shortage of manpower and the dramatically lessened numbers of unemployed. The factors were in any case closely related. For many nonpacifists and pacifists alike, the war emergency took priority over other kinds of social agitation, while the end of the Depression lessened the urgency of such work. Only those Catholic Workers who had adopted Day's whole radical Gospel ideology felt the necessity of carrying on the movement's complete program in the drastically altered circumstances. In the remaining Houses where the "Catholic Worker idea" still burned brightly, the work was managed as well as possible by women, war resisters, and those exempt from the draft by reason of age, physical handicap, or some other circumstance.[15]

Given the magnitude of the internal crisis and the altered social circumstances during and after the war, it is remarkable that the Catholic Worker survived at all; yet Day and her most ardent followers continued with the movement and the paper without fundamental changes. After World War II the movement differed in size and emphasis from what it had been in the thirties, but not in basic ideology or character.

Besides the development of the Catholic peace witness itself, the main effect of the pacifist emphasis was to underscore the radicalism of the movement's dissent. Although a radical minority, the Catholic Worker in the thirties had been a growing movement that reflected some of the broad social concerns of American Catholicism. While its radical social critique was unacceptable to most Catholics, the Catholic Worker's Gospel-based concern for the poor was in keeping with the recognized Christian ideals of the "counsels of perfection."

But pacifism, as Day's opponents in the movement recognized, was a much narrower principle, and one more out of line with the prevalent "mind of the Church." Striking as it did at the central political values of patriotism and national defense, it was not even granted the status of an "ideal" by the majority of Americans, particularly Roman Catholics. And instead of exerting a broad appeal, pacifism tended to attract only persons with a particular moral sensibility. In the postwar years, Day and other *Catholic Worker* writers continually stressed the comprehensive character of the movement, insisting that pacifism was no more the whole of the "Catholic Worker idea" than soup lines or unionization had been in the thirties. Through their efforts the *Catholic Worker* remained a broad intellectual forum, and the movement stayed involved in a variety of social causes. Catholic Workers fought for racial integration in the north in the forties, and participated in the southern civil rights movement in the fifties and sixties. They defended the civil rights of Communists and other dissenters during the McCarthy era, opposed capital punishment, and encouraged a variety of decentralist social experiments in the United States and abroad. Labor remained a concern, but it was now only small marginal unions or minorities that attracted direct Worker support: Catholic cemetery workers, domestic workers, retail employees, California farm workers, and so on. And of course the problems of the poor—unemployment, food, housing, health, day care—were still a primary concern, reinforced by the daily work in the Houses of Hospitality. Through its comprehensive ideology and diverse activities the Catholic Worker retained its identity as a broad social movement rather than a single-issue group. But after 1945 it was the issue of pacifism that most effectively represented the Catholic Worker's radical Gospel idealism.

II

With the beginning of Selective Service call-ups in 1941, the draft was no longer a question of public policy, but a matter for highly personal decision by each Catholic Worker eligible for induction. While the nonpacifists went into the military willingly, denying that conscription was coercive under the circumstances, the pacifists had to struggle with both conscience and the authorities. A number of Workers eventually chose to accept noncombatant status in the military, where they served as medics and ambulance drivers. A few extreme pacifists, strongly supported by Dorothy Day, favored refusal to register and outright resistance to the draft, which would lead to imprisonment. But most draft-age Workers were unwilling either to enter the military as noncombatants or to commit a felony, particularly because the new law appeared to provide a satisfactory option for them in the provisions for conscientious objection.[16]

As passed by Congress, the Burke-Wadsworth Act provided for conscientious objection to all war on religious grounds. Although this represented a change from the harsh World War I treatment of COs, the language of the statute made successful application extremely difficult for all but traditional peace-church objectors. Catholics, Jews, and non-peace-church Protestants were not excluded as they had been during World War I, but in the absence of an official pacifist stand by the applicant's church, each individual had to persuade a skeptical local draft board of his eligibility for the 4-E classification. Unsuccessful 4-E applicants faced the choice of military service or prison (though noncombatant status was sometimes offered as a "test of sincerity" by local boards). Among the Catholic pacifists imprisoned for draft violations were the poet Robert Lowell and novelist J. F. Powers; Powers had ties to the Minnesota Catholic Worker group and wrote for the *Catholic Worker*.

Even those Catholic objectors who successfully attained recognition as COs faced enormous difficulties. In close cooperation with the historic peace churches represented on the National Service Board for Religious Objectors, Selective Service organized a system of Civilian Public Service Camps (CPS) where recognized 4-E registrants would perform unpaid "labor in the national interest." The traditional pacifist sects and the mainstream Protestant denominations provided counsel and financial assistance for their members in CPS camps, but Catholic objectors were left isolated and vulnerable, with little encouragement and no financial assistance from their Church.[17]

Dorothy Day disagreed with registration and participation in CPS because, as she told one group of conscientious objectors in 1941, she considered it "a form of cooperation with the war and conscription." Yet she also committed the Catholic Worker to the support of those objectors who worked within the law because she respected their decision as an equally conscientious one. Beginning in 1939/40, the Catholic Worker provided information to potential conscientious objectors, and after the law went into effect, it developed a small network of sympathetic priests who would support Catholic claims before draft boards.

In mid-1940 this work was taken over by the Association of Catholic Conscientious Objectors, the successor to Pax. Essentially a Catholic Worker "front" run by Arthur Sheehan out of the Mott Street headquarters, the ACCO hoped to provide support and mutual assistance for Catholic pacifists. Original expectations for the organization were high. A survey of 54,000 Catholic college students in November 1939 had shown 36 percent claiming they would become conscientious objectors if the United States entered the war. Between September 1940 and April 1941, four hundred Catholics sent their names in to ACCO as war objectors, and Sheehan anticipated that at least several hundred more would register in the next year.[18]

Based partly on these high expectations, the ACCO announced in April 1941 that it was exploring the possibility of sponsoring a Catholic Civilian Public Service Camp like those run by other denominations. Although ACCO was the only nonofficial group participating with church agencies in the National Service Board for Religious Objectors, its proposal for a Catholic CPS camp was accepted by Selective Service. In July 1941 the first contingent of Catholic objectors, led by Catholic Worker Dwight Larrowe as camp director, arrived at an abandoned Forest Service camp in Stoddard, New Hampshire. Stoddard served as the primary center for Catholic conscientious objectors until November 1942, when the men were transferred to a supposedly better camp near Warner, New Hampshire.[19]

The Catholic CO camps were plagued with problems from the beginning. The expectations of substantial numbers of Catholic 4-E registrants proved false. Most Catholic "antiwar" sentiment had really been isolationist or anti-English, and it declined rapidly in 1941. Even true Catholic objectors had great difficulty getting their claims accepted by local draft boards. As a result, only some one hundred and fifty Catholic objectors were officially registered with CPS. Of these, sixty-one were assigned to the Stoddard-Warner camp by Selective Service. Although "Camp Simon," as Stoddard-Warner was dubbed, did serve as a symbolic focal point for Catholic antiwar dissent during World War II, the camp experience mocked the idealistic expectations of its founders. During their time in the remote mountain site, the Catholic COs endured rough conditions, poverty, loneliness, and conflict. The unpaid "work of national importance" at Stoddard-Warner consisted of largely make-work "fire prevention" and wood chopping. Unlike the well-financed camps run by the Quakers, Mennonites, and others, Camp Simon depended for funds entirely on the Catholic Worker, which was, as usual, poor and deeply in debt. Special appeals in the *Catholic Worker* brought in canned goods and clothing, but the men's meager diets were relieved only by food they raised themselves and occasional charitable gifts from Protestant CO camps.[20]

The isolation and poverty of the Catholic pacifists' camps underscored the loneliness of their social and religious position. "The Catholic CO knew himself to be in disagreement with the overwhelming majority of his fellow communicants on a critical public question," wrote Gordon Zahn, a sociologist who came to Camp Simon as a young Catholic pacifist in 1942. Alienated from country, Church, community, and often even their families, the Catholic COs struggled to give some social meaning to their lonely dissent. In several articles and a recent book, Zahn has provided a detailed social portrait of life in Camp Simon, with an emphasis on the fierce arguments among those who based their pacifism on various debatable "Catholic" grounds. Personal and intellectual conflict was heightened by the presence of non-Catholics and nonpracticing Catholics who resented the more pious Catholics, and by a half-dozen Coughlinites who had been classified 4-E by local draft boards even though their objection to the war was that the United States was fighting on the wrong side. Altogether, Camp Simon provided a hothouse atmosphere for the development of radical Catholic thought about the problem of war, even though the camp was regarded as a scandal by those who thought pacifists should be able to live in harmony at least among themselves.[21]

Warner was closed in March 1943, and the Catholic COs scattered to a number of locations, after Selective Service officials determined that the men were underfed. The officials were also apparently influenced in their decision by a letter from Bishop John Petersen of New Hampshire who said that "the Catholic Church has declared that participation in this war is an essential duty. While it respects the conscientious opinion of any individual who may think otherwise, it does not make the stand of such individuals its stand." Always sensitive to the possibility of public criticism of the CPS program, Selective Service officials took the local bishop's letter as a signal that the Catholic hierarchy was opposed to the existence of any Catholic CO camp and revoked ACCO's status as a sponsoring agency.[22]

Fearing complete dispersal, the Catholic COs successfully petitioned CPS for reassignment in small "detached units" in nonprofit institutions rather than individual relocation to other forest camps. Most Camp Simon veterans were assigned in groups of a dozen or so to places like the Alexian Brothers Hospital in Chicago and the Rosewood State

Training School for the Mentally Handicapped in Maryland. In these locations ACCO gained new life. Once relieved of the impossible assignment of trying to finance and operate the labor camps, the group could concentrate on its primary task of developing a collective Catholic peace witness. The new assignments were difficult and unpaid, but the work was clearly of social benefit, and the possibilities for collective action were more promising than in the New Hampshire woods. During the last years of the war, the young Catholic intellectuals at Rosewood and elsewhere made ACCO into an effective liaison among the scattered Catholic COs and tried to turn it into a practical expression of pacifist idealism. They publicized cases of hardship and maltreatment of COs in camps and prisons, worked to improve the treatment of the mentally ill and retarded under their care, and tried to formulate principles for a new kind of peace witness within American Catholicism.[23]

The medium for the Catholic pacifists' reflections during this period was the *Catholic CO*, the ACCO quarterly that appeared from 1943 to 1948. There and in the *Catholic Worker* they tried to come to better intellectual terms with the novel phenomenon of American Catholic pacfism. Their major accomplishment was a decisive break with the just war tradition. Although the Catholic Worker's personalist appeal to the radical Gospel had already pointed the way to such a rejection, a more elaborate rationale was clearly required to undermine the intellectual prestige of the just war.[24]

From the standpoint of the just war theory, World War II presented sharp paradoxes. On the one hand the war against Hitler appeared to be precisely the sort of righteous and defensive cause the theory allowed. Even most pacifists acknowledged that if any war had a just cause, it was probably the anti-Nazi conflict. But just war theory required that the means of war also be just, even against the most evil enemy. Yet before World War II was over, the Allies had resorted to policies like the mass-terror bombing of civilians that would have condemned their cause according to a strict application of the just war criteria. Significantly, a small number of nonpacifist Catholic moral theologians, notably the Jesuit John C. Ford of Catholic University, followed precisely this dogmatically formal line of reasoning to a moral condemnation of the American cause, thereby setting off a minor theological uproar.[25]

The younger Catholics associated with the ACCO, while applauding the "consistent" application of the just war criteria to the Allied cause by Ford and others, were increasingly persuaded that the just war theory could not bear the heavy moral burden laid on it. The formal and legalistic moral reckoning demanded by the just war tradition was academically distant from the real world of irrational passions generated by war, they contended, while psychologically the theory was incapable of inspiring a sustained antiwar movement under the best of circumstances. Men who believed war fundamentally acceptable, argued the *Catholic CO*, would seldom apply strict moral criteria to their own nation-states. They would, instead, multiply casuistic distinctions— such as that between "intended" and "unintended" civilian casualties of strategic bombing—in order to avoid opposing their own state during wartime. The historic function of the just war theory, the *Catholic CO* argued, had been to provide moral rationalizations for the belligerence of the state, and it could never form an adequate basis for a significant reconsideration of the Catholic attitude toward war. One must either accept or reject modern war as it is, the argument concluded, and not try to judge it solely according to a moral theory developed in premodern conditions.[26]

Such hardening opposition to the whole rationally intricate just war tradition was part of an increasingly radical mood that swept through the whole Civilian Public Service system in 1944 and 1945. Most conscientious objectors had initially accepted their classification on the assumption that it represented an honorable way to witness to the sincerity of their pacifist convictions while performing a useful service to American society as provided by the law. But their experiences in CPS suggested that the real purpose of their classification and assignment was that stated by Selective Service Director General Lewis B. Hershey to a congressional committee: "The CO is best handled if no one ever hears of him." Recalling its unhappy experiences with imprisoned religious pacifists during World War I, the government had apparently hit on a more agreeable solution in which the historic peace churches would "cooperate" in helping "solve" the "CO problem." The mostly meaningless unpaid labor in the isolated forest camps, the continued hardship and poverty faced by CO families, the thinly veiled military control of the ostensibly "civilian" system, and the constant efforts of the historic peace churches in the National Service Board for Religious Objectors to "walk the second mile" in avoiding direct conflict with the government—all these factors contributed to a deepening conviction among many COs that an effective antiwar witness was impossible within the CPS system.[27]

At Camp Simon some of the Catholic COs had already engaged in periodic work stoppages. Usually these were to protest specific grievances, but they actually reflected a growing disaffection with the entire CPS setup. By the time the Warner camp closed, a minority of the objectors were in open rebellion against CPS, with particular bitterness reserved for the pacifist leadership in Washington. Next to some of the nonreligious war resisters in CPS, the Catholics developed a reputation as the greatest "troublemakers" in the system. Throughout the history of CPS, Zahn noted, much of the agitation that disturbed the tranquility of CPS found its origin, or certainly its most vocal support, in Catholic camps and units.[28]

Beginning in 1944, a series of militant demonstrations, walkouts, and hunger strikes rocked CPS camps across the country, as well as the federal prisons where noncooperators were held. The Catholic COs decided not to strike on the grounds that their work in nonprofit institutions genuinely served the needy, but they shared the growing rejection of the system. "The CPS was built on lies and has brought about a form of slavery incompatible with Christian ethic," editorialized the *Catholic CO*. The protests escalated when COs continued to be held in camps and prisons after the end of World War II in August. In October 1945, the members of ACCO voted three to one to end all cooperation with the National Service Board, and along with the Quakers and Evan Thomas's War Resisters League, to organize active resistance to the CO system. They could no longer, they said, support "a system where pacifists aid in the smooth functioning of conscription, and thus make things easier for the warmakers."[29]

III

The Catholic pacifists' disillusioning experience with the government during World War II convinced them that a postwar Catholic peace movement must be less piously moralistic and more politically radical. The initial opposition to war had turned many modest young Catholics into radical advocates of sweeping social change. As the pacifists returned to American society in 1946, Arthur Sheehan observed, they "were agreed that something drastic must be done to reform the social order . . . even when, as they often were, they were the only persons in their home towns who dared to be different." The mood of radical alienation from prevailing American Catholic opinion was reflected in the pages of the *Catholic CO*, which in its last years increasingly tied pacifism to radical labor and racial causes. It called for the infiltration of society by the "Catholic extremist," defined as "one who goes to such riotous excess he is called a fool for Christ's sake as he shakes up moderate, sane, dull American society." Even Catholic COs who disagreed with some of the anarchist articles in the journal were willing to say that "the Christian must now become a political radical . . . [and] tear down the new idols, the golden calf of materialistic capitalism, the Moloch of nationalism, the hydra-headed monster of bourgeois respectability." [30]

Few of the pacifists who left the camps in 1947/48 stuck by these militant declarations, although some became socially progressive gadflies in their local parishes and communities. It was the small group of intellectuals associated with the *Catholic CO* who did the most to develop a broader foundation for postwar American Catholic pacifism. The best known of these was Gordon Zahn, who combined an academic career in sociology with peace writing and political activism. In Zahn's scholarly studies of the Catholic Church's relation to war, notably *German Catholics and Hitler's Wars*, *In Solitary Witness*, and *War, Conscience, and Dissent*, as well as in his numerous articles in Catholic and non-Catholic periodicals, he made the case for a new Catholic peace witness in intense but reasonable tones. Personally irenic and attentive to the whole range of opinion in the American and European Church, Zahn was immune to the emotional ups and downs of the more passionate antiwar activists. As the respected scholar of the postwar Catholic peace movement, he became a sturdy bridge between the broad concern for peace that slowly developed in respectable sectors of American Catholicism in the postwar era and the more intense and boisterous commitment of the radical pacifist minority. Zahn's unspectacular but effective efforts in a wide range of peace activities provided a badly needed stability and intellectual depth to the Catholic antiwar cause in America. [31]

If Zahn represented the sober and scholarly side of Catholic pacifism in the postwar years, its defiantly radical wing was exemplified by Robert Ludlow. The son of a Scranton, Pennsylvania, coal miner, Ludlow became a supporter of the Catholic Worker after hearing Day and Maurin speak at St. Thomas College in 1937. After being fired from a high school teaching position for criticizing U.S. foreign policy, he worked as a librarian at Catholic University until he was drafted into CPS in 1942. Ludlow's wartime pieces in the *Catholic Worker* and *Catholic CO* earned him a reputation as the most articulate radical among the Catholic pacifists, and after his release from CPS in 1947, he headed for St. Joseph's House of Hospitality in New York.

In the late forties and early fifties, Ludlow was the dominant intellectual presence at the *Catholic Worker*. In many ways he was the perfect Catholic Worker propagandist: steeped in traditional Catholic philosophy and culture (he was of the Eastern Rite); conversant with contemporary history, politics, psychology, and economics; and a skillful debater in the scholastic style that still dominated Catholic moral reflection at that time. Day herself called him "doctrinaire and dogmatic, and yet the mildest of mortals, meek and disciplined in his personal life."

While admitting that she did not always follow his detailed arguments, Day strongly endorsed Ludlow's attempt to establish a firmer intellectual foundation for the Catholic Worker's anarchism and pacifism. Ludlow's elaborate arguments for a perfectionist Catholic anarchism followed the lines of Paul Hanley Furfey's views in the thirties, but went further in assessing the Catholic Worker's relation to prior Catholic social thought. In condemning anarchism, Ludlow contended, earlier Catholic theologians and philosophers had failed to distinguish sufficiently between society and the state, and between the state as an administrative social arrangement and the state as a belligerent, self-aggrandizing power. An anarchism that preserved social cohesion and authority while discarding coercive state violence was at least permissible according to Catholic social theory, Ludlow argued, and might even come to be the Church's preferred form of society.[32]

While Ludlow's interpretations of Catholic Worker personalism essentially built on longstanding principles of the movement, his contribution to Catholic pacifism was original, and made an enduring contribution to the Worker's religious social vision. Ludlow was the first Catholic pacifist really to understand and appropriate the Gandhian theory of nonviolence as a comprehensive method of religious peacemaking. He was also the first to see Catholic pacifism not simply as the witness of a small minority to the counsels of perfection, but as the forerunner of a possibly historic shift in the whole Catholic Church's attitude toward war.

Gandhi's general ideas were already familiar to American pacifists in the thirties, especially after the publication of Richard Gregg's seminal *The Power of Nonviolence* in 1935. The spectacular success of nonviolent techniques in disrupting CPS and the federal prison system at the end of the war, as well as Gandhi's final achievement of Indian independence, contributed to the enormous prestige and appeal of these ideas in the postwar years. Many younger American pacifists like David McReynolds, Bayard Rustin, Roy Kepler, and David Dellinger enthusiastically publicized and experimented with Gandhian techniques as weapons for bringing about "revolutionary" social change.

Like A. J. Muste and Martin Luther King among Protestant pacifists, Ludlow saw an essentially religious core in Gandhian nonviolence and attempted to interpret the meaning of its principles for Western Christians. For most adherents of nonviolent direct action, Gandhianism was attractive because it promised to be both politically effective and morally uncompromised. But for Ludlow and the other religious activists, Gandhianism was appealing because it rested on an essentially spiritual vision of life.

In a series of articles in the *Catholic Worker* in 1949 and 1950, Ludlow hailed *satyagraha* as "a new *Christian* way of social change." *Satyagraha*, he said, incorporated the religious view of the sanctity of life and the dignity of the person that was at the heart of Christ's peace teaching, but went beyond most earlier Christian pacifism's individualism, passivity, and sentimentality. By acknowledging and, indeed, insisting upon the elements of power and conflict in social relations, *satyagraha* effectively refuted the standard critiques of Christian pacifism. Gandhianism suggested that it was possible to resist violent power, not by responding in kind or by helplessly turning the other cheek, but by transforming it through the spiritual practices of disciplined social struggle and suffering. "*Satyagraha* does not mean cooperation with evil," wrote Ludlow. "It does not subscribe to the false concept of love which reduces it to imbecility." Yet Gandhianism also insisted on the essential humanity of one's opponents and thus avoided the "Manichean moralism" which, Ludlow observed, tended to afflict pacifists of all kinds.

> In the international sphere pacifists take the correct stand of refusing to divide people and nations into absolute good and evil, yet in our social habits we only too easily slip into regarding ourselves as more virtuous than our non-pacifist fellows, of being excessively moralistic. We must strive to achieve a non-moralistic attitude, at the same time not surrendering our principles out of a mistaken charity, in which case we would have no opinions on anything.[33]

Like other advocates of the new nonviolence, Ludlow emphasized that it was especially appropriate for a peace movement, because the very means of nonviolent struggle against warmakers exemplified how the end of abolishing war among nations might be accomplished.

Ludlow also provided Catholic pacifists with a more satisfactory interpretation of their own increasingly insistent departure from the Church's prevailing positions on war. While some pacifists saw their position only as a witness of personal conscience, Ludlow argued that war would turn out to be an instance of Cardinal Newman's theory concerning the development of Catholic dogma: The Church arrives at many tentative judgments on the way to truth and may even tolerate for a time such un-Christian practices as human slavery, which was long permitted but eventually condemned. In such an evolutionary course, Newman had observed, some within the Church must risk going beyond the official positions of the time. Ludlow argued that this was true of war and that Catholic pacifists should not fear to differ with leaders of the Church on a matter not defined in terms of formal doctrine. "We act in accordance with the belief that war will eventually be condemned," he wrote, "and must try by our actions to add our very small contributions to the time when pacifism may be the norm of society." The moral progressivism of this approach appealed to American Catholic pacifists, who wanted to be not only prophetic but effective. The idea that their radical pacifist witness was not only a counsel of perfection intended for a few saints, but somehow represented the true "mind of the Church" better than its current voices, gradually shaped the pacifists' self-understanding and relations with their fellow Catholics.[34]

Part of the reason for Ludlow's optimism was that the American peace movement as a whole experienced a brief flowering from 1946 to 1949. The dropping of the atomic bomb shocked many Americans who had never questioned conventional war into some form of "nuclear pacifism." In the immediate postwar period, calls for the end of nuclear testing, the abolition of atomic weapons, and even the dissolution of the sovereign nation-state itself were heard from reputable quarters of society. Newly formed groups like the Federation of Atomic Scientists, the United World Federalists, and the World Citizen movement gained membership and public attention. Pacifists like the Catholic Workers benefited momentarily from this mood of national anxiety, for their pessimistic predictions about the threat of yet another war—this time with the Soviet Union—seemed to be coming true.[35]

Nevertheless, the activities and concerns of the absolute pacifists remained somewhat removed from the popular antiwar movement, which tended to play heavily on public fears about the new nuclear weapons. Radical pacifists were the only members of the peace movement who spoke more of the immorality of bombing others than of the danger of being bombed. Reflecting a more pessimistic assessment of the world political situation, as well as their own wartime experience, the pacifists also concentrated their energies on opposing conscription rather than the issues of atomic arms control and world government.

In 1946 and 1947 the Catholic Worker joined for the first time with other non-Catholic pacifist groups—the Protestant Fellowship of Reconciliation, the non-religious War Resisters League, the radical Peacemakers, and the Committee on Nonviolent Revolution—in a campaign against President Truman's proposed peacetime draft and Universal Military Training (UMT). The Catholic Worker printed and distributed 150,000 copies of Father John Hugo's booklet *The Immorality of Conscription*, originally published in the *Catholic Worker* in 1944, which rehearsed all the arguments against compulsory military service, while adding peculiarly Catholic complaints about family disruption and the possibility of women in combat. When the peacetime draft was passed in 1948 (without UMT), the *Catholic Worker* advised noncooperation and gave publicity and support to men prosecuted for draft resistance. The case of Larry Gara, a Bluffton College, Ohio, history professor who was imprisoned in 1949 for urging a student to refuse to register if it violated his conscience, drew particular attention. Along with other peace groups, Catholic Workers picketed the White House and worked for Gara's release. Their efforts attracted the attention of a number of Catholic priests and intellectuals, notably the Jesuit attorney and later Congressman Robert Drinan, who publicized Gara's case in Catholic journals.[36]

This brief flurry of postwar peace activities ended in the early 1950s under the impact of the Cold War, McCarthyism, and the Korean War. As during World War I and World War II, the moderate peace organizations collapsed or changed their emphasis, while the radicals encountered increased public hostility. The Catholic Worker fared better than most pacifist groups during this period. Perhaps because of its protective coloring of Catholicism, it stayed off the "lists" of McCarthy and the Attorney General and never came under sustained political attack. The *Catholic Worker* and Day's incessant speaking tours also helped sustain the movement's substantial constituency. Although only eight Houses of Hospitality were in operation in 1950, the paper's circulation had recovered from a low of 50,000 during World War II and remained steady at about 60,000 during the early fifties. Even during the height of McCarthyism, Ludlow kept up his eloquent polemics against the state in the *Catholic Worker* while Day criticized the silence of Catholic publications about the anticivilian tactics of the United Nations in Korea.[37]

Although the Workers staged only a few small public demonstrations against Korea, the movement became the rallying point for the small number of Catholic COs and draft resisters who appeared during that conflict. Michael Harrington, a member of the Army Reserve, was one of those who slowly converted to pacifism under the influence of the Worker:

> In January, 1951, I transferred to a New York unit. In February I joined the Worker. On drill nights I felt myself an outcast. I would wait until everyone was at dinner and then sneak out of the House in my uniform, the livery of my compromise. There was constant discussion of how I could be so unprincipled. One gentle CW pacifist, Hector Black, was particularly persuasive.[38]

Although he claimed it was finally the army itself that turned him into a conscientious objector, Harrington's conversion to radical Catholic pacifism illustrates the Catholic Worker's moral appeal even during the height of the Cold War.

Despite such individual gains, the early fifties was a difficult time for the little band of Catholic radicals. Dwight Macdonald's 1952 *New Yorker* articles effectively portrayed the group's stubborn adherence to their idealistic vision in an unfavorable period. But many were discouraged by the seemingly permanent Cold War and the fierce opposition they encountered in the American Church. "With the growing monism of our times we are confronted with compelling evidence of the futility of the pacifist and libertarian positions," Ludlow lamented after surveying the response to the Korean War. He blamed "liberals of the *New Leader, New Republic, Commonweal* variety" for supporting the drift toward a centralized state built on a permanent war-preparation economy. But it was apparent, too, that the radicals, for all their intellectual effort, had failed to influence events. Pacifism, it seemed, might have to remain a politically irrelevant moral preference. In 1954, personally and politically exhausted, Ludlow himself left the Catholic Worker for a quiet private life.[39]

IV

Keeping the Catholic peace witness alive in such difficult times required an exceptionally hardy breed of activist. Man and moment were well met, therefore, when Ammon Hennacy brought his "One Man Revolution" to the Catholic Church and the Catholic Worker in 1952. A truly singular character, this old-time anarchist and radical was already fifty-nine years old when he came to New York. Hennacy was a thoroughly American, midwestern rebel whose simple life-style and single-minded devotion to righteousness would, no doubt, have pleased his Quaker and abolitionist ancestors. In his *Autobiography of a Catholic Anarchist* (later retitled with typical immodesty *The Book of Ammon*), Hennacy recalled that his family often pointed with pride to a farm near his birthplace in Negley, Ohio, that had been owned by the Coppac brothers who died at Harper's Ferry. "A bewhiskered picture of John Brown hung in our parlor," Hennacy said, "and I was ten years old before I knew the difference between God, Moses, and John Brown."[40]

Although his father had mellowed into a Bryan Democrat, it was no surprise when the sixteen-year-old Ammon joined the Ohio Socialist Party and the Industrial Workers of the World in 1910 (a feat which was possible until the 1912 Socialist Convention forbade such joint membership). During three years of college, one each at Hiram College, the

University of Wisconsin, and Ohio State, Hennacy used most of his abundant energy and salesmanship to organize student Socialist clubs and import radical speakers like Emma Goldman and Randolph Bourne. In 1916 Hennacy left school to become a full-time Socialist organizer in Ohio, the stronghold of the party's militant left wing. When World War I came a year later, Hennacy advocated draft resistance, and in July 1917, he was sentenced to five years in an Atlanta federal prison for conspiracy. There he met Alexander Berkman, the well-known anarchist who had stabbed steel magnate Henry Clay Frick. Berkman completed Hennacy's conversion from Socialism to anarchism. In June 1918, the young rebel was put in solitary confinement for organizing several effective prison protests.[41]

During seven months in solitary, under extreme pressure to recant his anarchism and inform on fellow inmates, Hennacy underwent a spiritual crisis and a conversion to the ethics of the Sermon on the Mount. "Gradually I came to gain a glimpse of what Jesus meant when he said, 'The kingdom of God is within you!' . . . This kingdom must be in everyone; in the deputy, the warden, the rat and the pervert—and now I came to know it in myself. . . . The warden said he did not understand political prisoners. He and the deputy, in plain words, did not know any better. It was my job to teach them another method, that of good will overcoming evil intentions, or rather habits." In July 1919, after resisting further pressures and winning the begrudged admiration of prison authorities, Hennacy was released on parole.[42]

During the twenty years following his release from prison, Hennacy was a minor but colorful figure in the little world of American anarchism. He traveled around the country with his common-law wife for several years visiting radical communes before taking up farming in Wisconsin. In the thirties he was a social worker in Milwaukee. All the time he wrote for obscure anarchist and pacifist journals in the U.S. and abroad—*The Fellow Worker, Freedom, The World Tomorrow, Retort, Challenge, Mother Earth,* and *Man!*—and corresponded with all sorts of independent radicals, including Emma Goldman and Gandhi.[43]

In these years Hennacy called himself a "Tolstoyan anarchist Christian," though "not a very orthodox one, spelling God with a small g and two oo's." Witty and irreverent, incapable of following any church or party line, Hennacy enjoyed preaching pacifism and religion to revolutionary anarchists and anarchism and revolution to Christians and pacifists. Being a revolutionary pacifist, he admitted, was like "wanting to eat the chicken without killing it." But there would be no point to revolution, "if, in the gaining of it through violence, the ideal is lost sight of." While proclaiming his own personal resistance to authority,

Hennacy stressed patience and tolerance as the critical virtues necessary to create a new society. "We must not be in a hurry to see immediate results," he told his fellow anarchists. Anarchists should favor democracy, Hennacy argued, but real democracy meant not "pushing each other around through politics" or rounding up temporary majorities, but rather "the organic growth of thought and action by small voluntarily federated groups of society, where the right of the individual to disobey and secede is granted." Hennacy publicly announced that he was a one-man demonstration of the practicality of anarchist and pacifist principles and shortly gained something of a reputation in Milwaukee for defusing violent situations by his personal courage and quick tongue. "Long before I read of the method of 'moral jiu-jitsu' described by Gandhi I had used it myself," he said in explaining how he disarmed hostile welfare clients and political vigilantes. "When a person wishes to attack you, the clear, unexpected answer throws him off base." [44]

A subscriber of the *Catholic Worker*, Hennacy began frequenting the Milwaukee House of Hospitality after hearing Day and Maurin speak there in 1937. Although he openly disdained all churches, Hennacy admired the Catholic Worker's uncompromising radicalism. When he learned of Pearl Harbor in December 1941, Hennacy immediately wrote the U.S. district attorney to say he would again refuse to register for the draft or pay taxes for the war. "I speak for the time when all shall realize they are Sons of God and brothers," his letter said. "When all the world is filled with hatred, this is the time when I must not be silent." The government declined to prosecute the forty-eight-year-old draft resister, but his public appeal to all pacifists to resist war taxes aroused some publicity and official concern. When Dorothy Day proved to be the only prominent pacifist figure who would endorse his call for tax resistance, Hennacy wrote to thank her, and sent along his dramatic account of his World War I resistance. The resulting article, entitled "God's Coward," evoked considerable reader response when it was printed in the May 1942 *Catholic Worker*. [45]

In order to fulfill his pledge and avoid federal withholding taxes, Hennacy quit his job to work as a migrant day laborer in the fields of Arizona and New Mexico. He also lived for a time among the Hopi Indians, whose communal way of life and still-active hostility to the American government he found congenial. From 1944 to 1950 Hennacy's lively accounts of his "life at hard labor" and his skirmishes with the Bureau of Internal Revenue appeared regularly in the *Catholic Worker*. He grew closer to the movement and to Dorothy Day, who introduced him to a number of radical priests and lay persons when she visited the Southwest in 1949. [46]

After an extended speaking tour before mostly Catholic audiences, Hennacy came to the new Chrystie Street House of Hospitality in August 1952. In November he was baptized by the anarchist priest Marion Casey, with Robert Ludlow as his godfather. His conversion came, Hennacy explained, because he "felt the handicap of a lack of spirituality" in his activist life and realized that "I was not hurting the Church by remaining outside. I was only hurting myself." The old radical found personal satisfaction in the practice of penance and daily Mass, and he seriously tried to emulate the integral spirituality of Dorothy Day—the only person whose moral integrity and courage Hennacy would admit were superior to his own. But he never really caught on to the Catholic Worker's complete fusion of orthodox Catholic tradition and social radicalism, and his painfully earnest attempts at piety were constantly undermined by his skeptical temperament and instinctive dislike of all institutional compromise. He eventually left the Catholic Worker and the Church in 1962 and opened his own Joe Hill House of Hospitality in Salt Lake City.[47]

But during the decade he was with the Catholic Worker Hennacy was a whirlwind: writing, picketing, traveling around the country to spread the Catholic Worker message, always just out of jail or on his way back in. His flamboyant language, weatherbeaten Indian appearance, and Spartan feats of physical endurance all appealed to younger Catholic Workers who thought the movement had lost its flair for creative radical action. At the same time Hennacy's ongoing tax resistance and lively run-ins with local police and judges made him good newspaper copy wherever he went. (Told by a judge, "You can't change the world," Hennacy quipped, "No, but I'm damn sure it can't change me." Arrested for disturbing the peace, Hennacy pleaded that he was "disturbing the war.") So guileless and engaging was Hennacy's personal style of radicalism that the authorities frequently came to respect and befriend him: Wives of FBI agents assigned to tail him baked him birthday cakes, generals and sheriffs inquired after his health during his frequent fasts, Atomic Energy Commission and Bureau of Internal Revenue employees wrote him fan letters.[48]

Hennacy's personal idiosyncrasies and intellectual deficiencies made the "one man revolution" a somewhat dubious hero for the Catholic Worker. Many old-time Workers found him hopelessly lacking in Catholic piety and fretted that the movement was losing its religious bearings. Dorothy Day herself became exasperated with such incorrigible Hennacy behavior as referring to Pope Pius X in a public speech as "that Italian gangster." But Day also recognized in Hennacy a different, nonchurchly sort of piety: the innocent sense of unbounded individual liberty and moral perfectionism that had been so much a part of the older American radicalism. Although she found it difficult to explain to fellow Catholics, Day saw in Hennacy, for all his weaknesses and self-promotion, certain qualities of individual integrity and moral courage that belonged to a properly American Catholic radical movement.

Hennacy proved the value of his activist mettle in short order. While others talked, it was his fearless absolutism that helped pull American pacifism out of its doldrums in the early fifties and into an effective campaign of nonviolent civil disobedience against compulsory air-raid drills. The annual Civil Defense drill presented an inviting target to radical pacifists. Once every year all citizens had to take shelter for ten minutes during a hypothetical nuclear attack because, as U.S. Civil Defense Director Val Petersen warned the nation, "the balance of victory may well rest with the nation whose population can best manage the effects of atomic attack by getting up off the ground organized and ready." [49]

In 1953 and 1954, the first years of the drill, Hennacy picketed alone during the alert without incident. But in 1955 the program was made compulsory nationwide, and the New York State Defense Emergency Act made failure to take shelter a misdemeanor subject to one-year imprisonment and a $500 fine. In response, Hennacy led the Catholic Worker and other pacifists into the first significant pacifist civil disobedience campaign of the post-Korea period. On June 15, 1955, twenty-eight persons, ten of them Catholic Workers, were arrested in City Hall Park for refusing to take shelter when the air-raid sirens went off. Their arrest, trial, and five-day jail sentence received considerable publicity, especially after Judge William Hamilton told Hennacy and Dorothy Day that they were, in effect, "guilty of the murder of three million people" in the supposed attack on New York City. Day's imprisonment brought new attention to the Catholic Worker, helped stir other pacifists from their Cold War despair, and led journals like *Commonweal* and the *New Republic* to question the value of the compulsory drill and its strict enforcement. [50]

The next year Hennacy, Day, and twenty others were arrested again. The Catholic Workers pleaded guilty as before and returned to jail for ten days, but others in the group appealed the case all the way to the Supreme Court, which denied *certiorari* in 1961. The demonstrators returned for their by now ritual arrests in 1957 and 1958, but public and media attention dwindled, except for an annual eloquent editorial in John Cogley's *Commonweal*. In 1959, however, there were signs of renewed interest in the civil defense issue. Several leaders of the reviving pacifist movement in the New York area, notably David McReynolds of the War Resisters League, turned out for the demonstration and arrest that year, and the media again covered it as a major event.[51]

The breakthrough came in 1960. Massive predemonstration publicity and organization by the Catholic Worker, the Fellowship of Reconciliation, the War Resisters League, and other pacifist groups drew over a thousand persons to the park on May 3, 1960. The helpless police made only twenty-seven arrests and pointedly ignored the pacifist leaders. "It looks as if we have been like the little Dutch boy, holding our fingers in the dike until help came along," exulted Hennacy. Even more help appeared in 1961, when the New York antidrill action was merged into a national antinuclear demonstration by A. J. Muste's Committee for Nonviolent Action. Twenty-five hundred people demonstrated throughout New York City, and others marched in a dozen East Coast cities and college campuses. The law had become a dead letter, and there were no attempts at enforcement. The Office of Emergency Preparedness in the new Kennedy administration declared an end to all public air-raid drills and announced, instead, a new civil defense program of individual backyard fallout shelters.[52]

The air-raid demonstrations were important to the peace movement for several reasons. First, they represented the first major attempt to apply to the issue of nuclear war the principles of radical nonviolence that had been discussed since the war. The regular summer arrest of a few pacifist militants was a long way from the mass resistance of the Gandhian theory, but it was one important sign that nonviolent civil disobedience, the principal tactic of the growing civil rights movement, could also play a part in the peace movement.

Second, the crescendo of protest from Hennacy's lonely pickets in the early fifties to the large-scale movement seven years later symbolized as almost nothing else the rebirth of the American peace movement after the lean years of 1949 to 1955. After disillusionment and decline, pacifist organizations, including the Catholic Worker, experienced a revival of membership and morale in the late fifties. For the first time since 1940 the number of Worker Houses of Hospitality began to rise, to a dozen in 1960. Through new Houses in places like Memphis, Chicago, and Oakland the movement gathered a growing number of adherents. The *Catholic Worker*'s circulation also crept up to 65,000, as a new generation of readers discovered the paper, and new audiences heard Day, Hennacy, or other Worker speakers. The public still rejected pacifist arguments, but a growing uneasiness about the official assurances concerning national security created a new audience for dissenters.

Finally, the success of the Catholic Worker–inspired civil defense campaign confirmed Dorothy Day's status as second only to the venerable A. J. Muste among the leaders of American pacifism. Among non-Catholics, Day's personal example was considerably more important than the actual efforts of her movement, however determined. As the Worker's diminishing role in the large-scale demonstrations of 1960 and 1961 proved, the movement was too small and religiously idiosyncratic to carry much weight in the swelling national peace movement. Among peace-conscious activists and writers, however, Day and her followers exercised an influence far out of proportion to their numbers or political importance.

V

Besides the civil defense campaign, the Catholic Worker engaged in a number of other activities that brought it closer to the general postwar American peace movement. Although the Workers had enjoyed cordial relations with A. J. Muste's brand of Protestant pacifism since before World War II, the Catholics' cooperative efforts were previously limited to a few demonstrations and an annual gathering with the Committee on Nonviolent Revolution, a small radical pacifist-anarchist group formed after the war. In the late fifties, while taking care to preserve their own Catholic identity and distinctive outlook, the Catholic Workers began to work closely with Protestant and nonreligious groups in the national movement against nuclear weapons and testing.

The antinuclear campaign of the late fifties and early sixties, like most major peace activities, was carried out by a diverse coalition. Acting under the same broad umbrella were the Committee for a Sane Nuclear Policy (SANE), which had the respectable membership, moderate aims, and conventional political tactics of a normal American lobbying group, and A. J. Muste's Committee for Nonviolent Action (CNVA), a coalition of pacifists who were more socially radical and inclined toward unconventional methods of demonstration and civil disobedience. Dorothy Day, Ed Turner, and Ammon Hennacy of the CW sat on the Executive Committee of CNVA, where they helped plan a series of nationwide demonstrations to dramatize the antinuclear cause.[53]

CNVA's first action was a demonstration set for August 1957 at the Atomic Energy Commission's Nevada nuclear test site, where a large hydrogen bomb was to be detonated. Typically, Ammon Hennacy arrived several weeks early to conduct one of his solitary picketing fasts. (After 1950 he had fasted and picketed the nearest government installation to commemorate Hiroshima Day and each year had increased the days of the fast to equal the years since the bombing.) The Las Vegas vigil, carried on in blistering heat, received national attention when a technical failure aborted the scheduled H-bomb. Lt. Col. James Hunter, the AEC official in charge of the project, reportedly told the old rebel, "Hennacy, you stopped this one; now you had better go back to New York and let us get back to work." Hennacy did leave after Hiroshima Day, but a dozen demonstrators from the Catholic Worker and other pacifist groups were arrested on August 9 for entering the test site.[54]

From this small beginning, the CNVA went on to a series of headline-making actions which alerted the nation to the intensity of pacifist dissent on the nuclear question. Catholic Workers did not participate in the most spectacular demonstrations, the sailing of the ships *Golden Rule* and *Phoenix* into South Pacific test areas in 1958. But they were present at most of the other peace protests of the period, including the extended "Polaris Action" at New London, Connecticut, in 1959/60, where pacifists tried unsuccessfully to dissuade workers from building nuclear submarines. In August 1959, Ammon Hennacy and a young Chicago Catholic Worker, Karl Meyer, were among those arrested for "going over the fence" at Strategic Air Command headquarters near Omaha; Hennacy served six months in a Minnesota federal prison as a result. In 1961 two dozen CNVA activists, including Meyer as a representative of the Catholic Worker, walked the distance from San Francisco to Moscow, preaching unconditional disarmament to Westerners and Communists alike. Their final tense demonstration in Red Square in October had no effect on the Soviets, but the effort enhanced the credibility of the CNVA campaign in the United States.[55]

Demonstrations, civil disobedience, and political actions like the international "General Strikes for Peace" in 1961 and 1962 gained publicity and new recruits for the American peace movement and may have contributed to the political atmosphere leading up to the limited Nuclear Test Ban Treaty between the United States and the U.S.S.R. in 1963. But the very sense of total moral commitment and dramatic confrontation that fueled such demonstrations tended to reduce the taste for critical or theoretical reflection within the peace movement. There was often a loss of intellectual perspective, especially among newer recruits caught up in the excitement and moral passion of the moment. The peace movement, *Catholic Worker* writer Thomas Cornell complained, "often appears to be made up of sensitive victims of emotionalism." Of course, he said, emotions are important, and it did not matter if people came to the cause for personal or psychological reasons. "But after that there should be a growth, an integration and maturing of their pacifism based upon study and hard thinking as well as action. . . . Emotional pacifism, sometimes called religious or spiritual pacifism, but certainly neither, is unexamined pacifism, and like the unexamined life, not worth living." The person who fails to probe the intellectual foundations of his cause, Cornell continued, "will not realize himself as a full person and an effective peacemaker."[56]

Throughout the period of growing peace agitation, the Catholic Worker stood out among peace groups for its insistence that the less-visible "intellectual front" was just as important to the cause of peace as the attention-getting demonstrations and political pressure. The *Catholic Worker* in particular remained a forum for demanding reflection about the troubling moral and political dilemmas of modern war, violence, and social revolution, especially after Cornell and the brilliant Martin Corbin, an older Fordham graduate and Air Force veteran, became managing editors of the paper in 1962. Picket-line heroes like Hennacy received their share of attention in the paper, but meanwhile the intellectuals associated with the Catholic Worker continued to emphasize that a Catholic approach to peace must be thought out as well as acted out.

A good example of the *Catholic Worker*'s capacity for promoting critical thought among pacifists came after the Hungarian revolt of 1956. Worker Edmund Egan observed that the events in Hungary challenged some articles of the pacifist faith. The most prominent forms of violence around the world, he noted, included just such popular rebellions against oppression. "The position of philosophical pacifism has of late lost some of its tangential props," Egan said. "What is happening is not one of those conflicts between the masters of states in which the people are dragged in to wage the battles of power-hungry leaders. It is rather the revolution of an entire people against a government which has dared every extreme of cruelty in order to re-assert itself." The spectacle of civilian students and workers attacking armored divisions with clubs and pistols removed the standard objection to the immorality of means used in warfare, Egan noted, while the customary scruples concerning the surrender of individual moral discretion to military authority were lacking in this spontaneous revolt, which was "a violent individual action communally channeled." Under such circumstances, how could one remain a pacifist?[57]

Egan acknowledged the difficulties of any response, but he presented *Catholic Worker* readers with an ingenious argument that illustrated the close connection of political and moral concern in postwar pacifism. A popular revolution that relied on the apparently justified means of small-scale violence simply could not succeed, Egan claimed. "This revolution points up a contention central to pacifist thought, especially in the Catholic theological context, namely, that in armed conflict there is an insuperable advantage on the side of the less morally scrupulous combatant, an advantage which the other side must meet in kind if it hopes to win the war." This was the "dialectic of force," which appeared in Hungary during the period when the rebels gained control and engaged in mass shootings and hangings of captured Communist officials. Such violence gave the rebels a temporary advantage, but brought the most severe reprisals when their enemies regained control. Therefore, unless the popular rebels could become as militarily strong as their opponents—an unlikely prospect—their best hope for success lay in "a combination of spontaneous action, political pressure, and the moral superiority of their cause." By far the most important weapon was the moral one which, as the Russians' fears about their own troops showed, had enormous potential for demoralizing the enemy. But by resorting to arms, Egan claimed, the rebels had diluted their strongest weapon, moral pressure, without bringing to bear enough violence to win. Since the popular revolt of men against tanks was closer in spirit to *satyagraha* than war, why not insist on a completely nonviolent struggle which, while also unlikely to win, would use the strongest weapons available and sustain the righteousness of the cause?[58]

Those who accepted collective violence in principle would probably not be convinced of either the moral or political advantages of *satyagraha* against an armed enemy. Yet arguments like Egan's show how some postwar pacifists were taking account of complex political reality and social conflict in advancing their religious ideals. The radicals' Gandhian principles were constantly called into question by contemporary circumstances, particularly by what they saw as the urgency of bringing social justice to the poor in the non-European world. The Catholic Workers were prominent among those who tried to engage firmly held religious ideals with the harsh facts of modern social and political life.

Radical Catholic intellectuals felt less ambiguity about nuclear war, which remained the major focus of attention in the peace movement until 1963. In the late fifties and early sixties, prominent American and European Catholic scholars like Pierre Regamey, James Douglass, Bede Griffiths, Karl Stern, E. I. Watkin, Thomas Roberts, and Gordon Zahn developed a detailed critique of nuclear war from the standpoint of Catholic moral philosophy. While sometimes simply appealing to the radical Gospel and historic examples of Christian pacifism, these modern Catholics also stressed the unprecedented situation created by nuclear weapons. Like University of Chicago president Robert Hutchins and others in the early postwar era, they declared that the atomic bomb was "the good news of damnation" which now required mankind to face up once and for all to the outmoded institution of war. "For centuries the church has accepted that violence is a normal way of settling international disputes," wrote Griffiths, an English Dominican, in the *Catholic Worker* in 1963. But the providentially coincident development of both nuclear war and nonviolent methods of struggle meant that "the entire moral theology of war ought to be revised." Psychologist Karl Stern, a Catholic convert and close friend of the Catholic Worker, argued that in contrast to all previous technological improvements in war, nuclear weaponry completely undermined the Thomist "principle of double effect" concerning civilian casualties—i.e., that civilians could be killed only as an inadvertent byproduct of assaults on military targets.[59]

Writers friendly to the Catholic Worker predictably lined up against the defenders of limited nuclear war like Henry Kissinger, John Courtney Murray, and Paul Ramsey. Noting that some American Protestant theologians like Ramsey were appropriating and refining the Catholic just war tradition in the context of the Cold War, *Catholic Worker* editor Edward Morin wrote:

> Dr. Ramsey contends that the just war tradition is based on obligations in charity toward the society one defends without regard for the assessed guilt of the enemy. This "neighbor-regarding love" is easier to argue for than the Suarezian idea of punitive war recently revived by John Courtney Murray, but in the age of the permiable state, when the enemy is difficult to identify as an "aggressor," the justice one sovereign state assumes it has the right to inflict upon another lacks political responsibility and legal jurisdiction.

The problem with the just war theorists, the pacifists claimed, was that they expected the churches to teach some kind of nuclear morality to the state, yet most of them took no account of the state's patent unwillingness to be morally instructed. The Murray-Ramsey idea that nuclear war could be physically limited, and hence morally justified, came, said Morin, from the same "happy if imaginary land" where there were also "clean bombs" and "contained radioactivity." Far better were the unthinkable thoughts of a Herman Kahn, who clearly understood nuclear strategy and the consequences of any nuclear exchange. As for the elaborate theories of deterrence, the Catholic radicals quoted Protestant theologian John C. Bennett, a nonpacifist disciple of Niebuhr, who said that "those who believe in deterrence in a real crisis tenaciously presuppose a degree of rationality under stress that calls for almost as much faith as the oft-ridiculed optimism of the idealists who presuppose virtue in all men."[60]

Unfortunately for the pacifists, such arguments received a severe blow when the 1962 Cuban missile crisis apparently demonstrated that the nuclear operators could, indeed, play their hand perfectly in the high-stakes game of superpower strategy. But while most Americans' faith in the deterrent system was increased by President Kennedy's dramatically successful gamble, the growing number of antiwar Catholic intellectuals were not dissuaded from their belief in the moral unacceptability of maintaining national security through nuclear deterrence.

VI

The most eminent convert to the Catholic peace movement in this period was the Trappist monk Thomas Merton. When he turned to writing about war and peace in the early sixties, Merton was already one of the best-known figures in contemporary American Catholicism. After *The Seven-Storey Mountain*, his best-selling account of his youthful conversion and entry into the Trappist order, Merton had written numerous volumes of essays and poetry. Although he had worked in Baroness Catherine de Hueck's Catholic Worker–inspired Friendship House movement for a period before entering the monastery, Merton's early Catholic writings were devoid of social content. In the mid-fifties, however, there was a softening of the world-weariness and triumphalism that marked Merton's early work and a growing appreciation of what modern literature, philosophy, and psychology could do in association with traditional Catholic spirituality. From his Abbey of Gethsemani in Kentucky Merton began to correspond with Catholic intellectuals and activists about social problems. "I am deeply touched by your witness for peace," he said in a letter to Dorothy Day in 1959. "You are very, very right in going at it along the lines of *satyagraha*. I see no other way, though of course the angles of the problem are not all clear." [61]

In 1960 Merton brought out *Disputed Questions*, a collection of essays that focused on the nuclear question as a cause and symbol of contemporary alienation from God. Although Merton's initial approach to the problem of peace was mostly pious and speculative, his sense of urgency about the atomic age, his critical stance toward the political structures that had led the way to a possible Armageddon, and his conviction that religion had something special to offer in this situation were all in the tradition of radical Catholic Worker pacifism. In the next five years Merton published more than a dozen essays on topics related to peace, many of them appearing first in the *Catholic Worker*. During this period he also corresponded with Dorothy Day, with whom he shared a traditional Catholic religiosity. [62]

Much of Merton's early peace writing reflected standard religious pacifist views. He decried the nuclear confrontation, characterizing the United States and the Soviet Union in terms of the twins Gog and

Magog of the biblical Apocalypse, "each with great power and little sanity, each telling lies with great conviction." He joined those who criticized the just war tradition as applied to the confrontation of the superpowers. "The twofold weakness of the Augustinian theory," he wrote, "is its stress on the subjective purity of intention, which can be doctored or manipulated with apparent 'sincerity,' and the tendency to pessimism about human nature and the world, which is used as a justification for resort to violence." John Courtney Murray's defense of limited nuclear war showed how elastic just war analysis was, Merton contended, for Hiroshima-sized weapons were now (1962) considered small-scale, while preemptive strikes might be "defensive" under certain circumstances. The tendency toward such reasoning was inherent in the just war theory, the monk said, and it showed that the theory would always tend to rationalize existing military-political strategies.[63]

Despite such arguments and his association with the pacifists at the Catholic Worker, Merton was reluctant to accept the pacifist label for himself. He endorsed the papal statements that some kinds of defensive wars could be legitimate and criticized some pacifists for attempting to turn their moral convictions into an article of Christian faith. He also expressed more sympathy than most Catholic radicals of that time for the claims of revolutionary violence. "If the oppressed try to resist by force—which is their right—theology has no business preaching non-violence to them," Merton wrote in *Faith and Violence*. A theology of love must not be allowed to serve the interests of the rich and powerful. "Mere blind destruction" by the downtrodden was futile and immoral, Merton said, but desperate efforts to overturn an unjust social order could not be condemned, especially by those with some complicity in the injustice.[64]

Such comments stemmed in part from Merton's deep concern about the war in Vietnam, which dominated his thoughts during the last years of his life. Although he resolved in early 1965 to stop writing about contemporary issues and return to purely spiritual subjects, he saw Vietnam as "an overwhelming atrocity" that required extraordinary commitments by Americans, particularly those in the religious community. Merton was especially stirred by his growing interest in Asian thought in general and Zen Buddhism in particular. In 1966, through friends in the American peace movement, Merton made personal connections with Vietnamese Buddhists who were active in opposing the war. In "Nhat Hanh Is My Brother," one of Merton's last pieces, he described the special affinity he felt for a Buddhist contemplative who had come to the U.S. to plead for peace. "We are both monks, both poets," Merton said, and he spoke of "the bonds of a new brotherhood which is beginning to be evident on all five continents and cuts across political, religious, and cultural lines." It was on behalf of this vision of international spiritual unity that Merton set off in 1968 on a religious pilgrimage to India, Burma, and Thailand, where he was accidentally electrocuted.[65]

Merton's influence on the Catholic peace movement was considerable. Daniel Berrigan said it was "one of his essays in the *CW* that set me on fire," and Patricia McNeal, a historian and participant in the Catholic peace movement, stated that "although it cannot be documented, it would not be an overstatement to say that every Catholic peace activist of the sixties read Merton's writings on peace."[66] Merton's real importance, however, probably lay more in what he was than in what he said. As with many of the religious who became rather suddenly involved in social questions in the 1960s, Merton's moral aspirations exceeded his knowledge of the world. Not surprisingly for one who had led a cloistered life, Merton displayed only cursory awareness of the secular literature on war and peace, tended to confuse the issues of individual and collective violence, and remained naive about the dilemmas of even the most righteous politics.

But while Merton's monastic life weakened his political analysis, as he himself recognized, it strengthened his relations with many Catholic activists, including some who were drifting away from the institutional Church. "He simply changed people's lives," wrote James Forest, a young Catholic Worker, after Merton's death. "Men were turned inside out. He brought together politics and the spiritual life, and helped give resistence a contemplative dimension." In 1962, Forest related, he and another Worker had gone to Merton's abbey from the furious activism of the CNVA campaigns:

> In a climate of such urgency and exhaustion it is not surprising that we at the Catholic Worker were showing signs of strain. Then to be at a Trappist monastery in a remote part of Kentucky with a man who, despite distances and solitude, was more conscious of the agonies being decried than we were. . . . He spoke of the problem of consciousness, how accidental and minor is the "I" we speak of, how far from the real essence. He talked of the need for silence and the uncluttering of the mind, even more important for us than for monks. "Inside yourselves you shouldn't be running all the time," he said.[67]

Such connections between nonviolent activism and Catholic contemplative spirituality had long been a part of the Catholic Worker's understanding of Catholic radicalism. But the centrality of the inner life for political activists received added emphasis through Merton's association with the Catholic peace movement in his later years. Like Dorothy Day, he made an interior peace the basis for promoting external peace in the world. "You are so right about prayer being the main thing," he wrote to Day. "It is the realm that cannot be closed to us, and cannot be got at."[68] As a monk and mystic who also came to care for man's worldly strife, Merton was a powerful symbol of the distinctive Catholic contribution to American pacifism.

Merton's closest disciple among the Catholic radicals was James Douglass, one of those who learned "the power of contemplation in the world" from the monk, but concentrated more specifically on the intellectual problems of Catholic pacifism. A graduate of the University of Santa Clara, Douglass met Merton while teaching theology at Jesuit Bellarmine College in Kentucky. Merton put him in touch with the Catholic Worker. Although he never joined the movement, Catholic pacifism soon absorbed his personal and intellectual energies. "With many American Catholics I have come to know and love the Church through Dorothy Day and the Catholic Worker movement," Douglass said. "It is impossible to say where I would be personally without the Catholic Worker."[69] In his writings in the *Catholic Worker* and elsewhere, Douglass applied the perspective of religious radicalism to the thorny moral problems of the nuclear age.

Douglass combined the moral passion of the pacifist movement with a formal theological background and a thorough knowledge of nuclear strategy, a field which in its speculative ambiguity and apocalyptic implications proved congenial to the professional theologian. Along with Paul Ramsey and Justus George Lawler, Douglass was one of the small number of American religious thinkers who became versed themselves in the think-tank world of nuclear strategy, with its arcane jargon and elaborate scenarios of conflict. Douglass was therefore able to comprehend the technical issues raised in the works of nuclear theorists like Bernard Brodie, Herman Kahn, and Henry Kissinger, while he evaluated the moral and religious dimensions of these theories, which many experts declined to discuss. In a review of physicist Ralph Lapp's *Kill and Overkill*, for instance, Douglass noted how "the author's own evident concern does not prevent him from making the morally ambiguous strategy recommendation of a shift from counterforce to a more clearly retaliatory system of anti-city warfare." Lapp's work showed, Douglass concluded, that even the most well-intentioned strategic analysis was inadequate without an explicit moral dimension.[70]

While Douglass's own conclusions invariably pointed toward radically Gandhian approaches to the nuclear stalemate, his assumptions and methods illustrate how different postwar religious pacifists were from the naively optimistic "children of light" so effectively attacked by Niebuhr and others in the thirties. Now it was Douglass, the pacifist, who frequently chastised the establishment nuclear strategists and conventional peacemakers for their underlying complacency and reluctance to face the ugly realities of the world. War had deep-rooted causes in human institutions and beliefs, Douglass insisted, and there was no reason to believe that the present generation of American leaders was any cleverer or wiser than previous ones that had eventually stumbled into war and used all the readily available means of destruction. "The issues [in the Cold War] as well as the intentions and fears behind them are real and run deep," Douglass wrote in 1964. Peace, he said, "must indeed be sought, but it must be suffered for, too, given this world, and not some more serene creation of the liberal mind."[71] For Catholic radicals like Douglass, only a firm grounding in religion could sustain both the realistic pessimism concerning the prospects of avoiding future wars and the strength to endure the "suffering" that would have to accompany efforts to prevent them.

Douglass's work also showed the continuing preoccupation of Catholic pacifists with the just war doctrine, despite their own professed rejection of it. The just war revival had actually begun with Protestant theologians in the late fifties and early sixties who saw in it the most politically relevant Christian approach to the new moral dilemmas facing the United States. A few of the just war adherents, like Walter Stein and Justus George Lawler, eventually arrived at a nuclear pacifism based on the traditional moral reasoning. But others, notably Paul Ramsey and the theorists associated with the Catholic Association for International Peace, held that the just war criteria left room, not for the reality of nuclear war, but for the political-military strategy of deterrence. Deterrence, they claimed, was not subject to just war moral condemnation because it threatened doomsday only in order to preserve the peace. While the radical Catholic pacifists had long before abandoned the premises of the just war debate, they were prepared to refute the just war theorists on their own ground. Douglass's critique of Ramsey on the deterrence question was typical:

> Ramsey's case for the just deterrent illustrates the strains placed on even the most brilliant effort to maintain the justice of war in the nuclear era. It is a case dependent at every step on a distinction between the threat of a massive evil and the saving possibility of an opposite moral intention by those judged to be

making the threat. The deterrent theory preserves our good conscience, first, because the millions of deaths threatened by our counterforce policy are beyond our intention: simply collateral civilian damage; second, because the city destruction threatened by our weapons is also beyond our intention: "the dual use of the weapons themselves"; third, because the genocide that might result from our national policy of massive retaliation is beyond our good intentions: "our leaders' bluff." At no point in the theory is our intention permitted to correspond with the substance of the threat attributed to us by the enemy. Populations, cities, societies are threatened with destruction, but from a moral point of view there is no one threatening them: just indirect effects, the inherent ambiguity of the weapons, and a policy of bluff. And if by chance, in "the fury or fog of war," the worst should somehow come to pass and a world be buried in flame, we would at least have the consolation of knowing we were not responsible.[72]

Many of those concerned about nuclear war undoubtedly considered such intricate moral debates irrelevant. So thick was the tangle of disputed facts, religious and moral assumptions, and military and political contingencies that it seemed impossible to take an intelligent stand, much less affect the course of events, in less than three hundred pages. Such people, probably a majority in all sectors of the American peace movement, tended to retreat from the complexity of intellectual discussion and make moral imperatives alone the basis of their action.

But a minority of pacifists, including many of those associated with the Catholic Worker, believed that an effective Christian peace witness in the modern era required not just a return to biblical simplicity or evangelical fervor, but a full engagement with the most difficult contemporary intellectual and moral dilemmas. Catholic pacifists like Douglass and the Catholic Workers were Christian moralists, but perhaps because their religious tradition had long held to a sturdy realism about human nature and the structures of power, they had an easier time than their Protestant counterparts in avoiding the naive optimism and sentimentality of some earlier religious antiwar rhetoric. Ultimately, their case still rested on a bedrock of Christian spirituality and anthropology; yet they recognized that the Gospel message of peace could only be taken seriously if it confronted the complexity of the whole modern situation and did not allow itself to be dismissed as a mere "religious" sentiment.

VII

The confluence of the new nonviolent activism and the deepening American Catholic reflection about war among both pacifists and nonpacifists led to the formation of a new Catholic peace group, Pax, in 1962. (There was no connection with the pre–World War II group of the same name.) Most Catholic peace activists and writers up to that time had been connected with the Catholic Worker in some way. But by the early sixties some of them felt the need for an organization which would deal exclusively with the peace question and avoid some of the extremist rhetoric and actions that kept the Catholic Worker from having much direct influence on the mainstream clergy and laity of the American Catholic Church. Following the familiar route by which the Catholic Worker spun off new groups, a dozen peace workers met at the Chrystie Street House of Hospitality in September to consider whether to form a Catholic Peace Fellowship as part of the Protestant-dominated Fellowship of Reconciliation or to create a separate Catholic group. Despite the friendly relations many Catholic activists had been developing with their Protestant counterparts in the previous decade, denominational suspicion remained strong even among Catholic radicals. "They just want to use us," one participant reportedly said. The FOR proposal was rejected, and Pax was established as a Catholic organization specifically dedicated to altering the Church's attitudes toward war.[73]

In its first year Pax enlisted about a hundred members, including a number of well-known clergy and lay persons. The director was Eileen Egan, a longtime associate of Dorothy Day with extensive connections among socially conscious Catholics. Eschewing direct action and civil disobedience, Egan made Pax a small but active lobby for peace within the Church. By steering clear of the pacifist question, the Pax leaders were able to attract a number of concerned Catholics who wanted a reduction of armaments and a repudiation of nuclear war on just war grounds. Throughout the 1960s, Pax held conferences to promote its goals, spread peace propaganda at Catholic gatherings, and put out a semischolarly quarterly, *Peace*.[74]

Pax faced serious obstacles in trying to alter the peace positions of the Catholic Church in the United States. The American hierarchy was dominated at that time by conservative bishops like Francis Spellman of New York and Patrick O'Malley of Washington, D.C., while the Catholic Association for International Peace continued to advocate only cautious and officially approved peace initiatives. Nevertheless, Pax could make the appealing argument that it was more in line with the new peace directions of the universal Church than the American hierarchy was. Pope John XXIII's 1963 encyclical *Pacem in Terris* in particular became the charter for Catholics in all countries who hoped to see their Church take the lead in global peacemaking. The pope's eloquent plea for peace clearly departed from the crusading anti-Communism and militant defensiveness that had dominated Rome's pronouncements on international affairs for a generation. It appealed, instead, to "all men of good will" to recognize their "common brotherhood" and lay aside force as a means of settling international disputes. In keeping with customary encyclical practice, *Pacem in Terris* never descended from its eloquent but lofty rhetorical plane to discuss the thorny problems of promoting peace in a world where neither goodwill nor brotherhood were much in evidence. Nevertheless, some politicians, peace activists, and churchmen recognized that this last testament of a beloved pope lent encouragement to those who wanted strong Western initiatives to reduce Cold War tensions and break the nuclear stalemate.[75]

In 1964 and 1965 Pax had a unique opportunity to influence the views of the worldwide Church on this matter during the Third and Fourth Sessions of Vatican II, where the assembled prelates were to formulate Rome's official peace position in the "Pastoral Constitution on the Church in the Modern World." While Dorothy Day joined a group of pilgrims to the conference in fasting and praying for peace, Eileen Egan, Gordon Zahn, Philip Scharper, and James Douglass of the American Pax cooperated with European Catholic peace groups in lobbying for a strong antiwar statement in Schema 13, the section dealing with international relations. Their actions alarmed groups like the CAIP, whose president warned before the conference that "the European pacifist influence in Rome may need to be offset. Here, too, we need to speak out because of Pax. Like all extremists, they may have the most persistent, devoted, and persuasive adherents."[76]

The Pax representatives did prove to be devoted and persistent advocates during their months in Rome. Though their direct influence was limited by their unofficial status and the reluctance of many bishops to tackle the difficult matter, they lobbied effectively to secure the strongest possible peace statement from the Council. The political maneuvering on this controversial issue was, naturally, intense. An early draft of Schema 13 proposed by a committee condemned all "uncontrollable weapons," but this was rejected in the assembly after American and British bishops successfully argued that the "controllability" of weapons was a technical question that could only be decided by experts and that the Church should therefore not speak to it. Working closely with a number of friendly European bishops, however, including the

arch-conservative Cardinal Ottaviani, the Pax representatives successfully shifted the focus of the condemnation from the weapons themselves
to their effects, thus finessing the objections of technical incompetence.
After extensive debate the Council passed the language proposed by a
Swedish bishop, but actually written by Douglass, which said that "any
act of war aimed at the indiscriminate destruction of entire cities and
their inhabitants, and *a fortiori* at the practically total destruction of
whole areas is, of its nature, objectively a crime against God and against
man himself; it is to be vigorously and unhesitatingly condemned."[77]

There were further sharp debates over nuclear deterrence. Most
American bishops, led by Cardinal Spellman, wanted it explicitly endorsed as the best means of maintaining peace. Cardinal Joseph Ritter of
St. Louis and the Pax lobbyists wanted an explicit condemnation. Both
efforts failed, and the Council came up with the weak statement that
"whatever be the facts about this method of deterrence," an unlimited
arms race is to be deplored. Although this result proved to some peace
activists that, as the Protestant observer Robert McAfee Brown commented, "prophetism does not thrive on majorities," the peace movement had reason to be pleased with the results. The worldwide publicity
surrounding the debate had highlighted the trend within the Catholic
Church, particularly outside the United States, toward raising critical
questions about modern war and nuclear weapons. Within the United
States, Vatican II and Schema 13 contributed to a noticeable increase in
concern among Catholic elites about the effectiveness and morality of
American nuclear policy, an attitude subsequently reflected in the yearly
Pacem in Terris conferences sponsored by the Center for the Study of Democratic Institutions.[78]

After its notable efforts in Rome, Pax itself continued throughout the 1960s as a small pressure group, working without much success
to get the U.S. Catholic Conference and other official bodies to come out
in favor of nuclear disarmament and against the Vietnam war. Pax's patient, nondemonstrative approach to peace was not well suited to the
mood of the decade, and the group struggled for members and funds. In
1971 it was reconstituted as the American affiliate of Pax Christi, the
official worldwide peace organization of the Catholic Church.

VIII

The problems that preoccupied Pax—the arms race, atomic
testing, the danger of total war between the superpowers—were the
predominant ones in all segments of the American peace movement in

the early sixties. But even as the final sessions of Vatican II were drawing to a close, such issues were being overshadowed by the quite different issue of Vietnam. While most peace activists were struggling to arouse public alarm about the danger of a potential nuclear war, they were suddenly confronted with a real war that created a radically new environment for social activism. While many pacifists continued to see the nuclear issue as primary, they were forced to direct their attention to the immediate conflict. Some saw in Vietnam a superb opportunity to arouse the American public about the danger of war in general. But older peace workers who remembered that their cause had seldom prospered during wartime saw that the explosive political environment created by the Vietnam War presented special dangers.

What was at first a small guerrilla action in Southwest Asia received little attention from pacifist groups like the Catholic Worker until 1961. Day had written on the unhappy history of Western intervention in Vietnam in 1954, and some Catholic radicals were informed on the situation in the country because some members of the American hierarchy, notably Spellman, were involved in the anti-Communist cause. But it was only after the first significant American military commitment in 1961/62 that pacifists began to divert some of their limited energy and resources to opposing the war. From 1962 to 1965 the Catholic Worker was one of only a handful of pacifist and radical groups to work against American involvement in Vietnam. Although Catholic opponents of the war were still not very visible in the nation, the Catholic Worker's early opposition and dramatic practice of civil disobedience, especially with respect to the draft, put it in the vanguard of the anti-Vietnam War movement in this country.[79]

The first Catholic Worker action of the Vietnam era occurred in Washington Square in November 1962, when Thomas Cornell, a young Catholic Worker activist and editor, led twenty-five men in burning their draft cards, a form of radical protest not seen since the anticonscription campaign of 1947. The demonstration received little public attention, but its dramatic symbolism stirred interest in radical circles in New York City. The rising draft calls in 1963 and 1964 expanded the constituency for actions aimed at conscription, and on May 12, 1964, Cornell and Christopher Kearnes of the Catholic Worker again helped organize a card-burning rally.[80]

The Gulf of Tonkin Resolution three months later was a final signal to pacifists of the urgency of the Vietnam issue, and across the country Catholic Worker Houses began direct action and propaganda campaigns against the war. Largely because of the interest aroused by these activities, sales of the *Catholic Worker* rose dramatically from 65,000 in 1960 to around 85,000 five years later, while growing numbers of young Catholics came to Houses of Hospitality to work for the antiwar cause. New Houses began to open as rapidly as they had in the thirties; by the middle of the 1960s there were about twenty-five Houses and farms at some level of activity. Catholic Workers appeared prominently among organizers of the nation's first major anti-Vietnam demonstrations in late 1964 and early 1965. On February 18, 1965, they were among about three hundred who gathered in New York's Union Square to call for a halt to American intervention in the war. In Oakland, California, several Catholic Workers were arrested along with other demonstrators for sitting down in front of troop trains. Also in February the Catholic Worker sponsored a "Declaration of Conscience Against the War in Vietnam," signed by more than fifty Catholic theologians, scholars, and activists, which condemned American participation in the war and called for noncooperation in the war effort, including draft resistance, refusal to do war-related work, and other nonviolent acts of civil disobedience. These small early protests failed to halt the rapid escalation of the war, but among the minority of Americans puzzled or skeptical about Vietnam, such actions, even when not approved, helped raise questions and cast doubt on official assurances about the conflict.[81]

Catholic Workers remained highly visible in the small but growing anti-Vietnam cause throughout the important year 1965. Because groups like the Catholic Worker, the Fellowship of Reconciliation, and War Resisters League were first on the antiwar scene and possessed some resources of money, publicity, and experienced leadership, they led for a time a movement whose many newcomers were mostly nonpacifists. Ignoring warnings that their tactics were counterproductive, the pacifists at first concentrated on the draft as the Achilles heel of the war effort, organizing draft resistance and leading demonstrations at such places as Whitehall, the Selective Service Headquarters in New York. On August 9, thirty-two Catholic Workers were among those arrested at a Washington anti-draft and antiwar demonstration. Photographs of draft card burnings in front of the Capitol appeared in the Luce publications and led to swift passage through Congress of the Rivers Act which for the first time made destruction of a draft card a federal crime. On October 15, at a Whitehall demonstration, David Miller, a young Catholic Worker, burned his card in front of cameras and note-taking FBI agents. The widely printed photographs of the well-groomed young Catholic blatantly defying the law caused a wave of emotional reaction in Congress and the media. Miller was quickly arrested, tried, and sentenced to five years in the Lewisburg, Pennsylvania, penitentiary. Miller's action helped stir similar protests elsewhere, as draft resistance grew along with more conventional forms of opposition to the war.[82]

The last occasions when pacifists could still claim leadership of the anti-Vietnam movement were the mass rallies in New York City in October and November of 1965. On November 6 several thousand people watched a group of war resisters, including a number of Catholic Workers, destroy their draft cards. The Workers' statement for the occasion said, "Fellow Americans—sincere and conscientious soldiers—leave their families to go to Vietnam risking their lives. We who have dedicated ourselves to the war on war, to nonviolence as an effective means to resist tyranny, cannot shrink from the consequences of our conscientious act." A. J. Muste and Dorothy Day, the two venerable leaders of American pacifism, were principal speakers at the demonstration. Over chants of "Moscow Mary" and "Burn yourselves, not your cards," from counterdemonstrators, Day said, "I speak today as one who is old, and who must endorse the courage of the young who themselves are willing to give up their freedom. I speak as one whose whole lifetime has seen the cruelty and hysteria of war in the last half century. . . . I wish to place myself beside A. J. Muste, to show my solidarity of purpose with these young men, and to point out that we, too, are breaking the law." Despite this invitation, the government chose not to prosecute the aged religious pacifists. By the following year, with both the war and political opposition to it escalating rapidly, the leadership of the antiwar movement passed largely out of pacifist hands.[83]

The failure of demonstrations to stop the escalation of the war caused despair among some young pacifists. On November 9, 1965, Roger LaPorte, a twenty-one-year-old former Trappist novice who had worked at the Catholic Worker only a few months, burned himself to death in front of the United Nations building, in apparent imitation of Buddhist immolations in Vietnam and Quaker Norman Morrison's suicide in front of the Pentagon a week earlier. Comment even from sources normally sympathetic to the Catholic Worker was critical. The *National Catholic Reporter* condemned the "dangerous" effects of radical pacifist rhetoric on "young and tender consciences" and called on the Catholic Worker to repudiate ideas that might encourage such acts. From Kentucky, Thomas Merton fired off a telegram to the New York Worker headquarters: "Just heard tragic death of Roger LaPorte. Deeply shocked and concerned about current developments in the peace movement. Will these do grave harm to cause of peace? Do they represent a right understanding of nonviolence? I think not."[84]

The Workers were also badly shaken by LaPorte's action and engaged in a good deal of private soul searching. But they denied that the movement was responsible for the youth's death and tended to absolve him of the guilt Catholics normally attached to the "sin" of self-destruction. "The indignation of the young is a terrible thing," said one *Catholic Worker* writer. "Even if we must view this as a unique action never again to be imitated by a Christian for fear of destroying its purity and of making it a monstrous parody through pride of fanaticism, it stands out as an impulse of extraordinary innocence." Another said that such a "mysterious witness" should not be simply dismissed, but should lead to "a harsh inquiry into why these things are happening among us."[85]

In 1965 harsh inquiry was, indeed, beginning among Catholics as well as other Americans about the war in Vietnam. Unlike all previous American wars, Vietnam precipitated a serious opposition and division in the American Catholic community. For the first time substantial numbers of Catholics began to question not simply a particular article of American foreign policy, but the essential premises of their nation's relations with the rest of the world. In their divided reaction to the war, Catholics mirrored fully the experience of their countrymen.

This reaction was a consequence of the general changes within the Roman Catholic Church after Vatican II, as well as the vast social, economic, and educational transformation that had occurred among American Catholics since World War II. Once relatively secure from the turmoil of American culture within the institutions and values of the Catholic ghetto, Catholics in the sixties completed their full entry into American social, political, and intellectual life. As they did, they discovered that they faced all the moral and cultural dilemmas of modern America as well. Catholics found they could no longer afford, even if they wanted to, the luxury of passing remote and superior judgment on an American culture in confusion; it was their own culture as well.

One immediate result of this change for some American Catholics was a loss of Catholic identity. Where once Catholics had asked what it meant to be American, now some Americans were asking what it meant to be Catholic. The components of American Catholic identity had always been complex and various, but had usually included somewhere a belief that Catholicism had something of unique value to bring to society. With that assumption in question, the reasons for acting publicly under the label *Catholic* seemed suddenly less clear.

Accordingly, the difficulties of talking about "Catholic" activities in this period are compounded. Catholics who participated in social movements were, in this respect, no different from those who participated in government, business, academic, or journalistic life. For example, a young Catholic named Thomas Hayden from Charles Coughlin's Shrine of the Little Flower in Royal Oak, Michigan, became a nationally known leader of the very secular Students for a Democratic Society. Michael Harrington, who had known Hayden as a young radical at the University of Michigan and later in New York, observed that in earlier decades a like-minded young Catholic would probably have gravitated to one of the Catholic social movements. The presence of numerous persons of Catholic background like Hayden in all segments of the antiwar activities of the sixties requires a distinction between Catholics in the peace movement and the Catholic peace movement. It was only the latter that retained the belief that American Catholics had a responsibility as a religious community, and not simply as individual citizens, to act on the question of war.[86]

The principal organization of the radical Catholic peace movement in the mid-1960s was the Catholic Peace Fellowship. The Protestant Fellowship of Reconciliation had tried for a number of years to establish a Catholic affiliate, but it was only after Vatican II encouraged ecumenical cooperation that Catholics responded favorably. The CPF grew out of a Christian Peace Conference in Prague, Czechoslovakia, in October 1964, where FOR staff member John Heidbrink brought together leading Catholic peace activists who wanted an alternative to Pax's institutional lobbying and its tactical use of the just war argument. Father Daniel Berrigan agreed to spearhead the new Catholic FOR affiliate and to contribute his lecture fees as seed money. James Forest, a former Catholic Worker, became the director.[87]

For several months CPF existed largely on paper. Then in November 1964 Thomas Merton conducted a retreat at his Abbey of Gethsemani on the theme "Spiritual Roots of Protest." Among those attending were the Berrigan brothers, Forest, Thomas Cornell, A. J. Muste, and Mennonite theologian John Howard Yoder. With Merton's encouragement, the Catholics reaffirmed their commitment to a new peace group that would concentrate on grass-roots activity and war resistance. Additional funding was secured from the FOR and the War Resisters League, and the CPF became active in the spring of 1965.[88]

The birth of the CPF was timely, for the Vietnam escalation was just getting underway and many Catholics were looking for ways to express their concern about the war. Seldom finding leadership from ordinary Church sources, they readily turned to an unofficial but expressly Catholic group like the CPF. The organization was quickly overwhelmed by requests for information, direction, and assistance from Catholics across the country. Priests frequently directed those troubled about the draft to CPF; by 1967 the New York office alone was handling two dozen draft inquiries a week. To answer the growing demand for information, CPF put out printed material on Catholic teaching about war and conscience, reprinted articles by Day, Ludlow, Merton, Zahn, and others, distributed tapes and films, and published a bimonthly bulletin. CPF leaders were also in demand as speakers before all sorts of Catholic groups, and wherever they went they found people in the churches ready to form local Catholic peace groups.[89]

The exact character of these local groups varied considerably. Some were established as local chapters of CPF; others simply drew informally on the resources and literature of the national organization. Some were bitterly opposed by the regular clergy and became associated with so-called underground churches; others received open or covert support from local priests and even bishops. Some groups focused on turning the Church against the war, some on direct political action, and others on the draft. In several cases the prosecution of a local Catholic conscientious objector or draft resister became the catalyst for Catholic peace activity. By 1966 some sort of Catholic peace group existed in almost every major city outside the South, and everywhere their numbers and commitment escalated in proportion to the growing war in Vietnam. Although little noticed at first by news organizations, these local groups formed a strong foundation for the more visible protests of nationally prominent Catholic activists.

The growth of the CPF into a substantial Catholic antiwar organization, following closely on the creation of Pax, marked what might be called the coming of age of the American Catholic peace witness. Previously, the Catholic concern for peace had been identified almost exclusively with a single group, the Catholic Worker. Pax and CPF still had close ties with the Catholic Worker, but they were forerunners of the great variety of Catholic antiwar activity that soon appeared. This diversity reflected the growing breadth of Catholic concern about war and the growing internal diversity of American Catholicism in general. The days when American Catholics—even Catholic social activists—could be assumed to have a single outlook on significant social questions were over. The Catholic Worker's comprehensive radical Gospel vision was no longer the focal point of the growing peace witness within American Catholicism. Henceforth, a commitment by Catholics to the cause of peace no longer meant, as it had for three decades, an encounter with Dorothy Day and her movement.

To be sure, the Catholic Worker's presence was still felt. All three national co-chairmen of the Catholic Peace Fellowship, for instance, had connections with the movement. Thomas Cornell and James

Forest were typical Catholic Worker alumni of the sort that had been coming out of the movement since the 1930s. Cornell had come to the movement in the early fifties after reading Day's autobiography while a student at Jesuit Fairfield College. A talented organizer and propagandist, he was prominent in Catholic Worker civil rights and peace activities of the early sixties, until he left the movement for marriage and CPF in 1964. Forest was a former naval intelligence officer who converted to Catholicism and pacifism in 1960. He moved directly from the navy to the Catholic Worker, where he quickly became a well-known writer and activist. Both Cornell and Forest remained close to Day and the Catholic Worker after their departure, and the movement remained an important influence on their later work and thought.[90]

But the influence of the Catholic Worker on the third member of the CPF leadership, Daniel Berrigan, was remoter and, therefore, more typical of its influence on the new Catholic peace movement. Berrigan's father, an Irish-American farmer and laborer in Syracuse, New York, was a reader of the paper, but Daniel's "progressive Catholicism" really developed during the fifties when he encountered the worker-priest movement in France. Only after he had become a well-known Catholic poet and civil rights activist in the late 1950s did he become acquainted with the Catholic Worker in more than a casual way. It is probable that reading Dorothy Day and Thomas Merton helped change Berrigan from a "chubby, smug, talky liberal priest" into an ascetic radical activist. Certainly his close association with Catholic Workers Forest and Cornell in CPF educated him in the history and techniques of radical pacifism. Yet Berrigan was as much a product of the broader progressive trends within American and international Catholicism as of the specifically Catholic Worker tradition. Although the *Catholic Worker* ran a number of Berrigan's articles on Vietnam in 1964 and 1965, he was always a quite independent center of Catholic peace activity.[91]

The connections between the Catholic Worker and prominent Catholic activists of the sixties suggest that the emergence of the new Catholic Left was partly due to the Catholic Worker's years of patient labor within the American Church. In some cases, certainly, the Catholic Worker laid the groundwork for the new Catholic activism. At a 1966 Catholic peace meeting in New Jersey, for example, about one-third of those present indicated that they were readers of the *Catholic Worker*. "I belong to a Church that is known definitely only for being against birth control and for bingo," said one man. "If it had not been for reading the *Catholic Worker* I would have left long ago."[92]

But the Catholic Left attracted many people who knew Day and the Catholic Worker, if at all, as symbols of the past. Day was sometimes hailed as a pioneer of Catholic dissent, but the dominant mood within "progressive" sectors of the American Church in the mid-sixties was favorable to neither religious tradition nor the style of reflective and intellectual radicalism cultivated by the Catholic Worker. Many Catholic religious and lay persons who became socially active in the sixties were too caught up in their own novelty and what they saw as immediate moral imperatives to explore the considerable religious and intellectual heritage built up over the previous thirty years by Day's Catholic radical movement. Even as they criticized American values, many Catholic dissenters showed that they had thoroughly assimilated one fundamental American trait: absorption in the present and disdain for the past. This lack of historical depth and perspective had unfortunate consequences a few years later when the Catholic Left, like the New Left as a whole, faced severe crises within and without.

Yet it is also true that the tradition of Catholic radicalism represented by the Catholic Worker gave least guidance precisely where the Catholic Left made its strongest efforts—in the area of politics. In steering directly into the violent political storms of Vietnam, the Catholic Left followed the course increasingly taken by American peace activists in the twentieth century. Even the Catholic Worker, which disdained conventional politics and stressed the primacy of moral and religious transformation in ending war, engaged in campaigns of nonviolent direct action that could be interpreted in political terms. Indeed, the surprising and heady success of nonviolent movements in the decade from 1955 to 1965 led some pacifists to believe that they were on the verge of developing a broad Gandhian movement in America that would bring closer the ideals of peace and social justice.

Such expectations were misguided. Consistent ideological pacifists in America were never more than a small faction, far outnumbered even in the peace campaigns they led by those for whom nonviolence was a useful tactic, not a moral necessity. The weakness of the radical nonviolent movement was demonstrated during the war in Vietnam. Not only were pacifists helpless to stop the unpopular war, but they could not even retain control of the antiwar movement, which passed into nonpacifist hands as it became a truly mass affair. Millions of Americans wanted an end to the Vietnam War, but not under the banner of those who would rule out all war on religious or moral grounds. Unable to compete effectively with liberal and New Left war opponents for public support, consistent pacifists had to either suppress their principles in order to remain politically effective in the anti-Vietnam movement or retreat to the transcendental and personal sources of their beliefs. In either case their goal of ending war through nonviolence receded.

From one perspective, then, the evolution of the Catholic peace movement up to 1966 simply demonstrated anew the validity of Reinhold Niebuhr's criticism of pacifism for its inability to take seriously the real world of political power and international violence. But for radical pacifists, assuming political responsibility could only mean plunging into the compromises and imperfections of existing politics and, thus, eroding pacifist ideals. To some pacifists, including those at the Catholic Worker, Gandhianism seemed to point a way out of this impasse. But its impressive theories remained only theories. The viability of mass nonviolence as a substitute method of international relations could not be tested so long as most men believed in the necessity of war, and most men would continue to believe war was necessary until some alternative proved workable. During the Vietnam War, certainly, pacifists had no convincing response to the charge that their proposed substitute for war was a chimera.

It was typical of contemporary uncertainty, however, that while pacifists were condemned as utopian radicals, many of their essential arguments were echoed by realistic men of affairs. "Let us have no part in making millions of women and children and noncombatants hostages for the behavior of their governments," said George Kennan in 1959. "If this means defeat, I can only reply that I am skeptical of the meaning of victory and defeat in their relation to modern war." And General Douglas MacArthur stated, "The progress and survival of civilization are dependent upon the realization of the utter futility of force as an arbiter of international issues." Yet no matter how much realistic men recoiled from war, they recoiled even farther from the pacifists' suggestion that there should be a unilateral repudiation of war and the instruments of war, beginning with the individual's declared unwillingness to take up arms for the state. Pacifist arguments for such a course had little effect in an armed and hostile world.[93]

So practical men pursued peace by practical means; but meanwhile they tolerated preparations for war. They therefore made it difficult to refute the pacifist contention that even the best-intentioned practical men would eventually be drawn into war, as they always had been in the past. This was why pacifists insisted that the path to peace required more than a purely political or rational approach. "People want peace, but not the things that make for peace," Dorothy Day frequently said. And A. J. Muste warned that "those who do not undergo a spiritual revolution will, after a period of protesting that war simply must not be, find in the event of crisis a moral justification for engaging in it." The history of peace activity after World War II suggested that until more men underwent such a spiritual revolution, or until politics somehow changed in radically unforeseen ways, stopping war would remain a utopian dream.[94]

Yet if the Catholic radicals, like American pacifists in general, had not succeeded by 1966 in moving any closer to their goal, they could claim some more modest achievements. The practice of nonviolent civil disobedience against war and armaments by the radical pacifists remained, in Thomas Merton's phrase, a "sign of contradiction" to national policies and presented at least a minor annoyance to the authorities. Paradoxically, the very lack of political ambition and sophistication among religious pacifists like the Catholic Workers may have made them more effective witnesses in this regard than the more politically sophisticated war objectors. The continued readiness of many Catholic radicals to accept prison terms for draft resistance, for instance, testified to their sincerity among nonpacifists and pricked the conscience of those war objectors who took the safe escape routes provided by the state.

The Catholic Worker had also helped create a small but growing peace witness within the American Catholic Church and had brought a distinctively Catholic religious and intellectual outlook to American peace activity. Catholic Workers and their fellow travelers had led the intellectual assault on the ancient just war doctrine by which the Christian churches justified their toleration of war and had thereby contributed in some measure to the ethical reevaluation of war by modern theologians, moral philosophers, and social thinkers. Pacifism by no means emerged triumphant from this reconsideration. The just war idea proved resilient, constantly reappearing in new forms. Yet the pacifists could take some satisfaction from the revival of just war thinking, for that ancient Catholic idea at least acknowledged the necessity of applying moral standards to international violence. When applied universally, as by some Americans during Vietnam, the teaching concerning just war could present serious challenges to modern war and nationalism. As with many significant contemporary moral debates, the questions were clearer than the proposed answers. But the perspectives of the Catholic radicals added to Americans' social thought about war and reminded them of the momentous consequences of their personal and national decisions.

CHAPTER SEVEN

Catholic Spiritual Radicalism in America

Drawing historical conclusions about the Catholic Worker is difficult because the movement does not fit easily into conventional categories. It was at once a social and political movement, a utopian experiment, and a force for change within American Catholicism. In these areas the Catholic Worker was provocative but not especially successful. What made the group of greater interest was its function as a movement of intellectual and spiritual renewal. By raising some basic religious questions with singular vigor and intelligence, the Catholic Worker carved a unique place for itself in American culture.

As a radical social movement, the Catholic Worker had only a small impact. From union organizing in the thirties to anti-Vietnam protests in the sixties, Day's followers were part of larger American movements for social change. Along with other small groups of American religious and ethical radicals, the Workers added some new and interesting twists to what Max Weber called "the ethic of ultimate ends" as applied to American public life. Although never the dominant presence in social movements, religious groups like the Catholic Worker were among those that contributed to a heightened moral sensitivity in recent American society and occasionally aroused a "moral constituency" that moved the centers of power.

The Catholic Worker's most measurable success in this regard probably came with the publication of Michael Harrington's *The Other America*. Although written after Harrington left the movement, *The Other America* clearly stemmed from his Catholic Worker experience. Besides its direct policy consequences in the War on Poverty, *The Other America* had a deeper impact in stimulating a permanent public awareness of the persistence of poverty in affluent America. It was fitting that the Catholic Worker, which had so long concerned itself with aiding "our

241

invisible poor," should thus have contributed to making poverty more visible to the whole nation.

Still, by conventional measures, the Catholic Worker's years of social activism yielded few great results. At no time were any of the movement's distinctive principles adopted by any substantial constituency. Whatever moral and intellectual weight the religious and ethical radicals like the Workers may have added to American concern for labor, civil rights, anti-poverty, and peace, such groups were unable to effect any significant transformation in American political attitudes or institutions.

To some extent the political ineffectuality of religious social movements like the Catholic Worker can be considered part of the larger failure of American radicalism, which has always functioned more as a moral goad than as an effective force in national life. But religious-ethical radicals have been even less successful than other radicals because they belong to a tradition that consistently subordinates attainable social goals to ethical purity. Even though the Catholic Worker attempted to influence public affairs, it never operated according to normal political motives or judgments. On the few occasions when a modest social influence was in view, it was rejected in order to defend the group's higher ethical ideals. In the particular tradition of the radical Gospel followed by the Catholic Worker, political failure was justified by the mysterious language of religious paradox: losing one's life to find it, taking up the cross, the first shall be last and the last first. This apparent indifference to practical results was a great source of strength for the Catholic Worker during periods of isolation and failure, such as World War II and the McCarthy era. But its transcendental logic clearly places the group outside the ordinary boundaries of the political sphere.

The Catholic Worker might therefore be considered not primarily as a movement for social change, but as a movement of utopian dissent. These typically express their disaffection with the larger society not through direct social action but through attempts to criticize the values of that society, often by creating enclaves that are expected to serve as alternative social models. This impulse was clearly present in the Catholic Workers' communal Houses and farms, which incorporated many of the themes prevalent in American utopian experiments and movements since the nineteenth century: personal freedom and dignity, economic communism, social equality, an emphasis on nonmaterial values, smaller-scale social relations, and closer relations with nature. Like most such ventures, the Catholic Worker communities only partially lived up to their ideals, but they deserve a place in American history alongside other small but noteworthy American experiments, such as the Shaker settlements, Brook Farm, and Oneida. And even though they did not precipitate the wave of American dissent and alternative intentional communities in the sixties, the Catholic Workers can be counted among the small number of "utopian" social critics of the thirties, forties, and fifties who saw that the apparent triumph of the values of big organization, production, and efficiency in industrial America was by no means final and that competing American values would have their day.

Still, despite some similarities to other utopian and communitarian movements, the Catholic Worker does not fit comfortably among them. Because they appeal to individuals who are dissatisfied with the dominant social values yet choose to express their dissent by withdrawal from the whole culture, alternative communitarian movements are, in the long run, susceptible to fragmentation and loss of identity. These tendencies in turn generate pressures for complete sectarian isolation or authoritarian leadership as the only way of holding the dissenting community together. While such pressures were present in the Catholic Worker's history, the group was remarkably successful over a long period in avoiding loss of identity, isolation, or authoritarian leadership.

This was partly due, no doubt, to Dorothy Day, whose long tenure as charismatic leader might be said to fit the utopian pattern of strong personal direction. Yet the strength of Day's leadership was exercised as much through her role as spiritual writer and exemplar as through her position as head of the movement. As this study has tried to show, the Catholic Worker was a multifaceted anarchist affair, with a variety of other leaders and tendencies. The continued existence into the 1970s of more than fifty Catholic Worker Houses and farms suggests that the movement rested on more than the personal appeal of even such an imposing figure as Dorothy Day.

The Workers also avoided sectarianism by carefully preserving their connections with the common life of the larger society. The strongest of these connections was the religious one—loyalty to the Roman Catholic Church. For the Catholic Worker, Catholicism represented not simply a denominational tie, but a rich religious heritage extending through time and across national boundaries. By being staunchly Catholic, the Catholic Worker remained catholic as well. The Worker also maintained social connections with the surrounding society through its acts of charity, economic connections through its dependence on contributions, and political connections through its involvement in public issues. Therefore, even though the Workers did partially secede from

American society in order to express their dissenting values, their relationship with that society seems more subtle, intimate, and enduring than those maintained by most utopian experiments.

The Catholic Worker may also be considered in terms of its effects on American Catholicism. Dorothy Day's primary achievement in this regard was to introduce the social perspectives of the radical Gospel into the American Church. This was a considerable achievement because, until Vatican II, modern Catholicism, unlike Protestantism, had few theological pegs on which to hang such an interpretation of the faith. The Workers, therefore, acted with only a minimum of clerical backing. In slowly gaining a wider recognition of the legitimacy of a radical Gospel witness within American Catholicism, the Workers functioned in somewhat the same way—though on a smaller scale—as the Mennonite, Quaker, and radical Social Gospel movements within Protestant tradition.

The Catholic Worker was also ahead of its time in such areas of Catholic churchlife as lay leadership, social involvement, intellectual openness, and ecumenical spirit. Although these traits were once highly controversial, the Worker's grass-roots Christianity was closer to present-day American Catholic theological understandings of what the Church should be than the strictly institutional and hierarchical models of earlier times. The Catholic Worker also nurtured several generations of socially concerned lay Catholics who strengthened the already vigorous liberal social tradition of the American Church. As an example of deeply committed but completely independent lay Catholicism in the United States, the Catholic Worker provided an alternative model of what American Catholicism might be.

Although the Catholic Worker was unquestionably one of the early forces for change within American Catholicism, its direct influence in this respect should not be exaggerated. Even at its high points, the movement never reached more than a minority in the Church. The changed relations of American Catholics to their Church in the 1950s and 1960s owed more to their altered social and educational condition and to their broader historical experience in America than to specific movements like the Catholic Worker. To take one example, the election of John Kennedy was probably a greater stimulus to change in the American Church, particularly among lay persons, than any overtly Catholic force.

Furthermore, despite her devotion to Catholic doctrine and the Catholic community, Dorothy Day herself paid relatively little attention to Church affairs as such. The Catholic Worker disturbed American Catholic waters somewhat simply by the way it acted, but it had almost nothing to say either before or after Vatican II about such liberal ecclesiastical concerns as democratizing Church governance, changing sexual teachings, enhancing the position of women, and loosening the dogmatic approach to Catholic education. Except in the areas of social justice, ecumenical relations, and liturgical reform—where its concern was with deepening the corporate character and social implications of worship rather than with such things as the vernacular—the Worker's stance on Church issues can be described as moderately conservative. Dorothy Day's steady posture as "the angry but obedient daughter of holy mother Church" makes her an ambiguous symbol for those in the United States or elsewhere who look for substantial changes in Catholic moral teaching or institutional practices.

In its approaches to politics, cultural criticism, and specifically Catholic affairs, then, the Catholic Worker was a lively but not especially influential force. If its reputation rested on its achievements in these areas alone, it would have a rather slender claim to historical significance. The Catholic Worker's other activities are finally important because they were part of its functions as an intellectually alert movement of spiritual renewal.

A spiritual movement may be defined as one that positively addresses the spiritual dilemmas of a period and thereby opens the possibility of new cultural approaches to religion. The history of the Catholic Worker can be seen as an attempt to confront certain fundamental issues that have prevented religion from exerting a great effect on modern American civilization: the social timidity of religion in the United States, its lack of a vital contemplative tradition, and its intellectual isolation from the mainstream of American life. Although the Catholic Worker's own solutions to these problems were accepted only by a few, the group's integrity, courage, and self-sacrifice underscored the importance of religious questions at a time when history had made them of considerable interest.

That modern Americans in general and many intellectuals in particular had difficulty dealing intelligently with religious questions was evident, for example, in a 1950 *Partisan Review* symposium, "Religion and the Intellectuals." Although the intellectuals surveyed differed in their attitudes toward religion, most stressed that any statement or inquiry they might make was hampered by what they saw as the social and spiritual weakness of American religion—particularly its intellectual segregation from other areas of American life. "Piety in the large active sense . . . fails to inspire the religious community as a whole enough to affect civil affairs in a decisive way," stated Meyer Schapiro, one of the participants. "The churches know that religion is unable to create a moral order." William Phillips noted that the symposium's American participants, including himself, tended to see religion as primarily a private or personal affair, while "in Europe the church has a more vital relation to the public lives of the people, and generally the assertion of a religious position, far from being a literary act, has serious social consequences."[1]

Even at the personal level the participants found it difficult to say what religious commitment meant. "I have not been able to observe any difference between the way of life of those who profess some religious belief and those who do not," said Phillips. Robert Gorham Davis contended that "only an infinitesimal minority of Christians act as if God had really become man and spiritualized human existence." One result was that even when intellectuals developed a positive interest in religion, they found few points of contact between religious ideas and the rest of American life. "The great intellectual converts . . . had solutions good for themselves," stated William Barrett, "but the very isolation of their experience from any roots in the common religious and social life of the culture give it a kind of abstract and formal quality." The problem with the postwar "religious revival" among some intellectuals, agreed Phillips, was that "it has very little to do with American life as a whole. What we have now in America is not so much a turn to religion but a turn to religiosity, which is not the same thing. There has been virtually no serious presentation of the problems of belief, faith, creed, the value of existing religious institutions. Only T. S. Eliot has made such an effort, but he has done so in terms of British institutions and traditions."[2]

Although Dorothy Day set out only to start a Catholic paper for the unemployed, her searching spiritual radicalism forced her to cope with these basic American religious problems. The Catholic Workers addressed the problem of religion's social weakness by practicing radical Gospel Christianity with a "harsh and dreadful love" that embraced both personal sacrifice and collective protest against some major American institutions and values. They addressed the problem of spiritual apathy by attempting to develop a synthesis of traditional Catholic spirituality and American social ideals, bringing together the ancient religious goal of communion with God and the modern goal of transforming the world by social commitment. The problem of intellectual weakness was met by the *Catholic Worker*, which carried on a sophisticated discussion of religious and moral issues from the perspective of a committed effort to reconstruct American society.

It was this spiritual and intellectual vigor that attracted wider interest in a small and politically isolated Catholic movement. Although the Catholic Worker had a following from all walks of life, it found particular admirers among intellectuals. The movement was naturally most attractive to American Catholic intellectuals, who shared much of the Catholic Worker's distinctively Catholic tradition and vocabulary. But the Worker also drew the attention of persons with quite different religious and political outlooks: James Farrell, Dwight Macdonald, T. S. Eliot, Hannah Arendt, Lewis Mumford, James Wallis, Claude McKay, and W. H. Auden, to name only a few. Since 1950, articles on the movement have appeared in a wide variety of Catholic and non-Catholic journals.

Some of this interest can be attributed to the *Catholic Worker* itself, which was an important meeting place of European and American Catholic thought, even apart from its ideological presentation of "the Catholic Worker idea." Yet what made the Catholic Worker unique was not ideas or social theory alone, but the way these were intimately linked with religion. And what made the Workers' religion interesting was their total commitment to living it out. Simply by persevering in their efforts through some of the most tumultuous years of American history, the Workers opened at least one bridge between the higher religious and ethical ideals of the Christian heritage and the actual experience of American society.

Some intellectuals felt the need for such links even more strongly by the end of the 1960s. In the forties and fifties the stirrings of intellectual interest in religion were little affected by conditions within American society itself. Two world wars and a Cold War had shaken many Americans' earlier faith in human progress and self-sufficiency, but their doubts seldom reached basic American institutions or "the American way of life," which was practically apotheosized during the popular religious revival of the 1950s. But in the sixties doubts about the foundations of American culture were no longer the property of a few intellectuals. Beneath the particular social conflicts of the time there developed a basic loss of confidence in culture that to such contemporary observers as Paul Goodman, Daniel Bell, Richard Hofstadter, and Sydney Ahlstrom took on the character of a religious crisis.[3]

One participant in that crisis was the American Catholic Church. No longer isolated from the general American experience and unable to escape the spiritual upheavals of modernism, American Catholicism experienced what historian John Tracy Ellis frankly called "a crisis of faith."[4] The dimensions of that crisis were complex and its impact difficult to discern in detail, but one obvious result was an upheaval in the values and self-understanding of practically every major Catholic institution.

Amidst all this turmoil, perhaps the most unchanged thing in American Catholicism was the Catholic Worker. While much of the American Church scrambled to adapt to new circumstances, the Catholic Worker proceeded with little alteration in its basic outlook or practices. It was as if this most radical Catholic movement had already come to terms with the forces that elsewhere caused so much disruption.

Certainly Day had built into the Catholic Worker from the beginning a subtle relationship with the values of modern American culture. Many of the conditions that the rest of Catholicism had to struggle with—the free-swinging intellectual exchanges, the questioning of values, the radical sense of freedom and equality, the voluntarism in religion—came as no surprise at the Catholic Worker, where they had always been part of the landscape.

But Day had worked out this relationship with American culture in ways that did not undercut the Catholic Worker's deeper commitment to the spiritual values of Catholicism. It was this inner wholeness of religious and social outlooks that perhaps most distinguished the Catholic Worker from many other religious dissenters. While professing respect for the Catholic Worker, many of the newcomers to Catholic protest either dismissed or failed to understand at all some of the movement's distinctive ideas. One Catholic Leftist, for example, who called himself a "spiritual stepchild" of the Catholic Worker, also said that "it is crucially important to me that people understand that Christianity is political. A religious ideology must lead to a political ideology."[5] Whatever the validity of this view, it could not have been fathered by the Catholic Worker, which had worked out a quite different and subtle approach to the relationship of religion and society. Similarly, the Catholic Worker's extremely subtle pattern of relations with institutional religion—the Church—was misunderstood even more often than it was rejected.

Certainly the Catholic Worker had some old-fashioned ideas, and plenty of foibles and failings, too. In matters concerning women, for example, the movement did not show the same capacity for positive social criticism it displayed in other areas of social thought. But seeing the Catholic Worker's weaknesses made it too easy to overlook the fact that many of its seemingly peculiar qualities were the result of a thoughtful, sophisticated effort to adapt ancient religious values to use in the modern world. The practices of voluntary poverty and direct personal charity to the poor preserved the uniquely Christian character of the movement and guarded against laxity or politicization. The emphasis on traditional prayer, liturgy, and practices like fasting connected both individuals and group to the common faith and life of the whole Catholic community. And the respect for Catholic tradition in social thought, the arts, literature, philosophy, and theology guarded against narrow moralism, anti-intellectualism, and thoughtless innovation.

These factors may account for the Catholic Worker's notable steadiness in an age of rapid change, when it was often difficult to distinguish between genuine cultural innovation and bored faddishness. In the wake of the political upheavals and disillusionment of the sixties, some Catholics and other Americans developed an interest in the kind of matters that had long been a part of the Catholic Worker tradition: the practice of spirituality in daily life, the subtle dialectic of contemplation and social action, the interest in spiritual links between non-Western religions and Christianity. The growing intellectual interest in Thomas Merton as an example of a socially engaged contemplative was an indirect tribute to the Catholic Worker, for Merton's own social awakening owed much to Dorothy Day.

The fundamental importance of the Catholic Worker, then, was that it offered within contemporary American culture a model of socially and intellectually engaged Catholic spirituality. In so doing, it signaled the beginning of a deeper relationship between Catholicism and American culture, a mark of the maturing of the American Catholic community. It also raised in a pointed fashion the questions every society must ask about religion and social values.

It did not make the answers any easier to give. Dorothy Day and the Catholic Workers found a way within Catholic and American tradition to integrate religion and politics, spirituality and social concern. But it was by no means clear what the Workers' experience implied for persons in other religious traditions or conditions of life, much less for a whole society. The radical Gospel remained as problematic as ever when presented not simply as a personalist ethical ideal but as a model for the reconstruction of a complex modern society like the United States. Since the radical Gospel necessarily pointed to social failure even for those like the Catholic Workers who strove hardest to live up to it, a great deal of subtle religious interpretation would be required to uncover the larger social implications of the movement. In any case those who might look to the Catholic Worker for simple solutions to all the dilemmas of the age would surely be disappointed.

The Catholic Worker was never a mass movement, and the number of those directly influenced by it is not likely to be large either. Yet history affords examples of spiritual and intellectual minorities affecting culture far out of proportion to numbers. It is too soon to know whether anything more will come of Dorothy Day's lonely pilgrimage through modern America. Henry Adams ended his *Education* with the wish that he might return after thirty years to witness the judgments of posterity on his generation. A similar interval may have to pass before definitive conclusions can be reached about the Catholic Worker. But in the meantime, in a world that sensitive and timid natures still had to regard with a shudder, it was one small sign of hope.

Notes

Chapter One

1. *Catholic Worker* 1 (May 1933): 2 (hereinafter cited as *CW*).
2. *New York Review of Books* 19 (December 14, 1972): 3.
3. Dorothy Day, *The Long Loneliness* (New York: Harper & Row, 1952), p. 20.
4. Dorothy Day, *The Eleventh Virgin* (New York: Boni, 1924), p. 304.
5. Richard Sennett, *Families Against the City: Middle Class Homes of Industrial Chicago, 1872–1890* (New York: Vintage, 1970), pp. 184–217. Dorothy was the third of five children; the two oldest and the youngest were boys. In contrast to the cold, distant father, Day's mother, Grace Satterlee Day, was a kind, open woman who remained close to Dorothy throughout her life; but she, too, lacked the emotional warmth young Dorothy sought
6. Day, *Long Loneliness*, p. 27.
7. Ibid., p. 30. The senior Day had intellectual aspirations of a sort. He filled his sports columns with biblical and Shakespearean allusions, published in the *Saturday Evening Post*, and at one point quit his job to write a novel.
8. Ibid., pp. 30–31.
9. Dorothy Day, "Eviction," *Jubilee* 6 (November 1958): 29.
10. Day, *Eleventh Virgin*, p. 20; Day, *Long Loneliness*, p. 36.
11. Day, *Long Loneliness*, pp. 42–43.
12. Ibid., pp. 36–42.
13. Ibid., p. 25.
14. Ibid., p. 42.
15. Ibid., p. 43.
16. Ibid., p. 46.
17. Ibid., pp. 48–49; Day, *Eleventh Virgin*, pp. 61–87. William D. Miller, *Dorothy Day: A Biography* (San Francisco: Harper and Row, 1982), pp. 31–53. Among Day's close friends at the university was Rayna Prohme, later a Communist heroine and comrade of Mikhail Borodin in China.
18. Day, *Long Loneliness*, p. 47.
19. Ibid., p. 46.
20. John Diggins, *The American Left in the Twentieth Century* (New York: Harcourt,

Brace, 1973), pp. 77–78; Henry F. May, *The End of American Innocence* (Chicago: Quadrangle, 1964).

21. *New York Call*, December 12, 1916. The "Diet Squad" reports appeared in the *Call* on December 3, 10, 12, 15, 18, 21, 27, 1916.

22. Day, *Long Loneliness*, p. 58.

23. Ibid., February 21, 1917, p. 2. The interview with Trotsky is in the *Call* for January 16, 1917, p. 1. On muckraking journalism, see Richard Hofstadter, *The Age of Reform* (New York: Vintage, 1955), pp. 186–214; and Alfred Kazin, *On Native Grounds* (Garden City: Doubleday, 1942), pp. 74–79.

24. *New York Call*, February 3, 1917, p. 1.

25. Dorothy Day, *From Union Square to Rome* (Silver Spring: Preservation of the Faith Press, 1938), p. 74. Day covered the entire Sanger story, from the opening of an illegal birth control clinic to Mrs. Byrne's release from prison. Other reports in the *Call* were January 9, 14, 15, 16, 18, 20, 23, 24, 26, 27, 28, 29, 30, 31, and February 1, 2, 3, 8, 9, 12, 14, 1917. For the whole Sanger-Byrne affair, see David M. Kennedy, *Birth Control in America* (New Haven: Yale University Press, 1970), pp. 84–87.

26. Floyd Dell, *Homecoming: An Autobiography* (New York: Farrar and Rinehart, 1933), p. 296.

27. Day, *From Union Square to Rome*, pp. 77–124. Day, *Eleventh Virgin*, pp. 59–122.

28. Dorothy Day, "Doing My Bit for Ireland," *The Masses* 9 (August 1917): 37; see also Day, "Mary Maclane," *The Masses* 9 (September 1917): 31; Day, "Upton Sinclair's *King Coal*," *The Masses* 10 (November–December 1917): 31; Day, "Sherwood Anderson's *Marching Men*," *The Masses* 10 (November–December 1917): 33. For Day's portrait of Eastman, Dell, and others, see *Eleventh Virgin*, pp. 148–179.

29. Day, *Long Loneliness*, p. 68. See also Day, *Eleventh Virgin*, pp. 94–96.

30. *From Union Square to Rome*, p. 80. For the trial, see Floyd Dell, "The Story of a Trial," *Liberator* 1 (1918): 17–23.

31. Malcolm Cowley, *Exile's Return* (New York: Viking, 1951), p. 69.

32. For the relationship between Day and O'Neill, see Arthur and Barbara Gelb, *O'Neill* (New York: Harper and Row, 1962), pp. 358–368; and Miller, *Dorothy Day*, pp. 106–113.

33. Interview with Sue Brown, Dorothy Day-Catholic Worker Papers, Marquette University Archives, Milwaukee, Wisconsin (hereinafter cited as CW papers).

34. Day, *Long Loneliness*, pp. 109–110; Day, *From Union Square to Rome*, pp. 90–108; Day, *Eleventh Virgin*, pp. 221–245.

35. Day, *Eleventh Virgin*, pp. 246–306; Interview with Sue Brown, CW Papers; Miller, *Dorothy Day*, pp. 125–142.

36. Day, *Eleventh Virgin*, pp. 309–311.

37. Interview with Sue Brown, CW Papers; Day, *Long Loneliness*, pp. 110–111; Miller, *Dorothy Day*, pp. 143–147.

38. Day, *Long Loneliness*, pp. 111–124; Miller, *Dorothy Day*, pp. 147–159. For an example of her journalism in this period, see Dorothy Day, "Floyd Dell's *Janet March*," *Liberator* 6 (1923): 30–31. The convoluted history of radical journals and their contributors during this period is traced in Daniel Aaron, *Writers on the Left* (New York: Harcourt, Brace, 1961), pp. 5–118.

39. Dorothy Day, "Girls in Jail," *The New Masses* 4 (1928): 8; Day, *Long Loneliness*, pp. 113–121.

40. *New Orleans Item*, January 14, February 3, 5, 7, 1924.

41. Day, *Eleventh Virgin*, p. 297.

42. Interviews with Sue Brown and Jack English, CW Papers; Miller, *Dorothy Day*, pp. 136–137.
43. Walter Rideout, *The Radical Novel in the United States, 1900–1934* (Cambridge, Mass.: Harvard University Press, 1956), pp. 274–280.
44. Dorothy Day, "Having a Baby," *The New Masses* 4 (1928): 5; Day, *Long Loneliness*, pp. 124–170; Miller, *Dorothy Day*, pp. 166–188.
45. Day, *Long Loneliness*, p. 91.
46. Ibid., p. 77.
47. Ibid., p. 92.
48. Ibid., p. 155.
49. Robert Coles, *A Spectacle Unto the World* (New York: Viking, 1973), pp. 28–29.
50. Dorothy Day, "A Human Document," *Sign* 12 (November 1932): 223–224.
51. Day, *Long Loneliness*, p. 151.
52. CW Papers, D-3. She also stated, "Somehow I always associated joy and happiness with the religious life. I felt that no religious experience was valid unless there came with it a deep sense of confidence and joy."
53. Ibid., p. 161.
54. David J. O'Brien, *American Catholics and Social Reform: The New Deal Years* (New York: Oxford University Press, 1968), p. 194; Day, *From Union Square to Rome*, p. 80; Day, *Long Loneliness*, p. 130.
55. Richard Hofstadter, *Anti-Intellectualism in American Life* (New York: Vintage, 1963), p. 25. (*italics mine*)
56. CW Papers, D-3. Day often stated Dostoevski's importance for her: "Peter was not a reader of Dostoevsky, but the fact that I have always been such a student of the Russian helped me understand Peter as one of the meek, whom Dostoevsky loved to portray" (Dorothy Day, unpublished manuscript, CW Papers, W-3.1 [n.d.]).
57. Quoted in Coles, *Spectacle*, p. 26.
58. Dorothy Day, unpublished manuscript, CW Papers, D-2.
59. Dorothy Day, "A Reminiscence at 75," *Commonweal* 98 (1973): 424.
60. For some of Day's writing during this period, see Dorothy Day, "Guadalupe," *Commonweal* 11 (1930): 477–478; "Spring Festival From Mexico," *Commonweal* 12 (1930): 296–297.
61. Dorothy Day, *Loaves and Fishes* (New York: Harper and Row, 1963), p. 14.
62. For Day's reporting during this time, see Dorothy Day, "East 12th Street," *Commonweal* 17 (1932): 128–129; "A Human Document," *Sign* 12 (1932): 277–279; "Real Revolutionaries," *Commonweal* 17 (1933): 293–294; "Communism and the Intellectual," *America* 48 (1933): 401–403; "For the Truly Poor," *Commonweal* 17 (1933): 544–545; "St. John of the Cross," *Commonweal* 18 (1933): 287–288.
63. Day, *Long Loneliness*, pp. 187–189.

Chapter Two

1. André Siegfried, *America Comes of Age* (New York: Harcourt, Brace, 1927), p. 33.
2. Martin Marty, *Righteous Empire: The Protestant Experience in America* (New York: Dial, 1970), pp. 89–99.
3. Robert Baird, *Religion in America*, rev. ed. (New York: Harper and Row, 1970); Leonard Woolsey Bacon, *A History of American Christianity* (New York: Christian Literature, 1897), pp. 2, 419.

4. Quoted in Winthrop Hudson, *American Protestantism* (Chicago: University of Chicago Press, 1961), p. 139.

5. Kenneth Cauthen, *The Impact of American Religious Liberalism* (New York: Harper, 1962), pp. 9–32; William Hutchison, *The Modernist Impulse in American Protestantism* (Cambridge, Mass.: Harvard University Press, 1976).

6. Josiah Strong, *Our Country: Its Possible Future and Present Crisis* (1885; reprint ed., Cambridge, Mass.: Harvard University Press, 1963), pp. 201–218.

7. John Higham, *Strangers in the Land* (New Brunswick: Rutgers University Press, 1955), p. 5.

8. John Tracy Ellis, *American Catholicism* (Chicago: University of Chicago Press, 1968), pp. 150–157.

9. Robert Cross, *The Emergence of Liberal Catholicism in America* (Chicago: Quadrangle, 1958), pp. 22–70.

10. Thomas McAvoy, *The Great Crisis in American Catholic History, 1895–1900* (Chicago: Henry Regnery, 1957), pp. 76–77.

11. William M. Halsey, *The Survival of American Innocence* (Notre Dame: University of Notre Dame Press, 1980), p. 2.

12. Patrick McSweeney, "The Church and the Classes," *Catholic World* 47 (July 1888): 471–474.

13. *Christian Union*, October 27, 1875, p. 346.

14. William Hayes Ward, "Church Attendance," *North American Review* 137 (1883): 81. American workingmen were not necessarily alienated from religion—only from the churches. See Herbert Gutman, "Protestantism and the American Labor Movement," *American Historical Review* 77 (1966): 74–101.

15. Orvis Jordan, "What Must the Church Do to Be Saved," *Christian Century* 35 (December 5, 1918): 3–4; H. D. C. Malachen, "A Bourgeois Church in a Protestant World," *Christian Century* 37 (April 21, 1920): 9–12.

16. Jay Dolan, *The Immigrant Church* (Baltimore: Johns Hopkins University Press, 1975), pp. 52–53.

17. Liston Pope, "Religion and Class Structure," *Annals of the Academy of Political and Social Science* 256 (March 1948): 85–86; Hadley Cantrill, "Educational and Economic Composition of Religious Groups," *American Journal of Sociology* 47 (March 1943): 574–579; Herbert Wallace Schneider, ed., *Religion in Twentieth Century America* (Cambridge, Mass.: Harvard University Press, 1952), pp. 225–238; John J. Kane, "The Social Structure of American Catholics," *American Catholic Sociological Review* 16 (March 1955): 23–30; Andrew Greeley and Peter Rossi, *The Education of Catholic Americans* (Chicago: University of Chicago Press, 1966), pp. 28–29; Norval Glenn and Ruth Hyland, "Religious Preference and Worldly Success," *American Sociological Review* 32 (February 1967): 73–85. The phrase "a damn sight better than County Cork" is from Stephen Thernstrom's article, "Urbanization, Migration, and Social Mobility," in *Towards a New Past*, ed. Barton Bernstein (New York: Random House, 1968), pp. 161–162.

18. Samuel Lubell, *The Future of American Politics* (New York: Harper and Row, 1951), p. 86; Ellis, *American Catholicism*, pp. 116–119.

19. Robert Wiebe, *The Search for Order* (New York: Hill & Wang, 1967), p. 50.

20. William S. Anent, "Religion, Education, and Distinction," *School and Society* 26 (September 24, 1927): 399–406; Harvey Lehmann and Paul Witty, "Scientific Eminence and Church Membership," *Scientific Monthly* 33 (December 1931): 544–549; William Miller, "American Historians and the Business Elite," *Journal of Economic History* 9 (November 1949): 184–208; John Tracy

Ellis, "American Catholics and the Intellectual Life," *Thought* 30 (Autumn 1955): 351–388.

21. Henry F. May, *Protestant Churches and Industrial America* (New York: Harper, 1949), pp. 163–164; Aaron Abell, *The Urban Impact on American Protestantism* (Cambridge, Mass.: Harvard University Press, 1943), pp. 57–87.

22. Washington Gladden, *Recollections* (New York: Christian Literature, 1909), pp. 294–295.

23. Donald Meyer, *The Protestant Search for Political Realism* (Berkeley: University of California Press, 1960), p. 29; Charles Hopkins, *The Rise of the Social Gospel in American Protestantism* (New Haven: Yale University Press, 1940); W. A. Brown and Mark May, *The Education of American Ministers* (New York: Institute of Social and Religious Research, 1934).

24. For accounts of the conservative evangelical Christian responses to urbanization and industrialization, see Paul Boyer, *Urban Masses and Moral Order in America, 1820–1920* (Cambridge: Harvard University Press, 1978), pp. 132–142; and Norris Magnuson, *Salvation in the Slums: Evangelical Social Work, 1865–1920* (Metuchen, N.J.: Scarecrow Press, 1977), pp. 30–44, 165–178.

25. Washington Gladden, *The Nation and the Kingdom* (Boston: American Board of Commissioners for Foreign Missions, 1909), p. 4. See also Gladden, *Applied Christianity: Moral Aspects of Social Questions* (Boston: Houghton Mifflin, 1886).

26. Washington Gladden, *The New Idolatry and Other Discussions* (Boston: Houghton Mifflin, 1905), pp. 57–60; Walter Rauschenbusch, *Christianity and the Social Crisis* (1907; reprint ed., New York: Harper, 1964), p. 29.

27. Janet Forsythe Fishburn, *The Fatherhood of God and the Victorian Family: The Social Gospel in America* (Philadelphia: Fortress Press, 1982).

28. Paul Tillich, *The Protestant Era* (Chicago: University of Chicago Press, 1948), pp. 166–181.

29. Samuel L. Loomis, *Modern Cities and Their Religious Problems* (New York: Pilgrim Press, 1887), p. 99.

30. Aaron Abell, *American Catholicism and Social Action* (Notre Dame: University of Notre Dame Press, 1963), pp. 175–177. See also James Roohan, *American Catholics and the Social Question, 1865–1900* (New York: Arno Press, 1976).

31. Quoted in John O'Grady, *Catholic Charities in the United States* (Washington, D.C.: National Conference of Catholic Charities, 1931), pp. 106–107; see also pp. 235–271.

32. Abell, *American Catholicism*, p. 31.

33. Joan Marie Donahoe, *The Irish Catholic Benevolent Union* (Washington, D.C.: Catholic University Press, 1953); Philip Gleason, *The Conservative Reformers* (Notre Dame: University of Notre Dame Press, 1968), pp. 23–29.

34. James Cardinal Gibbons, *A Retrospect of Fifty Years*, 2 vols. (Baltimore: John Murphy Co., 1916), 1: 186–209; James Cardinal Gibbons, "Wealth and Its Obligations," *North American Review* 152 (1891): 385–394; James Cardinal Gibbons, "Some Defects in Our Political and Social Institutions," *North American Review* 145 (1887): 345–354; Roohan, *American Catholics*, p. 312.

35. Victor Greene, *The Slavic Community on Strike* (Notre Dame: University of Notre Dame Press, 1968), pp. 136–138; Richard Ely, "Socialism," *Inter-Denominational Proceedings* (Cincinnati: N.p., 1885): 12–14. See also Roohan, *American Catholics*, pp. 330–331.

36. Abell, *American Catholicism*, pp. 61–66.

37. Marc Karson, *American Labor Unions and Politics* (Carbondale: Southern Illinois University Press, 1956), pp. 224, 528.

38. Ibid., p. 264; Mary Harrita Fox, *Peter E. Dietz: Labor Priest* (Notre Dame: University of Notre Dame Press, 1953).

39. Francis Broderick, *Right Reverend New Dealer: John A. Ryan* (New York: Macmillan, 1963), pp. 48–75.

40. See John Ryan, *Declining Liberty and Other Papers* (New York: Macmillan, 1927), p. 24.

41. Marty, *Righteous Empire*, p. 177. For the rise of fundamentalism, see George Marsden, *Fundamentalism and American Culture: The Shaping of Twentieth Century Evangelicalism, 1870–1925* (New York: Oxford University Press, 1980).

42. George Herron, *The New Redemption* (New York: Thomas Y. Crowell, 1893), p. 21; George Herron, *The Christian Society* (New York: Johnson reprint, 1969); George Herron, *The Christian State* (New York: Johnson reprint, 1968); George Herron, *The Meaning of Religious Experiences* (New York: Thomas Y. Crowell, 1896).

43. Quoted in Hopkins, *Rise of the Social Gospel*, p. 235.

44. Meyer, *Protestant Search for Political Realism*, pp. 145–159, 292–306.

45. Gleason, *Conservative Reformers*, p. 4.

46. T. Wharton Collens, "View of the Labor Movement," *Catholic World* 10 (March 1870): 794–798.

47. Robert Doherty, "Thomas J. Hagerty, the Church, and Socialism," *Labor History* (Winter 1965), pp. 43–46.

48. Aaron I. Abell, "The Reception of Leo XIII's Labor Encyclical in America, 1891–1919," *Review of Politics* 9 (October 1945): 479.

49. Myth here refers not to a fiction, but to a cultural expression of otherwise inexpressible features of reality. See Mircea Eliade, *The Sacred and the Profane* (New York: Harper, 1957), pp. 14–18, 201–213.

50. Ernst Troeltsch, *The Social Teachings of the Christian Churches*, 2 vols. (London: George Allen, 1931), 1:51–58.

51. Ibid., p. 58.

52. Ibid., p. 336.

53. See Lawrence Foster, *Religion and Sexuality: Three American Communal Experiments of the Nineteenth Century* (New York: Oxford University Press, 1981).

54. Pope Pius IX, "*Syllabus errorum*," in *Church and State Through the Centuries*, ed. Sidney Z. Ehler and John Morrall (London: Burns and Oates, 1954), p. 285.

55. Martin Marty, *The Modern Schism* (New York: Harper, 1969), p. 98.

56. See Bernard Weisberger, *They Gathered at the River* (Boston: Little, Brown, 1958), pp. 160–219; Timothy L. Smith, *Revivalism and Social Reform in Mid-Nineteenth Century America* (Nashville: Abingdon Press, 1957).

57. Gutman, "Protestantism and the American Labor Movement," pp. 74–101.

58. William G. Sumner [Christian Reid], "The Doctor's Fee," *Catholic World* 52 (February 1886): 610.

59. Sydney Ahlstrom, *A Religious History of the American People* (New Haven: Yale University Press, 1972), p. 782.

60. T. J. Jackson Lears, *No Place of Grace: Antimodernism and the Transformation of American Culture, 1880–1920* (New York: Pantheon, 1981).

61. Robert Handy, ed., *The Social Gospel in America* (New York: Oxford University Press, 1966), p. 267.

62. Cauthen, *Impact of American Religious Liberalism*, p. 182. Fishburn, *Fatherhood of God*.

63. Handy, *Social Gospel in America*, p. 200.

64. Paul Conkin, *The New Deal* (New York: Thomas Crowell, 1967), p. 51.

65. Eldon G. Ernst, *Moment of Truth for Protestant America: Interchurch Campaigns Following World War One* (Missoula, Mont.: American Academy of Religion and Scholars' Press, 1974), pp. 115–151.

66. Meyer, *Protestant Search for Political Realism*, pp. 160–185.

67. H. Richard Niebuhr, "Inconsistency of the Majority," *World Tomorrow* 17 (January 18, 1934): 43–44; H. Richard Niebuhr, "The Grace of Doing Nothing," *Christian Century* 69 (March 23, 1932): 378–380.

68. Shailer Mathews, *Jesus on Social Institutions* (New York: Macmillan, 1928). See also E. A. Cook, "The Kingdom of God as a Democratic Ideal," *Journal of Religion* 1 (November 1921): 626–640; and Henry J. Cadbury, *The Peril of Modernizing Jesus* (New York: Macmillan, 1938).

69. Charles Clayton Morrison, "Is There a Catholic-Protestant Rapprochement," *Christendom* 1 (August, 1936): 861. See also "Editorial," *Christian Century* 42 (March 12, 1925): 335–336; "The Coolidge Business Policy," *Christian Century* 44 (November 17, 1927): 1350–1352.

70. Meyer, *Protestant Search for Political Realism*, pp. 186–216.

71. Niebuhr, "The Grace of Doing Nothing."

72. Tillich, *Protestant Era*, p. 169.

73. Cross, *Emergence of Liberal Catholicism*, p. 63.

74. Troeltsch, *Social Teachings*, 2:698.

75. Jaroslav Pelikan, *The Riddle of Roman Catholicism* (Nashville: Abingdon, 1959), p. 162.

76. Garry Wills, *Bare Ruined Choirs* (New York: Delta, 1972), pp. 15–371.

77. For a typical statement, see Karl Adam, *The Spirit of Catholicism* (New York: Macmillan, 1929), pp. 28–29.

78. Quoted in O'Brien, *American Catholics and Social Reform*, p. 21.

79. See Hans Meier, *Revolution and Church: The Early History of Christian Democracy* (Notre Dame: University of Notre Dame Press, 1969).

80. James Hitchcock, "Postmortem on a Rebirth," *American Scholar* 49 (Spring, 1980): 211–225.

81. Michael D. Fogarty, *Christian Democracy in Western Europe, 1820–1953* (Notre Dame: University of Notre Dame Press, 1969); O'Brien, *American Catholics and Social Reform*, pp. 9–14.

82. Neil Betten, *Catholic Activism and the Industrial Worker* (Gainesville: Florida State University Press, 1976), p. 12.

83. John Ryan, *Distributive Justice* (New York: Harper, 1916), p. 196.

84. Jay P. Dolan, *Catholic Revivalism* (Notre Dame: University of Notre Dame Press, 1978).

85. Charles E. Curran, "American and Catholic: American Catholic Social Ethics, 1880–1965," *Thought* 52 (1977): 50–74.

86. William J. Walsh, "Quadragesimo Anno," *Catholic Charities Review* 15 (June 1931): 173.

87. O'Brien, *American Catholics and Social Reform*, pp. 150–181; Charles J. Tull, *Father Coughlin and the New Deal* (Syracuse: Syracuse University Press, 1965); Forrest Davis, "Father Coughlin," *Atlantic* 66 (November 1935): 659–668.

Chapter Three

1. Day, *The Long Loneliness*, p. 199; Dorothy Day, "I Remember Peter Maurin," *Jubilee* 1 (March 1954): 34–39.

2. Arthur Sheehan, *Peter Maurin: Gay Believer* (Garden City: Hanover, 1959), pp. 10–

39; Anthony Novitsky, "The Ideological Development of Peter Maurin's Green Revolution" (Ph.D. diss., State University of New York at Buffalo, 1977), p. 171; Marc Ellis, *Peter Maurin: Prophet in the Twentieth Century* (New York: Paulist Press, 1981).

3. John C. Cort, "The Worst Possible System" (unpublished manuscript), p. 19.
4. Alex Avitabile, John Cort, C. Smith, and Stanley Vishnewski, "The Maurin Dimension," *Commonweal* 98 (1973): 135–137.
5. Day, *Long Loneliness*, p. 199.
6. Ibid., p. 197.
7. *CW* 2 (June 1933): 4.
8. *CW* 2 (June 1933): 3.
9. Quoted in Joseph Zarella Interview, CW Papers.
10. William Miller, *A Harsh and Dreadful Love: Dorothy Day and the Catholic Worker Movement* (New York: Liveright, 1972), p. 19.
11. Zarella Interview, CW Papers. John Cogley, *A Canterbury Tale* (New York: Seabury, 1976), pp. 11–12.
12. Cort, "The Worst Possible System," pp. 15–16. Some of the controversy over Maurin can be traced in Kieran Dugan, "Apostolic Agitator," *Today* 15 (June 1960): 33–34; John Cort, "Memories of Peter Maurin," *Commonweal* 71 (1960): 463–464; Arthur Sheehan, "In Defense of Peter Maurin," *Ave Maria* 95 (1962): 3–5; Avitabile, Cort, Smith, and Vishnewski, "The Maurin Dimension," pp. 135–137; as well as in the full-length works by Sheehan, Cort, Novitsky, and Ellis cited above.
13. Day, *Loaves and Fishes*, pp. 101–102.
14. Dorothy Day, "I Remember Peter Maurin," p. 37.
15. Day to Father Wilbur, May 22, 1934, CW Papers, W-3.1.
16. Dorothy Day, "Peter Maurin," unpublished manuscript, n.d. (c. 1946), CW Papers, D-3.
17. Day to J. J. Tompkins, November 24, 1934, CW Papers, W-3.1.
18. Reprinted in Thomas C. Cornell and James Forest, eds., *A Penny a Copy* (New York: Macmillan, 1968), pp. 9–15.
19. Ibid.
20. Day, *Long Loneliness*, p. 198.
21. Day, *Loaves and Fishes*, p. 19. Day, "Peter Maurin," pp. 26–29: "He was used to poverty as a peasant is used to rough living, poor food, hard bed, dirt, fatigue, and hard and unrespected work. He was a man with a mission, a vision, and he had put off from him honors, prestige, recognition. . . . The impact Peter made on us all, from one end of the country to the other . . . was because he personally lived a life of poverty and work, and never asked anything for himself. . . . He was a pilgrim and a stranger on earth."
22. Day, "Peter Maurin," p. 25, CW Papers; *CW* 17 (March 1951): 1.
23. Dwight Macdonald, "Revisiting Dorothy Day," *New York Review of Books* 16 (January 28, 1971): 12.
24. Miller, *A Harsh and Dreadful Love*, pp. 72, 180.
25. Cornell and Forest, *A Penny a Copy*, pp. ix–x; Macdonald, "Revisiting Dorothy Day," p. 12.
26. *CW* 1 (June 1933): 2.
27. *CW* 3 (May 1935): 1–8.
28. Ade Bethune Interview, CW Papers.
29. John Hellman, *Emmanuel Mounier and the New Catholic Left, 1930–1950* (Toronto: University of Toronto Press, 1981), p. 3.

30. Joseph Amato, *Mounier and Maritain: A French Catholic Understanding of the Modern World* (University: University of Alabama Press, 1975), p. 13.
31. Hellman, *Emmanuel Mounier and the New Catholic Left*, pp. 3–11.
32. Day, "Peter Maurin," CW Papers.
33. John Hellman, "The Opening to the Left in French Catholicism. The Role of the Personalists," *Journal of the History of Ideas* 34 (July 1973): 387.
34. *CW* 18 (March 1952): 4.
35. See, for example, *CW* 2 (June 1934): 2.
36. See *CW* 17 (November 1950): 4; and *CW* 28 (February 1962): 3.
37. *CW* 17 (November 1950): 4.
38. *CW* 23 (July–August 1956): 4.
39. For this discussion of both Berdyaev's and Dostoevski's influence on the Catholic Worker I am indebted to Miller, *Harsh and Dreadful Love*, pp. 7–13. See also Michael Harrington, *The Accidental Century* (Baltimore: Penguin Books, 1966), pp. 154–163.
40. *CW* 1 (March 1934): 1; *CW* 2 (December 1934): 8.
41. Cogley, *Canterbury Tale*, p. 20; *CW* 2 (December 1934): 8.
42. *CW* 8 (April 1942): 2.
43. *CW* 24 (June 1958): 3.
44. Wills, *Bare Ruined Choirs*, p. 59.
45. Dwight Macdonald, *Politics Past* (New York: Viking, 1970), p. 362.
46. Joseph Zarella Interview, CW Papers.
47. Macdonald, "Revisiting Dorothy Day," p. 12.
48. Ammon Hennacy to Dorothy Day, June 18, 1954, CW Papers, W-2. Editors frequently consulted with Day on contributors and the choice of major articles. See Martin Corbin to Dorothy Day, November 13, 1967, CW Papers, W-2.
49. Edmund Egan Interview, CW Papers.
50. Dorothy Day, "Sharecroppers," *America* 54 (1936): 516.
51. Richard Deverall, "The Way It Was," *Social Order* 16 (1961): 49–57; *CW* 4 (August 1936): 1; *CW* 4 (March 1937): 1.
52. *CW* 20 (May 1954): 1.
53. *CW* 1 (December 1933): 2. Day raised her daughter in the communal setting of the movement.
54. Quoted in Miller, *Harsh and Dreadful Love*, pp. 116–117.
55. Erik Erikson, *Gandhi's Truth* (New York: Norton, 1969), p. 342.
56. Quoted in *National Catholic Reporter*, June 9, 1973, p. 7.
57. Stanley Vishnewski, "Days of Action," CW Papers, pp. 167–168.
58. Day to Supervisor of Home Relief, August 14, 1935, CW Papers.
59. *CW* 17 (January 1951): 1; Dorothy Day, "Letter: Blood, Sweat, and Tears," *Commonweal* 53 (December 29, 1950): 300–301.
60. *CW* 4 (April 1937): 4.
61. *CW* 12 (September 1945): 1.
62. Julia Porcelli Interview, CW Papers: "Dorothy has presence. . . . When she enters a room you are very much aware of her." Vishnewski, "Days of Action," p. 168.
63. Dorothy Day, "St. Joseph the Wonderworker," *Jubilee* 4 (1957): 37–40; Cort, "The Worst Possible System," p. 7.
64. Vishnewski, "Days of Action," p. 168. A physical condition may also have contributed to Day's demeanor. "Then, too, her seeming air of aloofness was partly due to the fact that her hearing in her right ear was impaired, and she had difficulty catching conversations, especially when there was a large group around."

65. Dorothy Day, "A Human Document," *Sign* 12 (November 1932): 223–224.
66. Dorothy Day to Father James McGuire, December 18, 1934, CW Papers, W-2.
67. Day, *Long Loneliness*, p. 206.
68. Ibid.
69. *CW* 10 (February 1943): 1; *CW* 18 (April 1952): 4; Dorothy Day, "A Catholic Speaks His Mind," *Commonweal* 55 (April 1952): 640. See Thomas Sugrue, *A Catholic Speaks His Mind on America's Religious Conflict* (New York: Harper, 1952), pp. 50–53. For a later reiteration of the same themes, see Dorothy Day, "A Reminiscence at 75," *Commonweal* 98 (1973): 424–425; and Day, *On Pilgrimage: The Sixties* (New York: Curtis, 1973), pp. 159–160. In speaking of the search for "holiness," Day wrote, "Naturally speaking people are filled with repulsion at the idea of holiness. We have so many sad examples of Pecksniffs in our midst." *CW* 12 (January 1946): 2.
70. Day, unpublished manuscript, CW Papers, D-3.
71. Helene Iswolsky, quoted in CW Papers, W-9.
72. For examples of Michel's work see Virgil Michel, "Social Aspects of the Liturgy," *Catholic Action* 16 (May 1934): 9–11; Virgil Michel, "The Liturgical Movement and the Future," *America* 54 (1935): 6–7; Paul B. Marx, *Virgil Michel and the Liturgical Movement* (Collegeville: St. John's Abbey–Liturgical Press, 1957), pp. 200–218. See also Leo Ward and Emersen Hynes, "Virgil Michel," *Commonweal* 29 (1938): 237; and Joseph McDonald, "A Liturgical Apostolate," *Orate Fratres* 12 (1938): 272–273. For an overview of the entire liturgical movement, which was international in scope, see Ernest B. Koenker, *The Liturgical Renaissance in the Roman Catholic Church* (St. Louis: Concordia, 1954), especially Chap. IX.
73. Day to Father Henry Borgmann, December 30, 1933, CW Papers, W-2.
74. Ibid.
75. *CW* 1 (September 1933): 2.
76. *CW* 2 (October 1934): 3; *CW* 6 (January 1939): 2.
77. *CW* 14 (May 1948): 52.
78. CW Papers, D-3. .
79. Day, *Long Loneliness*, p. 276.
80. Ibid., p. 277.
81. CW Papers, D-3.
82. Stanley Vishnewski Interview, CW Papers, W-9. Ade Bethune to Father John Hugo, February 23, 1942. Bethune to Hugo, March 27, 1942, CW Papers, W-3.2.
83. Karl Stern Interview, CW Papers, W-9.
84. Stanley Vishnewski Interview, CW Papers, W-9.
85. Sister Peter Claver Interview, CW Papers, W-9.
86. Day, "All Is Grace," unpublished manuscript, CW Papers, D-3.
87. Coles, *Spectacle Unto the World*, p. 52.
88. Dorothy Day, *Thérèse* (New York: Fides Press, 1960). Day, "A Reminiscence at 75," p. 474.
89. CW Papers, D-3.
90. CW Papers, W-3.1; *CW* 17 (March 1951): 1.
91. Day, *Long Loneliness*, p. 171.
92. Jack English Interview, CW Papers, W-9.
93. Day to "Friends" in Los Angeles, July 27, 1963, CW Papers, W-2.
94. Quoted in William Miller, "Dorothy Day, Christian Radical," CW Papers.

95. *CW* 42 (January 1976): 8.
96. Day to "Friends" in Los Angeles, July 27, 1963, CW Papers, W-2.
97. Day to Cardinal Spellman, March 4, 1949, CW Papers, W-6.2.
98. Quoted in Macdonald, *Politics Past*, p. 353.
99. James Forest, "Remembering Dorothy Day," *Fellowship* 47 (April–May 1981): 6.

Chapter Four

1. See Alfred Braunthal, *Salvation and the Perfect Society* (Amherst: University of Massachusetts Press, 1979), Frank Manuel and Fritzie Manuel, *Utopian Thought in the Western World* (Cambridge, Mass.: Belknap-Harvard, 1979).
2. Day, *Loaves and Fishes*, p. 19.
3. Ibid., p. 25.
4. Dorothy Day, *House of Hospitality* (New York: Catholic Worker, 1939), p. 236; *CW* 6 (May 1939): 1; Dorothy Day, "House of Hospitality," *Commonweal* 15 (1938): 683.
5. Peter Maurin, *The Green Revolution* (New York: Academy Guild Press, 1961), pp. 50–52.
6. Day, *Loaves and Fishes*, p. 85.
7. Dorothy Day, "It Was a Good Dinner," *Commonweal* 32 (August 23, 1940): 364–365.
8. Day, *Loaves and Fishes*, pp. 85–86.
9. *CW* 12 (February 1945): 1; Day, *House of Hospitality*, p. 54.
10. *CW* 13 (May 1946): 3.
11. Dorothy Day, CW Papers, W-3.1. See also *CW* 17 (September 1950): 1.
12. Day, *Long Loneliness*, p. 292.
13. Vishnewski, "Days of Action," p. 25.
14. Cort, "The Worst Possible System," p. 30.
15. *CW* 3 (September 1935): 5.
16. Cogley, *Canterbury Tale*, p. 20.
17. Joseph Zarella Interview, CW Papers, W-9.
18. Maurin, *Green Revolution*, pp. 8–11.
19. Ibid., p. 70.
20. Cornell and Forest, *A Penny a Copy*, pp. 17–18.
21. *CW* 14 (October 1947): 1.
22. Vishnewski, "Days of Action," p. 256.
23. *Chicago Catholic Worker* 4 (August 1941): 8.
24. John Cogley, "The Faceless Ones," *Today* 5 (December 1949): 14.
25. Vishnewski, "Days of Action," p. 257.
26. *Chicago CW* 2 (January 1940): 1–2.
27. Dorothy Day, "The Solemnity of St. Joseph," CW Papers, W-2.
28. *Chicago CW* 3 (January 1941): 3.
29. Gauchat to Day, March ?, 1940, CW Papers, W-4.
30. Day, "Peter Maurin," CW Papers.
31. Day to Buffalo House of Hospitality, n.d., CW Papers, W-4.
32. *CW* 7 (September 1939): 6.
33. Vishnewski, "Days of Action," p. 8.
34. Cort, "The Worst Possible System," p. 29.
35. *Chicago CW* 3 (January 1941): 3.
36. *Welfare*, A Frederick Wiseman film, 1975.
37. Cogley, *Canterbury Tale*, p. 21.

38. Day, "Peter Maurin," CW Papers.
39. Vishnewski, "Days of Action," p. 259.
40. Ibid.
41. Ammon Hennacy to Day, December 27, 1954, CW Papers.
42. *CW* 10 (May 1943): 9; *CW* 19 (April 1953): 1.
43. Vishnewski, "Days of Action," p. 304.
44. CW Papers, W-4; *CW* 7 (February 1940): 2; *CW* 10 (January 1943): 4.
45. For typical accounts, see Donald Gallagher to Day, March 17, 1936, CW Papers; and Cogley, *Canterbury Tale*, pp. 8–15.
46. CW Papers, W-4.
47. Quoted in Betten, *Catholic Activism*, p. 63.
48. Day to Buffalo House of Hospitality, n.d., CW Papers, W-4.
49. Day to Buffalo House, n.d., CW Papers, W-4.
50. Katherine O'Hearn to Day, February 25, 1939, CW Papers, W-4.
51. Jane Marra to Day, January 11, 1940, CW Papers, W-4. In 1946, after an exceptionally bitter internal struggle, Day withdrew her support from the Boston House and it closed. See *CW* 13 (February 1946): 2.
52. Arthur Sheehan to *Catholic Worker*, June 26, 1939, CW Papers; John Magee to Day, July 11, 1939, CW Papers, W-4.
53. Dorothy Day, "Traveling by Bus," *Commonweal* 51 (March 10, 1950): 577–579.
54. Notes of Meeting of Dorothy Day at St. Louis Catholic Worker, January 30, 1936, CW Papers.
55. Adele Butler to Day, Whit Wednesday, 1938, CW Papers.
56. James O'Connor to Friends of the Catholic Worker, April 1, 1939, CW Papers.
57. O'Brien, *American Catholics and Social Reform*, pp. 3–28.
58. Michael O'Shaughnessy, "Trade Associations New and Old," *Commonweal* 17 (January 25, 1933): 351–353.
59. O'Brien, *American Catholics and Social Reform*, p. 53; George Q. Flynn, *American Catholics and the Roosevelt Presidency* (Lexington: University of Kentucky Press, 1968), pp. 36–60.
60. O'Brien, *American Catholics and Social Reform*, pp. 52–53.
61. Quoted in Flynn, *American Catholics*, pp. 17, 49.
62. J. G. Brunini, "A Catholic Paper vs. Communism," *Commonweal* 18 (November 24, 1933): 96–98.
63. John Toomey, "Radicals of the Right," *America* 52 (February 2, 1935): 399.
64. Marieli Benziger, "Caritas Christi," *Catholic World* 144 (November 1936): 220–223.
65. *Brooklyn Tablet*, May 6, 1933, p. 1.
66. Lester P. Eliot, "Troubles of American Catholicism," *American Mercury* 34 (March 1935): 267–281.
67. *Daily Worker*, August 18, 1934, p. 2.
68. Maurin, *The Green Revolution*, pp. 50–52.
69. Ibid.
70. Ibid., pp. 17–20.
71. Cornell and Forest, *A Penny a Copy*, pp. 14–16.
72. Sheehan, *Peter Maurin*, p. 86.
73. Anthony Novitsky, "Ideological Development of Peter Maurin's Green Revolution," pp. 170–179 *passim*. Anthony Novitsky, "Peter Maurin's Green Revolution: The Radical Implications of Reactionary Social Catholicism," *Review of Politics* 37 (January 1975): 83–103; Ellis, *Peter Maurin*, pp. 26–72.

INSIGHT

17575 PACIFIC COAST HIGHWAY, PACIFIC PALISADES, CALIFORNIA 90272
AREA CODE 213   454-0688

Dick —

I enjoyed this. Chapter 1, 3, 4 & 7 are especially helpful, I think, in the area of overview, introduction.

Love

Bud

A PRODUCTION OF THE PAULIST FATHERS

74. Maurin, *Green Revolution*, pp. 23–26.
75. *CW* 7 (May 1940): 11.
76. For Koch and his paper *The Guildsman*, see O'Brien, *American Catholics and Social Reform*, p. 172. For Kenkel and the German Catholic Central Verein, see Gleason, *The Conservative Reformers*, pp. 91–102.
77. Maurin, *Green Revolution*, pp. 131, 135.
78. Day, *Loaves and Fishes*, p. 18; Day, *House of Hospitality*, pp. 140–149.
79. Stanley Vishnewski, "The Catholic Worker Story," unpublished manuscript, CW Papers. See also *CW* 2 (March 1935): 1; and *CW* 3 (June 1936): 4.
80. Day, *House of Hospitality*, pp. 180–188, 260–261; *CW* 4 (July 1937): 6.
81. *CW* 2 (March 1935): 1; *CW* 2 (April 1935): 1; *CW* 3 (April 1936): 1; *CW* 3 (June 1936): 1; *CW* 4 (April 1938): 1. See also Day, *Long Loneliness*, pp. 200–210.
82. *CW* 4 (February 1938): 6; Day, *House of Hospitality*, p. 263.
83. Maurin, *Green Revolution*, pp. 57, 70.
84. *CW* 1 (September 1933): 6; *CW* 1 (October 1933): 3; *CW* 1 (November 1933): 2; *CW* 1 (February 1934): 7; Day, *House of Hospitality*, p. 260.
85. Abigail McCarthy, *Private Faces, Public Places* (New York: Curtis, 1972), p. 24; Studs Terkel, *Hard Times* (New York: Pantheon, 1970), pp. 301–305.
86. Social Action Department, National Catholic Welfare Conference, *Organized Social Justice* (New York: Paulist Press, 1935), pp. 3–23.
87. *Brooklyn Tablet*, June 5, 1937, p. 11; July 31, 1937, p. 8; August 7, 1937, p. 6; *CW* 6 (March 1939): 3.
88. Dorothy Day to Rev. John Monaghan, September 24, 1934, *CW* Papers, W-2.
89. Raphael M. Huber, ed., *Our Bishops Speak* (Milwaukee: Bruce, 1952), pp. 98–101.
90. Dorothy Day, unpublished manuscript, n.d., CW Papers, W-3.1. This paper refers to the attacks on the movement by Catholic speakers at a communion breakfast at the Waldorf Astoria in 1936.
91. *CW* 2 (December 1934): 3; Day, *From Union Square to Rome*, p. 140.
92. O'Brien, *American Catholics and Social Reform*, pp. 86–87.
93. *CW* 6 (September 1938): 10.
94. John LaFarge, "With Scrip and Staff," *America* 56 (August 1, 1936): 129; John LaFarge, "Some Reflections on the Catholic Worker," *America* 57 (June 26, 1937): 275; John LaFarge, "Catholic Workers," *America* 57 (July 24, 1937): 371.
95. Dorothy Day to Monsignor Patrick Scanlan, December 8, 1934, CW Papers, W-2.
96. Day, *Long Loneliness*, p. 234.
97. *CW* 2 (October 1934): 5; *CW* 2 (February 1935): 7.
98. Day to Catherine de Hueck, May 30, 1936, CW Papers, D-1. Day, *Long Loneliness*, p. 205. Day was apparently aware of the scheming against her. She referred to the possibility that "I'll be asked to leave the work for the good of the cause." Day to de Hueck, n.d., 1936, CW Papers, D-1.
99. *CW* 5 (July 1937): 1; *CW* 5 (June 1937): 1.
100. *CW* 3 (February 1936): 2.
101. Betten, *Catholic Activism*, pp. 124–125.
102. Day, *House of Hospitality*, p. 260.
103. Day, *Long Loneliness*, p. 231.
104. Furfey to Day, August 4, 1934, CW Papers, W-2.
105. Paul Hanley Furfey, *Fire on the Earth* (New York: Macmillan, 1936), pp. 6–7.
106. Ibid., p. 92.
107. Ibid.

108. Ibid., pp. 117–136; Charles Curran, "The Radical Social Ethics of Paul Hanley Furfey," in *New Perspectives in Moral Theology*, Charles Curran, ed. (Notre Dame: Fides Press, 1976), pp. 87–121.
109. Betten, *Catholic Activism*, p. 78; *CW* 4 (February 1938): 6; *CW* 4 (May 1937): 7.
110. Day, *Loaves and Fishes*, p. 46; *CW* 6 (June 1939): 3; Sheehan, *Peter Maurin*, pp. 174–187.
111. Day, *Loaves and Fishes*, p. 48.
112. Stanley Vishnewski, "Life in Community," *Catholic World* 185 (August 1957): 346–351.
113. *CW* 3 (April 1936): 8.
114. *CW* 6 (May 1939): 2; Sheehan, *Peter Maurin*, pp. 131–133.
115. McCarthy, *Private Faces, Public Places*, pp. 110–132.
116. Day, *Long Loneliness*, p. 263.
117. Day, *Loaves and Fishes*, p. 57. Day, unpublished manuscript, c. 1946, CW Papers, W-3.1.
118. *CW* 19 (May 1953): 4–5; Day, *Long Loneliness*, pp. 260–263.
119. CW Papers. See issues of the *Mountain Worker*, published in the sixties at a Catholic Worker farm in Hamlin, West Virginia.
120. *CW* 3 (February 1936): 2; *CW* 6 (June 1938): 7; *CW* 7 (November 1939): 8; *CW* 7 (October 1939): 8; *CW* 7 (December 1939): 7. For a discussion of the farming issue in the fifties, see *CW* 19 (May 1953): 2.
121. *CW* 12 (November 1945): 3; *CW* 13 (May 1946): 4; *CW* 14 (March 1948): 1.
122. *CW* 3 (July–August 1935): 7; *CW* 21 (December 1954): 5.
123. CW Papers, W-6.1.
124. CW Papers, W-6.1; *CW* 20 (July–August 1954): 2.
125. John Cogley, *Catholic America* (Garden City: Doubleday, 1973), p. 88.
126. Ibid.
127. Winthrop S. Hudson, *Religion in America* (New York: Scribner's, 1965), p. 363. Nat Hentoff, ed., *The Essays of A. J. Muste* (Indianapolis: Bobbs-Merrill, 1967).
128. Hudson, *American Protestantism*, pp. 151–153.
129. For an attempt to explore such connections from the standpoint of political theory, see Mary C. Segers, "Equality and Christian Anarchism: The Political and Social Ideas of the Catholic Worker Movement," *Review of Politics* 40 (April 1978): 196–230.
130. Hentoff, *Essays of A. J. Muste*, p. 88.
131. Reinhold Niebuhr, *Moral Man and Immoral Society* (New York: Scribner's, 1932), pp. 261–271.
132. Reinhold Niebuhr, *The Nature and Destiny of Man* (New York: Scribner's, 1941); Reinhold Niebuhr, *Christianity and Power Politics* (New York: Scribner's, 1940); John C. Bennett, *Christian Realism* (New York: Scribner's, 1941).
133. Stanley Vishnewski, unpublished manuscript, CW Papers, W-3.2.
134. Edmund Egan Interview, CW Papers, W-9.
135. Quoted in Philip Gleason, "In Search of Unity: American Catholic Thought, 1920–1960," *Catholic Historical Review* 65 (April 1979): 185–205.
136. See Paul Hanley Furfey, "Why Does Rome Discourage Socio-religious Inter-Creedalism?" *American Ecclesiastical Review* 112 (1945): 365–374.
137. Cogley, *Canterbury Tale*, p. 21.
138. Niebuhr, *Moral Man and Immoral Society*, pp. 51–82.
139. *CW* 1 (April 1934): 3.

Chapter Five

1. Richard Deverall, "Over the Dam," *Christian Social Action* 6 (1941): 267.
2. Richard Deverall to Day, September 21, 1935; Day to Deverall, n.d., 1935, CW
    Papers; Deverall to Day, January 8, 1936, CW Papers. Thomas Barry, a Phila-
    delphia printer, was also in on the early stages of planning for *Christian Front*.
3. "Positions," *Christian Front* (hereinafter cited as *CF*) 1 (1936): 1–3; Richard Dever-
    all, "How Radical Must We Be?" *Chicago Catholic Worker* 1 (September 1938): 1.
4. Virgil Michel, "What Is Capitalism?" *CF* 1 (1936): 5–6. Paul Hanley Furfey, "Pru-
    dence—and Prudence," *CF* 1 (1936): 21–22.
5. "The State and Reconstruction," *CF* 1 (1936): 99–100.
6. Luigi Ligutti, "The Subsistence Homestead," *CF* 1 (1936): 103–105; Norman Mc-
    Kenna, "Fortitude Preferred," *Commonweal* 26 (1937): 397–399; John A.
    Ryan, "The Need for an Amendment," *CF* 1 (1936): 156–158.
7. "Labor on the March," *CF* 2 (1937): 51.
8. "NLRA," *CF* 3 (1938): 99–100; John Snobbig, "The Church and the CIO," *CF* 3
    (1938): 150–152; Richard Deverall, "OLPA," *CF* 4 (1939): 74–77; Norman
    McKenna, "Catholics and Labor Unions," *Catholic Mind* 37 (1937): 794–803.
9. "What We're Doing," *CF* 4 (1939): 8–10; Deverall, "Over the Dam," pp. 267–
    269; Richard Deverall, "The Way It Was," *Social Order* 11 (1961): 195–200.
10. Deverall to Day, June 22, 1953, CW Papers.
11. Frank Sicius, "The Chicago Catholic Worker Movement, 1936 to the Present,"
    (Ph.D. diss., Loyola University, 1979), pp. 55–68; *CW* 4 (June 1936): 3;
    CW 4 (February 1937): 2; Dan Herr, "The Chicago Dynamo," *Sign* 42 (1962):
    11–14+.
12. Sicius, "Chicago Catholic Worker," pp. 78–91.
13. John Cogley, "Storefront Catholicism," *America* 79 (1948): 447–449.
14. *CW* 6 (September 1938): 2.
15. *Chicago Catholic Worker* 1 (July–August 1938): 2 (hereinafter cited as *CCW*).
16. *CCW* 3 (December 1940): 8; Cogley, "Storefront Catholicism," pp. 447–449.
17. *CCW* 2 (January 1940): 1; *CCW* 3 (January 1941): 3; *CCW* 3 (December 1940): 8.
18. *CCW* 1 (September 1938): 1.
19. For an exception, see Catherine Reser, *CCW* 1 (May 1939): 4: "The Catholic Worker
    is a revolutionary movement. It intends the destruction of our present
    society."
20. *CCW* 3 (June 1941): 4.
21. Andrew Greeley, *The Catholic Experience* (Garden City: Doubleday-Image, 1969),
    pp. 251–279.
22. The Labor Theater was begun by Catholic Worker Philip Seaman at the Taylor Street
    House of Hospitality and was supported by Father Daniel Lord and others
    associated with the Chicago Catholic Workers. *CCW* 1 (March 1939): 3; *CCW*
    2 (March 1940): 1; *CCW* 3 (April 1941): 5.
23. Sicius, "Chicago Catholic Worker," pp. 86–120.
24. *CCW* 1 (November 1938): 4; *CCW* 2 (November 1939): 4; *CCW* 1 (May 1939): 4.
25. *CCW* 2 (September 1939): 2.
26. Day to "Fellow Workers," August 10, 1940, CW Papers.
27. Day to Cogley, n.d., 1940, CW Papers; Ed Marciniak to Day, "Feast of St. Philip
    Benizi, 1940," CW Papers.
28. Cogley to Day, September 26, 1940, CW Papers.
29. Cogley to Day, October 10, 1940, CW Papers.

30. Cort, "Worst Possible System," pp. 6–7, 30.
31. *CW* 4 (June 1936): 3; Day, *Loaves and Fishes*, pp. 135–136; Cort, "Worst Possible System," pp. 40–45.
32. Ibid., pp. 45–112; *CW* 5 (June 1937): 1.
33. Garry Wills, *Politics and Catholic Freedom* (Chicago: Henry Regnery, 1964), pp. 159–189; Cort, "Worst Possible System," pp. 75–78.
34. Richard Rovere, "Labor's Catholic Bloc," *Nation* 152 (January 1941): 13; Cort, "Worst Possible System," pp. 93–94, 132, 256; Michael Harrington, "Catholics in the Labor Movement," *Labor History* 11 (Fall 1960): 241–259; O'Brien, *American Catholics and Social Reform*, pp. 256ff.
35. Norman McKenna, "The Story of ACTU," *Catholic World* 169 (March 1949): 453–459; Betten, *Catholic Activism*, pp. 124–145.
36. John Cort, "Nine Years of ACTU," *America* 77 (April 1947): 4.
37. *CW* 10 (January 1943): 1; Ade Bethune, *Work* (Newport: John Sterns Press, 1942), pp. 1–30; Bethune, "Vocations," *Christian Social Art Quarterly* 3 (Spring 1940): 27–30. See also Etienne Borne and Francis Henry, *A Philosophy of Work* (New York: Sheed and Ward, 1937); and Dom Rombert Sorg, *Holy Work: Towards a Benedictine Theology of Labor* (St. Louis: Pio Decimo Press, 1953).
38. *CW* 12 (November 1945): 3; *CW* 14 (March 1948): 1; *CW* 5 (December 1937): 1.
39. *CW* 6 (January 1939): 1; D. Harald to Day, July 1, 1938, CW Papers; *CW* 14 (May 1947): 1.
40. John Cort, "Catholics in Trade Unions," *Commonweal* 30 (1939): 34–35.
41. John Cort, "Is Christian Industrialism Possible?" *Commonweal* 49 (1948): 60–62.
42. John Cort, "The Labor Movement," *Commonweal* 48 (1948): 597–598; "Is Christian Industrialism Possible?" *Commonweal* 49 (1948): 60–64; "Capitalism: Debate and Definitions," *Commonweal* 61 (1954): 221–223.
43. John Cort, "The Charms of Anarchism," *Commonweal* 56 (1952): 139–141.
44. John Cort, "The Catholic Worker and the Workers," *Commonweal* 55 (1952): 635–637.
45. Quoted in Charles Krauthammer, "The Humanist Phantom," *New Republic* 185 (July 25, 1981): 25.
46. Marciniak to Cort, February 4, 1950, Ed Marciniak Papers, Institute of Urban Studies, Loyola University, Chicago, Illinois; *CW* 21 (November 1954): 1.
47. Ed Marciniak, "The Dignity of Work I," *Work* 1 (1943): 2; Ed Marciniak, "The Dignity of Work II," *Work* 1 (1943): 1–2; Mike Schaefer, "Production, Always More Production," *Work* 5 (1948): 7; Ed Marciniak and Carol Jackson, "Industrialism: A Controversy," *Today* 5 (1949): 12–14.
48. Richard Deverall, "Catholic Radical Alliance," *Christian Front* 2 (1937): 141–143; Charles Owen Rice, "A Priest on Labor," *CF* 3 (1938): 105; Carl Hensler, "Bloodless Revolution," *CF* 3 (1938): 116–117; Charles Owen Rice, "Their Fight Is the Fight of Us All," *Work* 3 (1946): 8.
49. John J. Kane, *Protestant-Catholic Conflicts in America* (Chicago: Henry Regnery, 1955).
50. *Today*, 1–3 (1946–1948).
51. Rodger Van Allen, *The Commonweal and American Catholicism* (Philadelphia: Fortress Press, 1974), pp. 107–126.
52. Cogley, *Canterbury Tale*, pp. 46–47.
53. John Courtney Murray, *We Hold These Truths* (New York: Sheed and Ward, 1960).
54. Van Allen, *Commonweal and American Catholicism*, pp. 89–90.
55. John Cogley, "The Failure of Anti-Communism," *Commonweal* 52 (1950): 357.

56. John Cogley, "Cut off from the Maine," *Commonweal* 69 (1959): 599.
57. John Cogley, "The Catholic Worker," *Commonweal* 68 (1958): 180; "The Pacifists," *Commonweal* 59 (1953): 54; "Just a Gesture," *Commonweal* 65 (1957): 357.
58. Van Allen, *Commonweal and American Catholicism*, pp. 131–137.
59. Michael Harrington, *The Other America* (New York: Macmillan, 1963), p. 3.
60. Michael Harrington, *Fragments of the Century* (New York: Simon and Schuster, 1972), pp. 9–15.
61. Ibid., pp. 33–66.
62. Ibid., pp. 18–19.
63. CW Papers, W-3,1.
64. *CW* 18 (July–August 1952): 4; *CW* 19 (September 1952): 2.
65. *CW* 17 (June 1951), p. 5.
66. Harrington to John Randall, June 1, 1952, CW Papers, W-2.
67. *CW* 18 (July–August 1951): 2; *CW* 20 (February 1954): 3; *CW* 20 (March 1954): 1.
68. Harrington, *Accidental Century*, pp. 144–145; Harrington, *Fragments*, pp. 27–32.
69. Harrington, *Fragments*, pp. 70–78.
70. Ibid., pp. 174–175.
71. Ibid., p. 177.
72. Ibid., pp. 182–183.
73. Donald Demarest to Day, February 3, 1960, CW Papers, W-2; Van Allen, *Commonweal and American Catholicism*, pp. 152–178.
74. Marciniak to Egan, October 23, 1954, Ed Marciniak Papers.

Chapter Six

1. Dorothy Dohen, *Nationalism and American Catholicism* (New York: Sheed and Ward, 1967), p. 148; John Tracy Ellis, "American Catholics and Peace: A Historical Sketch," in *The Family of Nations*, James S. Rausch, ed. (New York: Huntington, 1970), pp. 13–39; Patricia McNeal, "Origins of the Catholic Peace Movement," *Review of Politics* 35 (July 1973): 346–374. I have benefited throughout this chapter from Patricia McNeal, *The American Catholic Peace Movement, 1928–1972* (New York: Arno Press, 1978); and John Leo LeBrun, "The Role of the Catholic Worker Movement in American Pacifism, 1933–1972" Ph.D. diss., Case Western Reserve University, 1973.
2. Roland H. Bainton, *Christian Attitudes Toward War and Peace* (Nashville: Abingdon, 1960), pp. 53–100; Geoffrey Nuttall, *Christian Pacifism in History* (London: Blackwell, 1958), pp. 1–31; *Catholic Encyclopedia*, s.v. "war." James T. Johnson, "Just War Theory," *Worldview* 19 (July–August 1976): 27–30; Michael Walzer, *Just and Unjust Wars: A Moral Argument with Historical Illustrations* (New York: Basic Books, 1977).
3. Gordon C. Zahn, "European Catholics' Work for Peace," *Catholic World* 187 (August 1958): 356–363.
4. McNeal, "Origins of the Catholic Peace Movement," pp. 347–363. The CAIP supported a speakers' bureau, maintained "study committees on world problems, and published works by its members, including John Eppstein's monumental *Catholic Tradition and the Law of Nations*. A good summary of CAIP's perspective is John A. Ryan's *Modern War and Basic Ethics* (Milwaukee: Bruce, 1943). The CAIP Papers in the Marquette University Archives include institutional histories by Raymond McGowan and Clarence Hohl, Jr. Illustrative of the

close ties between the CAIP and the United States government in later years is
the membership of the CAIP Arms Control Subcommittee: Alain Enthoven,
Deputy Secretary of Defense for Systems Analysis; Charles Herzfeld, Deputy
Director of Advanced Research, Defense Department; Edward Conway, Arms
Control and Disarmament Agency; William Nagle, State Department; William O'Brien, Chairman of the Institute of World Policy, Georgetown University; Col. Joseph Moriarty, U.S.A.F. (ret.).

5. *CW* 1 (October 1933): 1; *CW* 1 (April 1934): 5–6; *CW* 2 (May 1934): 1; *CW* 2 (June
1934): 8; *CW* 2 (March 1935): 3.

6. *CW* 2 (April 1935): 4; *CW* 3 (September 1935): 1; *CW* 3 (October 1935): 1; *CW* 4
(September 1936): 4; *CW* 4 (December 1936): 1, 2; *CW* 5 (June 1937): 7. See
also J. David Valaik, "American Catholic Dissenters and the Spanish Civil
War," *Catholic Historical Review* 53 (January 1968): 537–546; and J. David
Valaik, "Catholics, Neutrality, and the Spanish Embargo," *Journal of American
History* 54 (June 1967): 73–85.

7. *CW* 4 (October 1936): 1; *CW* 4 (December 1936): 2; *CW* 4 (February 1937): 3.

8. *CW* 5 (June 1937): 7; *CW* 2 (March 1935): 3; *CW* 3 (December 1935): 3.

9. *CW* 7 (September 1939): 1; *CW* 7 (November 1939); 1, 2.

10. *CW* 8 (December 1939–May 1940), *passim*. After Pearl Harbor, O'Toole arrived by
scholastic logic at support for the Japanese war, but not the war against Hitler.
O'Toole to Day, February 1, 1942, CW Papers; O'Toole to Day, April 15,
1942, CW Papers.

11. *CW* 7 (July–August 1940): 1. See also U.S., Congress, House, Hearings of the
House Committee on Military Affairs, July 30, 1940, *Report of the Hearings
anent H.R. 10132*, pp. 152–160, 299–323, 353–354.

12. *CW* 7 (July–August 1940): 1.

13. CW Papers, W-4.

14. CW Papers, W-2. *CW* 9 (February 1942): 1; Miller, *Harsh and Dreadful Love*,
pp. 168–174; Cogley to Day, October 10, 1940, CW Papers, W-2.

15. CW Papers, W-6.3; *CW* 9 (February 1942): 1; *CW* 8 (June 1941): 6.

16. *CW* 8 (February 1941): 1.

17. Philip Jacob and Mulford Q. Sibley, *Conscription of Conscience: The American State and
the Conscientious Objector, 1940–1947* (Ithaca: Cornell University Press, 1947);
Lawrence Wittner, *Rebels Against War: The American Peace Movement, 1941–
1960* (New York: Columbia University Press, 1969), pp. 34–96.

18. Gordon C. Zahn, *Another Part of the War: The Camp Simon Story* (Amherst: University
of Massachusetts Press, 1979), p. 45.

19. Ibid., pp. 37–82; *CW* 8 (April 1941): 1; *CW* 8 (October 1941): 2.

20. Zahn, *Another Part of the War*, pp. 36–55; McNeal, "Catholic Conscientious Objection During World War II," *Catholic Historical Review* 61 (April 1975):
221–225.

21. Zahn, *Another Part of the War*, pp. 83–177; Gordon C. Zahn, *War, Conscience, and
Dissent* (New York: Hawthorn, 1967), pp. 145–176; *CW* 9 (February–
November 1942), *passim*.

22. Zahn, *Another Part of the War*, pp. 210–211; *CW* 10 (December 1942): 2; *CW* 10
(February 1943): 3; *CW* 10 (March 1943): 3; Gordon C. Zahn, "Leaven of Love
and Justice," *America* 27 (November 11, 1972): 383–384; Wittner, *Rebels
Against War*, p. 54, attributes the move solely to poor finances, but the evidence of political motives is conclusive. Bishop Petersen's private attitude
toward the Catholic COs was sympathetic, but he urged them to remain "si-

lent." "That the present war, in savagery, brutality, and inhumanity out-brutalizes any that has gone before is sadly true. . . . Few, however, are able to understand it. . . . I counselled silence because sympathy with your cause is so rare that to defend your position serves only to weaken it." Bishop John Petersen to Dwight Larrowe, April 27, 1942, CW Papers, W-6.3. See also the letter from Petersen to New Hampshire Director of Selective Service, quoted in Zahn, *War, Conscience, and Dissent*, p. 163.

23. Zahn, *Another Part of the War*, pp. 212–215. The COs worked briefly in Oakwood, Md., before going to Rosewood, Md. Other contingents of Catholic COs ended up at the Alexian Brothers Hospital in Chicago, at Trenton, N.D., Big Flats, N.Y., and Mariensville, Pa.

24. *Catholic CO* 1 (September 1943): 1; *Catholic CO* 1 (April 1944): 3–4; *Catholic CO* 2 (April 1945): 1.

25. John C. Ford, "The Morality of Obliteration Bombing," *Theological Studies* 5 (1944): 261–309.

26. Paul Hanley Furfey, "The Bombing of Non-Combatants Is Murder," *Catholic CO* 2 (July 1945): 3–4; John Courtney Murray, "Remarks on the Moral Problem of War," *Theological Studies* 20 (1959): 40–61.

27. Zahn, *Another Part of the War*, pp. 38–44.

28. Ibid., pp. 73–82.

29. *Catholic CO* 2 (April 1945): 3; Wittner, *Rebels Against War*, pp. 62–96; *CW* 14 (April 1947): 1; *Catholic CO* 2 (January 1946): 1–2; *Catholic CO* 2 (July 1946): 2.

30. *Catholic CO* 3 (September 1947): 11–12; *Catholic CO* 4 (April 1948): 6–7; *CW* 15 (June 1948): 2; Zahn, *War, Conscience, and Dissent*, pp. 172–176.

31. *CW* 11 (May 1944): 3; *CW* 11 (October 1944): 1–6; *CW* 12 (May 1945): 4, 7; *CW* 14 (April 1947): 1; *CW* 14 (March 1948): 3; Gordon C. Zahn, *German Catholics and Hitler's Wars* (London: Sheed and Ward, 1963): Gordon C. Zahn, *In Solitary Witness: The Life and Death of Franz Jägerstätter* (Boston: Beacon, 1964).

32. John Cogley, "A Harsh and Dreadful Love," *America* 27 (November 11, 1972): 394; Day, *Long Loneliness*, pp. 262–263; *CW* 17 (April 1951): 1; *CW* 19 (April 1953): 1.

33. *CW* 15 (May 1949): 3; *CW* 16 (February 1950): 5; *CW* 16 (April 1950): 2.

34. *CW* 17 (March 1951): 1, 6; *CW* 18 (July–August 1951): 1; *CW* 19 (January 1953): 1; *CW* 20 (October 1953): 1.

35. Wittner, *Rebels Against War*, pp. 151–181.

36. *CW* 11 (November 1944): 1; John C. Hugo, *The Immorality of Conscription* (New York: Catholic Worker Press, 1944); *CW* 11 (January 1945): 1, 8; *CW* 12 (April 1945): 1, 3; *CW* 15 (April–October 1948), *passim*; *CW* 18 (May 1951): 3; Robert Drinan, "Is Pacifist Larry Gara a Criminal?" *Catholic World* 177 (March 1951): 410–415.

37. *CW* 27 (July–August 1950): 1; *CW* 27 (January 1951): 1, 3; Wittner, *Rebels Against War*, pp. 213–229; Dorothy Day, "Blood, Sweat, and Tears," *Commonweal* 53 (1950): 300–301; Edwin Halsey, "In Support of Dorothy Day," *Commonweal* 53 (1951): 470–472.

38. Michael Harrington, *Fragments of the Century* (New York: Simon and Schuster, 1973), p. 23.

39. *CW* 17 (January 1951): 1; *CW* 20 (February 1954): 2.

40. Ammon Hennacy, *The Book of Ammon* (Salt Lake City: n.p., 1965), originally published as *The Autobiography of a Catholic Anarchist* (New York: Catholic Worker Press, 1954), p. 1.

41. Ibid., pp. 3–17.

42. Ibid., pp. 18–32.

43. Ammon Hennacy Papers, Labadie Collection, University of Michigan Library, Ann Arbor, Mich.; Ammon Hennacy, "Inside or Outside?: The Relation of Pacifism to Revolutionary Movements," *World Tomorrow* 6 (July 1924): 18–21; Ammon Hennacy, "On Being Practical: The Viewpoint of the Christian Anarchist," *Freedom* 1 (May 1933): 7-8.; Ammon Hennacy, "In Praise of Roger Williams," *Freedom* 1 (March 1933): 5; Hennacy to Agnes Inglis, September 8, 1940, Hennacy Papers.

44. Ammon Hennacy, "Two Pacifist-Anarchists: Leo Tolstoy and Lloyd Garrison," *Man* 7 (November 1939): 3; Ammon Hennacy, "Real Democracy," *Man* 7 (September–October 1939): 4; Ammon Hennacy, "Gambling, Slavery, and Freedom," *Man* 7 (January 1939): 8; Hennacy, *Book of Ammon*, pp. 48–65.

45. Hennacy to U.S. Attorney, Milwaukee, December 19, 1941, Hennacy Papers; Hennacy, *Book of Ammon*, pp. 48–65; *CW* 8 (May 1941): 1.

46. Hennacy, *Book of Ammon*, pp. 86–141.

47. Hennacy to Day, January 21, 1954, CW Papers; Hennacy, *Book of Ammon*, pp. 262–279, 474–479.

48. Ibid., pp. 299–300.

49. Quoted in LeBrun, "Catholic Worker Movement and American Pacifism," p. 169.

50. Ibid., pp. 152–199; *Commonweal* 62 (1955): 363–364; *Commonweal* 65 (1957): 452; Dorothy Day, "Conscience and Civil Defense," *New Republic* 133 (August 22, 1956): 6; *New York Times*, June 16, 1955, p. 1.

51. *CW* 24 (September 1957): 1, 2, 6; *CW* 24 (October 1957): 3, 6; "Arrest of the Pacifists," *Commonweal* 46 (1957): 318; "Lonely Protests," *Commonweal* 46 (1957): 446; *New York Times*, May 7, 1958, pp. 1, 30; *CW* 25 (June 1959): 2, 6.

52. *New York Times*, May 4, 1960, p. 4; *New Yorker* 36 (May 14, 1960): 33–35; *CW* 26 (June 1960): 1, 2, 4, 7; *New York Times*, April 29, 1961, p. 1; *CW* 27 (May 1961): 2.

53. Wittner, *Rebels Against War*, pp. 247–256.

54. Hennacy, *Book of Ammon*, pp. 299–302; *CW* 23 (June 1957): 1; *CW* 23 (July–August 1957): 3; Peter Brock, *Twentieth Century Pacifism* (New York: Van Nostrand Co., 1970), p. 250; Wittner, *Rebels Against War*, p. 247.

55. *CW* 27 (April 1961): 3, 7; *New York Times*, July 2, 1961. Accounts of the walk also appeared in the *New York Times* on July 5, August 8, September 20, 29, 30, and October 3, 4, 7, 8, 9, 1961. Meyer, Hennacy's most ardent follower in the Catholic Worker during the 1960s, was the son of Congressman William Meyer of Vermont, a graduate of the University of Chicago, and a former employee of Dean Acheson's law firm. He was frequently arrested for demonstrations and tax resistance during the decade. See Karl Meyer, "Still Virgin Soil," in *Seeds of Liberation*, ed. Paul Goodman (New York: Braziller, 1964), pp. 162–164.

56. *CW* 29 (January 1963): 2.

57. *CW* 23 (December 1956): 1.

58. Ibid.

59. *CW* 28 (June 1961): 1; *CW* 28 (April 1962): 2.

60. *CW* 29 (July–August 1962): 2. For some of the extensive debate on these issues, see Walter Stein, ed., *Nuclear Weapons and Christian Conscience* (London: Merlin Press, 1961); John C. Bennett, ed., *Nuclear Weapons and the Conflict of Conscience* (New York: Harper, 1962); William E. Nagle, *Morality and Modern Warfare*

(New York: Helicon, 1960); Justus George Lawler, *Nuclear War: The Ethic, the Rhetoric, the Reality* (Westminster: Newman, 1965).

61. James Baker, *Thomas Merton: Social Critic* (Lexington: University of Kentucky Press, 1971); Merton to Day, July 9, 1959, CW Papers; Merton to Day, February 4, 1960, CW Papers.

62. Thomas Merton, *Disputed Questions* (New York: Farrar, Straus, 1960).

63. Thomas Merton, *Thomas Merton on Peace* (New York: McCall's, 1971) contains most of Merton's peace writings and a useful introduction by Gordon Zahn. See also Thomas Merton's *Breakthrough to Peace* (New York: New Directions, 1962), *Faith and Violence* (Notre Dame: University of Notre Dame Press, 1968), *Raids on the Unspeakable* (New York: New Directions, 1966), and *Contemplation in a World of Action* (Garden City: Doubleday, 1971). McNeal, *American Catholic Peace Movement*, pp. 125–166, contains a thorough discussion of Merton and his theology in relation to the Catholic peace movement. See also Merton to Day, August 23, 1961, and Merton to Day, June 16, 1962, CW Papers.

64. Merton, *Faith and Violence*, p. 8; Merton to Day, July 23, 1961, CW Papers.

65. Merton, *Faith and Violence*, pp. 107–108. Merton's growing interest in Eastern thought can be traced in Thomas Merton's *The Way of Chuang-tzu* (New York: New Directions, 1965), *Mystics and Zen Masters* (New York: Farrar, Straus, 1967), *Zen and the Birds of Appetite* (New York: New Directions, 1968), and *Asian Journal* (New York: New Directions, 1972).

66. McNeal, *American Catholic Peace Movement*, p. 161. See also Daniel Ostrow, *The FBI and the Berrigans* (New York: Coward, McCann, 1972), pp. 34–35; and Francine du Plessix Gray, *Divine Disobedience* (New York: Random, 1969), pp. 73–74.

67. James Forest, "The Gift of Merton," *Commonweal* 89 (1969): 463–464. See also Thomas Merton, "Christianity and Mass Movements," *Cross Currents* 14 (Summer 1969): 203–204.

68. Merton to Day, April 9, 1962, CW Papers.

69. James Douglass, *The Nonviolent Cross* (New York: Macmillan, 1966), p. viii.

70. James Douglass, "Peace and the Overkill Strategists," *Cross Currents* 14 (Winter 1964): 87–103; James Douglass, "War and Peace: Beyond Niebuhr and Murray," *Cross Currents* 17 (Winter 1967): 107–114.

71. James Douglass, "The Morality of Thermonuclear Deterrence," *Worldview* 6 (October 1964): 34; James Douglass, "Modern War and the Just War," *Worldview* 5 (September 1963): 27–29.

72. Douglass, *The Nonviolent Cross*, p. 164; Douglass, "War and Peace," p. 108.

73. James Forest, "No Longer Alone: The Catholic Peace Movement," in *American Catholics and Vietnam*, ed. Thomas Quigley (Grand Rapids: William Eerdmans, 1968), pp. 139–151.

74. Eileen Egan, "Pax in America," *Peace* 1 (Autumn 1963): 14; Joseph Cuneen, "The Need to Face the Question," *Peace* 1 (Autumn 1963): 41–42; Philip Scharper, "War: Apathy or Alternatives," *Peace* 2 (Spring 1965): 12.

75. John Courtney Murray, "Key Themes in the Encyclical," Introduction to Pope John XXIII, *Pacem in Terris*, American ed. (New York: America Press, 1963), p. 63; Douglass, *Nonviolent Cross*, pp. 81–98.

76. *CW* 31 (July–August 1965): 1; Harry W. Flannery to Victor Ferkiss, March 14, 1963, CAIP Collection, Marquette University Archives, Milwaukee, Wis.

77. Gregory Baum and Donald Campion, eds., *Pastoral Constitution on the Church in the Modern World* (New York: Paulist Press, 1967), pp. 209–226; Xavier Rhynne

[pseud.], *Letters from Vatican II: Background and Debates: The Fourth Session* (New York: Farrar, Straus, 1966); Robert Graham, "The Council, the Popes, and Peace," *America* 113 (October 2, 1965): 365–367.

78. Vincent A. Yzermans, ed., *American Participation in the Second Vatican Council* (New York: Sheed and Ward, 1967); Robert McAfee Brown, "A Response to the Pastoral Constitution on the Church in the Modern World," in *The Documents of Vatican II*, ed. Walter Abbott (New York: America Press, 1966), p. 309; Douglass, *Nonviolent Cross*, pp. 100–136; *New York Times*, October 8, 23, November 16, 17, December 3, 5, 7, 1965.

79. *CW* 20 (May 1954): 1.

80. *CW* 29 (December 1962): 8; *CW* 31 (December (1964): 1; *CW* 31 (March 1965): 1.

81. *CW* 31 (June 1965): 8; *CW* 31 (February 1965): 4.

82. *New York Times*, July 30, 1965, p. 2; *CW* 31 (September 1965): 1; *Life* 59 (August 20, 1965): 3; "Drafting Dissenters," *New Republic* 153 (November 6, 1965): 8; *Commonweal* 83 (1965): 136. See also the extensive file on the Miller case in CW Papers and the *New York Times*, October 16, 1965, p. 1, and October 17, 1965, p. 44.

83. *New York Times*, November 7, 1965, pp. 1, 3; *CW* 32 (November 1965): 1, 3.

84. *New York Times*, November 10, 1965, pp. 1, 5; November 11, p. 4; November 12, p. 4; *National Catholic Reporter*, November 18, 1965; Telegram, Merton to Day, November 11, 1965, CW Papers; Merton to Day, November 22, 1965, CW Papers.

85. *CW* 32 (November 1965): 1; *CW* 32 (October 1966): 1.

86. Harrington, *Fragments of the Century*, pp. 139–170.

87. John Deedy, "Behind the Catholic Peace Fellowship," *U.S. Catholic* 12 (August 1968): 15–16; "New Roman Catholic Peace Fellowship Created," *Fellowship* 30 (August 1964): 3.

88. *New Yorker* 42 (December 24, 1966): 23–25; Charles Palms, "Peace and the Catholic Conscience," *Catholic World* 202 (June 1966): 14.

89. CW Papers, W-6.3. McNeal, *American Catholic Peace Movement*, pp. 231–233.

90. *CW* 29 (December 1962): 1; Cornell and Forest, *A Penny a Copy*, pp. xi–xiii.

91. Gray, *Divine Disobedience*, pp. 60–87.

92. *CW* 32 (December 1966): 8.

93. George F. Kennan, "Foreign Policy and the Christian Conscience," *Atlantic* 203 (May 1959): 47–48; Douglas A. MacArthur, "The Surrender of the Right to Make War," *Vital Speeches* 12 (April 15, 1946): 389–391.

94. A. J. Muste, *Not By Might* (New York: Harper, 1947), p. 79.

Chapter Seven

1. "Religion and the Intellectuals," *Partisan Review* 17 (1950): 326, 481.

2. Ibid., pp. 315, 481.

3. See, for example, Daniel Bell, *The Cultural Contradictions of Capitalism* (New York: Basic Books, 1976), pp. 146–161; and Sydney Ahlstrom, *A Religious History of the American People*, pp. 1079–1096.

4. John Tracy Ellis, "The Church in Revolt," *Critic* 28 (January 1970): 21.

5. Gray, *Divine Disobedience*, p. 15.

Selected Bibliography

Manuscript Collections

Ann Arbor, Michigan. University of Michigan Library. Labadie Collection. Ammon Hennacy Papers.

Chicago, Illinois. Loyola University. Institute of Urban Studies. Ed Marciniak Papers.

Detroit, Michigan. Wayne State University Archives. Association of Catholic Trade Unionists Papers.

Milwaukee, Wisconsin. Marquette University Archives. Catholic Association for International Peace Collection.

Milwaukee, Wisconsin. Marquette University Archives. Dorothy Day-Catholic Worker Papers.

Swarthmore, Pennsylvania. Swarthmore College. Swarthmore College Peace Collection.

Periodicals

America, 1929–1973.
Brooklyn Tablet, 1933–1936.
Catholic CO, 1943–1948.
Catholic Worker, 1933–1973.
Catholic World, 1870–1967.
Chicago Catholic Worker, 1938–1941.
Christian Century, 1918–1935.
Christian Front (Christian Social Action), 1935–1942.
Commonweal, 1925–1973.
Cross Currents, 1953–1969.
Daily Worker, 1933–1935.

Fellowship, 1946–1967.
Freedom, 1933.
Jubilee, 1953–1958.
Labor Leader, 1938–1947.
Liberator, 1918–1923.
Man, 1935–1939.
Masses, 1917–1918.
National Catholic Reporter, 1965–1967.
New Masses, 1928.
New York Call, 1916–1917.
New York Review of Books, 1967–1973.
Peace, 1963–1966.
Today, 1946–1949.
Work, 1943–1950.
World Tomorrow, 1919–1931.

Articles

Abell, Aaron I. "The Reception of Leo XIII's Labor Encyclical in America, 1891–1919." *Review of Politics* 7 (October 1945): 461–485.

Anent, William S. "Religion, Education, and Distinction." *School and Society* 26 (1927): 399–406.

Bethune, Ade. "Vocations." *Christian Social Art Quarterly* 3 (Spring 1940): 27–30.

Cantrill, Hadley, "Educational and Economic Composition of Religious Groups." *American Journal of Sociology* 47 (March 1943): 574–579.

Collens, T. Wharton. "View of the Labor Movement." *Catholic World* 10 (March 1870): 794–798.

Cook, E. A. "The Kingdom of God as a Democratic Ideal." *Journal of Religion* 1 (November 1921): 626–640.

Curran, Charles E. "American and Catholic: American Catholic Social Ethics, 1880–1965." *Thought* 52 (1977): 50–74.

Davis, Forrest. "Father Coughlin." *Atlantic* 66 (November 1935): 659–668.

Day, Dorothy. "Eviction." *Jubilee* 6 (November 1958): 28–35.

———. "A Human Document." *Sign* 12 (November 1932): 223–224.

———. "I Remember Peter Maurin." *Jubilee* 1 (March 1954): 34–39.

———. "A Reminiscence at 75." *Commonweal* 98 (1973): 424–425.

Deedy, John. "Behind the Catholic Peace Fellowship." *U.S. Catholic* 12 (August 1968): 15–16.

Deverall, Richard. "The Way It Was." *Social Order* 16 (1961): 49–57.

Doherty, Robert. "Thomas J. Hagerty, the Church, and Socialism." *Labor History* 16 (Winter 1965): 43–46.

Dolan, Jay P. "A Critical Period in American Catholicism." *Review of Politics* 35 (1973): 523–536.

Douglass, James. "Modern War and the Just War." *Worldview* 5 (September 1963): 27–29.

——. "The Morality of Thermonuclear Deterrence." *Worldview* 6 (October 1964): 31–35.

Eliot, Lester P. "Troubles of American Catholicism." *American Mercury* 34 (March 1935): 267–281.

Ellis, John Tracy. "American Catholics and the Intellectual Life." *Thought* 30 (Autumn 1955): 351–388.

——. "The Church in Revolt," *Critic* 28 (January 1970): 21–23.

Ely, Richard. "Socialism." *Inter-Denominational Proceedings* (1885): 89–95.

Ford, John C. "The Morality of Obliteration Bombing." *Theological Studies* 5 (1944): 261–309.

Furfey, Paul Hanley. "Why Does Rome Discourage Socio-religious Intercreedalism?" *American Ecclesiastical Review* 112 (1945): 365–374.

Gibbons, James Cardinal. "Some Defects in Our Political and Social Institutions." *North American Review* 145 (1887): 345–354.

——. "Wealth and Its Obligations." *North American Review* 152 (1891): 385–394.

Gleason, Philip. "In Search of Unity: American Catholic Thought, 1920–1960." *Catholic Historical Review* 65 (April 1979): 185–205.

Glenn, Norval, and Hyland, Ruth. "Religious Preference and Worldly Success." *American Sociological Review* 32 (February 1967): 73–85.

Gutman, Herbert. "Protestantism and the American Labor Movement." *American Historical Review* 77 (1966): 74–101.

Harrington, Michael. "Catholics in the Labor Movement." *Labor History* 11 (Fall 1960): 241–259.

Hellman, John. "The Opening to the Left in French Catholicism: The Role of the Personalists." *Journal of the History of Ideas* 34 (July 1973): 381–390.

Herr, Dan. "The Chicago Dynamo." *Sign* 42 (1962): 11–14, 37–42.

Hitchcock, James. "Postmortem on a Rebirth." *American Scholar* 49 (Spring 1980): 211–225.

Johnson, James T. "Just War Theory." *Worldview* 19 (July–August 1976): 27–30.

Kane, John J. "The Social Structure of American Catholics." *American Catholic Sociological Review* 16 (March 1955): 23–30.

Kennan, George F. "Foreign Policy and the Christian Conscience." *Atlantic* 203 (May 1959): 47–48.

Lehmann, Harvey, and Witty, Paul. "Scientific Eminence and Church Membership." *Scientific Monthly* 33 (December 1931): 544–549.

Lobue, Wayne. "Public Theology and the Catholic Worker." *Cross Currents* 26 (Autumn 1976): 270–285.

MacArthur, Douglas A. "The Surrender of the Right to Make War." *Vital Speeches* 12 (April 15, 1946): 389–391.

Macdonald, Dwight. "Revisiting Dorothy Day." *New York Review of Books* (January 28, 1971): 12–13.

McDonald, Joseph. "A Liturgical Apostolate." *Orate Fratres* 12 (1938): 272–273.

McNeal, Patricia. "Catholic Conscientious Objection During World War II." *Catholic Historical Review* 61 (April 1975): 219–231.

———. "Origins of the Catholic Peace Movement." *Review of Politics* 35 (July 1973): 346–374.

McSweeney, Patrick. "The Church and the Classes." *Catholic World* 47 (July 1888): 471–474.

Miller, William. "American Historians and the Business Elite." *Journal of Economic History* 9 (November 1949): 184–208.

Murray, John Courtney. "Remarks on the Moral Problem of War." *Theological Studies* 20 (1959): 40–61.

Niebuhr, H. Richard. "Inconsistency of the Majority." *World Tomorrow* 17 (January 18, 1934): 43–44.

Pope, Liston. "Religion and Class Structure." *Annals of the Academy of Political and Social Science* 256 (March 1948): 85–95.

"Religion and the Intellectuals." *Partisan Review* 17 (1950): 310–490.

Rovere, Richard. "Labor's Catholic Bloc." *Nation* 152 (January 1941): 9–15.

Segers, Mary C. "Equality and Christian Anarchism: The Political and Social Ideas of the Catholic Worker Movement." *Review of Politics* 40 (April 1978): 196–230.

Valaik, J. David. "American Catholic Dissenters and the Spanish Civil War." *Catholic Historical Review* 53 (January 1968): 537–546.

———. "Catholics, Neutrality, and the Spanish Embargo." *Journal of American History* 54 (June 1967): 73–85.

Walsh, William J. "Quadragesimo Anno." *Catholic Charities Review* 15 (June 1931): 17–176.

Ward, William Hayes. "Church Attendance." *North American Review* 137 (1883): 79–85.

Books

Aaron, Daniel. *Writers on the Left*. New York: Harcourt, Brace, 1961.

Abell, Aaron. *American Catholicism and Social Action*. Notre Dame: University of Notre Dame Press, 1963.

————. *The Urban Impact on American Protestantism*. Cambridge, Mass.: Harvard University Press, 1943.

Adam, Karl. *The Spirit of Catholicism*. New York: Macmillan, 1929.

Ahlstrom, Sydney. *A Religious History of the American People*. New Haven: Yale University Press, 1972.

Amato, Joseph. *Mounier and Maritain: A French Catholic Understanding of the Modern World*. University: University of Alabama Press, 1975.

Bacon, Leonard Woolsey. *A History of American Christianity*. New York: Christian Literature, 1897.

Bainton, Roland H. *Christian Attitudes Toward War and Peace*. Nashville: Abingdon, 1960.

Baird, Robert. *Religion in America*. Rev. ed. New York: Harper & Row, 1970.

Baker, James. *Thomas Merton: Social Critic*. Lexington: University of Kentucky Press, 1971.

Baum, Gregory, and Campion, Donald, eds. *Pastoral Constitution on the Church in the Modern World*. New York: Paulist Press, 1967.

Bennett, John C. *Christian Realism*. New York: Scribner's, 1941.

————, ed. *Nuclear Weapons and the Conflict of Conscience*. New York: Harper, 1962.

Bernstein, Barton J., ed. *Towards a New Past*. New York: Random House, 1968.

Bethune, Ade. *Work*. Newport: John Sterns Press, 1942.

Betten, Neil. *Catholic Activism and the Industrial Worker*. Gainesville: Florida State University Press, 1976.

Borne, Etienne, and Henry, Francis. *A Philosophy of Work*. New York: Sheed and Ward, 1937.

Boyer, Paul. *Urban Masses and Moral Order in America, 1820–1920*. Cambridge: Harvard University Press, 1978.

Braunthal, Alfred. *Salvation and the Perfect Society*. Amherst: University of Massachusetts Press, 1979.

Brock, Peter. *Twentieth Century Pacifism*. New York: Van Nostrand Co., 1970.

Broderick, Francis. *Right Reverend New Dealer: John A. Ryan*. New York: Macmillan, 1963.

Brown, W. A., and May, Mark. *The Education of American Ministers.* New York: Institute of Social and Religious Research, 1934.

Cadbury, Henry J. *The Peril of Modernizing Jesus.* New York: Macmillan, 1938.

Carter, Paul A. *The Spiritual Crisis of the Gilded Age.* DeKalb: Northern Illinois University Press, 1971.

Catholic Encyclopedia. New York, 1912.

Cauthen, Kenneth. *The Impact of American Religious Liberalism.* New York: Harper, 1962.

Cogley, John. *A Canterbury Tale.* New York: Seabury, 1976.

————. *Catholic America.* Garden City: Doubleday, 1973.

Coles, Robert. *A Spectacle Unto the World.* New York: Viking, 1973.

Cornell, Thomas C., and Forest, James. *A Penny a Copy.* New York: Macmillan, 1968.

Cowley, Malcolm. *Exile's Return.* New York: Viking, 1951.

Cross, Robert. *The Emergence of Liberal Catholicism in America.* Chicago: Quadrangle, 1958.

Curran, Charles, ed. *New Perspectives in Moral Theology.* Notre Dame: University of Notre Dame Press, 1976.

Day, Dorothy. *The Eleventh Virgin.* New York: Boni, 1924.

————. *From Union Square to Rome.* Silver Spring: Preservation of the Faith Press, 1938.

————. *House of Hospitality.* New York: Catholic Worker, 1939.

————. *Loaves and Fishes.* New York: Harper, 1963.

————. *The Long Loneliness.* New York: Harper and Row, 1952.

————. *On Pilgrimage: The Sixties.* New York: Curtis, 1973.

————. *Thérèse.* Notre Dame: Fides Press, 1960.

Degler, Carl. *Out of Our Past.* New York: Harper, 1959.

Dell, Floyd. *Homecoming: An Autobiography.* New York: Farrar and Rinehart, 1933.

Diggins, John. *The American Left in the Twentieth Century.* New York: Harcourt, Brace, 1973.

Dohen, Dorothy. *Nationalism and American Catholicism.* New York: Sheed and Ward, 1967.

Dolan, Jay P. *Catholic Revivalism.* Notre Dame: University of Notre Dame Press, 1978.

————. *The Immigrant Church.* Baltimore: Johns Hopkins University Press, 1975.

Donohoe, Joan Marie. *The Irish Catholic Benevolent Union.* Washington, D.C.: Catholic University, 1953.

Douglass, James. *The Nonviolent Cross.* New York: Macmillan, 1966.

Ehler, Sidney Z., and Morall, John, eds. *Church and State Through the Centuries*. London: Burns and Oates, 1954.

Eliade, Mircea. *The Sacred and the Profane*. New York: Harper, 1957.

Ellis, John Tracy. *American Catholicism*. Chicago. University of Chicago Press, 1968.

Ellis, Marc. *Peter Maurin: Prophet in the Twentieth Century*. New York: Paulist Press, 1981.

Erikson, Erik. *Gandhi's Truth*. New York: Norton, 1969.

Ernst, Eldon G. *Moment of Truth for Protestant America: Interchurch Campaigns Following World War I*. Missoula, Mont.: American Academy of Religion and Scholars' Press, 1974.

Fishburn, Janet Forsythe. *The Fatherhood of God and the Victorian Family: The Social Gospel in America*. Philadelphia: Fortress Press, 1982.

Flynn, George Q. *American Catholics and the Roosevelt Presidency*. Lexington: University of Kentucky Press, 1968.

Fogarty, Michael D. *Christian Democracy in Western Europe, 1820–1953*. Notre Dame: University of Notre Dame Press, 1969.

Foster, Laurence. *Religion and Sexuality: Three American Communal Experiments of the Nineteenth Century*. New York: Oxford University Press, 1981.

Fox, Mary Harrita. *Peter E. Dietz: Labor Priest*. Notre Dame: University of Notre Dame Press, 1953.

Gelb, Arthur and Barbara. *O'Neill*. New York: Harper, 1962.

Gibbons, James Cardinal. *A Retrospect of Fifty Years*. Vol. 1. Baltimore: John Murphy Co., 1916.

Gladden, Washington. *Applied Christianity: Moral Aspects of Social Questions*. Boston: Houghton Mifflin: 1886.

———. *The Nation and the Kingdom*. Boston: American Board of Commissioners for Foreign Missions, 1909.

———. *The New Idolatry and Other Discussions*. New York: Macmillan, 1905.

———. *Recollections*. New York: Christian Literature, 1909.

Gleason, Philip. *The Conservative Reformers*. Notre Dame: University of Notre Dame Press, 1968.

Goodman, Paul, ed. *Seeds of Liberation*. New York: Braziller, 1964.

Gray, Francine du Plessix. *Divine Disobedience*. New York: Random House, 1969.

Greeley, Andrew. *The Catholic Experience*. Garden City: Doubleday-Image, 1969.

Greeley, Andrew and Rossi, Peter. *The Education of Catholic Americans*. Chicago: University of Chicago Press, 1966.

Greene, Victor. *The Slavic Community on Strike*. Notre Dame: University of Notre Dame Press, 1968.

Halsey, William M. *The Survival of American Innocence*. Notre Dame: University of Notre Dame Press, 1980.

Handy, Robert, ed. *The Social Gospel in America*. New York: Oxford University Press, 1966.

Harrington, Michael. *The Accidental Century*. Baltimore: Penguin Books, 1966.

————. *Fragments of the Century*. New York: Simon and Schuster, 1973.

————. *The Other America*. New York: Macmillan, 1962.

Hellman, John. *Emmanuel Mounier and the New Catholic Left, 1930–1950*. Toronto: University of Toronto Press, 1981.

Hennacy, Ammon. *The Book of Ammon*. Originally published as *The Autobiography of a Catholic Anarchist*. New York: Catholic Worker Press, 1954.

Hentoff, Nat, ed. *The Essays of A. J. Muste*. Indianapolis: Bobbs-Merrill, 1967.

Herberg, Will. *Protestant-Catholic-Jew*. Garden City: Doubleday, 1955.

Herron, George. *The Christian Society*. New York: Johnson reprint, 1969.

————. *The Christian State*. New York: Johnson reprint, 1968.

————. *The Meaning of Religious Experiences*. New York: Thomas Y. Crowell, 1896.

————. *The New Redemption*. New York: Thomas Y. Crowell, 1893.

Higham, John. *Strangers in the Land*. New Brunswick: Rutgers University Press, 1955.

Hofstadter, Richard. *The Age of Reform*. New York: Vintage, 1955.

————. *Anti-Intellectualism in American Life*. New York: Vintage, 1963.

Hopkins, Charles. *The Rise of the Social Gospel in American Protestantism*. New Haven: Yale University Press, 1940.

Huber, Raphael M., ed. *Our Bishops Speak*. Milwaukee: Bruce, 1952.

Hudson, Winthrop S. *American Protestantism*. Chicago: University of Chicago Press, 1961.

————. *Religion in America*. New York: Scribner's, 1965.

Hugo, John C. *The Immorality of Conscription*. New York: Catholic Worker Press, 1944.

Hutchison, William. *The Modernist Impulse in American Protestantism*. Cambridge, Mass.: Harvard University Press, 1976.

Jacob, Philip, and Sidney, Mulford. *Conscription of Conscience: The American State and the Conscientious Objector, 1940–1947*. Ithaca: Cornell University Press, 1947.

Kane, John J. *Protestant-Catholic Conflicts in America*. Chicago: Henry Regnery, 1955.

Karson, Marc. *American Labor Unions and Politics*. Carbondale: Southern Illinois University Press, 1956.

Kazin, Alfred. *On Native Grounds*. Garden City: Doubleday, 1942.

Kennedy, David M. *Birth Control in America*. New Haven: Yale University Press, 1970.

Koenker, Ernest B. *The Liturgical Renaissance in the Roman Catholic Church*. St. Louis: Concordia, 1954.

Lawler, Justus George. *Nuclear War: The Ethic, the Rhetoric, the Reality*. Westminster: Newman, 1965.

Lears, T. J. Jackson. *No Place of Grace: Antimodernism and the Transformation of American Culture, 1880–1920*. New York: Pantheon, 1981.

Loomis, Samuel. *Modern Cities and Their Religious Problems*. New York: Pilgrim Press, 1887.

Lubell, Samuel. *The Future of American Politics*. New York: Harper & Row, 1951.

Lynd, Alice, ed. *We Won't Go: Personal Accounts of Conscientious Objectors*. Boston: Beacon, 1968.

McAvoy, Thomas. *The Great Crisis in American Catholic History, 1895–1900*. Chicago: Henry Regnery, 1957.

McCarthy, Abigail. *Private Faces, Public Places*. New York: Curtis, 1972.

Macdonald, Dwight. *Politics Past*. New York: Viking, 1970.

McNeal, Patricia. *The American Catholic Peace Movement, 1928–1972*. New York: Arno Press, 1978.

Magnuson, Norris. *Salvation in the Slums: Evangelical Social Work, 1820–1920*. Metuchen, N.J.: Scarecrow Press, 1977.

Manuel, Frank and Fritzie Manuel. *Utopian Thought in the Western World*. Cambridge, Mass.: Belknap-Harvard, 1979.

Marsden, George. *Fundamentalism and American Culture: The Shaping of Twentieth Century Evangelicalism, 1870–1925*. New York: Oxford University Press, 1980.

Marty, Martin. *The Modern Schism*. New York: Harper, 1969.

———. *Protestantism*. Garden City: Doubleday, 1974.

———. *Righteous Empire: The Protestant Experience in America*. New York: Dial, 1970.

Marx, Paul B. *Virgil Michel and the Liturgical Movement*. Collegeville: St. John's Abbey-Liturgical Press, 1957.

Mathews, Shailer. *Jesus on Social Institutions*. New York: Macmillan, 1928.

Maurin, Peter. *The Green Revolution*. New York: Academy Guild Press, 1961.

May, Henry F. *The End of American Innocence*. Chicago: Quadrangle, 1964.

————. *Protestant Churches and Industrial America*. New York: Harper, 1949.

Meier, Hans. *Religion and Church: The Early History of Christian Democracy*. Notre Dame: University of Notre Dame Press, 1969.

Merton, Thomas. *Asian Journal*. New York: New Directions, 1972.

————. *Breakthrough to Peace*. New York: New Directions, 1962.

————. *Contemplation in a World of Action*. Garden City: Doubleday, 1971.

————. *Disputed Questions*. New York: Farrar, Straus, 1960.

————. *Faith and Violence*. Notre Dame: University of Notre Dame Press, 1968.

————. *Mystics and Zen Masters*. New York: Farrar, Straus, 1967.

————. *Raids on the Unspeakable*. New York: New Directions, 1966.

————. *The Seven Storey Mountain*. New York: Harcourt, Brace, 1948.

————. *Thomas Merton on Peace*. New York: McCall's, 1971.

————. *The Way of Chuang-tzu*. New York: New Directions, 1965.

————. *Zen and the Birds of Appetite*. New York: New Directions, 1968.

Meyer, Donald. *The Protestant Search for Political Realism*. Berkeley: University of California Press, 1960.

Miller, William D. *Dorothy Day: A Biography*. San Francisco: Harper and Row, 1982.

————. *A Harsh and Dreadful Love: Dorothy Day and the Catholic Worker Movement*. New York: Liveright, 1972.

Murray, John Courtney. *We Hold These Truths* (New York: Sheed and Ward, 1960).

Muste, A. J. *Not by Might*. New York: Harper, 1947.

Nagle, William E. *Morality and Modern Warfare*. New York: Helicon, 1960.

Niebuhr, Reinhold. *Christianity and Power Politics*. New York: Scribner's, 1940.

————. *Moral Man and Immoral Society*. New York: Scribner's, 1932.

————. *The Nature and Destiny of Man*. New York: Scribner's, 1941.

Nuttall, Geoffrey. *Christian Pacifism in History*. London: Blackwell, 1958.

O'Brien, David J. *American Catholics and Social Reform: The New Deal Years*. New York: Oxford University Press, 1968.

O'Grady, John. *Catholic Charities in the United States*. Washington, D.C.: National Conference of Catholic Charities, 1931.

Ostrow, Daniel. *The FBI and the Berrigans.* New York: Coward, McCann, 1972.

Pelikan, Jaroslav. *The Riddle of Roman Catholicism.* Nashville: Abingdon, 1959.

Pope John XXIII. *Pacem in Terris.* New York: America Press, 1963.

Quigley, Thomas, ed. *American Catholics and Vietnam.* Grand Rapids: William Eerdmans, 1968.

Rausch, James S., ed. *The Family of Nations.* New York: Huntington, 1970.

Rauschenbusch, Walter. *Christianity and the Social Crisis.* Reprint of 1907 ed. New York: Harper, 1964.

Rhynne, Xavier [pseud.]. *Letters from Vatican II: Background and Debates: The Fourth Session.* New York: Farrar, Straus, 1966.

Rideout, Walter. *The Radical Novel in the United States, 1900–1934.* Cambridge, Mass.: Harvard University Press, 1956.

Robinson, Jo Ann Oviman. *Abraham Went Out: A Biography of A. J. Muste.* Philadelphia: Temple University Press, 1982.

Roohan, James. *American Catholics and the Social Question, 1865–1900.* New York: Arno Press, 1976.

Ryan, John A. *Declining Liberty and Other Papers.* New York: Macmillan, 1927.

———. *Distributive Justice.* New York: Harper, 1916.

———. *A Living Wage.* New York: Macmillan, 1906.

———. *Modern War and Basic Ethics.* Milwaukee, Bruce: 1943.

Schneider, Herbert Wallace, ed. *Religion in Twentieth Century America.* Cambridge, Mass.: Harvard University Press, 1952.

Sennett, Richard. *Families Against the City: Middle Class Homes of Industrial Chicago, 1872–1890.* New York: Vintage, 1970.

Sheehan, Arthur. *Peter Maurin: Gay Believer.* Garden City: Hanover, 1959.

Siegfried, André. *America Comes of Age.* New York: Harcourt, Brace, 1927.

Smith, Timothy L. *Revivalism and Social Reform in Mid-Nineteenth Century America.* Nashville: Abingdon Press, 1967.

Social Action Department. National Catholic Welfare Conference. *Organized Social Justice.* New York: Paulist Press, 1935.

Sorg, Dom Rombert. *Holy Work: Towards a Benedictine Theology of Labor.* St. Louis: Pio Decimo Press, 1953.

Stein, Walter, ed. *Nuclear Weapons and Christian Conscience.* London: Merlin Press, 1961.

Strong, Josiah. *Our Country: Its Possible Future and Present Crisis.* 1885; reprint ed. Cambridge: Harvard University Press, 1963.

Sugrue, Thomas. *A Catholic Speaks His Mind on America's Religious Conflict*. New York: Harper, 1952.

Terkel, Studs. *Hard Times*. New York: Pantheon, 1970.

Tillich, Paul. *The Protestant Era*. Chicago: University of Chicago Press, 1948.

Troeltsch, Ernst. *The Social Teachings of the Christian Churches*. 2 vols. London: George Allen, 1931.

Tull, Charles J. *Father Coughlin and the New Deal*. Syracuse: Syracuse University Press, 1965.

Van Allen, Rodger. *The Commonweal and American Catholicism*. Philadelphia: Fortress Press, 1974.

Walzer, Michael. *Just and Unjust Wars: A Moral Argument with Historical Illustrations*. New York: Basic Books, 1977.

Weisberger, Bernard. *They Gathered at the River*. Boston: Little, Brown, 1958.

Wiebe, Robert. *The Search for Order*. New York: Hill & Wang, 1967.

Wills, Garry. *Bare Ruined Choirs*. New York: Delta, 1972.

————. *Politics and Catholic Freedom*. Chicago: Henry Regnery, 1964.

Wittner, Lawrence. *Rebels Against War: The American Peace Movement, 1941–1960*. New York: Columbia University Press, 1969.

Yzermans, Vincent A., ed. *American Participation in the Second Vatican Council*. New York: Sheed and Ward, 1967.

Zahn, Gordon C. *Another Part of the War: The Camp Simon Story*. Amherst: University of Massachusetts Press, 1979.

————. *German Catholics and Hitler's Wars*. London: Sheed and Ward, 1963.

————. *In Solitary Witness: The Life and Death of Franz Jägerstätter*. Boston: Beacon, 1964.

————. *War, Conscience, and Dissent*. New York: Hawthorn, 1967.

Unpublished Materials

Cort, John C. "The Worst Possible System." Unpublished manuscript. Author's possession. Nahant, Massachusetts.

LeBrun, John Leo. "The Role of the Catholic Worker Movement in American Pacifism, 1933–1972." Ph.D. dissertation, Case Western Reserve University, 1973.

Novitsky, Anthony. "The Ideological Development of Peter Maurin's Green Revolution." Ph.D. dissertation, State University of New York at Buffalo, 1977.

Sicius, Frank. "The Chicago Catholic Worker Movement, 1936 to the Present." Ph.D. dissertation, Loyola University, 1979.

Index